CURRENT TRENDS IN PROGRAMMING METHODOLOGY

VOLUME IV

Data Structuring

CURRENT TRENDS IN PROGRAMMING METHODOLOGY

VOLUME IV

Data Structuring

RAYMOND T. YEH, *Editor*

Department of Computer Sciences
The University of Texas at Austin

PRENTICE-HALL, INC., Englewood Cliffs, New Jersey 07632

Library of Congress Cataloging in Publication Data

Main entry under title:

Current trends in programming methodology.

Includes bibliographies.
CONTENTS: v. 1 Software specifications and design.—v. 4. Data structuring.
1. Programming (Electronic computers) I. Yeh, Raymond Tzuu-Yau (date)
QA76.6.C87 001.6′42 76–46467
ISBN 0–13–195735–X

Printed in the United States of America

10 9 8 7 6 5 4 3 2 1

PRENTICE-HALL INTERNATIONAL, INC., *London*
PRENTICE-HALL OF AUSTRALIA PTY. LIMITED, *Sydney*
PRENTICE-HALL OF CANADA, LTD., *Toronto*
PRENTICE-HALL OF INDIA PRIVATE LIMITED, *New Delhi*
PRENTICE-HALL OF JAPAN, INC., *Tokyo*
PRENTICE-HALL OF SOUTHEAST ASIA PTE. LTD., *Singapore*
WHITEHALL BOOKS LIMITED, *Wellington, New Zealand*

CONTENTS

PREFACE

The introduction of "structured programming" by Edsger Dijkstra [1972] has revolutionized the programming practice and, with it, the birth of programming methodology as an academic discipline. In his famous paper, "Notes on Structured Programming," Dijkstra has lucidly pointed out our human inability to cope with the complexities of large software systems. He suggested the use of abstraction to decompose the programming task into "intellectually manageable" parts, and the disciplined use of control structures in the development of more reliable and understandable software. Although data structuring is implicitly an integral part of such a methodology as evidenced by the levels of representations in program design, the emphasis in programming methodology in its earlier phase was on the structure of algorithms represented by program texts.

It is pointed out by C.A.R. Hoare [1972] that the subjects of program composition and data structuring are inseparably intertwined in software design, and hence data structuring must be studied with the same rigor and depth as its algorithmic counterpart. Indeed, any programming methodology, as a scientific and systematic approach to the design and construction of programs, has bearings primarily on large, complex programs involving complicated sets of data as pointed out by Nicklaus Wirth [1976]. Research efforts in data structuring have been increasing in recent years, mainly in the development of a theory of abstract data types, a methodology for the implementation of data abstraction in programming languages, and in formal models of data structures. It is the intention of this volume to bring out some of the major recent accomplishments in data structuring research so that it may contribute in a more meaningful way to the existing methodology in programming.

The organization of this volume of ten chapters may be divided into four groups: Chapter 1, Chapters 2 to 5, Chapters 6 and 7, and Chapters 8, 9 and Chapter 10.

In Chapter 1, Hoare surveys the problems and difficulty of achieving data reliability, and suggests a methodology for the structured design and description of data. In this methodology, a restricted set of primitives are introduced for data structuring purposes so that simplicity of the resulting structure can be achieved. The primitives suggested by Hoare are analogous to the control structure primitives suggested by Dijkstra [1972]. Hoare also suggests that unrestricted use of reference pointers for data structuring is dangerous.

Chapters 2 to 5 emphasize the need for a formal approach to data structures. Central to these chapters is the notion of an abstract data type which is a formal and precise characterization of a concept. Such an approach provides a representation for independent specification of data, and hence is valuable as an organizational and conceptual tool. The advantages of a formal approach to data structuring have been eloquently expressed by Standish in Chapter 3, and I quote him here:

"1. To permit clear, rigorous definition of the concept of data representations and data types.
2. To specify precisely the requirements on data representations.
3. To specify precisely the requirements on programs that manipulate data representations.
4. To permit the widest possible selection of implementation detail.
5. To simplify program maintenance . . . by allowing changes in superstructure or underpinnings to be made independently.
6. To extend the basis for proofs of correctness of programs.
7. To permit concise definition of the semantics of data definition facilities.
8. To establish a framework for tackling the problem of automatic synthesis or selection of data representations.
9. To capture the behavior of composite information structures that are pervasive in programming.
10. To offer a better basis for machine independence."

In Chapter 2, Mealy proposes to reconsider data yet again in the context of program development. His paradigm for program development consists of (1) the formulation of a theory, and (2) bridging the gap between the abstract and concrete. It is pointed out that in the passage from abstract to concrete, we must initially start with some abstract mental objects which Mealy calls *notions*. "Notions are fuzzy data objects." The contribution of the chapter comes in the realization that notions can be characterized by properties in the form of sets and relations. It is through such formalization (in the context of a theory of classes) that most of the problems in data semantics and control can potentially be treated in a uniform and rigorous manner.

In Chapter 3, Standish proposes an axiomatic data theory. In this theory, "the notion of a *data type* in programming corresponds to a representation-independent axiomatic specification of abstract behavior requirements for a system of data objects and data operators . . . Thus, a *data representation* for a *data type* is just a model for its axioms which also obeys some *basic data axioms*." In this chapter, Standish first introduces a set of *ground axioms* which characterizes some rudimentary behaviors of composite information structures. Using this set of axioms, he explores classes of models for the axioms and studies related characterizations of controllable composite objects from the literature. Standish also examines the problem of synthesizing data representations starting from axiomatic characterizations of higher order data types.

In Chapter 4, Guttag, Horowitz, and Musser are concerned with the design of data types using a formal approach following the same philosophy as expounded by

Standish in Chapter 3. The authors here explore the algebraic specification techniques for data types, and exhibit such specifications for a number of commonly used data types. It is shown in this chapter that the algebraic technique is useful in providing a representation-independent specification which does not put any constraints on the choice of implementation. The authors also indicate how such kinds of specifications can be further used for proving the correctness of implementations and for testing, at design time, large software systems.

In Chapter 5, Goguen, Thatcher, and Wagner present a comprehensive formal treatment of abstract data types based on initial algebra. The basic thesis of this chapter is that an "abstract data type is an algebra." The significance of this chapter lies in the fact that an algebra captures the concept of abstraction precisely. Indeed, the concept of isomorphism in algebra makes explicit that the abstraction is representation-independent. Furthermore, this chapter is concerned with a whole spectrum of problems in data abstraction from specification, verification to implementation. It also presents a first formal treatment on the handling of exception conditions.

The previous four chapters, in summary, have provided a formal basis for the specification, design, verification, and implementation of data abstractions. Although many challenging theoretical problems remain, it seems that a new methodology on the structured design of data has emerged and can be incorporated into programming languages. It should be pointed out that although these chapters cover a wealth of material from basic algebraic concepts needed to the application of algebra to the design and implementation of abstract data types, the readings have been made easier and more instructive by the numerous examples introduced.

Chapters 6 and 7 are concerned with programming language design. It is shown that many of the problems of concern in previous chapters are also considered extensively in these two chapters.

In Chapter 6, Mitchell and Wegbreit introduce a notation and semantics for parameterized implementation mechanisms called *schemes*. Schemes are type-parameterized definitions which are useful implementation techniques in that once a scheme is correctly programmed, that concept need not be coded again. A scheme may also be regarded as providing one possible implementation of some abstract specifications. Thus, a set of schemes may be used to provide alternative realizations of a single abstraction, having different performance characteristics for example. Many examples are given in this chapter to illustrate these new constructs.

In Chapter 7, Schwartz is concerned with various phases of program design from abstract to concrete with the design of programming language in mind. The author first points out various circumstances of programming; clean-slate programming, i.e., the design and development of programming systems from scratch, adaptive programming, and programming for non-programmers. This chapter concentrates on clean-slate programming. The evolution of the programming process from a Protoprogram to a final program is well discussed. Programming discipline and very high level features of future languages such as data structuring, are discussed in detail. Special attention has been paid to data structuring based on set theoretical concepts.

Chapters 8 and 9 are concerned with formal models of different data structures.

In Chapter 8, Fleck proposes two formal models for string pattern generation and then uses them in structuring collections of strings. Through these formal models, the author leads us to a deeper understanding of patterns and the pattern machining process. As a consequence of the conceptual simplicity of such a formal treatment, we are in a better perspective position to examine existing programming features using patterns in languages such as SNOBOL4 in which the patterns "although extremely flexible and powerful, are notoriously difficult to explain and use."

In Chapter 9, Bang and Yeh investigate relations of finite ranks through decomposition and synthesis. A relational data structure is proposed based on the theoretical foundation. It is pointed out that the proposed data structure is advantageous since it is a unified treatment of many different types of data, such as sets, graphs, binary relations, lists, etc., which we encounter in various applications in pattern description, natural language processing, and data management systems.

In Chapter 10, Rosenberg provides an in-depth survey to the problem of allocating storage for multidimensional arrays that can expand dynamically. The author provides a most lucid exposition, illustrated by many examples of the many exciting aspects of *computed-access* array storage mappings. Future directions for research in this area are also discussed.

I would like to take this opportunity to thank all contributing authors, and to express my gratitude to the following persons who have acted as referees for various chapters in this volume: Bob Channon, Mike Conner, John Laski, David Musser, Charles Reynolds, and Larry Yellowitz.

RAYMOND T. YEH

Austin, Texas

CURRENT TRENDS IN PROGRAMMING METHODOLOGY

VOLUME IV

Data Structuring

CHAPTER 1

DATA STRUCTURES

C. A. R. HOARE
Department of Computer Science
The Queen's University of Belfast
Belfast, Ireland

Abstract

In this chapter we survey the problems of data design and find them more severe than those of program design. We then outline some of the conceptual and methodological tools which are available for the solution of these problems, including the concept of type, direct product, union, sequence, recursion, and mapping. We touch on the top-down design of data and programs and argue that references or pointers are to be avoided.

Key Words and Phrases

software reliability, data structuring, abstraction and representation, avoidance of references

1.1. FLOWCHARTS AND DATA DIAGRAMS

The most widely accepted and practiced method for the design and documentation of computer programs is the flowchart (Figure 1.1). But more recently the disadvantages of flowcharts have become apparent. Here are some of them:

1. They use too much paper: As soon as they overflow a few pages, the extra page turning and cross referencing form a significant barrier to understanding.
2. They cannot conveniently be input to a computer or output from it.
3. They do not enable you to understand the whole in terms of its parts, and so they become intellectually unmanageable when applied to large problems.
4. The slightest fault in an arrow or box has unpredictable and global consequences on the whole program.

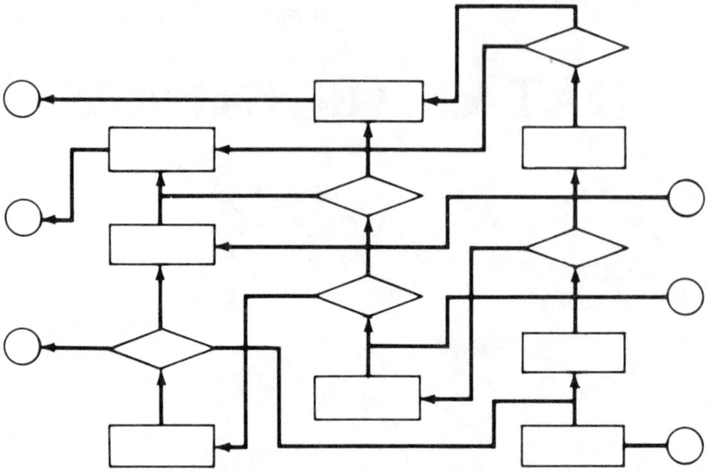

Figure 1.1. Flowchart.

5. These problems are greatly magnified if the structure is changed during program execution, for example, by assigned go to's in FORTRAN or ALTERs in COBOL.
6. The physical realization of an arrow by a jump is surprisingly expensive on modern machines, with cache stores, instruction pipelines, and virtual memory.

It is also accepted practice to use diagrams in the design of data (Figure 1.2). However, these diagrams seem to suffer all the disadvantages of flowcharts but to an even greater degree. For example,

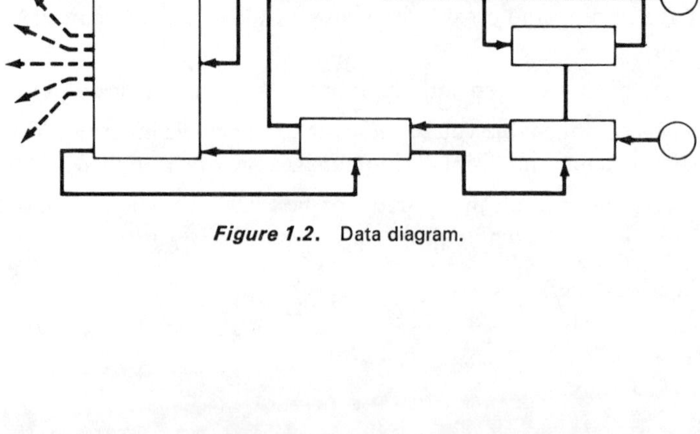

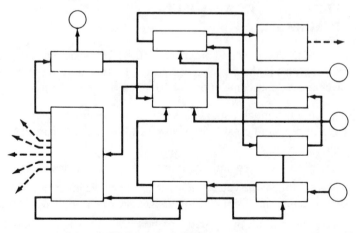

Figure 1.2. Data diagram.

7. Change in the structure at run time is now the rule rather than the exception.
8. Physical realization of an arrow by a reference or pointer is expensive in storage.
9. Cache stores and instruction pipelines are especially ineffective against a program which is chasing down a chain of indirect addresses.
10. The diagram, instead of being an actual representation of the whole program, is only an imagined example of only part of the actual data structure at some instant in time.

A simple example with a picture is of great advantage in confirming our understanding of a complex problem, but as the sole means of developing and communicating such an understanding it is woefully inadequate.

1.2. DATA RELIABILITY

The problems of program reliability are notorious, but reliability problems which arise with long-term data storage are even more severe; some of the reasons are as follows:

1. Programs expressed in a suitable high-level language can be analyzed rigorously by a compiler so that a running program is known to be meaningful even if it does not do what the programmer wanted. Input data are nothing but an unstructured stream of characters, chards, or bits; they may be meaningless, and even if meaningful, the information conveyed may be false.
2. If a program behaves incorrectly on a particular run, this does not affect other programs or even subsequent runs of the same program. However, if a bug is introduced on one run into a data base, it remains there and can actually propagate itself as later correct programs operate on the data.
3. If the hardware fails in the middle of a run of a program, it can safely be run again from the beginning, but the same fault in the midst of updating a data base may leave it in a partially or wholly unusable condition.
4. From bitter experience, users can learn to avoid the bugs in unreliable software. But as soon as bugs appear in a data bank, its users lose confidence and will withdraw their data for private keeping. Now they no longer have any motive to keep their banked data up-to-date. A run on a data bank is as catastrophic as a run on an ordinary bank which deals merely in money.

This theoretical analysis shows that in the design of data we have been using weaker design methods to tackle problems more serious than those of the design of programs. Practical experience in the design of data bases seems to confirm the theoretical analysis. In this chapter we shall survey some of the improved methods for data design and description which are now becoming available and shall point out the analogies with some of the improved methods of design and description which are being applied to programs and which have been packaged and marketed under the brand name *structured programming*.

Programmers benefit from these methods largely because they reject flowcharts and deliberately confine themselves to a range of structuring disciplines with the following desirable properties:

1. They are few in number.
2. They are logically simple.
3. They are amenable to simple proof techniques.
4. They can be applied on a large scale or on a small scale.
5. They assist in top-down design or in bottom-up design.
6. They are easy to implement.
7. The easy implementation is also efficient.

Structuring principles for data should have the same properties.

1.3. TYPE

To develop the analogy between program and data structuring methods, we must introduce the concept of *type*. A type determines a class of values, which may be stored in a variable (declared to be of that type), passed as a parameter (specified as of that type), or given as the result of an expression or function (of that type). The primitive types of a programming language, such as the *integer* of ALGOL 60 and FLOAT of FORTRAN, are obvious examples. But the concept of a type can be usefully generalized to cover structured data, whose pattern can be specified by the programmer himself by means of a *type declaration*.

A program or procedure may also be regarded as determining a certain class, namely the class of all computations which may result from a particular run of the program or call of the procedure. All these computations will be similar in their overall structure, even though the exact size and values involved will vary from computation to computation. In the case of a well-structured program, the overall pattern of the class of possible computations is so clearly revealed in the pattern of the program itself that it is possible to understand and prove the correctness of such a program without even thinking of the large class of potential computations involved. A type declaration should use similar clear patterns to define the structural properties of all possible data instances of that type, independent of their size or the component values involved.

1.4. DIRECT PRODUCT

The first and simplest structuring method is known by mathematicians as the direct or Cartesian product. For example, a mathematician can define the space of complex numbers as a product of real and real, as follows:

$$\text{complex} =_{\text{df}} \text{real} \times \text{real}.$$

By this definition, he states that each value of the type complex is a structure with exactly two components, a first component which is real and a second component which is also real—or, in other words, an ordered pair of reals. Furthermore, the two reals are entirely independent of each other; their only connection consists of their grouping together in the specified order as a single complex number.

The same structuring method is just as familiar in data processing, where it is known as a record definition. For example, a record which specifies an insertion may be defined as

$$\text{insertion} =_{\text{df}} \text{partnumber} \times \text{partdetail},$$

or as it is expressed in a COBOL-like language,

```
01  INSERTION
  02 PARTNUMBER
    03    . . .
  02 PARTDETAIL
    03    . . . ,
```

where the items with level number 03 (and higher) indicate the substructure of PARTNUMBER and PARTDETAIL components.

The direct product method of data structuring has close analogies with the method of constructing a program by composition (the compound statement). For example, a particular program or procedure may be composed of two statements:

```
begin q:=q+1; r:=r−y end
```

This means that every computation evoked by this compound statement also consists of two disjoint parts; the first adds 1 to q, and the second subtracts y from r. Furthermore, the only connecting relationship between these parts consists of their grouping together in the specified order.

One of the most important advantages of a good structuring method is that it can be applied to components of any size or substructure. The method of program composition can be applied equally to atomic instructions as to complete programs; for example, the following is a very common structure for scientific programs:

```
begin input; calculation; output end
```

Similarly, a large data base may be described as the direct product of the files which it contains, for example,

$$\text{database} =_{\text{df}} \text{salesledger} \times \text{inventory} \times \text{payroll} \times \text{catalogue}.$$

1.5. DISCRIMINATED UNION

The next simple structuring method is the discriminated union, which specifies that a choice is to be made from a selection of alternative structures. In the simplest case, the alternatives are just indicators of some condition, for example, a possible malfunction of a peripheral device:

$$\text{exception} =_{\text{df}} \text{parity fault} \mid \text{empty} \mid \text{manual}.$$

This states that the type "exception" consists of exactly three values with the names indicated and that every exception variable has one of these three values. As a more substantial example, consider a transaction record for a traditional file-updating program. If record definitions have already been made for deletions, insertions, and amendments, a transaction can be defined as being a choice of exactly one of these alternatives:

$$\text{transaction} =_{\text{df}} \text{insertion} \mid \text{deletion} \mid \text{amendment}.$$

A similar specification can be given in COBOL by multiple record definitions:

```
01  INSERTION
  02      . . .
01  DELETION
  02      . . .
01  AMENDMENT
  02      . . .
```

At levels lower than 01, the REDEFINES clause permits a similar effect.

But a discriminated union differs from the mathematical union of sets (and from COBOL), in that each value retains an inspectable "tag," indicating the alternative to which it belongs.

The discriminated union is closely analogous to the conditional or case construction in programming. A conditional of the form

<u>if</u> B <u>then</u> T <u>else</u> E

evokes computation of exactly one of the alternatives T or E, the selection to be made in accordance with the value of B.

1.6. SEQUENCE

The third major data structuring method is called the *sequence*. A sequence consists of none or more components of data, arranged in some meaningful order. In mathematical notation a sequence is frequently denoted by an asterisk, as follows:

$$\text{string} = \text{character}^*,$$

which defines a string as a sequence of none or more characters, for example,

```
A
B7Y
A SLIGHTLY LONGER STRING
```

(The fourth example has no character and is therefore invisible. Mathematicians sometimes use the symbol $\wedge$ to denote the empty sequence.)

In data processing, a sequence is usually known as a *file* and might be defined as

$$\text{transaction file} = \text{header} \times \text{transaction}^* \times \text{trailer},$$

where "header," "trailer," and "transaction" have previously been given record definitions. A similar, but less precise, specification of a file can be given in the COBOL file description:

```
DATA RECORDS ARE HEADER,
INSERTION, DELETION, AMENDMENT, TRAILER;
```

A sequence corresponds to the iterative program structure, using while:

```
while B do L.
```

The computation of this structure consists of a sequence of none or more computations of the program component L; the sequence is not bounded in advance, but its length on any given occasion must be finite.

1.7. TYPES AND RECURSION

A procedure declaration in a programming language is a means of packaging a complex program structure, possibly evoking long and elaborate computations, and enabling it to be regarded and used many times by procedure calls, as though it were a single primitive unit of action. Thus, the procedure declaration is one of the most powerful tools provided in a high-level programming language for mastering the complexity of a large problem.

A similar benefit can be extended to the design and description of data by the *type* declaration of PASCAL, the *mode* declaration of ALGOL 68, or, perhaps best of all, by the *class* declaration of SIMULA 67.

A type declaration associates a complex structure description with the type name. This name can be used repeatedly to declare new variables of the type, for example, using PASCAL notation,

```
X, Y :complex;
```

will declare two new variables X and Y of type complex; each of these will display the structure of a complex number, and each will consist of two separate real numbers, but the programmer can regard it as a single unit of data. On a larger scale, two files might be declared:

```
oldmaster, newmaster :masterfile.
```

The analogy with procedure declarations suggests the question: 'Is there any place for recursion in the definition of data structures?'. Again the answer is yes. The occurrence of a type name inside its own definition denotes an occurrence of a (smaller) instance of a value of that type as a component. This is exactly analogous to the computation of a recursive procedure, which contains a (smaller) computation of that same recursive procedure in place of each of the recursive calls.

Examples of recursive types occur frequently in programming language definition and processing and also in general symbol manipulation. For example, the traditional data structure of LISP may be declared:

$$\text{list} =_{\text{df}} \text{atom} \mid \text{list} \times \text{list};$$

or, in other words, a list is either an atom (defined elsewhere) or an ordered pair, whose first and second components are themselves lists.

An example drawn from data processing applications is the catalogue of parts and components which is used in a parts explosion analysis. A part is either bought in (and has no components), or is an assembly. Each assembly has assembly data, followed by a sequence of the parts from which it is made. These facts can be expressed formally in the type declarations

$$\text{part} =_{\text{df}} \text{bought in} \mid \text{assembly}$$

$$\text{assembly} =_{\text{df}} \text{assembly data} \times \text{part}^*.$$

It is unfortunate that no well-known programming language permits this simple use of recursion in data structuring.

1.8. OPERATIONS

The preceding sections have been based on an oversimplified view of the concept of type, which concentrates solely on the values and their structure. A more balanced view regards a type as a set of values (for variables, functions, and parameters) *together with* the primitive operations which can be applied to these values. Thus, the concept of the integer type consists not only of a certain range of integer values but also of the availability of the primitive operators of addition, subtraction, multiplication, and division, which are defined on integer arguments and give integer results. It is far better, for conceptual clarity as well as machine independence, to regard the integer type as a set of abstract values on which these operations are defined, rather than as being structured out of the component binary digits, which are used in most machines to represent an integer.

A similar abstraction is highly desirable when the programmer is constructing new types. For example, the complex type too is better regarded as an abstract number space over which certain arithmetic operations are defined, rather than in terms of its representation, say, in polar coordinates. But in this case it is the programmer rather than the hardware designer who must declare the functions or procedures which actually implement these operations. Furthermore, once these operations are implemented, they should be the *only* means of processing and updating complex numbers, and from then on the programmer should cease to think of them in terms of the pair of real components from which they have been made.

It is this resolve to hide the details of a representation which provides in data structuring the same power of abstraction that is offered by procedures and parameters. The caller of a procedure is encouraged to be unaware of the details of the computation which it invokes and the nature and names of the local data which are needed temporarily during the computation. The only aspect of the procedure with which he is concerned is its effect on the actual parameters (arguments) which he has passed. Similarly, the user of a type should be concerned only with the effect of the operations which have been made available by the implementor of the type, and not with the details of their internal structure.

1.9. MAPPINGS

The survey of data structuring methods given above deals only with the most important structures, which can be easily and efficiently mapped onto machine representations, and it is not intended to be complete. For example, it omits one very useful concept of a finite mapping. A finite mapping, in the mathematician's sense, is a function which is defined only on a finite range of arguments of type A and which maps each argument onto a value from type B.

In mathematical notation, this may be expressed with an arrow:

$$A \longrightarrow B.$$

To the programmer, the most familiar example of a finite mapping is the array, which maps a finite range of integers, say [a. . b], onto values of some type, for example, real. Using mathematical notation this may be written

$$\text{vector} =_{\text{df}} [a..b] \longrightarrow \text{real}.$$

In the case of a multidimensional array, it is a Cartesian product of such ranges over which the array is defined:

$$\text{matrix} =_{\text{df}} [a..b] \times [c..d] \longrightarrow \text{real}$$

But the concept of a finite mapping is more general than that, and the range of arguments may be any finite set or subset of values of any type. For example, a sparse matrix may be regarded as a mapping given only by its (finite number of) nonzero elements:

$$\text{sparse matrix} =_{\text{df}} \text{integer} \times \text{integer} \longrightarrow \text{real}.$$

In a more commercial environment, a price list may be regarded as a finite mapping which assigns a price to each product;

$$\text{pricelist} =_{\text{df}} \text{product} \longrightarrow \text{price}.$$

Similarly, in a compiler, we require a symbol table which maps each identifier onto its decode (type, address, etc.):

$$\text{symboltable} =_{\text{df}} \text{identifier} \longrightarrow \text{decode}.$$

And finally, to illustrate the application of this concept on a large scale, consider a telephone directory. In the simplest view, this is nothing but a finite (but very large) mapping:

$$\text{telephone directory} =_{\text{df}} \text{subscriber} \rightarrow \text{telephone number}.$$

1.10. TOP-DOWN DESIGN

The concept of mapping offers a very abstract way of looking at a large random-access file and does not give any help or insight into the way in which the structure is going to be implemented in some combination of storage levels on a large computer. In fact, all the real problems of implementation remain. It is totally unrealistic to suppose that any high-level language or automatic process (or even a generalized integrated data base management system) will be able to produce a satisfactory implementation from such an abstract definition.

However, I would suggest that this abstract definition, devoid of all implementation detail, will be helpful to the programmer in the early stages of design of his system. He can design his abstract program as though it operates on the abstract data structure and can thereby complete a consistent design, without being confused by the details of the representation of his data; then, when he knows more exactly how these data are going to be processed, he may choose the most suitable representation and implement it by coding the fundamental operations required. In this way, the design and implementation may proceed in an orderly fashion, from the top downwards, or even from the bottom up, if preferred.

But in practice, progress may not be so orderly. If it appears that there is no acceptably efficient method of representing the data, it may be necessary to reconsider the abstract program. However, the clear separation of decisions and details relevant to the two stages (or more) will probably clarify the task of the designer or designers and will almost certainly help him to communicate and discuss his problems with his colleagues and successors.

1.11. REFERENCES AND POINTERS

One remarkable feature of the structuring methods introduced here is that they make no mention of the reference or pointer, which are traditionally regarded as the prime means of structuring data. In this respect, references seem similar to go to statements, which have traditionally played a major role in computer programming and which seem to be going rapidly out of fashion. In fact the analogy goes deeper. In the implementation of data structures use may be made of machine addresses, just as jumps are used in machine code to implement conditionals, and while loops and procedures. The major structuring disadvantage of the jump is that it creates new wide interfaces between distant parts of a program, which look as though they should be separate, and the slightest change in a program can propagate errors rapidly and uncontrollably along these interfaces. I suspect that the same is true of a reference, pointing from one part of a data structure to another distant part, which ought to be disjoint. And I expect that there will be yet another analogy—the recommendation to remove references from data structuring will meet as much controversy as that to remove go to's from programming.

1.12. CONCLUSION

The methods of data structuring and description which have been summarized in this chapter are in principle capable of representing all data whatsoever. The proof of this is trivial and depends on the finitude of the computation which constructs a data value. Each data value can in principle be represented by a history of the computation which constructs it, and all such computational histories can be described using the given structuring methods.

But this theoretical proof does not guarantee that the methods will be convenient or efficient in practice; this can be established only by a determined effort to apply them to the design of data in some reasonably typical large-scale projects. If these experiments are successful, it would be very interesting to design a simple data base description language and management scheme along the lines indicated by the theory, avoiding the explicit introduction of references and making the clearest possible distinction between abstraction and representation.

Nevertheless, I believe that the problems of data structure and representation are likely to remain more severe than those of program structuring. In addition to the problems summarized in the first two sections, the peculiar timing and storage characteristics of high-volume magnetic stores, together with real-time response constraints, will often force the programmer to violate the structure of his problem and his program in the interests of efficiency, and there always remains the possibility of the wholly unstructured problem, which permits no structured solution. So the methods described in this chapter can be recommended not as a panacea for the control of arbitrary complexity but rather as a discipline for elucidating and preserving any possible underlying grain of simplicity. And simplicity is the unavoidable price which we must pay for reliability.

CHAPTER 2

NOTIONS

GEORGE H. MEALY
Center for Research in Computing Technology
Harvard University
Cambridge, Massachusetts

"That is not an *idea* in this system."

T. E. Cheatham, Jr.

"What we need is young men with old ideas."

Mort Sahl

"Here is one more system of philosophy. If the reader is tempted to smile, I can assure him that I smile with him, and that my system—to which this volume is a critical introduction—differs widely in spirit and pretensions from what usually goes by that name. In the first place, *my system is not mine, or new*. I am merely attempting to express for the reader the principles to which he appeals when he smiles. There are convictions in the depths of his soul, beneath all his overt parrot beliefs, on which I would build our friendship."

George Santayana
Scepticism and Animal Faith

2.1. INTRODUCTION

While the content of this chapter is largely motivated by a series of investigations into the nature of data and computational semantics [1, 4, 6, 7, 8, 10, 11, 12, 13], its immediate setting is that of a *program manipulation system* or PMS [3, 5, 9]. Structured programming, whatever else one may believe it to be, is the study of the transition from an initial idea of a program to a refined version which is acceptable to a conventional programming system. The goal of a PMS is to render the computer useful during this passage from an idea in the mind of man to a runnable program. The ultimate criterion of correctness of a program must be its faithful rendition of the mental concept: "Program *P* does the following: . . .."

From this standpoint, programming is usefully visualized as a process of abstraction followed by making a series of choices of algorithms and representations that deliver a concrete version of the initial or revised abstraction (backtracking is, of course, involved along the way). In a very real sense, the initial step is formulation of a *theory* which, the programmer believes, models the relevant features of a particular problem area. If the reader grants me the validity of this characterization of the programming process, she may then understand why it is that the practicing programmer (the good one, at least) spends such a relatively small part of her time coding and debugging. What is by no means clear is that the aforementioned goal can be realized to any very significant extent, for I seem to be discussing mental and psychological phenomena. We shall see.

My paradigm for program development, then, is (1) formulation of a theory and (2) bridging the gap between the abstract and the concrete. The goal of a PMS is to offer use of the computer as a significant aid in bridging this gap. A correctness proof is a plausible argument that the concrete form of the program is a model, in the sense of logic, of its abstract form.

Let us explore the idea of a PMS in just a bit more detail. Any given PMS is realized on a given *base system*. The PMS under investigation at Harvard, for instance, uses the PDP-10 implementation of the ECL system [2, 14, 15, 16]. A program developed using PMS is intended to be run on a possibly different *target system*. The goal of program portability, taken together with one's feeling that the gap is bridged by a series of specializations (refinements, restrictions) which are selected by making deliberate choices, leads quite naturally to the idea of a choice tree. A program is *portable* between target systems S and T precisely when its realizations on S and T are among the terminal nodes of its choice tree. Further, the portable form of that program with respect to S and T is that (usually nonterminal) node of the tree which is the least remote common ancestor of the two realizations.

Our ambitions with regard to portability add poignancy to the following dilemma: On the abstract side of the gap, *systems should not constrain the programmer's formulation of her theory in any nontrivial respect*. But, on the opposite shore of this sea of mixed metaphor, the target system is itself based on a specific theory, and, in the medium distance, the PMS and its base system have their own theories. Thus, the programmer's task is made more difficult by the fact that her theory must be made to square with those of the PMS and the target system(s).

Recoiling from the Procrustean nature of this task, a classics scholar would no doubt remind us that the way out of a dilemma is to grasp both horns firmly and, like the Cretan bulldancer, somersault gracefully over its head. Thereby the horns become lemmas, or useful tools. The key to this evolution in our current strait is, I claim, to reconsider data yet again.

When we achieve any concrete realization of a program, we have a collection of data objects, including the code itself, represented in the target system. During our passage from the abstract to the concrete, the predecessors of these data objects must be represented by PMS on the base system. Initially, however, we start with abstract mental objects, and these I shall call *notions*. *Notions are fuzzy data objects*. Thus, we may say that the programmer's first task is to formulate an abstract theory whose objects are notions. Her remaining task is to refine them so that they become concrete data objects in a given target system.

In many current programming systems a data type is itself embodied as a data object. Borrowing from the terminology of ALGOL 68, as did ECL, I shall call these concrete data objects *modes*. For their abstract form as notions, I shall use the conventional term *type*. Thus, while notions are fuzzy data objects, types are that subset of notions which are fuzzy modes.

And now for the leap: While the mathematical concepts of class and relation go back a mere century, disputation on the nature of various notions and their types was a Greek innovation, as far as we know. You and I can point to a computer without seriously misunderstanding which object it is that we point at, but notions evade such direct demonstration. The leap taken early in the history of Greek philosophy was, instead, to discuss *properties* of the notion in question. By "property," I mean a predicate which asserts that the notion possesses a certain *attribute* and that such and such is the *value* of that attribute (or, we employ a predicate which is the logical conjunction of such primitive predicates, sometimes using the full power of propositional logic with quantification). Thus, we communicate a notion by asserting its properties; we may then argue about whether or not and under what circumstances a given property is possessed by the notion at issue. Frege and his successors, in developing the abstract theory of classes (or sets) and relations, formalized this convention of Greek thought.

The implication of the above for a PMS is that *notions may be represented by their properties in the form of sets and relations*. That is, a notion can be represented in a PMS by a list of attribute and value pairs—for instance, the property list of IPL-V and LISP.

Having set the stage, I am ready to end this prologue. In Section 2.2 I shall present a formalization of notions, types, and classes (of types). The style is that of algebra, and the basic trick consists of maintaining that types form a lattice. The formal definition of classes follows immediately, given the lattice. I shall then suggest how types may presume to describe notions.

I have insisted that the first task of the programmer is to construct a theory. Part of this job consists of the design of types and a class theory which interrelates them. (Data structures are the crucial components of the overall design of any program or system.) A PMS itself requires a minimal and nonconstraining class theory to establish a base for the programmer's construction of his own theory. In Section 2.3, I shall describe a sample class theory for a PMS. This I call FREECL, for it is a freely eclectic generalization of the class theory of ECL.

In Section 2.4 I shall consider control and semantics, indicating how the lines of thought described earlier may be extended to bring the subject of control into their framework.

ECL is used as a source of examples in the body of this chapter. Several features of the system conspire to make this a reasonable choice. First, it uses modes as data objects in their own right. Second, mode procedures are used to define data semantics. Third, it incorporates a general treatment of pointer data, unions, and user mode definition. By contrast with ALGOL 68, it possesses a relatively accessible (understandable) description of its syntax and semantics [2, 14, 15, 16]. While a number of ideas in this chapter were inspired by ECL, they are applicable much more generally.

2.2. NOTIONS AS A FORMAL SYSTEM

There is an innate human urge to classify things, and we explain any system of classification by appealing to properties of the things being classified. By this rubric, x and y belong to some class if they share the properties common to all things of that class; we call them identical when they cannot be distinguished on the basis of having different values for some attribute which is significant in the current universe of discourse.

Data types are thus classes of notions—for example, vectors of length 6 or the more restricted integer vectors of length 6 are types. Recalling that a type is itself a notion in some systems, we can economize on storage in these systems by storing the common properties of the notions of each type in the type rather than in each of its notions. In this sense, *types describe notions.*

In a wider sense also, notions of a given type have attributes whose values may differ, and if a type is to describe its notions, it should have something to say about such attributes. In the forthcoming formal system, we shall explicitly assume that each type has a property, the *descriptor*, which specifies the latter, variable, properties.

In set theory, classes are partially ordered by the relation of set inclusion. Similarly, we should be able to partially order types by appealing to their properties. The question here is what semantic burden we should place upon the ordering. The answer to this question will be developed gradually in the following.

It is well to keep in mind that we are headed toward FREECL and other class theories, so the abstract objects and maps (or data) of the formal system are supposed to have direct interpretations in the context of a PMS or a target system. There will be the set P of *primitive values* which are interpreted as being the values of certain data objects in the base system. Among them are the subset A of P used as *attributes* or *selectors* and the subset I of A used as *identifiers*. The set N of *notions* is, by definition, disjoint from P.

To talk about pointers and shared values, we need a concept which specializes to the idea of a storage location or a byte pointer. I use the term *site* and assume a set of sites (of values) S. Notions have *shared values* precisely when their values occupy the same site. A *pointer* is a notion whose dereferenced value is the notion which it references. Hence, notions themselves must be storable as values.

Along with primitive values and notions, we need a kind of value which corresponds to compound data objects such as rows and structures; their components are selected by an index or some other selector. We can thus view compound values as sets of values which are indexed by subsets of A. Equivalently, a compound value is a set of ordered pairs, $\langle a, v \rangle$,where a is a selector and v is the corresponding selected value. $\langle a, v\rangle$ is an element of the direct product of the sets A and V. But the elements of V must be all values: primitive, notions, and compound; V must be defined recursively.

As to the maps we need, it is useful to recall the way we implement the identifier environment for a block-structured language. The usual method is to employ one or more run-time stacks. Among the stack entries are those which store information associated with the bindings of identifiers, be they free variables, formal parameters, or local variables. While the details are idiosyncratic to a given implementation, we should think of these stack entries as being among the notions. There are four important pieces of information associated with each stack entry or notion: its identifier, or *name*; its *type*; the *site* of its (bound) value; and the *value* itself. The maps in the formal system will correspond to these. The above is summarized in the following definition:

A *data system* is an ordered 9-tuple

$$D = \langle N, P, I, A, S, \nu, \tau, \sigma, \upsilon\rangle$$

where N and P are disjoint and $I \subseteq A \subseteq P$. The last four data are maps:

$\nu : N \dashrightarrow I$	*name*
$\tau : N \dashrightarrow N$	*type*
$\sigma : N \dashrightarrow S$	*site*
$\upsilon : S \dashrightarrow V$	*value*

where V is defined recursively:

(a) P and N are subsets of V.

(b) If X is a subset of V, then every subset of $A \times X$ is a subset of V.

As a notational convenience, I shall write $x.\nu$ rather than $\nu(x)$, *etc.*; for example, if we interpret the notion x as any stack entry associated with a binding, this notation suggests selection of the name of x.

Note that the doctrine that types lurk among the notions has been implemented in the definition of the type map. We define the set of types as the image of this map:

$$T == \tau(N)$$

Note also that the set of values (the range of the value map υ) is a disjoint union, by set theory and the disjointness of N and P. We can classify notions accordingly:

$B == \{x : x.\sigma.\upsilon \in P\}$	*basic* notions
$\Pi == \{x : x.\sigma.\upsilon \subseteq N$	*pointer* notions
$C == \{x : x.\sigma.\upsilon \in A \times V\}$	*compound* notions

[Please note that these are *not* the classes to be defined further below. These are classes of notions and are defined by the structure of their *representation* as sets. The classes of types to be defined later are classes according to the *behavior* (semantics) of the notions of each type.]

As a set-theoretic detail, we need to guarantee that the result of selection is unique. This is provided by

Axiom I

Selectors are functions: If $x \in N$ and $\langle a, u\rangle$ and $\langle a, v\rangle$ are in $x.\sigma.\upsilon$, then $u = v$.

Thus, we could treat a selector as a map, but the selection notation will be used:

$$\mathsf{x.a} == \{\mathsf{v}: \langle \mathsf{a}, \mathsf{v}\rangle \in \mathsf{x}.\sigma.\upsilon\}$$

(Equally well, I could have used the notation of indexing: $x[a]$.) If x is not a compound notion, an essay at selection will deliver the empty set, which corresponds to a compile-time diagnostic or a run-time fault; this is a consequence of set theory and the above definitions.

We wish to refine notions in order to ultimately obtain well-defined data objects. This leads in turn to the idea of ordering types. I wish to say that $\boldsymbol{s} \geq \boldsymbol{t}$ precisely when $\boldsymbol{t}$ can be said to be a *restricted* version of $\boldsymbol{s}$. What we need is a formalization of this idea. That characterization must be related to the Greek device of discussing properties of notions.

If we wish an ordering, it can surely be at best a partial ordering. Hence, we naturally (as suggested by the work of Scott [13]) try to define a lattice (a partially ordered set in which each pair of elements has both a least upper bound and a greatest lower bound in terms of the ordering). So far, however, the data and axioms of our system do not provide the means for proving that types form a lattice, so we must memorialize this intuition as an axiom. What is also missing is assurance that there exist limits in the lattice (in the sense of Scott [13]; the lower limit is available in ECL as the mode ***none***; as we shall see, the ECL mode ***any*** is not a type within the intended interpretation of the axioms).

While we could define types as classes determined by predicates (that is, by their properties) in the familiar style of logic and then define the ordering in terms of logical implication, this would lead to an overpopulated universe of types. Since we need only a finite stock of types at any time, I prefer a bold axiom to the effect that $\langle T, \geq\rangle$ is a lattice and that the limits exist. The axiom will also provide for the existence of the pointer constant *nil* and its dereferenced value *nothing*. In ECL, the latter is interpreted as being the *empty value*, not to be confused with the empty set.

Axiom II

Types form a lattice: Types are partially ordered by $\geq$, and $\langle T, \geq\rangle$ is a lattice. There exist types ***all*** and ***none*** such that for all types $\boldsymbol{t}$

(a) $\mathbf{all} \geq \mathbf{t} \geq \mathbf{none}$

There exist unique notions *nil* and *nothing* such that

(b) $\mathsf{nothing}.\tau = \mathbf{none}$

(c) $\mathsf{nil}.\sigma.\upsilon = \mathsf{nothing}$

Now that the lattice exists, we can define classes in terms of the partial ordering (they are the ideals in the lattice):

$$\mathsf{Class}(\mathbf{s}) == \{\mathbf{t}: \mathbf{s} \geq \mathbf{t}\}$$

Types are supposed to describe notions, and types are themselves notions. We shall assume that all types have the same type, ***type***. We shall also assume that they are compound notions and possess a *descriptor* component which is selected by the selector δ. We then consider the earlier classification of notions:

> If x is basic, then its value is primitive, and we assume that the system knows everything it needs to know about x, given $x.\tau$. $x.\tau.\delta$ is hence left unconstrained by the axioms.
>
> If x is a pointer, we wish to know the possible types of its dereferenced value and therefore require that $x.\sigma.\upsilon.\tau \in x.\tau.\delta$. That is, $x.\tau.\delta$ is the set of types of any notions which x may validly reference.
>
> Otherwise, x is compound, and we wish to know which selectors are legal for it as well as the types of the selectable components. If a is a legal selector for x, we require that $x.\tau.\delta.a = x.a.\tau$.

This information is packaged in the following definition and axiom:

Prop(x, a) == x.a is not the empty set

We say that x *has property* a when x is compound and a is a valid selector for x.

Axiom III

Types describe notions: If $\boldsymbol{t} \in T$, then

(a) **type** == **t**.τ is unique
(b) Prop(**t**, δ)
(c) p $\in \Pi$ implies p.$\sigma.\upsilon.\tau \in$ p.$\tau.\delta$
(d) x $\in$ C and Prop(x.$\tau.\delta$, a) implies x.$\tau.\delta$.a = x.a.τ

It is important to note that types may have selectors other than δ and that compound notions may have selectors not specified by their type—the latter remark is important only in the context of PMS; the idea here is that one may decide that a notion will have a certain property or component earlier than the point in design at which the type of that notion is fully specified—such a property may persist in remaining illegal for some time.

The connection between the type properties and the ordering must now be explored. Our final axiom will specify this in terms of how order is preserved by the type descriptors, considered as mappings.

Consider two arbitrary notions x and y of types $\boldsymbol{x}$ and $\boldsymbol{y}$, respectively, and such that $\boldsymbol{x} \geq \boldsymbol{y}$. If x is a pointer, then y must be one as well and we require that $\boldsymbol{y}.\delta \subseteq \boldsymbol{x}.\delta$. On the other hand, suppose that the notions are compound and that a is a property of $\boldsymbol{x}.\delta$ and thus, by Axiom III(d), of x. $\boldsymbol{y}$ is supposed to be a restriction of $\boldsymbol{x}$. We can ensure this if we require that a be a property of $\boldsymbol{y}.\delta$ and that the same order hold for the types of the respective selected components of x and y. For instance, $x.a$ might be a set and $y.a$ an ordered set (a more restrictive type). We thus require that $\boldsymbol{x}.\delta.a \geq \boldsymbol{y}.\delta.a$.

We can also obtain restricted types by adding new properties; they are more restricted in the sense that the conditions for a notion having the type are stronger and, hence, fewer notions may qualify.

There is yet another way to obtain restricted types. To see this, notice that Axiom III(b) provides for only one standard type selector, but types may have other selectors (properties). The descriptor δ describes the variable properties of notions of a given type, in the sense that when a property varies in its values between notions of a given type then each value must be stored as a component of the individual notion. On the other hand, a property value which is constant for all notions within a type should be stored as a component of the type, if storage efficiency means anything at all. Thus, the descriptor describes the *variable properties* of notions of the type, and the other components of the type describe the *constant properties* of its notions. Consider, for instance, variable-length rows of integers as opposed to integer rows of a given, fixed length. The upshot of this argument is that we may also restrict a type by holding a variable property constant.

Our final axiom has thus been motivated:

Axiom IV

Description preserves order: Let $x = x.\tau$, $y = y.\tau$, and $x \geq y$. Then

(a) x, y ϵ Π implies y.$\delta \subseteq$ x.δ

(b) x, y ϵ C and Prop(x.δ, a) imply either Prop(y.δ, a) and x.δ.a $\geq$ y.δ.a or Prop(y, a) and x.δ.a $\geq$ y.a.τ but not both.

To some extent, the comprehensiveness of an axiom set is a matter of individual taste. My intent has been to require the minimum necessary to avoid overconstraining the construction of user and system class theories; if the formalization is reasonable, it must be justified in terms of its usefulness for such constructions. In and of itself, it does not explain many things that we might normally assume about types and their classes. This is the job of a class theory, and our next agenda item is to indicate how a PMS class theory might be constructed. (The user defines his class theory by declaring types. Each declaration is, in effect, a further axiom.) Issues of representation and semantics, for the most part absent in the above formal system, now come to the fore.

2.3. FREECL

In this section we shall not pretend to fully define FREECL. Rather, we shall attempt to indicate the basic ideas involved in such a way that the reader can fill in the details if she wishes and is already sufficiently familiar with ECL (otherwise she may refer to [2]).

Class Conflict

The lattice trick of the last section has at the same time connected the idea of type with those of restriction and refinement and given us an immediate formal definition of class. While properties have been used in establishing these connections, we are still starkly confronted by the horns of our dilemma. To reiterate my earlier maxim, the user's class theory must not be significantly constrained by that of the PMS, its base system, or the target system. We need to turn another trick. It will develop that we must effect a divorce of class from representation.

Let me give an example to drive this point home. Suppose you are constructing a class theory in which ***point*** is to be a type, together with restricted versions of ***point*** (other members of that class of types) according to dimensionality and representation by rectangular or angular coordinatization. Surely, from a mathematical point of view, Figure 2.1 might well be that local part of the type lattice which you wish to define. Unfortunately, current systems usually force us to first define ***pair*** and ***triple*** (of reals). Only then may we explain the lower types in the figure as subclasses of these. Finally, we can define the remaining types as unions of these subclasses, as shown in Figure 2.2. This, for instance, might be a natural definitional pattern using ECL. In both figures, the ordering is that imposed by our axioms. Should we blame them or ECL?

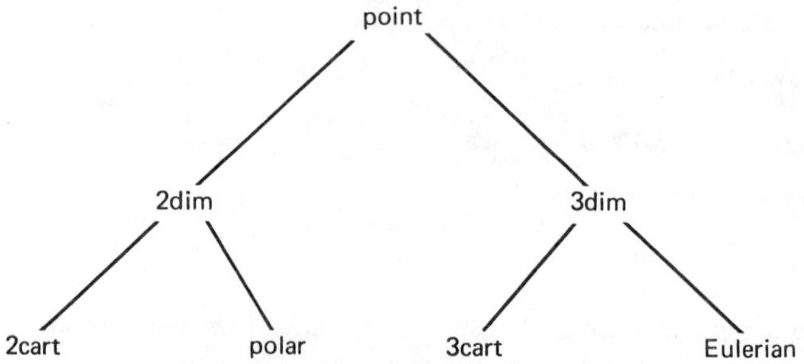

Figure 2.1. Abstract types.

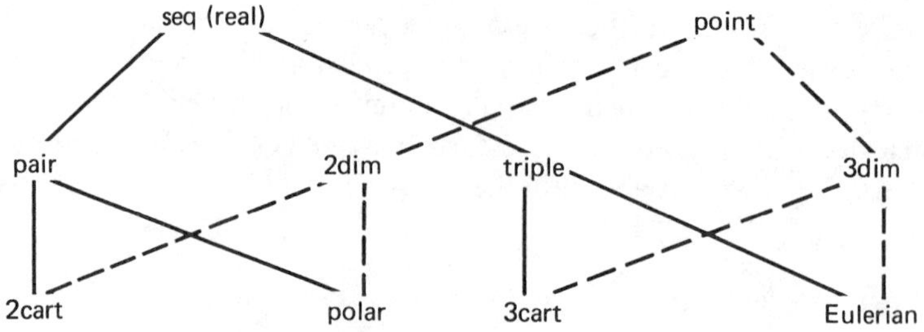

Figure 2.2. ECL types.

Neither, I believe. The class theory of ECL, as is the case with other systems which are not so self-conscious about class distinctions, is founded on the idea that storage representation is the major determinant of classhood. In ECL, revealingly enough, ***polar*** would have ***pair*** as its "underlying representation," and both are of class ***row***. ***2dim*** would be defined, on the other hand, as a union of the types ***polar*** and ***2cart***. Far from being a contrived example, Figure 2.2 is quite instructive. Why? Because we can easily see that for each pair of types at the top two levels of the figure the one on the left might well be viewed as being the storage representation for notions whose type is the one on the right!

This is to say that the mathematical idea of representation, as exhibited in Figure 2.1, is conformable to the idea of type restriction. That of storage representation is orthogonal to these concepts, or should be. ***triple*** might be a representing type for ***Eulerian*** in both ECL and FREECL, but in the former ***Eulerian*** is also called an *extension* of ***triple***. This terminology is reminiscent of extension of a field k to the field $k[x]$, but the former is a *restriction* of the latter, algebraically speaking, and to call k the underlying representation of $k[x]$ is contrary to mathematical usage.

The use of the term *extension* in extensible languages is quite different from its use just above. An extended mode in ECL, obtained by use of restriction or union, is a *definitional* extension; the technical vocabulary has been extended, not the basic power of the system. Extension of the rationals to obtain the field of algebraic numbers is quite another matter.

So, in FREECL we shall effect the divorce of class from storage representation. Class will be defined by the partial ordering, but representation will be independent of it.

Type Definition

Figure 2.2 illustrates two different ways of defining new types in terms of old ones. I shall call these *restriction* and *union*, respectively, and they correspond to the solid and the broken lines in the figure. The first method amounts to application of Axiom IV. The second amounts to declaring that the new type is an immediate cover of types already in the lattice. Thus, given an initial stock of types, the existence of others is asserted by declaration, using restriction and/or union.

My use of the term *union* should not be confused with the idea of a lattice join (least upper bound), even though in the lattice of subsets of a set the two ideas coincide. Consider Figure 2.3, for example: ***circular*** is asserted as a union of ***polar*** and ***Eulerian*** (the double arrows give the underlying representations of ***point***, *etc.*). No ordering relation between ***point*** and ***circular*** is defined, nor are these two types considered to be identical.

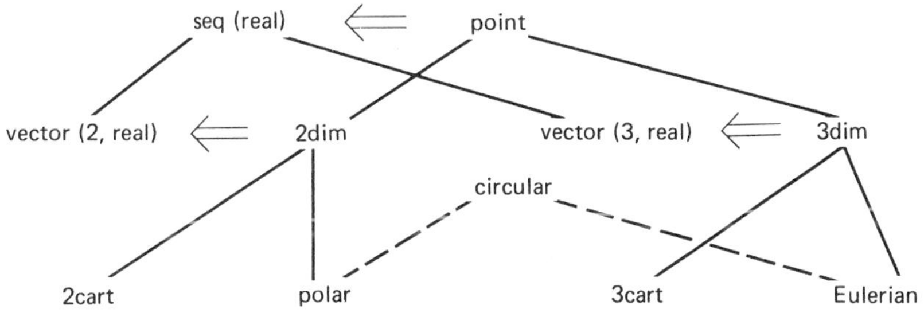

Figure 2.3. FREECL types.

Consider the following schemata for type declaration by restriction:

```
DECL t:type like s(a:b, c:d, . . . );
DECL t:type like s(a:b, c:d, . . . )
        with w:x, y:z . . . ;
```

In the above, properties are given by the pairs separated by colons, with the identifier on the left and the value on the right. The identifier is used, as throughout this chapter, to name both the property and its attribute part. *t* evaluates to an identifier, the name of the new type, ***t***, while *s* evaluates to an existing type ***s***, and we wish to have $\boldsymbol{s} \geq \boldsymbol{t}$. *a* and *c* are to be variable properties of *t*, and *w* and *y* are to be constant properties. By Axiom IV, *b* and *d* must evaluate to types, but *x* and *z* may evaluate to arbitrary notions. (The reader familiar with ECL will recognize *with* as being essentially the double colon operator with reversed arguments; it takes precedence over the colon following the name of the new type.)

The standard, or default, method of constructing the new type ***t*** is first to make a copy of ***s***. Then the properties given by the declaration are processed, restricting old properties and adding new properties as indicated, while checking that Axiom IV(b) is satisfied at each step.

In addition to *desc* (the *descriptor*, or variable property, field of any type), each type may have the standard property *cover*, which has a type as its value. The purpose of this property is to record the source type in the case of definition by restriction. In the examples above, we make the assignment ***t***.*cover* ::= ***s***.

In addition, the standard type property *ur* (for *underlying representation*) is used. Its value is normally inherited during definition by restriction, as indicated above.

Among the constant properties of notions of any fixed type are *type procedures*, used to define semantics of the type. This idea goes back to Hoare [8] and Wegbreit [2, 16]. As an example, we shall require that each type have a *tfn* (*type construction procedure*) property. Namely, given ***s*** above, the procedure ***s***.*tfn* is applied to the data in the declaration and delivers ***t*** as its result. One motivation for this is the fact that the syntax of the base language of PMS may well offer different sugaring for the definition of various classes of types. In ECL, for instance, we have the variants

```
STRING::SEQ(CHAR)
HWD::VECTOR(18, BOOL)
DTPR::STRUCT(CAR:FORM, CDR:FORM)
MODE::PTR(DDB)
ARITH::ONEOF(INT, REAL)
```

The last example is the ECL version of definition by union. These variants all boil down to type construction.

In a type construction procedure, as well as in other type procedures, it is often necessary to attribute a related type to a notion of a given type, using either the *ur* or the *cover* chain. The built-in procedures *LIFT*, *LOWER*, *RESTRICT*, and *RELAX* are used for this purpose. Suppose, for instance, we have the notion *x* of type ***x***, ***x***.*cover* is ***c***, and ***x***.*ur* is ***sr***. Then *LOWER*(*x*) returns a notion of type ***sr*** whose value is shared with *x*, *LIFT*(*LOWER*(*x*)) = *x*, *RELAX*(*x*) returns a notion of type ***c*** whose value is shared with *x*, and *RESTRICT*(*RELAX*(*x*)) returns *x*. *RESTRICT* and *RELAX* require, however, that both types involved have the same underlying representation.

As an aside, the declaration schemata above imply that type definitions may have strictly local scope, whereas in ECL types are absolutely global, although they may be bound to local identifiers. In the context of compilation, requiring global definition for types offers significant efficiencies. In the context of a PMS, on the other hand, local definitions are the thing, for we may wish to collect arbitrary packages of code into one program without worrying about identifier conflicts. Thus, for PMS, static (lexicographic) scoping of identifiers seems to be indicated. If the target system, like ECL, requires dynamic scoping or global types, the PMS must offer renaming facilities which bridge these particular gaps.

Generic "Types"

The idea of a union is quite different from that of restriction. An act of restriction delivers a new type in the sense of the axioms. Union, on the other hand, is used in contexts in which a notion whose type is one of the alternatives of the union is acceptable. This manner of speaking is used in declaring procedure formals, result types, and locals. If the formal x is typed ***any*(*int*, *real*)**, then we mean that it can be bound to an ***int*** or to a ***real*** and will be typed accordingly. But, there are no notions whose type is a union according to our axioms.

To formalize unions, we would add a set G of generic "types" to the lattice and extend the partial ordering to include them. Each generic would have a descriptor which is the set of alternative types for that generic. The generic ***any*** would have T as its descriptor value. The ordering between generics is defined by set inclusion on their descriptors, and $\boldsymbol{g} \geq \boldsymbol{t}$ when $\boldsymbol{t} \in \boldsymbol{g}.\delta$. ***all*** and ***none*** would remain the upper and lower limits in the lattice.

Pointer Types

Pointer notions are not freely available, lest the system twist slowly, slowly from its own references. We shall provide for explicit definition of pointer types in terms of the allowable types of their dereferenced notions. In all cases of type declaration, it will be up to the system to check that the axioms are satisfied.

Pointer types, like generic types, form a special class. ***ptr*** possesses a type constructor whose arguments are types. ***ptr*(*int*, *real*)**, for instance, is a pointer type whose dereferenced value may be an ***int*** or a ***real*** (or, implicitly, ***none***, for *nil* may be assigned to a notion of any pointer type).

The built-in type ***ref*** is synonymous to ***ptr***; pointers of this type may reference notions of any type whatsoever. The sequence of declarations

```
DECL symbol : type like ptr(atom) ;
DECL list : type like ptr(dtpr) ;
DECL form : type like ptr(atom, dtpr, ref) ;
```

might suggest an alternative rendering of ***form*** as

```
DECL form : type like
        any(symbol, list, ptr(ref)) ;
```

except that the latter version of ***form*** would be generic, whereas the former is not.

A pointer's type tells us what the type of the dereferenced pointer may be; we infer that when the descriptor for the pointer type is a set with more than one element we must look at the storage representation of the pointer itself to find the type after dereferencing. That is, the type of a dereferenced pointer is generic.

Base Types

Except for generic types, we must have a way of creating notions of each type. The methods of type definition treated above assume that some types already exist, so we need to start out with them already built into the system. Given a type, we assume the existence of a *notion generation procedure* which is given by the standard type property *gfn*; its value is a procedure which generates notions of that type (or, in the case of generic types, either evokes an error fault or generates a notion of a nongeneric type). Thus, ***int***.gfn will generate an ***int***.

We need built-in types whose type procedures are procedures of the base system and whose notion generation procedures generate data objects of the base system to represent the corresponding notions. Given these, new types may be defined by restriction and will carry along the base type procedures, if they are not overridden by new type procedures.

FREECL will have the built-in types ***int***, ***real***, ***char***, ***bool***, ***ptr***, ***seq***, ***vector***, ***struct***, ***all***, ***any***, and ***none***. Each of these (except ***all***) is a mode or a class (with a type constructor) in ECL proper. We can now generate FREECL data objects for notions of each of these types (except for ***any***, of course), and these types yield our initial stock of storage representations.

The type ***set*** is not so easily come by. It is to be represented, say, by the base ECL type ***hashtable***. But, this is defined by restriction from ***struct***, and my intent is to end up with ***set*** $\geq$ ***struct***! In FREECL, in fact, I desire to have ***set*** refinable to any type which is not a generic, basic, or a pointer type. We shall declare ***set*** in the form

```
DECL set:type like all with ur:hashtable, . . .
```

with the proper set of type procedures, whatever they may be.

To continue filling in the structure of the class ***set***, I wish its upper reaches to be as follows (using an indented display rather than a figure):

```
set
   iset                       (indexed sets)
      vstruct                 (variable-length structures)
         tdb                  (type definition block)
         struct               (fixed-length structures)
            atom              (global identifier bindings)
            dtpr              (linked list elements)
            subr              (built-in machine language routines)
            cexpr             (compiled routines)
            hashtable
            fds               (descriptors for procedure formals)
            fhb               (file header blocks)
   oset                       (ordered sets)
      seq                     (variable-length rows)
         string               seq(char)
         vector               (fixed-length rows)
```

The pointer class might then have this structure:

```
ptr
    type        ptr(tdb)
    symbol      ptr(atom)
    list        ptr(dtpr)
    port        ptr(fhb)
    routine     ptr(dtpr, subr, cexpr)
        proc    (strongly typed procedures)
    form        ptr(dtpr, atom, ref)
```

It is worth noting that the *cover* property of a type is quite insufficient for exhibiting the complete structure of the type lattice—that property merely exhibits some of its subtrees. Thus, for instance, if we allow (as ECL does, and hence so will FREECL) the possibility of indexing components of structures, they may also be viewed as being vectors with additional properties. The FREECL class theory does not attempt to completely define the structure of the type lattice; other class theories might well wish to achieve this degree of completeness.

Selection

Among the type procedures for indexed and ordered sets will be a *type selection procedure*, *sfn*, used to implement selection. One of the possibilities here is that a given selection procedure may implement a selector which is not actually a selector of the underlying (or base) representation. For instance, we might wish to have a class of strings which allow access to their length by means of a selection, but this selection is implemented by counting the components rather than by referring to the underlying representation (the string might be represented as a linked list). Should this *length* property be explicitly given as a variable property of the type? Since the practice may well aid error detection during symbolic evaluation or compilation, it appears to be good policy, although nothing said above seems to demand its adoption.

It is further worth noting that a notion need not be an indexed or ordered set to possess selectable components. The user may, for instance, wish to associate arbitrary variable or constant properties with each one of a restricted class of pointers. She might represent each pointer as a structure and store the pointer proper as one of its components. At the time such a pointer type is defined, she must, of course, supply appropriate type procedures. (Pointer types may have selection procedures as well. As in ECL, we assume that at most one level of automatic dereferencing will occur if the built-in default pointer type selection procedure is used.)

The idea of selection is normally associated with that of selecting a component of a compound notion. This, in turn, is based on a strong feeling that we are talking about fields in the storage representation of the notion in question. But, as we have seen, in the presence of a type selection procedure such components may be *virtual*. This fact argues for a relaxation of the usual definition of selection. *Prop*(x, a) means that x has the *variable property* a. We can formalize the idea of constant property as follows:

$$\text{Cprop}(x, a) == \text{Prop}(x.\tau, a) \text{ and not Prop}(x, a)$$

and we can then define selection as delivering the property *a* of *x* or of *x.τ* according to whether *a* is variable or constant and producing a fault otherwise. According to this definition, ***type*** has *no* constant properties!

Type Conversions (Coercion) and Generation

Some canonical situations in which an act of conversion must be attempted are these: I have in my left hand a notion of type ***t*** to which an assignment is to be made, or I am declaring a local of type ***t***, or I am binding to a formal of expected type ***t***; I have in my right hand a notion of type ***s*** to be used for assignment, initialization, or binding by value or by reference. (***s*** is meant to suggest *source type* and ***t*** to suggest target type.) How shall I proceed? It might seem that FREECL, being a looser class theory than that of ECL, would afford a generalization of the ECL rules for conversion and generation. Although I believed for several months that this was the case, correctness considerations intervened. The interested reader is invited, therefore, to refer to [2] for a description of the algorithms, ignoring the EL1 distinction between system and user type procedures.

2.4. SEMANTICS AND CONTROL

The reader has, I trust, noted the fact that FREECL has been discussed in some detail without the necessity of having a grammar. Syntactic detail has been only illustrative; we have been talking semantics, and primarily data semantics at that. What about semantics in the wider sense?

It is customary to draw a sharp distinction between data and control, just as many programmers still believe that the essential features of a language are captured by its grammar. Both ideas are, I believe, misguided. The character and appropriateness of a language are much more nearly captured by its semantics than by its grammar, although both are needed. If the gap mentioned in Section 2.1 is to be bridged by a PMS, it is surely most desirable that syntactic considerations enter the picture rather late in the series of refinements. But we must carry out correctness proofs at earlier stages. This seems, at first blush, to be a tall order, for correctness proofs usually argue using the proposed text of the program, and detailed proof methods generally concern themselves with certain control constructs. Dijkstra's methods, when applied during design, escape this criticism, although their use in conjunction with an existing program requires analysis of the text.

Hoare [8], as noted earlier, suggests that the semantics of a type is primarily dependent on its type procedures (although his development was based on an extension of the SIMULA 67 class theory, a similar argument holds generally) and only secondarily on representation. (One might hold, for instance, that data syntax is essentially storage representation.) This, in turn, suggests that data semantics can ultimately be explained by using Dijkstra's methods [12]. In this respect, at least, there is no clean separation between data and control.

Additionally, if one takes the McCarthy [10] view that semantics can be formalized by considering the action of an interpreter, it should be clear that what is data and what is program (or control) is relative to a given interpretation. Is the output of the ECL parser (a ***form***) data or program? It surely depends . . . .

If one believes that axiomatic semantics operates in the realm of notions and operational semantics in the realm of data and machines, then the idea of refinement leads from the first to the second. Thus, these views are mutually supportive rather than contradictory, and the work of Hoare and Dijkstra has tended to unify, rather than further separate, data and control. In this final section, I wish to suggest another point of view from which this rapprochement may be effected.

Control Types

The seminal idea here is due to G. H. Holloway (personal communication): In a PMS setting, at an early stage in design the user may wish to utter the text *FEE*(*FIE*, *FO*, *FUM*) without being sure whether he means that *FEE* is a macro, a procedure, or a data object. Thus, the system is unsure whether the method to be used for elaboration is macro expansion, procedure application, or selection. At a later stage of refinement, the choice will presumably be tied down. At this stage, however, all we can say is that *FEE* is a map, and the three aforementioned possibilities surely fit this rubric.

Iteration is another excellent application of Holloway's idea. Suppose *FOO* is a notion of class ***set***, and the user wishes to apply a procedure to each element of *FOO*. At an early stage of refinement, he should be able to specify this iteration without further knowledge of the type of *FOO*. If it turns out later, for instance, that *FOO* is a tree of some sort, then he may at that stage also wish to specify the order in which the treewalk will take place. If *FOO* turns out to be some sort of an ordered set, then the default method of iteration would probably be implemented using indexing. Many other possibilities suggest themselves.

If we abstract from these situations, taking note of the fact that refinement has been associated with the partial ordering in the type lattice, it is plausible that we should attempt to explain given patterns of control in terms of types. But where might these fit into the lattice?

Well, the situation is this: In ECL, input program text is converted by the parser to notions of type ***form***. A form may be interpreted by *EVAL* or be compiled (or be unparsed to character text). Thus, we might well arrange that if ***c*** is a control type, then ***form*** $\geq$ ***c***. We can construct a control class subtheory for FREECL forms which is based on the semantic properties of forms, whether given by Dijkstra's weakest preconditions or by the effect of them on the control and identifier environments of the interpreter.

Next, consider a PMS program development. Whatever the PMS class theory and the user extensions to it may be, at many stages in the development we may wish to pump out forms for symbolic evaluation, interpretation, and the like. This output may be produced by taking a notion of some control type (of class ***form***!) and operating on it with the relevant *type formulation procedure* (pardon the pun, please) to yield the desired output form. This is in some sense an act of translation or compilation. Since formulated programs may require arbitrarily structured data objects as initial data, there must exist type formulation procedures for all types, not just control types.

The underlying representations for control types need not be forms but can be data structures which hold various items to be used by the formulation procedures. For instance, a tree iteration control type might be designed in such a way that the particular method of walking the tree is a property of the type. The formulation procedure could then use this, and other information stored as properties of the notion to which the iteration is to be applied, to construct the output form.

FREECL Control Classes

We adopt, for the moment, the interpreter model view of semantics. The result of the parse is, as I have said, a ***form***. By its definition and the rules of type conversion, a ***form*** is convertible to a ***symbol***, a ***list***, or a doubly indirect reference to a notion constant, of which any constant in the grammer such as 5.6 is a special case. The corresponding interpretations by EVAL are

> ***Symbol:*** This is taken as an identifier, and the result is the notion most locally bound to the identifier according to the rules of scope.
>
> ***Constant:*** The result is the doubly dereferenced form.
>
> ***List:*** The first element of the list is evaluated to obtain either a built-in system routine or a ***routine***. In the former case, the system routine is called directly with the tail of the list as its argument. Otherwise, the system control routine *APPLY* is called with the given ***routine*** and the tail of the list as its arguments. Both of these cases amount to procedure application.

How, given a ***list***, do we recognize its control type? Easy: Evaluate its head, and look at the type of the result. Maybe this will have a constant property, *ctype*. (By default, we have a procedure application.) The control type for a ***macro*** might be named ***macro-expand***, for instance.

To be more specific, suppose we have the form $F(X, Y, Z)$ where evaluation of F gives a notion of type ***macro***. This notion gives us the macro definition among its properties. If we arrange that ***macro***.*ctype* is a (control) type, ***macro-expand***, then formulation of the above form is accomplished by applying ***macro-expand***.*ffn* to the form to obtain the expansion.

The control classes must evidently be subclasses of the list case above. Their organization is somewhat arbitrary—this is only a theory, remember, and thus is to some extent a matter of taste.

There are two kinds of interpretation which pervade programs which operate on data and forms. The first is the data object walk, controlled by interpretation of types of components encountered during the walk; it typically appears in input-output packages. The second is the control walk, typified by EVAL, the interpreter. It also appears in many system programs (for example, the compiler and the unparser); this kind of walk, or interpretation, is guided by the control types of the forms encountered during the walk. In both cases, type information is used to make the semantic interpretation. The idea of control types offers us an opportunity to treat control and data in an evenhanded manner. In short, semantic interpretation of a notion of any class is driven by its properties and that of its type. Control and data are *not* distinct ideas!

2.5. EPILOG

The main points I have tried to make in this chapter are these:

1. Program development builds a bridge between the notions which comprise the designer's theory of his subject matter and the final version of the program.
2. The class theory used arranges types in a lattice. The ordering in the lattice is strongly related to the ideas of refinement and restriction.
3. Storage representation should be independent of the structure of the class theory.
4. We can extend the idea of type to embrace distinctive patterns of control.

I wish to reemphasize that the above sketch of FREECL was solely for the purpose of illustration of these ideas. A more careful look at it by others may well disclose inconsistencies and inadequacies. Yet, it has a certain air of plausibility. Since it is only a theory, any belief that it is "correct" would be the sheerest illusion!

> "After life is over and the world has gone up in smoke, what realities might the spirit in us still call its own without illusion save the form of those very illusions which have made up our story?"
>
> George Santayana
> *The Last Puritan*

ACKNOWLEDGMENTS

This research was supported by the Advanced Research Projects Agency under Contract N-00039-76-C-0168 and by the Rome Air Development Center under Contract F-30602-74-C-0032.

My debt to others has been incompletely acknowledged in the epigraphs and by reference in the text. I am also indebted to M. Woodger and other members of the IFIPS Working Group 2.3 on Programming Methodology for the opportunity to present an earlier version of this material to the group in July 1976.

This work is dedicated to the memory of Edith M. Mealy.

CHAPTER 3

DATA STRUCTURES— AN AXIOMATIC APPROACH

THOMAS A. STANDISH
Computer Science Department
University of California at Irvine
Irvine, California

Un art ne saurait devenir une science sans une formalisation qui permette de définir ses concepts fondamentaux et d'étudier par la suite leurs propriétés.

Louis Nolin, from *Formalisation des Notions de Machine et de Programme*, Institut de Programmation, Paris, 1968

3.1. INTRODUCTION

Part of the art of programming is the art of organizing data representations. When we examine the specifications of contemporary computer programs of substantial size we often find that they tend to contain layers of separate representations that span the gap from the naked machine upwards to the problem domain. For example, in an airline reservation system the objects at the problem domain level may include flights, seats, schedules, dates, and names. At intermediate levels we might find objects such as records, files, tables, lists, directories, queues, strings, and numbers used to represent items in the problem domain, while at the lowest levels, we might find representations constructed from bits, bytes, and serially arranged sequences of machine words.

Programs are artifacts that organize the objects and operations available at given representational levels to exhibit behaviors required at higher levels, and in systems built according to contemporary disciplines of structured programming, the ultimate problem solving behaviors required may be synthesized from cascades of representational layers built hierarchically by *stepwise refinement* [Wirth (1971), Dahl et al. (1972)]. Some authors refer to the layers in such a representation cascade as *levels of abstraction*, and increased attention has been paid recently to the development of programming languages that permit the definition and use of *abstract data types*

[Wulf (1974), Liskov and Zilles (1974), Guttag (1976)]—i.e., specifications of data at a given level of abstraction independent of their representation by means of lower-order representational media.

A compelling reason for seeking such data abstraction capabilities is to assist programmers in the management of program complexity. As Dijkstra [Dahl et al. (1972)] and others have observed, the volume of detail encompassed by large computer programs we might wish to build exceeds that with which most programmers can cope at any single moment. It therefore becomes critical to learn how to organize complexity and detail into subsystems of manageable proportions.

Subroutines are devices by which arbitrarily complex compositions of operations can be packaged into units such that a programmer need know only descriptions of net effect in order to use them in building more complex operations. The quest for data abstraction has an analagous aim—the ability to define data such that a programmer need not know volumes of representational detail but need only know required behavioral characteristics in order to use defined data to organize larger collections of information and to program higher-order transformations on them.

To achieve this goal, it is necessary to find techniques for factoring the description of essential properties of data at a given level from the representational detail at lower levels organized to exhibit these properties. The axiomatic approach to data provides just this feature—a *representation-independent* specification of data. Therein lies its potential value as an organizational and conceptual tool.

What Is an Axiomatic Approach ?

Axioms express abstractly the relationships and behavioral laws that characterize classes of data and operations. The act of abstraction consists of focusing on properties thought to be essential, or characteristic, and of ignoring properties thought to be irrelevant. Axioms are stated in a language of relation and assertion, as opposed to the language of command with which (for the most part) we state low-level computer programs. This permits the use of *rules of inference* for deducing consequences of the axioms. All theorems proved from the axioms hold true for any system that satisfies the axioms.

This leads to the observation that axiomatic systems are an *economic* way of expressing knowledge in which (1) irrelevant detail is suppressed, (2) the labor of proving theorems needs to be performed only once, and (3) the results apply to every concrete situation where the axioms can be shown to hold. In short, more coverage is obtained for less labor. As Bertrand Russell once put it, "the advantages are the same as the advantages of theft over honest toil."

Mathematics has profited from this approach in geometry, algebra, topology, set theory, and logic. Computer science has begun to profit in the realm of axiomatic treatments of programming language semantics [Floyd (1967), Hoare (1969), Hoare and Wirth (1973)]. Recent exploration, which this chapter exemplifies, has been directed at examining potential advantages of an axiomatic approach to data structures [see also Dahl et al. (1972)].

Potential Advantages for Computer Science

More detailed contemplation of the potential advantages of an axiomatic approach to data leads to the considerations listed in Figure 3.1.

An axiomatic approach to data structures might eventually be expected

1. To permit clear, rigorous definition of the concepts of data representations and data types.
2. To specify precisely the requirements on data representations.
3. To specify precisely the requirements on programs that manipulate data representations.
4. To permit the widest possible selection of implementation detail.
5. To simplify program maintenance—by allowing changes in superstructure or underpinnings to be made independently.
6. To extend the basis for proofs of correctness of programs.
7. To permit concise definition of the semantics of data definition facilities.
8. To establish a framework for tackling the problem of automatic synthesis or selection of data representations.
9. To capture the behavior of composite information structures that are pervasive in programming.
10. To offer a better basis for machine independence.

Figure 3.1

Representations, Representation Independence, and Data Types

When we think of the data type **integer** in a programming language, we usually do not intend to commit ourselves to a particular *representation* of integers such as Roman numerals, radix notation, prime factor decompositions, two's complements, binary-coded decimals, strings of ones, or any other representation. Rather, we intend to commit ourselves to a set of *behaviors* for integers. These behaviors are usually given as a set of behavioral laws for operating on a set of abstract quantities (such as a, b, and c) under abstract operations (such as $+$, $-$, and $\times$). Indeed, the axioms for, say, an *integral domain* give a way of isolating relevant behaviors for integers independently of a commitment to any particular representation, as exemplified in Figure 3.2.[1]

A particular set of concrete objects and operations D is a *representation* of the integers if a correspondence can be established mapping the abstract objects and operations of the axioms for integers A into the concrete objects and operations D in such a way that the behavioral laws decreed in A are valid in D. This idea has been captured nicely in the notions of models, interpretations, and validity in contemporary mathematical logic [see, e.g., Mendelson (1964)]. Here, an *interpretation* I is a mapping

[1]Strictly speaking, the behavior of integers is specified by the Peano axioms. The integral domain axioms specify behaviors applicable not only to integers but also to rational numbers, real numbers, and numbers of the form $a + b\sqrt{3}$ (for integers a and b).

The Integral Domain Axioms

1. *Associative laws:*

$$a + (b + c) = (a + b) + c, \qquad a \times (b \times c) = (a \times b) \times c.$$

2. *Commutative laws:*

$$a + b = b + a, \qquad a \times b = b \times a.$$

3. *The distributive law:*

$$a \times (b + c) = a \times b + a \times c.$$

4. *The law for zero:* There exists a quantity 0 such that for any a,

$$a + 0 = a.$$

5. *The law for one:* There exists a quantity 1 such that $1 \neq 0$ and for any a,

$$a \times 1 = a.$$

6. *The additive inverse law:* For each a there exists an x such that

$$a + x = 0.$$

7. *The cancellation law:* If $c \neq 0$, then

$$\text{if } c \times a = c \times b, \quad \text{then } a = b.$$

Figure 3.2

from a set of axioms A into a domain of interpretation D which sends uninterpreted symbols in A onto concrete objects and operators in D. If the laws in A are valid in D (i.e. true for all legitimate combinations of values of variables) under the mapping I, then D forms a *model* for A. In our terms, then, a representation is just a model.

The position we take in this chapter is that the notion of a *data type* in programming corresponds to a representation-independent axiomatic specification of abstract behavioral requirements for a system of data objects and data operators. Thus, the *data types* for queues, stacks, finite sets, arrays, integers, rational numbers, and the like are specified by respective axiom sets that state behavioral requirements abstractly as relationships among compositions of operations on uninterpreted letters. A *data representation* for a *data type* is just a model for its axioms which also obeys some *basic data axioms.* These basic data axioms set forth additional properties required of computer data that are not required of representations in general. For example, in mathematics, we can use uncountable, continuous representations (such as real functions on compact intervals), but in digital computers, our representations must be countable and discrete.

Much discussion and debate on the nature of data types is found in the literature on programming languages [Mealy (1967), Earley (1971), Reynolds (1969), Childs (1968), Codd (1970), Holt (1965), Dahl et al. (1972), Liskov and Zilles (1974), Morris (1973), Guttag (1976)]. Paradoxically, the axiomatic view of data types is both old and new—old because it corresponds to the approach taken by mathematical logicians before the recent decade of debate on data types started—new because it differs f.om nearly all of the proposals to consider data types essentially as characterized by (1) directed graphs and their variants [Holt (1965), Earley (1971)], (2) sets or sets and relations [Reynolds (1969), Childs (1968), Codd (1970)], or (3) sets of storage structures and procedures packaged into modules (as in the Simula Class or the CLU Cluster) characteristic of recent work defining abstract data types in languages [Dahl et al. (1972), Liskov and Zilles (1974), Wulf (1974)].

Putting Our Axiomatic Approach in Perspective

Our first task in the development of an axiomatic data theory is to axiomatize some rudimentary behaviors of composite information structures. This leads to the formulation of the *ground axioms*.

The abstraction that the *ground axioms* express relies on four abstract characteristics of composite information structures formed by composing collections of parts.

The first characteristic is that this composition is *information lossless* in the sense that when parts are assembled into larger collections they are not altered or transformed but rather they retain their features. For example, composing the integers 6, 2, and 7 into a triple [6, 2, 7] is an information lossless composition since we can recover the individual components of the triple. However, adding $6 + 2 + 7$ to form the sum 15 is a form of composition in which the identity of the parts is lost since 15 cannot be decomposed uniquely back into integral summands.

The second characteristic of the abstraction we seek is that there exist (selector) operators for accessing the individual parts of each composite structure. The third characteristic is that we view all transformations of composite information structures as compositions of piecewise changes affecting only one part at a time. The fourth characteristic is that the parts used to form composite information structures are either atomic (i.e., indecomposable into parts) or are themselves composite objects. However, whether or not a particular object is atomic is viewed as *relative* to the set of selector operators under consideration in a particular subsystem. For example, in a subsystem that studies arrays of floating-point numbers, the floating-point numbers may be viewed as indecomposable with respect to the array element accessing operators, but these same floating-point numbers may participate simultaneously in another subsystem that allows them to be decomposed into signed integers representing, say, their respective mantissas and exponents. Atomicity is not a property of objects, therefore, but is rather a relationship between objects and decomposition operators.

Many (but by no means all) composite information structures used in computing have the four characteristics mentioned above. For example, a core memory can be viewed as a serial collection of words, each of which is a serial collection of bits. Many computers carry out net transformations on information structures in their memories a word at a time (i.e., by piecewise change in a composite object formed from parts). Files are often composed from collections of records, which, in turn, are composed from fields. Text is composed of pages which are composed of lines, which, in turn, are composed of characters. Card decks are composed of cards which are composed of columns, which, in turn, are composed of holes or nonholes. Some sorts of programs can be viewed as being composed from nested blocks which are ultimately composed from statements and declarations, which themselves are composed from various species of subexpressions. Our purpose in citing these examples is not to assert the universality of the four abstract characteristics we have mentioned but rather to suggest that at some representational levels in programming these characteristics are sufficiently pervasive to merit careful formalization and study. It is the purpose of the *ground axioms* to capture this level of behavior. Obviously, as we ascend representational levels in systems with multilayered representations, the behaviors encountered at each level change. At the lowest levels, we have brick-like, inelastic quantities that are serially arranged. At intermediate levels, we may have elastic quantities that can grow in length, or in depth by nesting, and that can be allocated in various sizes and shapes. At top levels, we may encounter an enormous variety of behaviors that bear little relation to the behaviors at widely separated lower representational levels. Therefore, because we deliberately organize the behaviors of available objects and operations on a given level to simulate the required behaviors at an immediately higher level, there is a shift in behaviors between the subsystem being imitated and the subsystem doing the imitating. In a cascade of representational layers, the cascading of small incremental behavioral shifts between layers may amount to a dramatic net shift in which, at the topmost layer, the properties of the lowest representational level are completely absent. For example, in a system designed to compute an orbit of a satellite, we deal at the topmost level with objects (i.e., orbits) that are essentially continuous motions of particles in continuously varying gravitational fields. The behaviors and properties of orbits bear little relation to the brick-like words and bytes used at the lowest representational levels in the computer that computes them. Thus, by focusing on *ground axioms*, we do not pretend to be characterizing behaviors of computer representations at all possible levels or even very many levels. Rather, we intend to work at the lowest abstract levels, whose behaviors, we freely acknowledge, may be washed out during ascent to higher representational levels.

In fact, in this chapter we must be even more modest than this. In particular, we deliberately avoid studying such advanced data structure phenomena as (1) shared, overlapping, or recursive substructures; (2) composite structures with simultaneous, nonunique, overlapping decompositions (such as arrays decomposable simultaneously into rows or columns or words decomposable simultaneously into bytes of various sizes which may overlap); and (3) content-addressable information structures wherein we access sets of parts by partial specification of their contents.

Our deliberate modesty is perhaps best justified by considering an analogy with axiomatic approaches in contemporary algebra. In particular, in algebra, we start by studying the simplest subsystems first. For example, we may begin with semigroups. We might then add the identity element together with its behaviors to semigroups to get monoids, and then by adding inverse elements, we get groups. Then we are prepared to progress to higher-order systems such as rings, fields, integral domains, and vector spaces, containing the simpler varieties as subsystems. It takes a text of moderate size to develop theories of all these algebraic systems, and it is too much to expect that all such systems could be covered in a single chapter. By analogy, it is reasonable for us to start with the study of only the simplest subsystems first when attempting to axiomatize data structures.

An eventual axiomatic treatment of data may well have an overall structure analogous to that of algebra. Namely, there may be elementary systems with just a few axioms (analogous to semigroups or partial orders in algebra), and there may be many nonelementary systems composed from several interacting subsystems of a simpler variety. For example, nonelementary data systems may characterize phenomena such as shared substructures or simultaneous, overlapping partitions, or they may capture the growth, combining, and decay laws of common systems of objects such as queues, lists, and finite sets. To complete the analogy, these nonelementary data systems may be thought to correspond to algebraic systems such as lattices, rings, and fields. Thus, it is the scope of this chapter to consider rigorously only the most elementary data systems and not to develop a complete axiomatic treatment of all data systems. In this respect, the chapter might be considered analogous to a chapter on semigroups in an algebra text. It is left to subsequent developments to explore higher-order axiomatic data systems. Horowitz and Sahni (1976) have initiated exploration in this direction.

Logical Foundations

As a logical foundation for our treatment, we assume we are working in a first-order predicate calculus with equality [Mendelson (1964, pp. 75–82)]. Informally, this means we assume the existence of an equality relation $x = y$ which has the following properties:

1. *Reflexivity:* $x = x$.
2. *Symmetry:* If $x = y$, then $y = x$.
3. *Transitivity:* If $x = y$ and $y = z$, then $x = z$.
4. *Substitutivity:* If equals are substituted for equals, the results are equal.[2]

When we talk about sets, we shall assume that we are using another notation for unary predicates. Thus, writing $x \in P$ means that P is a unary predicate for which $P(x)$ holds true, writing $x \in A \cup B$ means there exist predicates $A(x)$ and $B(x)$ such that $A(x) \vee B(x)$, writing $x \in A \cap B$ means there exist predicates $A(x)$ and $B(x)$ such that $A(x) \wedge B(x)$, and writing $A \subseteq B$ means there exist unary predicates $A(x)$ and $B(x)$ such that $\forall x[A(x) \supset B(x)]$. Because sets are viewed only as a notational convenience synonymous with unary predicates, we can avoid introducing separate set theory axioms.

The way is now paved for our study of the *ground axioms* and their consequences.

[2]To attain full precision in talking about substitutivity, we need to discuss well-formed formulas and various properties of free and bound variables with respect to quantifiers. Our preference is to develop the theory in the style of a contemporary axiomatic treatment of algebra, such as exemplified by Birkhoff and MacLane (1961). In what follows, we shall assume that all free variables are universally quantified, and we shall omit mention of universal quantifiers in most cases.

3.2. THE GROUND AXIOMS FOR DATA STRUCTURES

Let $D = (C, A, S, \Lambda, Selection, Assignment)$ be a system in which C is the set of *composite objects*, A is the set of *atoms*, S is the set of *selectors*, and Λ is *the null object*. Let O denote the set of all objects in the system $O = C \cup A$, and let *Selection* and *Assignment* be operators such that *Selection*: $O \times S \rightarrow O$ and *Assignment*: $O \times S \times O \rightarrow C$. We say that the system D satisfies the *ground axioms* provided the following relations hold:

1. *Axiom for atoms*: If x is an *atom*, then for every selector $s \in S$,
$$Selection(x, s) = \Lambda.$$
2. *Axiom for the null object*:
$$\Lambda \in C \cap A.$$
3. *Axiom for equality of composite objects*: For any two *composite objects* $c,d \in C$,
   if $Selection(c, s) = Selection(d, s)$ for every *selector* $s \in S$, then $c = d$.
4. *Axiom for assignment*[3]: For any selectors $s,t \in S$ and any objects $x,y \in O$,
$$\text{if } s = t, \quad \text{then } Selection\,(Assignment(x, s, y), t) = y$$
   and
$$\text{if } s \neq t, \quad \text{then } Selection(Assignment(x, s, y), t) = Selection(x, t).$$

Notation

We shall normally denote $Selection(x, s)$ by the expression $x[s]$, and we shall denote $Assignment(x, s, y)$ by $\alpha(x, s, y)$.

Strengthening the Statements of the Ground Axioms

In group theory, it is possible to state the associative, identity, and inverse laws in a form that gives only the left identity law and the left inverse law. It can then be shown that the right inverse law and the right identity law follow from the left identity and inverse laws; i.e., $\{ex = x \text{ and } x^{-1}x = e\}$ together imply that $\{xe = x \text{ and } xx^{-1} = e\}$. An analogous development holds for the ground axioms in that the weak form of the axioms stated in 1 through 4 above can be shown to imply the following stronger forms.

First, we can strengthen the axiom for the null object by showing that the null object Λ is the only object that belongs to both C and A.

[3]Historically, this axiom has its origins in a property of state vectors first observed and used by McCarthy (1962, p. 25).

Proposition 1

The only object that is both *composite* and *atomic* is the *null object*, $\{\Lambda\} = C \cap A$.

Proof: Suppose $x \in C \cap A$. Then $x \in A$, so that (by the axiom for atoms) for all $s \in S$, $x[s] = \Lambda$. Since $\Lambda \in A$ (by the null object axiom), we likewise have that for all $s \in S$, $\Lambda[s] = \Lambda$. Thus, $x[s] = \Lambda[s]$ for all $s \in S$. However, since both x and Λ belong to C and have identical decompositions under selection, we can apply the axiom for the equality of composite objects to conclude that $x = \Lambda$.

We can strengthen the axiom for atoms to the following if and only if (iff) condition:

Proposition 2

$x \in A$ iff $\forall s \in S, x[s] = \Lambda$.

Proof: Suppose that x is an object for which $x[s] = \Lambda$ for all $s \in S$. We note that x and Λ have identical decompositions under selection $x[s] = \Lambda[s]$ for all $s \in S$. Suppose x is not an *atom*. Then x is *composite*, and we can apply the axiom for the equality of composite objects to conclude that $x = \Lambda$, from which x must be an *atom* since Λ is.

We can strengthen the axiom for the equality of composite objects to the following iff condition:

Proposition 3

For any two *composite objects* $c,d \in C$,

$$c = d \quad \text{iff} \quad c[s] = d[s] \text{ for all } s \in S.$$

Proof: Let c and d be two *composite objects* such that $c = d$. Using the properties of equality in the underlying system of logic (a predicate calculus with equality), we can show (by reflexivity of equality) that $c[s] = c[s]$ for every $s \in S$ and therefore (by substituting equals for equals in equals) that $c[s] = d[s]$ for all $s \in S$.

By similar elementary reasoning, for any $x \in O$ and any $s,t \in S$ such that $s = t$, we have $x[s] = x[t]$. That is, identical selectors select identical components.

Figure 3.3 lists the strengthened form of the ground axioms.

Informal Observations

The operation of *Selection* is intended to apply a selector s to an object x in order to access what will be called the *s-component of x*. Proposition 2 asserts that objects are *atoms* if and only if they have no nonnull components. Proposition 3 shows that composite objects are identical iff they have identical decompositions under *Selection*.

Ground Axioms—Strong Form

1. *Axiom for atoms:* $x \in A$ iff $\forall s \in S$, $x[s] = \Lambda$.
2. *Axiom for the null object:* $\{\Lambda\} = C \cap A$.
3. *Axiom for equality of composite objects:* For $c, d \in C$,

   $$c = d \quad \text{iff} \quad c[s] = d[s] \text{ for all } s \in S.$$
4. *Axiom for assignment:* For $s, t \in S$ and $x, y \in O$,

   $$s = t \text{ implies } \alpha(x, s, y)[t] = y$$

   and

   $$s \neq t \text{ implies } \alpha(x, s, y)[t] = x[t].$$

Figure 3.3

Assignment is an operation which causes piecewise modification of an object. The assignment axiom says that after altering the s-component of an object x to be y, then selection by s yields y, but selection by any other selector $t \neq s$ yields the same result as selecting the t-component of x. In short, $\alpha(x, s, y)$ is a new object that differs from x only in its s-component, if it differs at all.

In certain models of the axioms in which only nonnull components of composite objects are represented explicitly, we can picture assignment and selection using tree notation. Let q, r, s, and t be selectors, let a, b, c, and d be nonnull objects, and let

$x =$ 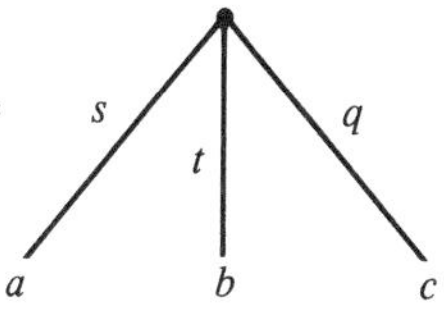

be a composite object. Then,

1. *Selection:*

$$x[s] = a \quad \text{and} \quad x[r] = \Lambda.$$

2. *Adding a component:*

$\alpha(x, r, d) =$ 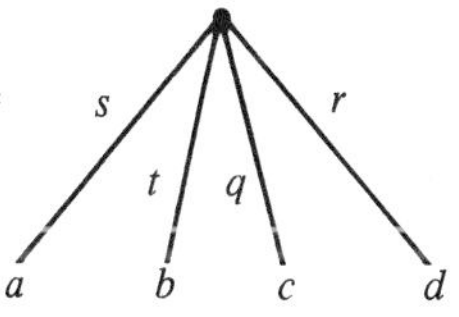

3. *Deleting a component:*

$\alpha(x, q, \Lambda) =$ 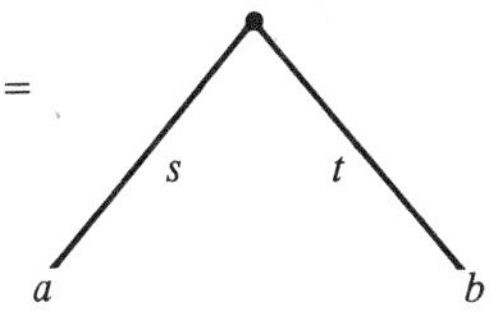

4. *Replacing a component:*

$\alpha(x, q, a) =$

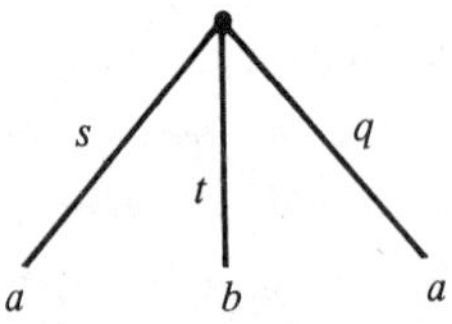

5. *Doing nothing:*

$\alpha(x, r, \Lambda) =$

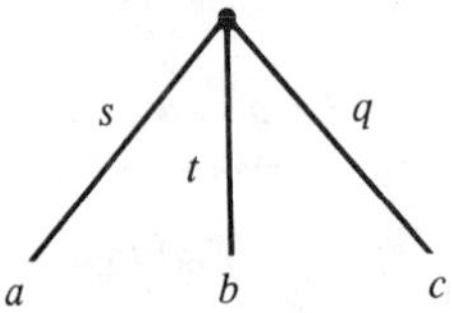

From these diagrams, we see that the composite objects in these tree models are elastic in the sense that they can grow or contract by taking on or dropping distinct nonnull components. This interpretation of $\alpha(x, s, y)$ holds only when x is a composite object. We have yet to discover what happens when x is an atom.

Assignment to Atoms

Proposition 4

Assignment of the null object Λ to be a component of an atom a produces the null object, whereas assignment of a nonnull object to be a component of a produces a composite object with a single nonnull component.

Proof: Consider $\alpha(a, s, b)$, where a is an *atom*.

Case 1: Let $b = \Lambda$. By the assignment axiom, for all $s, t \in S$, $t = s$ implies $\alpha(a, s, \Lambda)[t] = \Lambda$ and $t \neq s$ implies $\alpha(a, s, \Lambda)[t] = a[t]$. But $a[t] = \Lambda$ since $a \in A$. Hence, $\alpha(a, s, \Lambda)[t] = \Lambda$ for all $t \in S$. Thus, by Proposition 2, $\alpha(a, s, \Lambda) \in A$. However, by definition, *Assignment*: $O \times S \times O \longrightarrow C$, so $\alpha(a, s, \Lambda) \in C$. Hence, $\alpha(a, s, \Lambda) = C \cap A$. Applying Proposition 1, we conclude $\alpha(a, s, \Lambda) = \Lambda$.

Case 2: Now suppose $b \neq \Lambda$. Since $\alpha(a, s, b) \in C$ and since (by the first half of the assignment axiom) $\alpha(a, s, b)[s] = b$, it follows that $\alpha(a, s, b)$ is a nonnull composite object having b as its s-component. That $\alpha(a, s, b)$ has no other nonnull components follows from the second half of the assignment axiom.

3.3. COMPOSITE SELECTION AND ASSIGNMENT

Composite selection consists of repeatedly performing the operation of selection to select parts of parts of objects, and *composite assignment* consists of changing parts of parts of objects.

Informally, let $x[s_1, s_2, \ldots, s_n]$ stand for the expression $(\ldots((x[s_1])[s_2])\ldots)[s_n]$, and consider the following tree-like models of nested composite objects: Let

$x =$

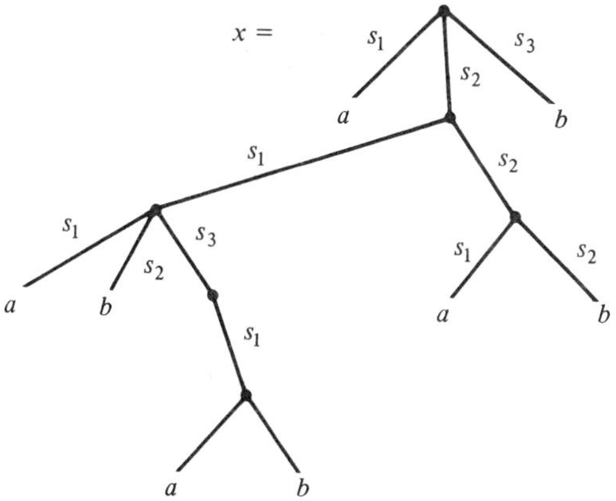

Then

$x[s_2, s_1, s_3] =$

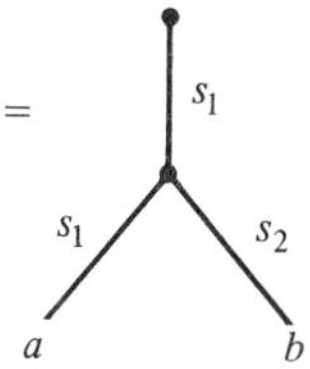

The result is Λ if the selection path does not lie in the object. For example, $x[s_1, s_3] = \Lambda$.

In these tree-like models we can visualize the effect of the composite assignment expression $\alpha(x,(s_1, s_2, \ldots, s_n), y)$ by inserting y at the end of the path $(s_1, s_2, \ldots, s_n)$ in the object x. If the selection path isn't in the object, we extend the object by putting in the path. For example, let

$x =$

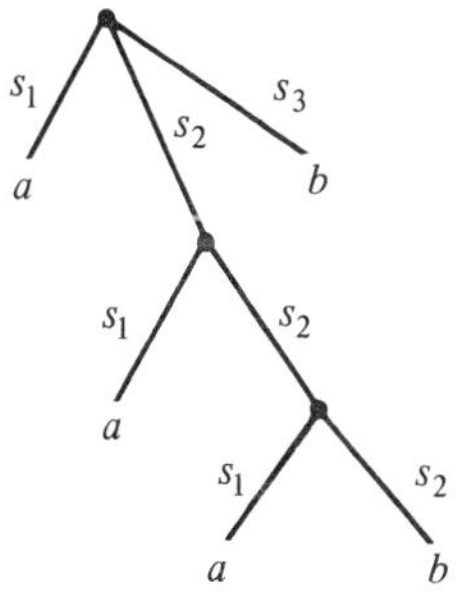

Then

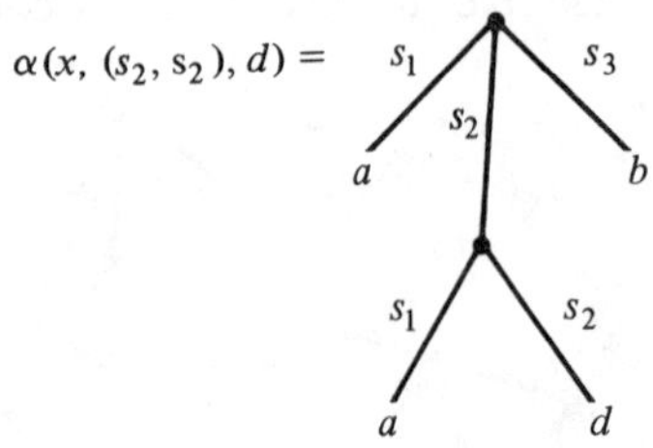

and

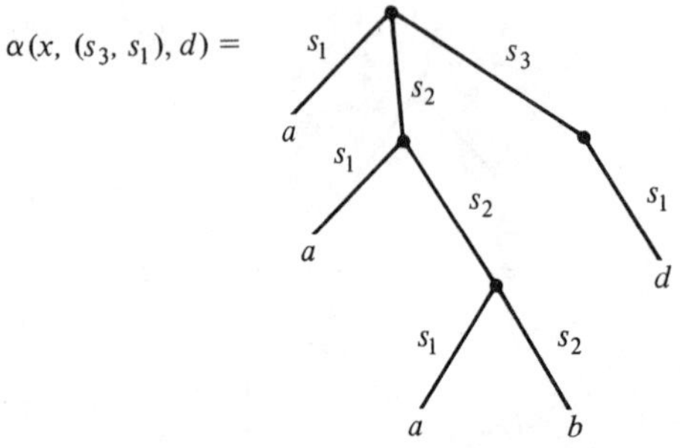

Under composite assignment these tree-like models exhibit elasticity because they can add and drop components at any level and thus can grow and shrink both in breadth and in depth by nesting.

We now proceed to extend the definition of *Selection* and *Assignment* to cover composite selection and assignment. Under the definitions we shall give, it will turn out that ground axioms 1, 2, and 3 are still valid when simple selection is replaced by composite selection. However, the ground axiom for assignment does not generalize directly but rather must be extended to cover four separate cases of composite assignment depending on whether the paths of selection and assignment are independent or share common segments in certain ways.

We denote the *composite selectors* over S by S^+, and we let S^+ consist of the set of strings over S under a binary, associative concatenation operator on selectors in S. We write composite selectors in the parenthesis-free form $s_1 s_2 \ldots s_n$ using juxtaposition to signify concatenation. If we adjoin to S^+ an identity element e, called the *empty selector*, having the properties $e \notin S$ and $es = se = s$ for all $s \in S$, we obtain S^* (which is just the free monoid over S with identity e). The expression $|u|$, called the *length of u*, consists of the number of nonempty selectors in u for any $u \in S^*$. In particular, we have $|e| = 0$, and $|uv| = |u| + |v|$ for all $u, v \in S^*$.

Definition 1. *Composite Selection*: The *Selection* function prescribed by the ground axioms is extended to the composite selection function *Selection*: $O \times S^* \to O$ as follows:

(a) $Selection(x, e) = x$ for all $x \in O$.

(b) $Selection(x, su) = Selection(Selection(x, s), u)$ for $s \in S, u \in S^*$, and $x \in O$.

Definition 2. *Composite Assignment*: The *Assignment* function prescribed by the ground axioms is extended to the composite assignment function *Assignment*: $O \times S^* \times O \rightarrow C$ as follows:

(a) $Assignment(x, e, y) = y$ for all $x, y \in O$.

(b) $Assignment(x, su, y) = Assignment(x, s, Assignment(x[s], u, y))$ for $s \in S, u \in S^*$, and $x, y \in O$.

We use the notations $x[u]$ and $\alpha(x, u, y)$ to denote composite selection and composite assignment for all $u \in S^*$.

Proposition 5

For any $x \in O$ and any $u, v \in S^*$,

(a) $x[uv] = (x[u])[v]$, and

(b) $\alpha(x, uv, y) = \alpha(x, u, \alpha(x[u], v, y))$.

Proof: These facts are a consequence of the associativity of functional composition (as can be established using induction on the length of u together with Definitions 1 and 2).

We shall now show that the strengthened versions of ground axioms 1 and 3 (cf. Figure 3.3) hold when the operation of *Selection* is replaced by *Composite Selection.*

Proposition 6 *Generalization of the Axiom for Atoms*

x is an *atom* iff $x[u] = \Lambda$ for any *composite selector* $u \in S^+$.

Proof: Since $S \subseteq S^+$, if $x[u] = \Lambda$ for all $u \in S^+$, then $x[s] = \Lambda$ for all $s \in S$, so by Proposition 2, $x \in A$. To go the other way, we use induction on the length of u. For $|u| = 1$, the result is the same as Proposition 2. If $|u| = n + 1$ and the result is true for all $v \in S^+$ such that $|v| = n$, then we can write $u = vs$ for some $v \in S^+$ and $s \in S$. Then

$x[u]$	$= x[vs]$	since $u = vs$
	$= (x[v])[s]$	by Prop. 5(a)
	$= (\Lambda)[s]$	by the inductive hypothesis
	$= \Lambda$	by the axiom for atoms and the fact that $\Lambda \in A$.

Proposition 7 *Generalization of the Axiom for Equality of Composite Objects*

For any two *composite objects* $c,d \in C$, $c = d$ iff $c[u] = d[u]$ for every $u \in S^+$.

Proof: Since we can substitute equals for equals, if $c = d$, then substituting d for the second occurrence of c in $c[u] = c[u]$ gives us: $c = d$ implies $c[u] = d[u]$ for all $u \in S^+$. Conversely, since $S \subseteq S^+$, $c[u] = d[u]$ for all $u \in S^+$ implies $c[s] = d[s]$ for all $s \in S$, and the result follows from the axiom for equality of composite objects.

To discuss how to generalize the assignment axiom so it holds for *Composite Assignment* we must first introduce the following definitions.

Definition 3. Let $u, v \in S^+$. We say u is a *proper prefix* of v, written $u < v$, provided there exists a $w \in S^+$ such that $v = uw$.

Definition 4. Let $u, v \in S^+$. We say u and v are *independent*, written $u <> v$, if $u \neq v$ and neither $u < v$ nor $v < u$.

The axiom for assignment generalizes to cover *Composite Assignment* as follows.

Proposition 8 *Generalization of the Assignment Axiom*

For any $u,v \in S^+$ and any $x,y \in O$,

1. If $u = v$, then $\alpha(x, v, y)[u] = y$,
2. If $u < v$, then $\alpha(x, v, y)[u] = \alpha(x[u], w, y)$, where $v = uw$,
3. If $v < u$, then $\alpha(x, v, y)[u] = y[w]$, where $u = vw$, and
4. If $u <> v$, then $\alpha(x, v, y)[u] = x[u]$.

Proof: We proceed by cases.

Case 1: We first prove that $\alpha(x, u, y)[u] = y$ for all $u \in S^+$, and then (using substitutivity of equality) we substitute v for the first occurrence of u under the hypothesis that $u = v$. The induction proceeds as follows. For $|u| = 1$, the assignment axiom implies $\alpha(x, u, y)[u] = y$. Now suppose the result holds for $|u| = n$. Consider composite selectors of the form su for $s \in S$. Then

$$
\begin{aligned}
\alpha(x, su, y)[su] &= \alpha(x, s, \alpha(x[s], u, y))[su] && \text{by Prop. 5(b)}\\
&= (\alpha(x, s, \alpha(x[s], u, y))[s])[u] && \text{by Prop. 5(a)}\\
&= \alpha(x[s], u, y)[u] && \text{by the assignment axiom}\\
&= y && \text{by the inductive hypothesis.}
\end{aligned}
$$

Case 2: Now suppose $u < v$. Then, by definition, there exists $w \in S^+$ such that $v = uw$. Hence,

$$
\begin{aligned}
\alpha(x, v, y)[u] &= \alpha(x, uw, y)[u] && \text{by } v = uw\\
&= \alpha(x, u, \alpha(x[u], w, y))[u] && \text{by Prop. 5(b)}\\
&= \alpha(x[u], w, y) && \text{by Case 1 above.}
\end{aligned}
$$

Case 3: If $v < u$, then, by definition, there exists a $w \in S^+$ such that $u = vw$. So,

$$\begin{aligned} \alpha(x, v, y)[u] &= \alpha(x, v, y)[vw] && \text{by } u = vw \\ &= (\alpha(x, v, y)[v])[w] && \text{by Prop. 5(a)} \\ &= y[w] && \text{by Case 1 above.} \end{aligned}$$

Case 4: If $u <> v$, then let $h \in S^*$ be the longest common prefix of u and v. Then there exist u_1, u_2, v_1, v_2 such that $u_1 \neq v_1$,

$$u = hu_1u_2, \qquad \text{where } u_1 \in S \text{ and } u_2 \in S^*$$

and

$$v = hv_1v_2, \qquad \text{where } v_1 \in S \text{ and } v_2 \in S^*.$$

Hence,

$$\begin{aligned} \alpha(x, v, y)[u] &= \alpha(x, hv_1v_2, y)[hu_1u_2] && \text{by } u = hu_1u_2 \text{ and } v = hv_1v_2 \\ &= (\alpha(x, h, \alpha(x[h], v_1v_2, y))[h])[u_1u_2] && \text{by Props. 5(a) and 5(b)} \\ &= \alpha(x[h], v_1v_2, y)[u_1u_2] && \text{by Case 1 above} \\ &= (\alpha(x[h], v_1, \alpha(x[hv_1], v_2, y))[u_1])[u_2] && \text{by Props. 5(a) and 5(b)} \\ &= ((x[h])[u_1])[u_2] && \text{by } u_1 \neq v_1 \text{ and the assignment axiom} \\ &= x[hu_1u_2] && \text{by Prop. 5(a) (twice)} \\ &= x[u] && \text{by } u = hu_1u_2. \end{aligned}$$

Figure 3.4 summarizes the implications of the ground axioms for *Composite Selection* and *Composite Assignment.*

Consequences of Ground Axioms for Composite Selection and Composite Assignment

1. *Axiom for atoms:*

   x is an *atom* iff $x[u] = \Lambda$ for every *composite selector* $u \in S^+$.

2. *Axiom for the null object:*

   $$\{\Lambda\} = C \cap A.$$

3. *Axiom for equality of composite objects:* For any two *composite objects* $c, d \in C$,

   $c = d$ iff $c[u] = d[u]$ for every *composite selector* $u \in S^+$.

4. *Axiom for assignment:* For any $u, v \in S^+$ and any $x, y \in O$,

   if $u = v$, then $\alpha(x, v, y)[u] = y$

   if $u < v$, then $\alpha(x, v, y)[u] = \alpha(x[u], w, y)$, where $v = uw$

   if $v < u$, then $\alpha(x, v, y)[u] = y[w]$, where $u = vw$

   and

   if $u <> v$, then $\alpha(x, v, y)[u] = x[u]$.

Figure 3.4

3.4. MODELS FOR THE GROUND AXIOMS

Having explored elementary consequences of the axioms and having shown their implications for the defined operations of composite selection and assignment, we now turn to a discussion of some facts about models of the axioms.

The Trivial Models

A *trivial model* is a model $M = (C, A, S, \Lambda, \textit{Selection, Assignment})$ such that $C = A = \{\Lambda\}$ and such that for every $s \in S$, $\Lambda[s] = \Lambda$ and $\alpha(\Lambda, s, \Lambda) = \Lambda$. Up to isomorphism, the trivial models differ only in the number of selectors $|S|$ in their selector sets.

The Unbounded Models

Once we have just a small number of selectors, atoms, and composite objects in a model, it turns out that we can demonstrate that the model must contain an unbounded number of distinct objects as well. This is made precise by the following proposition.

Proposition 9 *Unbounded Models*

A system $M = (C, A, S, \Lambda, \textit{Selection, Assignment})$, which is a model for the ground axioms, contains an unbounded number of distinct objects provided either

(a) $|S| \geq 1$ and $|A| \geq 2$, or

(b) $|S| \geq 2$ and $|C| \geq 2$.

Proof: This is proved by exhibiting a 1-1 mapping between the natural numbers and a subset of distinct objects in M. Suppose x is a nonnull object and s is a selector. Then we denote the object $\alpha(\Lambda, s, x)$ by the expression $[s{:}\ x]$. The sequence of objects in M that we shall examine is of the form x, $[s{:}\ x]$, $[s{:}\ [s{:}\ x]]$, $[s{:}\ [s{:}\ [s{:}\ x]]]$, . . . , and so on. This sequence is put into 1-1 correspondence with the natural numbers by defining a mapping ρ, where $\rho(0) = x$ and $\rho(n) = \alpha(\Lambda, s, \rho(n-1))$ for $n \geq 1$. It can be demonstrated that ρ is 1-1 by using induction on n to show that $\rho(n) = \rho(m)$ implies $n = m$, provided $x[s] = \Lambda$ and $x \neq \Lambda$. To find such an x and s in the above two cases, we proceed as follows:

(a) Choose any $s \in S$ and choose $x \in A$ such that $x \neq \Lambda$.

(b) Choose $c \in C$ such that $c \neq \Lambda$. There exist distinct selectors $s, s' \in S$ such that $c[s'] \neq \Lambda$. If $c[s] = \Lambda$, choose $x = c$. Otherwise choose $x = \alpha(c, s, \Lambda)$.

The Finite Models

By Proposition 9, any nontrivial model M for the ground axioms contains (for nonempty S) an unbounded number of objects whenever $|A| > 1$ or $|S| > 1$. Therefore, the finite nontrivial models, if they exist at all, must have $|A| = |S| = 1$ and $|C| = n + 1$ for some $n \geq 1$. The following proposition characterizes these models.

Proposition 10 *Finite Models*

There are $n!$ models of cardinality $|C| = n + 1$ in which, up to isomorphism, each model corresponds to a distinct permutation on n symbols.

Proof: Let π be a permutation on n distinct nonnull composite objects. Let s be the only selector $s \in S$. Set $\Lambda[s] = \Lambda$, and set $c[s] = \pi(c)$ for each $c \neq \Lambda$. Define $\alpha(c, s, d) = \pi^{-1}(d)$ for each $d \neq \Lambda$ for any c, and set $\alpha(c, s, \Lambda) = \Lambda$ for any c. The resulting system is a model for the ground axioms. Since Λ is the only atom as a consequence of the fact that $|A| = 1$ and since s is the only selector as a consequence of the fact that $|S| = 1$, the verification of the axiom for atoms reduces to verifying $\Lambda[s] = \Lambda$. But this is true by construction. The null object axiom is taken true by construction also. The axiom for the equality of composite objects follows from the property that permutations are 1-1 mappings, so $\pi(c) = \pi(d)$ implies $c = d$. Since there is only one selector s, only the top half of the assignment axiom need be verified. This reduces to showing $\alpha(c, s, d)[s] = d$, which follows from the fact that $\pi(\pi^{-1}(d)) = d$. In any such finite model of the ground axioms, the fact that π must be a permutation follows from the fact that π is synonymous for selection by the only selector s in the model, which by the axiom for the equality of composite objects is forced to be 1-1 on the finitely many composite objects. But any 1-1 map on a finite set must be a permutation.

Models with Objects of Unbounded Extent

Sometimes it is convenient to represent objects of unbounded extent. For example, if $f(x)$ is a function on the positive integers, we might view f as an object whose ith component is specified by the value $f(i)$. In this case, assignment of y to be a new ith component of f could be represented by replacing f with a new function g such that $g(x) =$ (**if** $x = i$ **then** y **else** $f(x)$). The new function g satisfies the assignment axiom since it agrees with f on all but its ith component and since $g(i) = y$. Hash-coded arrays furnish another example of objects of unbounded extent. We can define the element $A[i]$ of the array A to be x if there exists a triple (A, i, x) in a hash table H; otherwise, the value of $A[i]$ is defined to be 0. If the table H is empty, $A[i] = 0$ for any i, and therefore A can be considered an object of unbounded extent. The assignment operation $A[i] \leftarrow x$ is represented by removing triples from H of the form (A, i, y) if any exist and then by inserting the triple (A, i, x). Models in which composite objects are represented by partial functions have been explored in Reynolds (1970) and MacLennan (1973).

Constructive Models

Let $M = (C, A, S, \Lambda, \mathit{Selection}, \mathit{Assignment})$ be a model for the ground axioms in which $|A| \geq 2$. The composite objects C of M are said to be *constructible* provided they satisfy the following property:

> No nonnull object is in C unless it can be shown to be in C by a finite sequence of one or more applications of the following rules:
>
> 1. If $a \in A$ and $s \in S$, then $\alpha(\Lambda, s, a) \in C$.
> 2. If $c \in C, d \in C \cup A$, and $s \in S$, then $\alpha(c, s, d) \in C$.

A *constructive model* of the ground axioms is a model whose composite objects are *constructible*.

In any model of the ground axioms for which $|A| \geq 2$ and $|S| \geq 1$ there is a subset $C' \subset C$ of the composite objects such that $(C', A, S, \Lambda, \mathit{Selection}, \mathit{Assignment})$ is a constructive model. C' is called the set of *constructed objects* of the model. It can be shown that the constructed objects have the following properties:

1. *Finiteness:* Each constructed object x has finite *breadth* and finite *depth*, where the *breadth* of x is defined to be the number of distinct selectors s for which $x[s] \neq \Lambda$, and the *depth* of x is defined to be the integer n such that there exists a composite selector $u \in S^+$, where $|u| = n$, for which $x[u] \neq \Lambda$ and such that for every $t \in S^+$ for which $|t| > n$, $x[t] = \Lambda$. (The null object and the atoms are defined to have *breadth* and *depth* 0.)
2. *Structural induction property:* If P is a proposition that holds for all atoms of a model, and if P holds for a constructed object x whenever it holds for all components of x, then P holds for all constructed objects. [See Burstall (1969).]

The Rosenberg-Thatcher Construction

Rosenberg and Thatcher (1975) have given a succinct characterization of constructive models of the ground axioms. Taking S^* to be the free monoid of composite selectors over S with identity e, we again denote the concatenation of $x, y \in S^*$ by xy. If $z = xy \in S^*$, then x is said to be a *prefix* of z. In particular, e is a prefix of every string.

A subset of composite selectors L is said to be *prefix-free* if no composite selector in L is a *proper prefix* of any other string in L (see Definition 3 for the meaning of *proper prefix*). We say that L is *prefix-closed* if whenever a composite selector $z \in L$, then so also are all proper prefixes of z. The *left quotient of L by x*, denoted L^x, is defined to be the set of composite selectors $\{y \mid xy \in L\}$. An *access domain D* over a selector set S is a finite, nonempty, prefix-closed subset of S^*. The *extension set* $E(x, D)$ of a composite selector $x \in D$ is the set of simple selectors $\{s \mid xs \in D\}$. We call $x \in D$ a *fiber* precisely when $E(x, D) = \varnothing$ (the empty set). The set of fibers of the access domain D is denoted $\Phi(D)$. Clearly, $\Phi(D)$ is prefix-free.

There is a correspondence between an access domain D and a rooted, directed tree with edges labeled by elements of S. Each composite selector in D corresponds to a node of the tree, and there is an edge labeled $s \in S$ from each node $u \in D$ to the successor node $us \in D$. The root of the tree corresponds to the empty selector e. The fibers in $\Phi(D)$ correspond to the paths from the root of the tree to the leaves. Thus, graphically, access domains are trees which indicate how to access component positions of multilevel data structures in which the fibers provide access to the atomic positions. If we take a mapping $\sigma: \Phi(D) \longrightarrow A$ which sends fibers of D onto atoms A, we get a representation for constructible composite objects. We can choose to denote this mapping by the *characteristic set* notation of the Vienna Definition Language [see Lucas (1968) and Wegner (1972)], $\{\langle x, \sigma(x)\rangle \mid x \in \Phi(D)\}$.

We shall now show how the constructible composite objects of a constructive model of the ground axioms correspond to the Rosenberg-Thatcher construction. Let $c \in C$ be a constructible composite object, and set $D = \{u \in S^* \mid c[u] \neq \Lambda\}$. That is, D is the set of composite selectors (including the empty selector e) that access nonnull components of c. We must first prove that D is an access domain by showing it to be finite, nonempty, and prefix-closed. D is nonempty because it contains e, and it can be shown finite when c is constructible using structural induction and the finite breadth and depth properties of constructible objects. To show that D is prefix-closed, suppose, to the contrary, that there exist composite selectors x and y such that x is a proper prefix of y for which $y \in D$, but $x \notin D$. Since x is a proper prefix of y, there exists a nonempty composite selector z such that $y = xz$. Thus, $c[y] = c[xz]$, and by Proposition 5, the latter can be rewritten $c[xz] = (c[x])[z]$. Since $x \notin D$, we have $c[x] = \Lambda$, and by Proposition 6 and the fact that Λ is an atom, $\Lambda[z] = \Lambda$. Hence, $c[y] = \Lambda$, which contradicts the assertion that $y \in D$. Therefore, if $y \in D$, so also is any proper prefix of y, so that D must be prefix-closed.

Now, we observe that any fiber in D selects an atom from c. Let $x \in \Phi(D)$. Then, by definition, for any $s \in S$, $xs \notin D$, so that $c[xs] = \Lambda$. Thus, by Proposition 5, we can write $(c[x])[s] = \Lambda$ for all $s \in S$, which implies that $c[x]$ is an atom, by Proposition 2. Therefore, given a nonnull, constructible, composite object c, we can readily find the corresponding Rosenberg-Thatcher representation by, first, constructing the access domain D from the set of all composite selectors that select nonnull components of c; second, choosing the fibers $\Phi(D)$; and, third, constructing the function σ that sends fibers onto atoms by defining $\sigma(x) = c[x]$ for $x \in \Phi(D)$.

Composite selection and assignment can be especially succinctly stated in the Rosenberg-Thatcher representation. Given an object represented by a mapping σ: $F \longrightarrow A$ from a prefix-free set of fibers F into atoms A and given a composite selector x, we can define

$$\textit{Selection}(\sigma, x) = \sigma', \qquad \text{where } \sigma': F' \longrightarrow A \text{ such that } F' = F^x \text{ and } \sigma'(y) = \sigma(xy).$$

Given two composite objects $\sigma: F \longrightarrow A$ and $\sigma': F' \longrightarrow A$, together with x, a composite selector, we can define composite assignment as $\textit{Assignment}(\sigma, x, \sigma') = \sigma''$, where $\sigma'': F'' \longrightarrow A$ is a new mapping such that

1. $F'' = (F - \{x\}F^*) \cup \{x\}F'$.
2. For all $z \in F''$,

$$\sigma''(z) = \begin{cases} \sigma(z) & \text{if } z \in F - \{x\}F^* \\ \sigma'(y) & \text{if } z = xy \text{ for some } y \in F'. \end{cases}$$

Graphically, given a Rosenberg-Thatcher object $\sigma: F \longrightarrow A$, where F is a prefix-free set of fibers, we first take the prefix closure of F by adding to F all proper prefixes of fibers in F to obtain an access domain D, and then we can construct a rooted, directed tree corresponding to σ by letting nodes correspond to the distinct elements $x \in D$, by letting edges s be drawn from nodes x to nodes $xs \in D$, and by labeling the leaves with atoms $\sigma(x)$ for each fiber $x \in F$. *Selection*(σ, x) then corresponds to choosing the subtree of the graph of σ rooted at the end of the path x, and assignment of σ' at position x in σ corresponds to replacing the subtree rooted at x in the graph of σ with the graph of σ'.

The Rosenberg-Thatcher construction provides the bridge between the Vienna Objects [Lucas (1968), Wegner (1972)] and constructive models of the ground axioms, with one minor difference. Namely, in the Vienna Definition Language, the Vienna null object Ω is not taken as atomic, even though it has the property that $\Omega[s] = \Omega$ for all selectors s.

3.5. HIGHER-ORDER AXIOM SETS

Once we have defined and studied the elementary algebraic systems, such as semigroups or partial orders, we can progress to the definition and study of higher-order systems, such as rings, fields, and lattices, that use the elementary systems as subsystems. For example, in a ring, we study the interaction of an additive group and a multiplicative semigroup related to each other under a distribution law. By analogy, having defined the ground axioms and having studied their consequences, we can progress to the study of higher-order data systems having subsystems that obey the ground axioms. We should be clear that the ground axioms are not the only characterization of elementary subsystems of potential interest. We may well be interested in additional characterizations of elementary subsystems, such as total orderings on keys used in a file or various methods for characterizing the behavior of pointers, links, or references. Just as we would not proclaim semigroups to be the only subsystem of interest in algebra, so we cannot proclaim models of the ground axioms to be the only data subsystem of interest to an eventual, well-evolved, axiomatic theory of data structures. Rather, we should expect other axiomatic characterizations of elementary properties of data subsystems to merit attention in the study of higher-order systems.

Once we give axioms for a higher-order data type, such as binary trees, stacks, queues, strings, lists, arrays, or finite sets, we may find that it is possible to organize the objects and operations of lower-order subsystems of data to provide a faithful representation. Further, using axiomatic properties of the subsystems, we can often prove that a representation composed from subsystems obeys the axioms defining the required properties of the higher-order type. For example, Guttag (1976) has shown that the axioms for symbol tables in a block structured language can be satisfied by an implementation using stacks of arrays. The stack and array axioms are used to prove the correctness of the underlying implementation. Thus, it is demonstrable that the axiomatic approach provides a framework helpful for proving the correctness of programs and data representations. Further examples of axiomatic characterizations of over a dozen familiar higher-order data types are given in Horowitz and Sahni's book on data structures [Horowitz and Sahni (1976)].

Beyond correctness proofs lies the intriguing problem of *representation synthesis.* Given a representation-independent characterization of a data type in the form of axioms, we might like to know how we might go about synthesizing a suitable underlying representation for it. In this section, we shall examine two higher-order axiom systems—those for *queues* and those for *finite sets*—with an eye toward discovering how we might synthesize representations for a data type.

Synthesizing Representations for Queues

To study the representation synthesis problem for queues, we proceed in two steps. First, we devise a representation-independent axiomatic characterization for queues. As usual, this consists of writing down what we conceive to be the required abstract behaviors in the form of relationships between abstract operations applied to abstract quantities. We might also check the axioms for such properties as consistency, completeness, and independence. (Generally speaking, devising formal proofs of these properties can be quite challenging.) Second, we transform the axioms to yield both function definitions for the operations and a data model for the ground axioms.

Let Q be a class of (first-in, first-out) queues with elements in a set A. The following operations are defined on queues:

1. enq : A × Q ⟶ Q . . . puts an element a onto a queue q.
   firstout : Q ⟶ A . . . removes the element a from the queue q that was placed in q before any other.
   deq : Q ⟶ Q . . . produces the remainder of the queue after removal of the element first put in.

This system of objects and operations obeys the following *queue axioms*:

2. There exists a special queue Λ called the *empty queue* such that

$$\Lambda \in Q.$$

3. firstout(enq(a, Λ)) = a . . . if an element a has been placed on the empty queue, then the first element that can be removed is a.
4. q ≠ Λ ⊃ firstout(enq(a, q)) = firstout(q) . . . if an element a is the most recent element placed in a nonempty queue q, then the first element that can be removed from the resulting queue is identical to that which can first be removed from q.
5. deq(enq(a, Λ)) = Λ . . . the remainder of a queue consisting of a single element after removal of that element is the empty queue.

6. $q \neq \Lambda \supset$ deq(enq(a, q)) = enq(a, deq(q)) ... the remainder of a queue formed by placing an element a on a nonempty queue q is the same as placing a on the remainder of q.

Let us now consider the following data representation problem.

Problem: *The Representation Synthesis Problem for Queues*

Given the abstract behaviors for queues specified by the queue axioms above, find a representation which satisfies both the ground axioms and the queue axioms.

To solve this synthesis problem, we proceed as follows. First, take axiom 3, namely, firstout(enq(a, Λ)) = a, and rewrite it as

7. $q = \Lambda \supset$ firstout(enq(a, q)) = a.

Then, taking axiom 4, $q \neq \Lambda \supset$ firstout(enq(a, q)) = firstout(q), and combining it with step 7, we get

8. **if** $q = \Lambda$ **then** firstout(enq(a, q)) = a **else** firstout(enq(a, q)) = firstout(q).

Now, we factor out firstout(enq(a, q)) from step 8 using the transformation

$$\textbf{if } B \textbf{ then } f = X \textbf{ else } f = Y \Rightarrow f = (\textbf{if } B \textbf{ then } X \textbf{ else } Y)$$

to generate

9. firstout(enq(a, q)) = (**if** $q = \Lambda$ **then** a **else** firstout(q)).

Our objective is to produce a function definition in the form firstout(x) = $E(x)$ in which the left-hand side is a function of a parameter x and the right-hand side $E(x)$ is an expression whose free variable is also x. Thus, letting x = enq(a, q), we could rewrite firstout(enq(a, q)) as firstout(x). To eliminate a and q from the right-hand side of step 9 we must postulate the existence of two functions, say g and h, such that $a = g(x)$ and $q = h(x)$. Then, we can rewrite step 9 in the required form:

10. firstout(x) = (**if** h(x) = Λ **then** g(x) **else** firstout(h(x))).

A similar series of transformations gives us a definition for the function deq(x). First, we rewrite axiom 5, namely, deq(enq(a, Λ)) = Λ, as

11. $q = \Lambda \supset$ deq(enq(a, q)) = q,

and we combine step 11 with axiom 6 to yield

12. **if** $q = \Lambda$ **then** deq(enq(a, q)) = q **else** deq(enq(a, q)) = enq(a, deq(q)).

Now, by factoring out deq(enq(a, q)) from step 12, we get

13. deq(enq(a, q)) = (**if** $q = \Lambda$ **then** q **else** enq(a, deq(q))).

Exactly the same set of substitutions used to transform step 9 into step 10 can be used to transform step 13 into the required function definition form deq(x) = $G(x)$. Namely, taking enq(a, q) = x, $a = g(x)$, and $q = h(x)$, enables us to write step 13 as

14. deq(x) = (**if** h(x) = Λ **then** h(x) **else** enq(g(x), deq(h(x)))).

We observe that we have succeeded in transforming the axioms into valid function definitions—step 10 for firstout(x) and step 14 for deq(x)—but in so doing we generated a subproblem. Namely, find functions enq, g, and h satisfying the constraints enq(a, q) $= x$, $a = g(x)$, and $q = h(x)$. These constraints can be composed to give us the following two relations:

15. a = g(enq(a, q)) and q = h(enq(a, q)).

These relations tell us that if we take objects $a \in A$ and $q \in Q$ and apply the operation enq, we produce an object from which we can recover a by applying the operator g and from which we can recover q by applying the operator h. Thus, enq is an information lossless composition for which we can readily find a suitable ground axiom model. For instance, taking any two distinct selectors, such as {*first*, *second*}, we could write

16. enq(a, q) = α(α(Λ, *first*, a), *second*, q).
17. g(x) = x[*first*].
18. h(x) = x[*second*].

Using the assignment axiom, it is easy to show that steps 16–18 satisfy the relations in step 15. Letting Q' be the range of the mapping enq: $A \times Q \rightarrow Q'$, representing the empty queue by the null object Λ, and setting $Q = \{\Lambda\} \cup Q'$, we obtain a ground axiom model that satisfies the requirements of queue axioms 1 and 2. A finished form of the function definitions 16, 14, and 10 can be obtained by substituting 17 and 18 into 14 and 10 and making a minor simplification in 14. This gives

19. firstout(x) = (**if** x[*second*] = Λ **then** x[*first*] **else** firstout(x[*second*])).
20. deq(x) = (**if** x[*second*] = Λ **then** Λ **else** enq(x[*first*], deq(x[*second*]))).
21. enq(a, q) = μ_0(⟨*first*: a⟩, ⟨*second*: q⟩).

Here, we have used the Vienna Definition notation $\mu_0(\langle s\colon x\rangle, \langle t\colon y\rangle)$ to define enq(a, q), which builds a composite object whose *first* component is a and whose *second* component is q, since the μ_0 function has a slightly more pleasing visual appearance than the equivalent nested assignment expression α(α(Λ, *first*, a), *second*, q) [see Wegner (1972) for details].

The representation for queues we have synthesized above is clearly nonunique. Intuitively, the above representation adds a new item a to a queue q by building a new composite object whose *first* component is a and whose *second* component is q. The object selected by firstout(x) is retrieved by finding the most deeply nested *second* component (whose own *second* component is Λ) and by extracting its *first* component. The remainder of the queue after removal of the least recently entered element is obtained by replacing the most deeply nested *second* component by the null object Λ.

Another equally valid representation could be produced by letting enq(a, q) place a as the new *first* component of a new *second* component of deepest nesting and by letting firstout(x) pick the head of x. The functions specifying this second representation are as follows:

22. firstout(x) = x[*first*].
23. deq(x) = x[*second*].
24. enq(a, q) = (**if** q = Λ **then** α(Λ, *first*, a) **else**
α(α(Λ, *first*, q[*first*]), *second*, enq(a, q[*second*])).

It is easy to verify that these function definitions satisfy the queue axioms. For example, suppose we wish to show that axiom 6 is satisfied—namely, $q \neq \Lambda \supset$ deq(enq(a, q)) = enq(a, deq(q)). We first rewrite deq(enq(a, q)) applying the above definitions

$$\text{deq(enq(a, q))} = (\textbf{if } q = \Lambda \textbf{ then } \alpha(\Lambda, \textit{first}, a) \textbf{ else}$$
$$\alpha(\alpha(\Lambda, \textit{first}, q[\textit{first}]), \textit{second}, \text{enq}(a, q[\textit{second}])))[\textit{second}].$$

Using the transformation (**if** B **then** X **else** Y)[S] $\Rightarrow$ (**if** B **then** $X[S]$ **else** $Y[S]$) to distribute the selector across the arms of the conditional expression, we get

$$\text{deq(enq(a, q))} = (\textbf{if } q = \Lambda \textbf{ then } \alpha(\Lambda, \textit{first}, a)[\textit{second}] \textbf{ else}$$
$$\alpha(\alpha(\Lambda, \textit{first}, q[\textit{first}]), \textit{second}, \text{enq}(a, q[\textit{second}]))[\textit{second}]).$$

Under the hypothesis that $q \neq \Lambda$, we need consider only the **else** arm of the conditional expression. This yields

$$q \neq \Lambda \supset \text{deq(enq(a, q))} = \alpha(\alpha(\Lambda, \textit{first}, q[\textit{first}]), \textit{second}, \text{enq}(a, q[\textit{second}])))[\textit{second}].$$

Applying the assignment axiom to the right-hand side and rewriting $q[\textit{second}]$ as deq(q), we obtain the desired result

$$q \neq \Lambda \supset \text{deq(enq(a, q))} = \text{enq(a, deq(q))}.$$

While the manipulations we used to transform the queue axioms into the first of the above representations (19–21) seem straightforward enough, it is quite challenging to devise a set of transformations mapping the queue axioms into the second of the above representations (22–24). Thus, we must consider the possibility that the manipulations have a built-in "bias" so to speak that exhibits a tendency to find certain sorts of representations while missing others that are equally valid. In fact, as we shall show in the next section, this "bias" can lead to the discovery of valid representations that human programmers would likely never consider (because of intolerable inefficiency, for instance).

Synthesizing Representations for Finite Sets

Consider a class of data S with elements in A having the following operations:

1. has : S × A ⟶ {*true, false*} . . . has(s, a) is *true* iff $a \in S$.
2. insert : A × S ⟶ S . . . insert(a, s) adds element a to set s.
3. delete : A × S ⟶ S . . . delete(a, s) removes a from set s.

The following are the *finite set axioms*:

4. There exists a set Λ called the *empty set* such that $\Lambda \in S$.
5. $\sim$has(Λ, a).
6. has(insert(a, s), a).
7. $\sim$has(delete(a, s), a).
8. $a \neq b \supset$ has(insert(a, s), b) = has(s, b).
9. $a \neq b \supset$ has(delete(a, s), b) = has(s, b).

Essentially, these axioms specify the relationships between the set membership predicate, has(s, x), and the incremental element insertion and deletion functions. The relationship between the set membership predicate and the usual set theoretic notions of union, intersection, and equivalence can be specified by giving further axioms. In particular, letting has(s, x) be denoted by $x \in s$, we have

10. $x \in S \cup T$ iff $(x \in S) \vee (x \in T)$.
11. $x \in S \cap T$ iff $(x \in S) \wedge (x \in T)$.
12. $S \equiv T$ iff ($\forall a \in A$, $a \in S$ iff $a \in T$).

Once these axioms have been given, we can prove theorems such as the following:

13. insert(a, s) $\equiv$ insert(a, insert(a, s)).
14. $\Lambda \equiv$ delete(a, Λ).
15. delete(a, s) $\equiv$ delete(a, delete(a, s)).
16. if a $\neq$ b then delete(a, insert(b, s)) $\equiv$ insert(b, delete(a, s)).
17. insert(a, insert(b, s)) $\equiv$ insert(a, s) $\cup$ insert(b, s).

Since such consequences are provable directly from the axioms, they hold for all models of the axioms. We stress this point in advance because the representation about to be derived may seem counterintuitive with respect to such properties as 13–17 at first contact. In synthesizing our representation, we shall work only with axioms 4–9.

The solution proceeds as follows. Rewrite axiom 5 first as

5a. x = Λ $\supset$ has(x, b) = *false*

and again as

5b. has(x, b) = **if** x = Λ **then** *false*.

Rewrite axiom 6 as

6a. a = b $\supset$ has(insert(a, s), b) = *true*

and rewrite axiom 7 as

7a. a = b $\supset$ has(delete(a, s), b) = *false*.

Then taking axioms 6a and 8 together, we obtain

10. **if** a = b **then** has(insert(a, s), b) = *true* **else** has(insert(a, s), b) = has(s, b),

from which, by factoring out has(insert(a, s), b), we get

10a. has(insert(a, s), b) = (**if** a = b **then** *true* **else** has(s, b)).

To transform the latter result into function definition form, has(x, b) = $H(x, b)$, we take x = insert(a, s) and postulate the existence of functions g and h such that $a = g(x)$ and $s = h(x)$. Then we write

11. has(x, b) = (**if** g(x) = b **then** *true* **else** has(h(x), b)).

A similar sequence of transformations maps 7a and 9 into

12a. has(delete(a, s), b) = (**if** a = b **then** *false* **else** has(s, b)).

By taking $x = \text{delete}(a, s)$, $a = g(x)$, and $s = h(x)$, we get

13. has(x, b) = (**if** g(x) = b **then** *false* **else** has(h(x), b)).

We now observe that $x = \text{insert}(a, s)$, $a = g(x)$, and $s = h(x)$ imply

14. a = g(insert(a, s)) and s = h(insert(a, s))

and, similarly, that $x = \text{delete}(a, s)$, $a = g(x)$, and $s = h(x)$ imply

15. a = g(delete(a, s)) and s = h(delete(a, s)).

Conditions 14 and 15 are again recognized as the circumstances that suggest we can construct a model of the ground axioms in which insert(a, s) and delete(a, s) each construct composite objects having components a and s and in which g and h can be represented by selector functions. However, in contrast to the situation for queues, we have an additional subproblem to solve. Namely, definitions 11 and 13 for has(x, b) differ in effect depending on whether $x = \text{insert}(a, s)$ or $x = \text{delete}(a, s)$. This suggests that we could unify the two definitions 11 and 13 into one if only we could discriminate these two cases. Combining this requirement with the idea that insert and delete can each be modeled by constructors for composite objects, we settle on the idea of a *constructed discrimination*. Namely, we can agree to add, say, a *tag* component such that insert(a, s) has a tag + and delete(a, s) has a tag −. Hence, we could agree to represent insert and delete as follows:

16. insert(a, s) = μ_0(⟨tag : +⟩, ⟨first, a⟩, ⟨second, s⟩).
17. delete(a, s) = μ_0(⟨tag : −⟩, ⟨first, a⟩, ⟨second, s⟩).

Then we can also write

18. g(x) = x[*first*].
19. h(x) = x[*second*].

Finally, $x[tag] = +$ and $x[tag] = -$ are synonyms for the conditions $x = \text{insert}(a, s)$ and $x = \text{delete}(a, s)$, respectively. Proceeding, now, to unify the two definitions 11 and 13, we rewrite 11 and 13 as

11a. has(x, b) = **if** x[*tag*] = + **then** (**if** x[*first*] = b **then** *true* **else** has(x[*second*]))
13a. has(x, b) = **if** x[*tag*] = − **then** (**if** x[*first*] = b **then** *false* **else** has(x[*second*]))

Then we get the unified version

20. has(x, b) = **if** x[*tag*] = + **then**
    (**if** x[*first*] = b **then** *true* **else** has(x[*second*], b)) **else**
    if x[*tag*] = − **then**
    (**if** x[*first*] = b **then** *false* **else** has(x[*second*], b)).

Now, by noting that 16 and 17 cause mutually exclusive tagging constructions, whence $x[tag] = -$ iff $x[tag] \neq +$, we can apply the transformation

if B **then** C **else if** $\sim B$ **then** $D \Rightarrow$ **if** B **then** C **else** D

to 20 to get

21. has(x, b) = **if** x[*tag*] = + **then**
    (**if** x[*first*] = b **then** *true* **else** has(x[*second*], b))
    else
    (**if** x[*first*] = b **then** *false* **else** has(x[*second*], b)).

Now, a further simplifying transformation applies to yield

22. has(x, b) = **if** x[*first*] = b **then** x[*tag*] = + **else** has(x[*second*], b).

The latter equation may now be unified with 5b to give the final definition of has(x, b):

23. has(x, b) = (**if** x = Λ **then** *false* **else**
if x[*first*] = b **then** x[*tag*] = + **else** has(x[*second*], b)).

This definition, together with definitions 16 and 17, constitutes a representation for finite sets satisfying axioms 1–9, provided we identify the empty set Λ with the null object and provided we set S equal to the union of $\{\Lambda\}$ with the ranges of the constructor functions insert and delete.

If one were to denote insert(x, a) by the expression $+a\,|\,x$ and delete(x, a) by the expression $-a\,|\,x$, then, intuitively, the finite sets in this representation would be denoted by formal expressions such as $+a\,|-c\,|+d\,|+c\,|\,\Lambda$, which record for each set the sequence of insertions and deletions used to create it, starting with the null object. The function has(x, b) can then be visualized as searching left to right through the formal string for x to find the leftmost occurrence of b (if there is one), this being the occurrence of b that was inserted or deleted most recently in the formation of x. If the leftmost occurrence of b in x is prefixed by $+$, then b was inserted and has(x, b) is *true*, whereas if b is prefixed by $-$ or if b occurs nowhere in x, then has(x b) is *false*. It is clear intuitively as well as formally that this representation is valid. It is equally clear that the representation is of dubious efficiency, so much so, in fact, that we are led urgently to seek techniques for transforming inefficient, directly synthesized representations into more optimal relatives.

An interesting development in this direction results from studying ways to eliminate redundant information from formal set expressions. It is possible to devise sets of theorems, such as delete(a, Λ) $\equiv \Lambda$ and insert(a, insert(a, s)) $\equiv$ insert(a, s), which, when applied in a preferred direction, will simplify formal set expressions. Under certain conditions, these theorems can be packaged into Church-Rosser systems, which converge on unique, minimal output expressions no matter the order in which applicable constituent simplifications are carried out. For example, the following collection of simplification theorems, written in the formal notation of the last paragraph, constitutes a Church—Rosser (1936) system:

1. simplify(x) $\longrightarrow$ x $\cup$ Λ.
2. +a | x $\cup$ y $\longrightarrow$ −a | x $\cup$ +a | y.
3. −a | −a | x $\longrightarrow$ −a | x.
4. −a | +a | x $\longrightarrow$ −a | x.
5. a $\neq$ b $\supset$ −a | +b | x $\longrightarrow$ +b | −a | x.
6. −a | Λ $\longrightarrow$ Λ.
7. Λ $\cup$ y $\longrightarrow$ result(y).

This maps an input expression simplify(x) into an output expression result(y) such that y has neither negative elements nor redundant positive elements. For example, the following are successive simplifications of an input expression using the above system of rewriting rules:

```
simplify( +a|-b|-a|+a|+c|-b|-c|Λ) —→ by 1 and 2
-a|-b|-a|+a|+c|-b|-c|Λ ∪ +a|Λ     —→ by 6 used twice
-a|-b|-a|+a|+c|Λ         ∪ +a|Λ     —→ by 4
-a|-b|-a|+c|Λ            ∪ +a|Λ     —→ by 5 used thrice
+c|-a|-b|-a|Λ            ∪ +a|Λ     —→ by 6 used thrice
+c|Λ                     ∪ +a|Λ     —→ by 2
-c|Λ ∪ +c|+a|Λ                      —→ by 6
   Λ ∪ +c|+a|Λ                      —→ by 7
     result(+c|+a|Λ)
```

Since the Church-Rosser simplification system was composed from a collection of theorems that can be proved from the finite set axioms 1–12, the properties of the system are representation-independent and apply to all models of the finite set axioms. In particular, to any finite set composed from a sequence of insertions and deletions starting with Λ, the Church-Rosser system finds an equivalent set composed from a minimal length sequence of insertions of distinct elements. Applying this result to our synthesized representation, we see that the Church-Rosser simplifier can be used to condense constructed representations into irredundant, deletion-free form. Seen in this light, the synthesized representation is perhaps less ludicrous than at first suspected. There may be circumstances in which we wish to handle large batches of "orders" for insertions and deletions of items for which no sensible total ordering function exists. Only periodically might we wish to "consolidate" the insertions and deletions, and only after consolidation do we wish to test a few items for set membership in the consolidated sets. If storage space is plentiful and cheap and if there is a high premium on spending the least possible time processing new "orders" for deletions and insertions to a large number of sets, then the synthesized representation may perform better than competing set representations at which effort is spent at insertion and deletion time maintaining minimally redundant set representations.

For example, the following three functions are a valid representation for finite sets which maintain irredundant, deletion-free set representations but which require more insertion and deletion processing time, on the average, than the synthesized representation:

```
insert(a, s) = (if s = Λ then μ0(⟨first: a⟩, ⟨second: Λ⟩) else
                if s[first] = a then s else
                 μ0 (⟨first: s[first]⟩, ⟨second: insert(a, s[second])⟩))

delete(a, s) = (if s = Λ then Λ else
                 if s[first] = a then s[second] else
                  μ0 (⟨first: s[first]⟩, ⟨second: delete(a, s[second])⟩))

has(a, s) = (if s = Λ then false else
              if s[first] = a then true else
               has(a, s[second]))
```

Many of the interesting set representations studied in the literature [see, for example, Aho et al. (1974)] are based on the use of other higher order data types, such as binary trees or hash coded tables, and many depend on additional requirements on the set elements, such as total orderings or element access frequency distributions. We have not studied the problems of data representation synthesis in these realms out of preference for learning to mount the challenges of the simpler domains first. Even in these simpler domains, we have not yet learned how to transform given representations into different ones with altered performance properties, nor have we learned how to avoid the "bias" of our preliminary representation synthesis derivations. A great deal evidently remains to be done before we can claim to have discovered a practical calculus for deriving data representations from axiomatic specifications of abstract behavioral requirements. Nonetheless, the representation synthesis problem is interesting for the reason that programming will remain an art, as opposed to a science, until methods are determined for discovering precisely what range of data representations is possible in the solution of a given programming problem and whether it is possible to select the optima from among them.

3.6. CONCLUSIONS

In this chapter we have studied the consequences of some basic axioms for data. We explored classes of models for the axioms, and we studied related characterizations of constructible composite objects from the literature. Finally, we examined the problem of synthesizing data representations starting from axiomatic characterizations of higher-order data types.

Much work remains if the axiomatic approach to data is to be brought to full fruition. A stiff challenge to the axiomatic approach is to characterize concisely data structures which, loosely speaking, are modeled easily by directed graphs with cycles or reentrancies. A further challenge is to extend axiomatic characterizations to capture data structures having two or more simultaneous decompositions (such as arrays decomposable by rows or by columns) and data structures with overlapping shared subsystems of components (perhaps accessible by different name spaces).

Yet it seems clear that the ice has been broken. The axiomatic approach can already provide us with rigorous, representation-independent definitions of certain data types, and it provides a framework for proofs of correctness of data representations. What is more, we can at least state precisely what we mean by the data representation synthesis problem, even if our first few steps toward its solution are a bit wobbly. Under the circumstances, it seems tantalizing to want to take further steps.

ACKNOWLEDGMENTS

I am indebted to G. H. Mealy, K. Walk, E. L. Wegbreit, P. Wegner, and S. N. Zilles for valuable discussions. S. N. Zilles discovered the facts proved in Propositions 9 and 10.

CHAPTER 4

THE DESIGN OF DATA TYPE SPECIFICATIONS

JOHN V. GUTTAG
ELLIS HOROWITZ
Computer Science Department
University of Southern California
Los Angeles, California

DAVID R. MUSSER
USC Information Sciences Institute
Marina del Rey, California

Abstract

In this chapter we are concerned with the design of data types in the creation of a software system; our major purpose is to explore a means for specifying a data type that is independent of its eventual implementation. The particular style of specification, called algebraic axioms, is exhibited by axiomatizing many commonly used data types. These examples reveal a great deal about the intricacies of data type specification via algebraic axioms and also provide a standard to which alternative forms may be compared. Further uses of this specification technique are in proving the correctness of implementations and in interpretively executing a large system design before actual implementation commences.

Key Words and Phrases

data type, specification, algebraic axioms, software design, recursive programming, program correctness

4.1. INTRODUCTION

Creating a software system is generally regarded as a four-stage process: requirements, design, coding, and testing. For some of these stages, tools and/or techniques that significantly enhance the process have been developed. Recently, concern has increased about developing aids for the design stage. Design is essentially a creative, synthetic process, and a fully automated tool is very unlikely. What has been suggested is a *methodology* or a style of working which is purported to yield improved designs.

Top-down design is a process whereby a task is transformed into an executable program. This process in its purest form calls for carefully refining, step by step, the functional requirements of a system into operational programs. Further guidelines regarding the choice of appropriate statements and the postponement of design decisions can be found in Dahl (1972).

The purpose of this chapter is to explore a complementary design strategy, the design of data types. A complete software system may contain a variety of types (lists, stacks, trees, matrices, etc.) and a variety of operations. One useful design procedure is to treat those operations that act primarily on a single data type as forming a unit and to consider the semantics of these operations as the definition of the type. This idea was implicit in the SIMULA 67 programming language [Dahl (1970)] in which the syntactic designation *class* denotes a collection of such operations. However, the class concept applies this principle at the programming language level rather than at design time. Each operation of a class is a directly executable program. It is also useful to consider a collection of operations at design time; then the process of design (of data types) consists of specifying those operations to increasingly greater levels of detail until an executable implementation is achieved. The idea we wish to explore here is how to create an initial specification of a data type.

A *data type specification* (or abstract data type) is a representation-independent formal definition of each operation of a data type. Thus, the complete design of a single data type would proceed by first giving its specification, followed by an (efficient) implementation that agrees with the specification. This separation of data type design into two distinct phases is very useful from an organizational point of view. Any process that needs to make use of the data type can do so by examining the specification alone. There is no need to wait until the type is fully implemented, nor is it necessary to fully comprehend the implementation.

There are two chief concerns in devising a technique for data type specification. The first is to devise a notation that permits a rigorous definition of operations but remains representation-independent, and the second is to learn to use that notation. There are many criteria one can use to measure the value of a specification notation, but the two major ones are as follows:

1. Can specifications be constructed without undue difficulty?
2. Is the resulting specification easy to comprehend?

As with programming, there are potentially a very large number of ways to specify an operation. A good data type specification should give just enough information to define the type but not so much that the choice of implementations based on it is limited. Thus, we say that a data type specification is an abstraction of a concept of which the eventual implementation is only one instance.

In this chapter our intent is to explore a particular specification technique, *algebraic specifications* [Goguen (1975), Guttag (1975), Zilles (1975)], by exhibiting specifications for a number of commonly used data types. Those we have chosen are typical of those that are discussed in a course on data structures; see Horowitz (1976). By supplying these examples we hope to convince the reader that the style of specification we discuss here is especially appropriate for designing data types and that it meets the two criteria previously stated. Secondly, we hope these example specifications will provide a standard by which other methods can be compared. We do not pretend to have supplied definitive specifications of the example data types. Both our choice of operations and the semantics we associate with some of the operations are somewhat arbitrary.

In the last section we shall indicate how these specifications can be further used for proving the correctness of implementations and for testing, at design time, large software systems. However, since these subjects are fairly lengthy, we shall limit our presentation here to an informal discussion of reading and writing data type specifications. The remaining subjects will only be hinted at here, but are dealt with in Guttag (1976b).

Many other people have been working on these and related areas, and we have profited from their ideas. A useful bibliography of this work is given in Liskov (1975). Some of the particular axiomatizations have already appeared in the literature, notably Stacks, Queues, and Sets; see Goguen (1975), Guttag (1976a), Liskov (1975), Spitzen (1975), and Standish (1973).

4.2. THE SPECIFICATIONS

How can one describe a data type without unduly constraining its eventual implemented form? One method is to define the object using natural language and mathematical notation. For example, a stack can be defined as a sequence of objects $(a_1, \ldots, a_n)$, $n \geq 0$, where insertions or deletions are allowed only at the right-hand end. This type of definition is not satisfactory from a computing standpoint, where it is preferable to define constructively a data type by defining the operations which create, build up, and destroy instances of the type. Since software designers generally know how to program, the use of a programming-like language for specification is especially desirable.

The features we choose permit only the following:

1. Free variables,
2. *if-then-else* expressions,

3. Boolean expressions, and
4. Recursion.

Moreover, we restrict the use of procedures to those which are single-valued and have no side effects. Note that many features normally presumed to be present in conventional programming languages (such as assignment to variables, iteration statements) are not permitted in this formalism. This approach may seem so arbitrary as to eliminate the possibility of ever achieving the previously stated goals, but actually it has several strong points to recommend it. First, the restricted set yields a representation-independent means for supplying a specification. Second, the resulting specifications can clearly express the desired concepts if the reader is comfortable with reading recursive programs. (Though many programmers are not so accustomed, a faithful reading of this chapter will serve as a tutorial on this subject.) Third, the separation of values and side effects lends clarity and simplifies a specification. Though requiring this separation may be too restrictive for an implementation, the criterion of efficiency can be relaxed at the specification stage. Fourth, the above features can be easily axiomatized, which is a necessary first step for successfully carrying out proofs of implementations; see Guttag (1976b).

```
type Stack[item]
    declare   NEWSTACK() → Stack
              PUSH(Stack,item) → Stack
              POP(Stack) → Stack
              TOP(Stack) → item ∪ {UNDEFINED}
              ISNEWSTACK(Stack) → Boolean;
    for all   s ∈ Stack, i ∈ item let
              ISNEWSTACK(NEWSTACK) = true
              ISNEWSTACK(PUSH(s,i)) = false
              POP(NEWSTACK) = NEWSTACK
              POP(PUSH(s,i)) = s
              TOP(NEWSTACK) = UNDEFINED
              TOP(PUSH(s,i)) = i
    end
end Stack
```

Figure 4.2.1

Let us begin with the very simple example of a Stack data type which is given in Figure 4.2.1. The operations which are available for manipulating a stack are (1) NEWSTACK, which produces an instance of the empty stack; (2) PUSH, which inserts a new item onto the stack and returns the resulting stack; (3) POP, which removes the top item and returns the resulting stack; (4) TOP, which returns the top item of the stack; and (5) ISNEWSTACK, which tests if a stack is empty. For each operation, the types of its input and output are listed in the ***declare*** statement. Notice that all operations are true functions which return a single value and allow no side effects. If stack operations are implemented by procedures with side effects, their effect can be specified easily in terms of the operations we have given. Extending the formalism in this way is discussed in Section 4.4.

At this point let us introduce the notational conventions we shall use throughout this report. All operation names are written in uppercase. Type names begin with a capital letter, e.g., Stack. Lowercase symbols are regarded as free variables, such as s and i in Figure 4.2.1, which are taken to be of type Stack and item, respectively. Type names can be modified by listing *parameters* within square brackets. These parameters may be type names or free variables whose range is a type; e.g., item is such a variable and indicates that the type Stack can apply to any other data type. The equations within the ***for all*** and ***end*** are the axioms which describe the semantics of the operations.

At first these axioms may seem difficult to comprehend. One aid is to interpret the axioms as defining a set of recursive functions. The empty stack is represented by a function with no input arguments, NEWSTACK. Then asking for the topmost element of NEWSTACK is regarded as an exceptional condition which does not result in an item; hence, we call it UNDEFINED. The only other stacks we can have must be of the form PUSH(s,i), where s is any stack and i is the most recently inserted item. Then, by line 12, the last element inserted is the first returned. Notice that we need not worry about expressions of the form TOP(POP(s)), since axioms 9 and 10

```
type  CircularList[item]
1.   declare  CREATE( ) → CircularList
2.            INSERT(CircularList, item) → CircularList
3.            DELETE(CircularList) → CircularList
4.            VALUE(CircularList) → item ∪ {UNDEFINED}
5.            ISEMPTY(CircularList) → Boolean
6.            RIGHT (CircularList) → CircularList
7.            JOIN(CircularList,CircularList) → CircularList
8.   for all  c, c1 ∈ CircularList, i, i1, i2 ∈ item let
9.            ISEMPTY(CREATE) = true
10.           ISEMPTY(INSERT(c,i)) = false
11.           DELETE(CREATE) = CREATE
12.           DELETE(INSERT(c,i)) = c
13.           VALUE(CREATE) = UNDEFINED
14.           VALUE(INSERT(c,i)) = i
15.           RIGHT(CREATE) = CREATE
16.           RIGHT(INSERT(CREATE,i)) = INSERT(CREATE,i)
17.           RIGHT(INSERT(INSERT(c,i),i1))
                    =INSERT(RIGHT(INSERT(c,1)),i)
18.           JOIN(c,CREATE) = c
19.           JOIN(c,INSERT(c1,i)) = INSERT(JOIN(c,c1),i)
     end
end CircularList
```

Figure 4.2.2

give us rules for expressing any value of type Stack in terms of only NEWSTACK and PUSH.

Unfortunately, the Stack example is far too simple in many respects to properly illustrate the intricacies of data type specification. A somewhat richer example is the data type Circularlist defined in Figure 4.2.2. This type has seven operations. Five of these, CREATE, INSERT, DELETE, VALUE, and ISEMPTY, have exact analogs in type stack. The RIGHT and JOIN operations introduce additional complexity by allowing us to rotate the list of stored elements, thus permitting access to both ends of the list, and to join two lists into one. This additional complexity is reflected in the recursion of axioms 17 and 19. This specification is similar to one given by Valdis Berzins [Berzins (1977)] for a *symmetric* circular list data type, which included a LEFT operation but not a JOIN operation.

We have now introduced almost the entire specification language used in writing algebraic axioms. All that remains is to introduce conditionals into the right-hand sides. This is done in the definition of type Queue, a first-in first-out list, in Figure 4.2.3. There are six operations: four produce queues, one returns an item, and one is Boolean-valued. An easy way to understand the axioms is to conceive of the set of all queues as being represented by the set of strings consisting of

$$\text{NEWQ } \textit{or } \text{ADDQ}(\ldots\text{ADDQ}(\text{ADDQ}(\text{NEWQ},i_1),i_2),\ldots,i_n),n\geq 1.$$

The item i_1 is at the front and i_n is at the rear. Then the axioms can be concretely thought of as rules which show how each operation acts on any such string. For

```
type Queue[item]
    declare NEWQ( ) → Queue
            ADDQ(Queue,item) → Queue
            DELETEQ(Queue) → Queue
            FRONTQ(Queue) → item ∪ {UNDEFINED}
            ISNEWQ(Queue) → Boolean
            APPENDQ(Queue,Queue) → Queue;
    for all q,r ∈ Queue, i ∈ item let
            ISNEWQ(NEWQ) = true
            ISNEWQ(ADDQ(q,i)) = false
            DELETEQ(NEWQ) = NEWQ
            DELETEQ(ADDQ(q,i)) =
                if ISNEWQ(q) then NEWQ
                   else ADDQ(DELETEQ(q),i)
            FRONTQ(NEWQ) = UNDEFINED
            FRONTQ(ADDQ(q,i)) =
                if ISNEWQ(q) then i else FRONTQ(q)
            APPENDQ(q,NEWQ) = q
            APPENDQ(r,ADDQ(q,i)) = ADDQ(APPENDQ(r,q),i)
    end
end Queue
```

Figure 4.2.3

example, taking the FRONTQ of the empty queue is UNDEFINED. Otherwise FRONTQ is applied to a queue whose most recently inserted item is i, and q represents the remainder of the queue. If q is empty, then i is the correct result; otherwise FRONTQ is recursively applied to q. A similar situation holds for the DELETEQ operation. Notice that none of the common forms of queue representation, e.g., as linked lists or in an array, is implied or precluded by this definition.

Let us consider a third familiar structure, the *binary tree* (Binarytree), and examine in more detail the virtue of regarding all values of the data structure as being represented by strings. Its specification is given in Figure 4.2.4.

```
type Binarytree[item]
    declare  EMPTYTREE( ) → Binarytree
             MAKE(Binarytree,item,Binarytree) → Binarytree
             ISEMPTYTREE(Binarytree) → Boolean
             LEFT(Binarytree) → Binarytree
             DATA(Binarytree) → item ∪ {UNDEFINED}
             RIGHT(Binarytree) → Binarytree
             ISIN(Binarytree,item) → Boolean;
    for all  l,r ∈ Binarytree, d,e ∈ item let
             ISEMPTYTREE(EMPTYTREE) = true
             ISEMPTYTREE(MAKE(l,d,r)) = false
             LEFT(EMPTYTREE) = EMPTYTREE
             LEFT(MAKE(l,d,r)) = l
             DATA(EMPTYTREE) = UNDEFINED
             DATA(MAKE(l,d,r)) = d
             RIGHT(EMPTYTREE) = EMPTYTREE
             RIGHT(MAKE(l,d,r)) = r
             ISIN(EMPTYTREE,e) = false
             ISIN(MAKE(l,d,r),e) =
                   if d=e
                         then true
                         else ISIN(l,e) or ISIN(r,e)
    end
end Binarytree
```

Figure 4.2.4

The operations included are EMPTYTREE, which creates the empty tree; MAKE, which joins two trees together with a new root; and operations which access the data at a node, return the left subtree or the right subtree of a node, and search for a given data item. Three operations which we might naturally wonder whether to include are the usual traversal methods (preorder, inorder, and postorder), which place the elements contained in the tree into a queue [Horowitz (1976)]. Perhaps the strongest reason for including them is the very fact that they are so succinctly stated by our recursive notation, e.g., INORD(Binarytree) → Queue and

```
INORD(EMPTYTREE) = NEWQ
INORD(MAKE(l,d,r)) = APPENDQ(ADDQ(INORD(l),d),INORD(r))
```

for l,r ∈ Binarytree and d ∈ item. The choice of which operations to include in a specification is arbitrary. We have omitted this operation because it makes significant use of the operations of another data type, Queue. However, this does give us the opportunity to experiment with the string representation. Let us present an example which starts with the binary tree

```
T = MAKE(MAKE(EMPTYTREE,B,EMPTYTREE),A,
         MAKE(EMPTYTREE,C,EMPTYTREE))
```

and applies the axioms to INORD(T) to obtain

```
INORD(T) = APPENDQ(ADDQ(INORD(MAKE(EMPTYTREE,B,EMPTYTREE)),A),
           INORD(MAKE(EMPTYTREE,C,EMPTYTREE)))
```

which by the definition of INORD becomes

```
APPENDQ(ADDQ(APPENDQ(ADDQ(NEWQ,B),NEWQ),A),
        APPENDQ(ADDQ(NEWQ,C),NEWQ))
```

and now using the axioms for APPENDQ, we obtain

```
APPENDQ(ADDQ(ADDQ(NEWQ,B),A),ADDQ(NEWQ,C))
```

and again applying APPENDQ, we obtain

```
ADDQ(APPENDQ(ADDQ(ADDQ(NEWQ,B),A),NEWQ),C)
```

which gives the final result:

```
ADDQ(ADDQ(ADDQ(NEWQ,B),A),C).
```

At this point the reader has seen three examples, and we are in a better position to argue the virtues of the specification notation. The number of axioms is directly related to the number of operations of the type being described. The restriction of expressing axioms using only the *if-then-else* and recursion has not caused any contortions. This should not come as a surprise to LISP programmers who have found these features largely sufficient over many years of programming. One criticism we have encountered is that recursion foices one into inefficient code, as evidenced by the FRONTQ operation, which finds the front element of the queue by starting at the last element. To this we reply that a specification should not be viewed as describing the eventual implemented program but merely as a means for understanding what the operation is to do. One might also suppose that the operation names are not well chosen and then wonder how easy it is to discern their meaning via the axioms. This is hard to respond to, especially when trying to imagine how other techniques would fare under this restriction. Nevertheless, we might ask the reader if he can determine what the operation MYSTERY does where MYSTERY(Queue) ⟶ Queue and

```
MYSTERY(NEWQ) = NEWQ
MYSTERY(ADDQ(q,i)) = APPENDQ(ADDQ(NEWQ,i),MYSTERY(q))
```

are the axioms which define it.

Let us pursue the binary tree example a bit further. In most applications the elements in the tree are somehow ordered. That is, the tree is built up from a series of INSERT operations that preserve some ordering relationship among the nodes of the tree. This nonprimitive INSERT operation can be programmed in terms of the primitive operations of type Binarytree. One drawback of such an approach to creating a restricted kind of binary tree is that we cannot rely upon a type-checking mechanism to guarantee that the desired ordering property is always maintained. If, on the other hand, we declare a type with INSERT as a primitive operation, we can achieve the desired level of security.

Consider type Bstree (binary search tree), defined to be a binary tree with data items at each node such that for any node its item is alphabetically greater than any item in its left subtree and alphabetically less than any item in its right subtree; see Horowitz, (1976). Some axioms have to be changed and a new operation added in order to transform the Binarytree specification into one for type Bstree.

The second axiom for ISIN is altered to read

```
ISIN(MAKE(l,d,r),e) =
        if d=e then true
              else if d<e then ISIN(r,e)
                                    else ISIN(l,e).
```

```
type Bstree[item]
     declare  EMPTYTREE( ) → Bstree
             *MAKE(Bstree,item,Bstree) → Bstree
              ISEMPTYTREE(Bstree) → Boolean
              LEFT(Bstree) → Bstree
              DATA(Bstree) → item ∪ {UNDEFINED}
              RIGHT(Bstree) → Bstree
              ISIN(Bstree,item) → Boolean,
              INSERT(Bstree,item) → Bstree;
     for all  l,r ∈ Bstree, d,e ∈ item let
              ISEMPTYTREE(EMPTYTREE) = true
              ISEMPTYTREE(MAKE(l,d,r)) = false
              LEFT(EMPTYTREE) = EMPTYTREE
              LEFT(MAKE(l,d,r)) = l
              DATA(EMPTYTREE) = UNDEFINED
              DATA(MAKE(l,d,r)) = d
              RIGHT(EMPTYTREE) = EMPTYTREE
              RIGHT(MAKE(l,d,r)) = r
              ISIN(EMPTYTREE,e) = false
              ISIN(MAKE(l,d,r),e) =
                    if d=e then true
                          else if d<e then ISIN(r,e) else ISIN(l,e)
              INSERT(EMPTYTREE,e) = MAKE(EMPTYTREE,e,EMPTYTREE)
              INSERT(MAKE(l,d,r),e) =
                    if d=e then MAKE(l,d,r)
                          else if d<e then MAKE(l,d,INSERT(r,e))
                                      else MAKE(INSERT(l,e),d,r)
     end
end Bstree
```

Figure 4.2.5

The new operation is INSERT(Bstree, item) ⟶ Bstree, which searches for an item in a binary search tree and if it is not there, inserts it appropriately. Note that this is the only way that a binary search tree can be created. This implies that the operation MAKE, present in the specification of type Binarytree, must not be accessible to the programmer in this new specification. If it were available, we could not guarantee that all binary search trees would be well formed. Thus we regard MAKE as a *hidden* function [Parnas (1972)] and attach a star to it in the new specification (Figure 4.2.5) to indicate that it is no longer accessible.

Let us consider another familiar type, String. In the specification of Figure 4.2.6, we have chosen five primitive operations: NULL, which creates the null string; ADDCHAR, which appends a character to a string; CONCAT, which joins two strings together; SUBSTR(s,i,j), which from a string s returns the j-character substring

```
type String
  declare  NULL( ) → String
           ISNULL(String) → Boolean
           LEN(String) → Integer
           ADDCHAR(String,Character) → String
           CONCAT(String,String) → String
           SUBSTR(String,Integer,Integer) → String
           INDEX(String,String) → Integer;
  for all  s,t ∈ String, c,d ∈ Character, i,j ∈ Integer let
           ISNULL(NULL) = true
           ISNULL(ADDCHAR(s,c)) = false
           LEN(NULL) = 0
           LEN(ADDCHAR(s,c)) = LEN(s)+1
           CONCAT(s,NULL) = s
           CONCAT(s,ADDCHAR(t,d)) = ADDCHAR(CONCAT(s,t),d)
           SUBSTR(NULL,i,j) = NULL
           SUBSTR(ADDCHAR(s,c),i,j) =
                  if j = 0
                     then NULL
                     else if j = LEN(S)-i+2
                              then ADDCHAR(SUBSTR(s,i,j-1),c)
                              else SUBSTR(s,i,j)
           INDEX(s,NULL) = LEN(s)+1
           INDEX(NULL,ADDCHAR(t,d)) = 0
           INDEX(ADDCHAR(s,c),ADDCHAR(t,d)) =
                  if INDEX(s,ADDCHAR(t,d)) ≠ 0
                     then INDEX(s,ADDCHAR(t,d))
                     else if c=d and t = SUBSTR(s,LEN(s)-LEN(t)+1,LEN(t))
                              then LEN(s)-LEN(t)+1
                              else 0
  end
end String
```

Figure 4.2.6

beginning at the ith character of s and INDEX(s,t), which returns the position of the first occurrence of a string t as a substring of a string s (0 if t is not a substring of s).

Notice that there are several types which make up this definition in addition to type String, namely, types Character, Integer, and Boolean. In general, a data type specification always defines only one type, but it may require the operations of other data types to accomplish this. Another question which arises again is when should an operation be part of the specification and when should it not, an issue we have already encountered with binary trees. The operations we have chosen here are basically those provided in PL/1.

So far we have concentrated primarily on how to read axioms. Now let us consider how to create them. As a general outline of attack we begin with a basic set of operations $f_1, \ldots, f_m$. A subset of these, say $f_1, \ldots, f_k$, $k \leq m$, has as output the data type being defined. Out of the k operations are chosen a subset which we call the *constructor set*, satisfying the property that all instances of the data type can be represented using only constructor set operations. Then the axioms which need to be written are those that show how each non-constructor-set operation behaves on all possible instances of the data type.

As a new example, consider the type Set in Figure 4.2.7. The operations whose range is of type Set are EMPTYSET, which has the usual meaning, and INSERT and

```
type Set[item]
  declare  EMPTYSET( ) → Set
           ISEMPTYSET(Set) → Boolean
           INSERT(Set,item) → Set
           DELSET(Set,item) → Set
           HAS(Set,item) → Boolean;
  for all  s ∈ Set, i,j ∈ item let
           ISEMPTYSET(EMPTYSET) = true
           ISEMPTYSET(INSERT(s,i)) = false
           HAS(EMPTYSET,i) = false
           HAS(INSERT(s,i),j) =
               if i=j then true else HAS(s,j)
           DELSET(EMPTYSET,i) = EMPTYSET
           DELSET(INSERT(s,i),j) =
               if i=j then DELSET(s,j)
                  else INSERT(DELSET(s,j),i)
  end
end Set
```

Figure 4.2.7

DELSET, which put an element into or delete one from the set, respectively. Out of these three operations we select EMPTYSET and INSERT as the constructors. Then an arbitrary set containing $n \geq 1$ items is given by the expression

$$\text{INSERT}(\ldots\text{INSERT}(\text{EMPTYSET},i_1),\ldots,i_n).$$

A very important feature of this definition is the fact that there is no ordering assumed on the items. Alternatively, the specification might insist that $i_1 < i_2 < \cdots < i_n$ also be true.

The next example, the Graph type in Figure 4.2.8, is interesting in several respects. The mathematical definition of a graph is generally in terms of two sets: nodes and edges. This is reflected in the constructors for this definition, which are EMPTYGRAPH, ADDNODE, and ADDEDGE. This definition allows for an unconnected graph and for nodes with no edges incident to them. An edge is given by the function

```
type Graph
  declare  EMPTYGRAPH( ) → Graph
           ADDNODE(Graph,Node) → Graph
           ADDEDGE(Graph,Edge) → Graph
           NODES(Graph) → Set(Node)
           EDGES(Graph) → Set(Edge)
           ADJAC(Graph,Node) → Set(Node)
           NODOUT(Graph,Node) → Graph
           EDGEOUT(Graph,Edge) → Graph;
  for all  g ∈ Graph, i,j,k,l,v,w ∈ Node let
           NODES(EMPTYGRAPH) = EMPTYSET
           NODES(ADDNODE(g,v)) = INSERT(NODES(g),v)
           NODES(ADDEDGE(g,REL(i,j))) = INSERT(INSERT(NODES(g),i),j)
           EDGES(EMPTYGRAPH) = EMPTYSET
           EDGES(ADDNODE(g,v)) = EDGES(g)
           EDGES(ADDEDGE(g,REL(i,j))) = INSERT(EDGES(g),REL(i,j))
           ADJAC(EMPTYGRAPH,v) = EMPTYSET
           ADJAC(ADDNODE(g,w),v) = ADJAC(g,v)
           ADJAC(ADDEDGE(g,REL(i,j)),v) =
               if v=i then INSERT(ADJAC(g,v),j)
                  else if v=j then INSERT(ADJAC(g,v),i)
                       else ADJAC(g,v)
           NODOUT(EMPTYGRAPH,v) = EMPTYGRAPH
           NODOUT(ADDNODE(g,w),v) =
               if v=w then NODOUT(g,v) else ADDNODE(NODOUT(g,v),w)
           NODOUT(ADDEDGE(g,REL(i,j)),v) =
               if v=i or v=j then NODOUT(g,v)
                  else ADDEDGE(NODOUT(g,v),REL(i,j))
           EDGEOUT(EMPTYGRAPH,REL(i,j)) = EMPTYGRAPH
           EDGEOUT(ADDNODE(g,v),REL(i,j)) =
               ADDNODE(EDGEOUT(g,REL(i,j)),v)
           EDGEOUT(ADDEDGE(g,REL(k,l)),REL(i,j)) =
               if REL(k,l) = REL(i,j) then g
                  else ADDEDGE(EDGEOUT(g,REL(i,j)),REL(k,l))
  end
end Graph
```

Figure 4.2.8

REL(i,j) (a constructor of the data type Edge), and it is not specified whether the edges are directed or not. Notice that three of the operations result in sets, and the parameter notation has been naturally extended to distinguish between sets with different types of elements. ADJAC finds all nodes which are adjacent to some vertex. NODOUT (g,v) removes the node v and all edges incident to v. EDGEOUT removes a single edge from the graph.

The next example is a sequential File data type (Figure 4.2.9). The operations include READ, WRITE, RESET, ISEOF (end-of-file check), and SKIP (past a specified number of records).

```
type File[record]
  declare  EMPTYFILE( ) → File
           WRITE(File,record) → File
           SKIP(File,Integer) → File
           RESET(File) → File
           ISEOF(File) → Boolean
           READ(File) → record ∪ {UNDEFINED}
  for all  f ∈ File, r,s ∈ record, i,j ∈ Integer let
           SKIP(EMPTYFILE,i) = EMPTYFILE
           SKIP(SKIP(f,j),i) = SKIP(f,j+i)
           RESET(EMPTYFILE) = EMPTYFILE
           RESET(WRITE(f,r)) = SKIP(WRITE(f,r),0)
           RESET(SKIP(WRITE(f,r),i)) = SKIP(WRITE(f,r),0)
           ISEOF(EMPTYFILE) = true
           ISEOF(WRITE(f,r)) = true
           ISEOF(SKIP(WRITE(f,r),i)) =
                  if i=0 then false else ISEOF(SKIP(f,i−1))
           READ(EMPTYFILE) = UNDEFINED,
           READ(WRITE(f,r)) = UNDEFINED,
           READ(SKIP(WRITE(f,r),i)) =
                  if ISEOF(SKIP(f,i))
                       then r
                       else READ(SKIP(f,i))
           WRITE(SKIP(WRITE(f,r),i),s)
                  if ISEOF(SKIP(f,i))
                       then WRITE(f,s)
                       else WRITE(SKIP(f,i),s)
  end
end File
```

Figure 4.2.9

Sequential file operations would not, in practice, be implemented as functions but rather as procedures with side effects, say READP (f,r) and WRITEP (f,r). The operations we have given can be used to specify the effects of these procedures: READP (f,r) means r ← READ (f), f ← SKIP (f,1); and WRITEP (f,r) means f ← WRITE (f,r). Note that the axioms imply that if a SKIP operation immediately

```
type Polynomial
   declare  ZERO( ) → Polynomial
            ADDTERM(Polynomial,Coef,Exp) → Polynomial
            REMTERM(Polynomial,Exp) → Polynomial
            MULTTERM(Polynomial,Coef,Exp) → Polynomial
            ADD(Polynomial,Polynomial) → Polynomial
            MULT(Polynomial,Polynomial) → Polynomial
            REDUCTUM(Polynomial) → Polynomial
            ISZERO(Polynomial) → Boolean
            COEF(Polynomial,Exp) → Coef
            DEGREE(Polynomial) → Exp
            LDCF(Polynomial) → Coef;
   for all  p,q ∈ Polynomial, c,d ∈ Coef, e,f ∈ Exp let
            REMTERM(ZERO,f) = ZERO
            REMTERM(ADDTERM(p,c,e),f) =
                   if e=f then REMTERM(p,f)
                       else ADDTERM(REMTERM(p,f)c,e)
            MULTTERM(ZERO,d,f) = ZERO
            MULTTERM(ADDTERM(p,c,e),d,f) =
                   ADDTERM(MULTTERM(p,d,f),c*d,e+f)
            ADD(p,ZERO) = p
            ADD(p,ADDTERM(q,d,f)) = ADDTERM(ADD(p,q),d,f)
            MULT(p,ZERO) = ZERO
            MULT(p,ADDTERM(q,d,f)) = ADD(MULT(p,q),MULTTERM(p,d,f))
            REDUCTUM(p) = REMTERM(p,DEGREE(p))
            ISZERO(ZERO) = true
            ISZERO(ADDTERM(p,c,e)) =
                   if COEF(p,e) = -c
                       then ISZERO(REMTERM(p,e))
                       else false
            COEF(ZERO,e) = 0
            COEF(ADDTERM(p,c,e),f) =
                   if e=f then c+COEF(p,f) else COEF(p,f)
            DEGREE(ZERO) = 0
            DEGREE(ADDTERM(p,c,e)) =
                   if e> DEGREE(p)
                       then e
                       else if e< DEGREE(p)
                              then DEGREE(p)
                              else if COEF(p,e) = -c
                                     then DEGREE(REDUCTUM(p))
                                     else DEGREE(p)
            LDCF(p) = COEF(p,DEGREE(p))
   end
end Polynomial
```

Figure 4.2.10

follows a WRITE, it means reset the file to its beginning and then skip past i records. Also, if a record is overwritten, the part of the file past that record is lost. For further study of the axioms note that all File values can be viewed as one of the following string forms:

EMPTYFILE or WRITE(WRITE(...(EMPTYFILE,r_1),...),r_n)
or SKIP(WRITE(WRITE(...(EMPTYFILE,r_1),...),r_n),i).

We shall conclude this section with a presentation of type Polynomial. The usual mathematical definition of a polynomial is an expression of the form

$$a_m x^m + a_{m-1} x^{m-1} + \cdots + a_1 x + a_0,$$

where x is an indeterminate and the a_i's come from some commutative ring. If $a_m \neq 0$, then m is called the degree, a_m the leading coefficient, and $a_{m-1}x^{m-1} + \cdots + a_1 x + a_0$ the reductum. A specification of Polynomials as a data type with 11 operations is given in Figure 4.2.10.

In this specification every Polynomial is either ZERO or constructed by applying ADDTERM to a Polynomial. Note the absence of assumptions about order of exponents, nonzero coefficients, etc., which are important as representation decisions but are not essential for the specification.

The real virtue of this specification is that a fairly complex object has been completely defined using only a few lines. The corresponding programs in a conventional programming language may be several times this size. (This will be especially true if some of the "fast" algorithms are used.)

4.3. CORRECTNESS OF IMPLEMENTATIONS

Algebraic specifications of data types can play a significant role in program verification. As with any axiomatic approach, they permit factorization of proofs into distinct, manageable stages; also, the use of pure functions and equations as the form of specification permits proofs to be constructed in large part as sequences of substitutions using the equations as rewrite rules. These points are developed at length in Guttag (1976b), which also describes a *data type verification system* (implemented in INTERLISP) capable of interactively assisting a human user in carrying through many of the steps of verifications automatically. In this chapter we shall confine our discussion of verification issues to a brief example of the implementation of one data type, Queue (Figure 4.2.3), in terms of another, CircularLists (Figure 4.2.2). We first give, in a notation very similar to that for the specifications, an implementation of the Queue type consisting of a *representation* declaration and a *program* for each of the Queue operations in terms of the representation. See Figure 4.3.1.

A proof of correctness of this implementation consists of showing that each of the Queue axioms of Figure 4.2.3 is satisfied. For some of the axioms this is quite

```
implementation QueueByCircularList[item]
  declare QREP(CircularList) → Queue
  for all  c,c1 ∈ CircularList, i ∈ item let
           NEWQ = QREP(CREATE)
           ADDQ(QREP(c),i) = QREP(RIGHT(INSERT(c,i)))
           DELETEQ(QREP(c)) = QREP(DELETE(c))
           FRONTQ(QREP(c)) = VALUE(c)
           ISNEWQ(QREP(c)) = ISEMPTY(c)
           APPENDQ(QREP(c),QREP(c1)) = QREP(JOIN(c1,c))
  end
end QueueByCircularList
```

Figure 4.3.1

trivial because of the close correspondence between the axiomatizations of some of the Queue and CircularList operations. For example, we show that the Queue axiom ISNEWQ(NEWQ) = ***true*** is satisfied by the following sequence of steps:

```
                  (ISNEWQ(NEWQ) = true)
=[by NEWQ program]⟹ (ISNEWQ(QREP(CREATE)) = true)
=[by ISNEWQ program]⟹ (ISEMPTY(CREATE) = true)
=[by ISEMPTY axiom]⟹ (true = true)
=[by equality axiom]⟹ true.
```

A more difficult case is the following APPENDQ axiom.

```
          [APPENDQ(q,ADDQ(r,i)) = ADDQ(APPENDQ(q,r),i)]
=[by substitution of q=QREP(c), r=QREP(c1)]⟹
     [APPENDQ(QREP(c),ADDQ(QREP(c1),i)) = ADDQ(APPENDQ(QREP(c),QREP(c1)),i)]
=[by ADDQ and APPENDQ programs]⟹
     [APPENDQ(QREP(c),QREP(RIGHT(INSERT(c1,i)))) = ADDQ(QREP(JOIN(c1,c)),i)]
=[by APPENDQ and ADDQ programs]⟹
     [QREP(JOIN(RIGHT(INSERT(c1,i)),c)) = QREP(RIGHT(INSERT(JOIN(c1,c),i)))].
```

The proof can now be completed by using the following theorem about the JOIN operation.

Theorem

```
JOIN(RIGHT(INSERT(c1,i)),c2) = RIGHT(INSERT(JOIN(c1,c2),i))
```

This theorem will be proved from the CircularList axioms using *data type induction*, i.e., induction on the number of operations of the data type which are performed to obtain an element of the type [called *generator induction* in Spitzen (1975)]. Proofs by data type induction are often simplified if one first proves a *normal form lemma* for the data type, which specifies a minimal set of constructors of the data type (cf. the discussion of constructors following the String data type example in Section 4.2). For circular lists we have the following:

Normal Form Lemma

For every c ∈ CircularList, (c=CREATE) or (∃c′ ∈ CircularList, i′ ∈ item such that c = INSERT (c′, i′)).

Proof: By data type induction. Let c be a circular list; then one of the following cases holds:

1. c = CREATE.
2. c = INSERT (c1, i1).
3. c = DELETE (c1).
4. c = RIGHT (c1).

for some c1, i1. In cases 1 and 2, the theorem is clearly satisfied. In case 3, we use the induction hypothesis to conclude that c1=CREATE or ∃c2,i2 such that c1=INSERT(c2,i2). If c1=CREATE, then c=DELETE(CREATE)=CREATE, by a DELETE axiom. Otherwise, c=DELETE(INSERT(c2,i2))=c2, by the other DELETE axiom. The induction hypothesis applies to c2, so c=c2= INSERT(c3,i3) for some c3 and i3. A similar argument proves the lemma for case 4.

Proof of Theorem

By data type induction. By the lemma, it is sufficient to consider the cases

1. c2 = CREATE.
2. c2 = INSERT(c3,i3) for some c3, i3.

In case 1 we have

```
            [JOIN(RIGHT(INSERT(c1,i)),CREATE) = RIGHT(INSERT(JOIN(c1,CREATE),i))]
=[by JOIN axiom]⟹          [RIGHT(INSERT(c1,i))=RIGHT(INSERT(c1,i))]
⟹ true.
```

In case 2 we have

```
  [JOIN(RIGHT(INSERT(c1,i)),INSERT(c3,i3)) = RIGHT(INSERT(JOIN(c1,INSERT(c3,i3)),i))]
=[by JOIN axiom]⟹
  [INSERT(JOIN(RIGHT(INSERT(c1,i)),c3),i3) = RIGHT(INSERT(INSERT(JOIN(c1,c3),i3),i))]
=[by RIGHT axiom]⟹
  [INSERT(JOIN(RIGHT(INSERT(c1,i)),c3),i3) = INSERT(RIGHT(INSERT(JOIN(c1,c3),i)),i3)]
=[by induction hypothesis]⟹
  [INSERT(RIGHT(INSERT(JOIN(c1,c3),i)),i3) = INSERT(RIGHT(INSERT(JOIN(c1,c3),i)),i3)]
⟹ true.
```

Thus the theorem has been proved, and the APPENDQ axiom has been shown to be satisfied. Many other useful theorems (or *invariants*) about data types can be proved from the axioms using the same techniques of case analysis and induction as in the foregoing proofs. In some cases these techniques can also be applied to prove theorems about an implementation. We used one such *implementation invariant* in the proof of the APPENDQ axiom without explicitly mentioning it, namely (∃c such that q=QREP(c)). This is easily proved from the Normal Form Lemma, the programs for CREATE and INSERT, and data type induction.

The proofs of the other Queue axioms for the circular list implementation require no additional techniques and will be omitted. All of these proofs have been carried through semiautomatically by the *data type verification system* described more fully in Guttag (1976b).

4.4. PROCEDURES AND BOUNDED TYPES

Until now all of the abstract data types that we have axiomatized have been unbounded. It is relevant to observe a parallel here between computer science and mathematics, i.e., that bounded types are often harder to define than unbounded ones. In this section we intend to deal with the added complications of specifying more realistic data types, in particular a type of bounded size. At the same time we shall relax the restriction that all operations be single-valued and permit a notation that resembles the conventional use of procedures, first introduced in Guttag (1976b).

It will now be permissible to include procedures in the specifications. A procedure P whose first argument, x, is altered as a result of its execution, but not its second argument, y, is syntactically declared as P(*var* x, y). If P is a pure procedure, i.e., it returns no value, then this is syntactically expressed by writing P(*var* x, y) ⟶. The definition of procedure P would be included in the semantic specification of the data type using it. A procedure has a body and an optional value part separated by a semicolon, e.g.,

P(*var* x, *var* y) = x ← F(x,y), y ← G(x) ; H(x,y)

is a possible definition of P where F,G,H are functions returning a value. Notice that simultaneous assignment to parameters is now permitted, but we continue to adhere to our earlier approach by requiring that the values returned by a procedure be expressed by single-valued functions. In some cases the latter operations will no longer be accessible by the user of the data type. We call them *hidden functions* and indicate them by placing a star next to their names.

As an example, we give in Figure 4.4.1 the specification of a queue of bounded size. Notice that in comparison with the unbounded queue of Figure 4.2.3, four new operations have been added. ADDQ and DELETEQ are now designated as hidden functions, and in their place the user will apply the pure procedure ENQ and the function DEQ, both of which have the side effect of altering their first argument. SIZE returns the number of elements contained in a bounded queue and LIMIT the maximum number of elements permitted. Notice also that we have augmented the UNDEFINED operation by allowing it to be qualified. This will facilitate the handling of errors by distinguishing their source.

```
type Bqueue[item]
  declare  NEWQ(Integer) → Bqueue
           *ADDQ(Bqueue,item) → Bqueue
           *DELETEQ(Bqueue) → Bqueue
           FRONTQ(Bqueue) → item ∪ {UNDEFINED}
           ISNEWQ(Bqueue) → Boolean
           APPENDQ(Bqueue,Bqueue) → Bqueue
           SIZE(Bqueue) → Integer
           LIMIT(Bqueue) → Integer,
           ENQ(var Bqueue,item) → ,
           DEQ(var Bqueue) → item;
  for all  q,r ∈ Bqueue, i ∈ item, in ∈ Integer let
           ISNEWQ(NEWQ(in)) = true
           ISNEWQ(ADDQ(q,i)) = false
           DELETEQ(NEWQ(in)) = NEWQ (in)
           DELETEQ(ADDQ(q,i)) =
               if ISNEWQ(q) then NEWQ (in)
                            else ADDQ(DELETEQ(q),i)
           FRONT(NEWQ(in)) = UNDEFINED[underflow]
           FRONT(ADDQ(q,i)) =
               if ISNEWQ(q) then i else FRONTQ(q)
           APPENDQ(q,NEWQ(in)) = q
           APPENDQ(r,ADDQ(q,i)) = ADDQ(APPENDQ(r,q),i)
           LIMIT(NEWQ(in)) = in
           LIMIT(ADDQ(q,i)) = LIMIT(q)
           ENQ(q,i) = if SIZE(q)<LIMIT(q)
                         then q ← ADDQ(q,i)
                         else q ← UNDEFINED[overflow]
           DEQ(q) = q ← DELETEQ(q) ; FRONTQ(q)
           SIZE(NEWQ(in)) = 0
           SIZE(ADDQ(q,i)) = 1+SIZE(q)
  end
end Bqueue
```

Figure 4.4.1

This technique of taking a specification of an unbounded data type and refining it into a bounded one can be applied in exactly the same way to yield specifications for bounded stacks, binary trees, strings, etc.

4.5. OTHER DIRECTIONS

In this chapter we have stressed the art of data type specification. Our major goal has been to explore a notation which is especially attractive for formally defining a data type without regard to its implementation. In this section we want to indicate briefly how these specifications can be used to design reliable software but to reserve a complete discussion for Guttag (1976b).

The first use of an axiomatic specification is as an aid in designing and implementing the type. A decision is made to choose a particular form of implementation. This implementation will be in terms of other data types, and we assume that their specifications already exist. For a complex data type this process may proceed through several levels before an executable implementation is achieved. The virtue of the specifications is that each stage is made clearer by organizing the types, values, and operations that can be used.

A second use of these specifications, and perhaps its most important, is for proving that an implementation is correct. Establishing correctness now becomes equivalent to showing that the original axioms are satisfied by the newly developed implementation. This process also lends itself quite readily to automation.

Another use of these specifications is for early testing. It would be very desirable if one could design a system in such a way that it could be tested before committing people to actually build it. Given suitable restrictions on the form that the axiomatic equations may take, a system in which implementations and algebraic specifications of data types are interchangeable can be constructed. In the absence of an implementation, the operations of the data type may be interpreted symbolically. Thus, except for a significant loss in efficiency, the lack of an implementation can be made completely transparent to the user. Interestingly, it is not necessary to spend many man-years developing this system; the capability is essentially available in LISP-based symbol manipulation systems such as SCRATCHPAD [Griesmer (1971)], REDUCE [Hearn (1971)], and MACSYMA [Martin (1971)]. The use of REDUCE for this purpose is discussed in Guttag (1976b), as are the essential ideas of a pattern-match compiler designed especially for compilation of algebraic axioms.

ACKNOWLEDGMENTS

This research was supported in part by the Defense Research Projects Agency under Contract No. DAHC15 72 C 0308 and by the National Science Foundation under Contract No. MCS76-06089. The views expressed are those of the authors.

This chapter is an expanded version of a paper given at the Second International Conference on Software Engineering, October 1976. A number of people made valuable comments on earlier drafts of this chapter, including Ed Lazowska, Ralph London, Mary Shaw, Tim Standish, Ron Tugender, Dave Wile, and the referees of the conference version. We are grateful to Betty Randall for her expertise and patience in typing many drafts of the chapter.

CHAPTER 5

AN INITIAL ALGEBRA APPROACH TO THE SPECIFICATION, CORRECTNESS, AND IMPLEMENTATION OF ABSTRACT DATA TYPES

J. A. GOGUEN
Computer Science Department
UCLA
Los Angeles, California

J. W. THATCHER
E. G. WAGNER
IBM Thomas J. Watson Research Center
Yorktown Heights, New York

Abstract

Abstract data types have been claimed a powerful tool in programming (as in SIMULA and CLU), both from the viewpoint of user convenience and that of software reliability. Recently algebra has emerged as a promising method for the specification of abstract data types; this makes it possible to prove the correctness of implementations of abstract types. It also raises the question of the correctness of the specifications and the proper method for handling run-time errors in abstract types. Unfortunately not all the algebra underlying these issues is entirely trivial, nor has it been adequately developed or explained. In this chapter we show how a reasonable notation for many-sorted algebras makes them just about as manageable as one-sorted (universal) algebras, and we present comparatively simple yet completely rigorous statements of the major algebraic issues underlying abstract data types. We present a number of specifications, with correctness proofs for some; the issue of error messages is thoroughly explained, and the issue of implementations is broached.

5.1. INTRODUCTION

Abstract data types have been claimed to be a powerful tool in programming (as in SIMULA and CLU), both from the viewpoint of user convenience and that of software reliability. As these points have been strongly presented in several places now [see, e.g., Liskov and Zilles (1974) or Guttag (1976)], we shall assume that the reader is already interested in knowing what abstract types are and how they are specified, proved correct, and implemented.

Recently algebra has emerged as a promising method for the specification of abstract types [e.g., see Zilles (1975), Guttag (1975), ADJ (1975a)], and in this chapter we shall continue in that direction. Algebraic specifications make it possible to treat the key issues in a concise and general manner, as we hope to convince you.

Perhaps the major technical feature of this chapter is its rigorous development of the algebraic fundamentals. We have tried to carefully motivate all major concepts and to rigorously prove all major results. A great deal of the mathematics is new, either in form or in content. In particular, we use throughout the notation of ADJ (1973) for many-sorted algebras, thus making them just about as manageable as the more usual one-sorted (universal) algebras. This is in contrast (we feel) with the more widely used notation associated with *heterogeneous algebras* [see Birkhoff and Lipson (1970) or Higgins (1963)].

In addition, we have tried to present a reasonably broad sampling of specifications of abstract types; we would have liked to have presented more of the many specifications that we have worked out, as well as correctness proofs for all of them, but there just wasn't enough time. We do hope that we have given a sufficient number of proofs so that the methods will be reasonably clear. Finally, we have tried to make clear what some of the major points are regarding errors and implementations, although many details lie outside the scope of the present chapter.

Among the features which distinguish our approach from other related ones are the following: (1) We treat everything in terms of standard universal algebra, and in particular, we show how to accomplish the effect of so-called *conditional equations* without having to build from scratch a new form of universal algebra using them. (2) We give a fairly thorough treatment of the very important issue of error messages. (3) We treat *parameterized* types, such as $\underline{\text{stack}(d)}$ for $\underline{d}$ any suitable type, in a uniform way. (4) We introduce some new results on how to prove correctness of specifications. (5) We clarify the notion of implementation for abstract types.

In the remainder of this introduction, we argue the following points: (1) that data types are algebras—the whole chapter depends on the reader accepting this idea; (2) that *abstract* refers, in the context of *abstract data types*, to "independence of representation" and that the notion of algebraic isomorphism captures this—moreover, the idea of *initial algebra* embodies it in a particularly elegant and convenient manner;

(3) that error messages are an essential aspect of abstract data types, presenting some subtle and important problems; and (4) that the notion of correctness is basic to the subject of abstract data types, both needing and deserving a careful treatment and new results. This introduction concludes with a discussion of related work.

5.1.1. Data Types Are Algebras

This is perhaps not so controversial a point as it might have been some years ago. Morris (1973) argues that "types are not sets," and several authors have already used algebraic models [ADJ (1975a), Zilles (1975), Guttag (1975)]. We shall here briefly recapitulate some of the main points, from the perspective of the chapter to follow.

To begin with, a data type, such as stack(int), stack of integers, may involve several different sorts[1] of thing, such as truth values (of sort bool), integers (of sort int), and stack states (of sort stack). All the things of sort s are lumped together into a set, called the carrier of sort s.

But this is certainly not enough to describe what is going on: We want to *use* stack(int) for something, so we want to be able to perform *operations*[2] on the various data representations involved. For example, we want to be able to POP the stack, to test if it is EMPTY, and to PUSH a new integer onto it. These operations are functions among the various carriers, and their arguments and values must be of the correct sorts. For example, POP: stack $\longrightarrow$ stack, means that POP is defined on stack states and yields stack states—similarly, PUSH: int stack $\longrightarrow$ stack and EMPTY: stack $\longrightarrow$ bool. The operations which are involved in a data type are its essence, even more than the data representations. (It is our purpose in the next subsection to clarify what is meant by "essence" in the previous sentence.)

Now, a collection A_s of carriers, one for each s in a set S of sorts, together with a collection Σ of functions among those carriers, is exactly a many-sorted algebra (more precisely, an S-sorted Σ-algebra), as defined in Section 5.2.

The observation that data types are algebras is only the starting point of this chapter. What is fascinating is that it supports precise and insightful discussions of the whole range of important issues surrounding data types, from abstraction to implementation.

5.1.2. Abstraction

There seems to have been some confusion about the meaning of the term *abstraction* in computer science. It has been used in at least three ways which are distinct but related. First, there is the meaning common to most of science: "abstraction" occurs whenever one creates a mathematical model or description of something. In particular, one speaks in computer science of an "abstract machine" as opposed to real hardware when referring to a mathematical model of a machine; similarly, one

[1]The names of sorts are generally underlined in this chapter, as a convenient notational convention.

[2]Throughout this chapter, operation names appear in capital letters.

speaks of an "abstract implementation" when one uses sets, sequences, or other mathematical entities to model some computational process or structure.

A second meaning, closely related to the first, refers to the process (or result) of generalizing, so that certain detailed features can be ignored. There are many examples in computer science, since one of the main advantages of mathematicization is to "abstract" some details out of view. In particular, finite state machine models of hardware, and fix-point models of software, permit us to ignore many details of how processes are actually carried out.

However, a somewhat different sense of "abstraction" has gradually come to play a more specific role, particularly in the theory of programming languages, for the several important cases where one wishes to consider a concept *independent of its representation.*

For example, "abstract syntax" considers syntactic structure independently of whether it is represented by derivation trees, parenthesized expressions, indented program text, canonical parses, or whatever. This notion of abstract syntax is useful, for example, in specifying the semantics of a programming language in a manner independent of how it is implemented [see ADJ (1975)].

More to the point, an abstract data type is supposed to be independent of its representation, in the sense that details of how it is implemented are to be actually hidden or "shielded" from the user: He is provided with certain operations, and he only needs to know what they are supposed to do, not how they do it. This permits modularization of programs to such an extent that implementations (and representations) can actually be changed underneath the user without his even knowing. This might, for example, be desirable if the statistical properties of a module's use indicate that a different implementation would be more efficient. Moreover, it can have the important effect of localizing a bug in the implementation to one place, so that extensive reprogramming is not required to fix it, for none of the places where the abstraction is used make any assumptions about how it is implemented.

Note that what is usually called an "abstract implementation," that is, an implementation described by sets, sequences, etc., is *not* an "abstraction" in the above sense; rather, it is a *particular*, but rather undetailed, implementation.

Perhaps the source of confusion here is the seemingly bewildering problem of how to describe something without being committed to some particular description. As you may have guessed, this is where "abstract" algebra comes to the rescue. For it is common, for instance, in group theory, to speak of an "abstract group" to mean an isomorphism class of groups, that is, an abstract group structure, independent of whether the elements are represented by matrices of one order or another, complex or real, etc.: The key idea here is that two algebras have the "same structure" iff they are *isomorphic.*

Thus, we want some way to specify an isomorphism class of algebras. One way is to give a representative, of the correctness of which we are already certain; however, this will not be applicable when the type is either very complicated or being defined for the first time.

The approach taken in this chapter involves several aspects. First, the concept of an "initial algebra," which has also played a similar role in our work on semantics [ADJ (1975)], has the key property of being defined uniquely up to isomorphism; it has, therefore, the notion of abstraction built into it. (The idea is essentially the same as that of "free" algebra used by other authors, but the "initiality" formulation emphasizes an aspect of the mathematical definition which we find particularly helpful in our theoretical development.)

This leaves the problem of how to specify the initial algebra we want. We define a *specification* to be a triple $\langle S, \Sigma, \mathcal{E} \rangle$, where S is the set of sorts, Σ is the set of operators of the type, and $\mathcal{E}$ is a set of equations which the algebra is to satisfy. The initial $(\Sigma, \mathcal{E})$-algebra is then the "best" Σ-algebra satisfying $\mathcal{E}$; i.e., it satisfies *only* what $\mathcal{E}$ requires and no more. (Note the uses of "the" in the previous sentence—"the initial algebra" and "the 'best' Σ-algebra"—which suggest that we are considering isomorphic algebras to be already "the same"; that is, we are talking about the abstraction, not any representation.)

The reader might well find it amazing that seemingly all data types can in fact be described in this way; however, among the many examples we have tried, it has always worked. Some subtle points have had to be overcome, however. One of these is discussed in the next subsection.

5.1.3. Errors

A data type may well have inherent in its structure certain cases where it "isn't meaningful" to perform certain operations. For example, it isn't meaningful to ask what is the TOP of the empty stack of integers. If we inadvertantly or otherwise[3] ask that the operation be performed anyway, we ought to get an *error message* saying what went wrong. This is *not* the same as saying that the operation is undefined, as might occur for a nonterminating computation; it is a specific constant in the algebra.

We contend that it is very much the responsibility of the specifier of a data type to say what error messages he wants, exactly when they shall occur, and how they shall subsequently be handled; it is then up to the implementer to do it just like that. If the specifier leaves some cases unspecified, and the implementer just does whatever seems easy, possibly different things on different machines, etc., the user may be in bad trouble, since she won't know what did happen or what might happen next. In any case, she should be provided with whatever debugging aids are feasible, including good error messages as part of abstract data types.

However, things may be even worse for the theoretician than the user, since attempts to ignore error messages, e.g., in $\underline{\text{stack}}(\underline{\text{int}})$, can lead to specifications which just don't do what we want them to. For example, they may add all kinds of odd things alleged to be integers (such as ERROR + 1) or force us to conclude that TRUE

[3] In some cases, we might want to consider such cases as "exceptions" rather than "errors" and might want certain particular additional consequences to follow; however, this change in viewpoint requires no change in the mathematics which we give.

must equal FALSE in our implementation of bool. Several instances of such phenomena are discussed in Section 5.3.

We believe that the proper treatment of errors (or exceptions) is essential to the proper treatment of abstract data types, and we make a start on the problems involved. We contend that the issue is considerably more difficult and complex than has been generally recognized, and we attempt to support this contention with examples of the subtle things that can happen.

5.1.4. Correctness

The whole idea of specifications is to be able to use them to check the correctness of implementations. If they are going to be used as standards in this way, one's first concern must be to be sure that they are themselves correct. It is often possible to check the specifications against some generally accepted mathematical model. We shall develop some new techniques for this and illustrate them on some of our specifications.

It should be emphasized that rigor is essential to this enterprise. If the specification is not absolutely definite and explicit, it cannot be useful as a standard. Similarly, to the extent that the method of proving correctness is informal, there is room for doubt that the specification really is correct. We have found, as have many others, that surprisingly subtle difficulties arise, which the intuition can easily gloss over, thus leading to correctness proofs for incorrect specifications! A rigorous mathematical methodology is a tremendous aid in catching these problems.

We hope that the reader takes this seriously enough to feel that it justifies all the mathematics which is to be found in this chapter. It appears that without exact definitions, precise theorems, and methodical proofs, there may not be much point in giving specifications for abstract data types at all.

An automated, or semiautomated, system for checking specifications and implementations certainly would be of help here. But, of course, the mathematics underlying it would have to be thoroughly understood before we could rely on its results. The present chapter can be viewed as providing some steps toward the foundations for such a system.

5.1.5. Discussion

We wish to briefly compare some aspects of our approach with that of others. Both Guttag (1975, 1976) and Zilles (1975, 1975a) use a framework of many-sorted algebras, though we found Guttag to be hampered by his reliance on the notation of Birkhoff and Lipson (1970). Both also seem to use initial (or free) algebras and equations. Zilles (1975a) uses a limited form of conditional equation, whereas Guttag (1976) seems to permit unrestricted conditional expressions on right-hand sides (this work is highly informal, so that it is hard to be sure).

Standish (1970), on the other hand, just gives "ground axioms" for Vienna Definition-like "composite objects" and then imposes "higher-order" axioms for "higher-order data structures." One problem with this approach is that there are *not* unique (up to isomorphism) models for the axioms; it is also somewhat unclear what classes of axioms are permitted. But there is justification, with respect to the problem of synthesizing representations, for starting from a standard model of the ground axioms. Clearly the general approach there is quite different from that in this chapter, yet there must be many underlying similarities; in particular, algebraic structures do seem to be implicit.

It seems to us that there may well be advantages to an approach based on a sufficiently broad notion of conditional equation, however, and we hope to explore this in some future work.

The subtle points regarding error messages do not seem to have been previously discussed in the literature, and (making suitable allowances for informality of approach) it appears to us that other authors have often given erroneous specifications of data types involving error messages.

Some points concerning correctness proofs and implementations also seem to be new in this chapter. We regard it as particularly important to be clear about what the specification language is and what method is being used to prove correctness, since otherwise the whole enterprise is in doubt. Exactly how to manipulate terms to prove correctness seems to be a quite complicated issue. However, we have been able to isolate one general and powerful method involving what we call canonical term algebras. Our precise notion of implementation also seems to be new; we do regret not being able to give further applications for it here.

We think it is reasonably convincing that an exciting new area is opening up, involving both interesting mathematical problems and important practical applications. We believe that algebra will continue to play a vital roll as the subject of abstract data types continues to develop.

5.2. ALGEBRAS

The basic language and model for data types in this chapter are algebraic. In this section we shall introduce the necessary machinery, along with a number of relevant examples. Certain technical definitions and nearly all proofs are banished to the appendix (Section 5.6), where they are treated with unflinching detail.

A (many-sorted) *algebra* A is essentially a family of sets A_s (called the *carriers* of the algebra) with a collection of *operations* (that is, functions) among them. Such algebras seem to arise very naturally in computer science. The index set S for the carriers is called the *sort* set and might be, for example $\{\underline{\text{real}}, \underline{\text{bool}}, \underline{\text{int}}\}$. An S-sorted algebra A for this sort S would have three carriers, $A_{\underline{\text{real}}}$, $A_{\underline{\text{bool}}}$, and $A_{\underline{\text{int}}}$, and might have among its operations EXP: $A_{\underline{\text{real}}} \times A_{\underline{\text{int}}} \to A_{\underline{\text{real}}}$ and COND: $A_{\underline{\text{bool}}} \times A_{\underline{\text{real}}} \times A_{\underline{\text{real}}} \to A_{\underline{\text{real}}}$, for exponentiation and conditional (if-then-else), respectively.

In this chapter we shall use a graphical notation to conveniently indicate sorts and operations; it is much clearer than the direct set-theoretic specifications of sources and targets of operations which is the actual mathematical definition in our development. For example, the above COND and EXP are captured by the graphical notation of Figure 5.2.1. The convention is as follows: The ovals indicate sorts (or, more suggestively, the carriers corresponding to the sorts), and the many-tailed arrows indicate operations. The head of the arrow indicates the sort of the value returned by the operation, and the tails of the arrows indicate the sorts of the arguments or inputs to the operation. Where possible, we draw the diagrams so that the left-to-right ordering (facing as the arrow points) of the tails is the same as the ordering of the arguments of the operation (see Figure 5.2.1). This is not always convenient, and in such cases

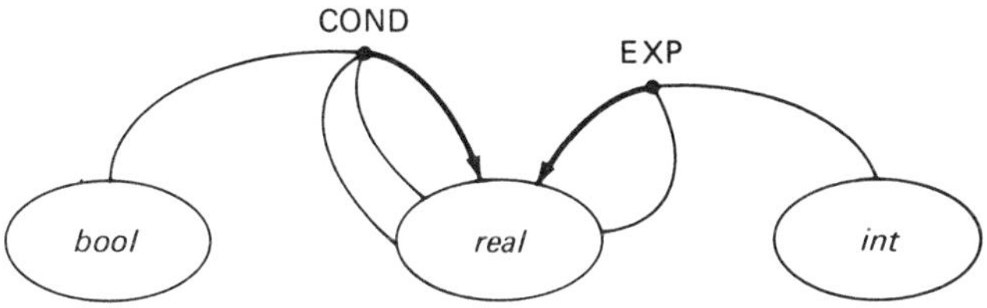

Figure 5.2.1

either the context of the figure or the numbering on the tails of the arrow will determine the order of the operands. The dot, where the tails meet the head, is labeled with the name of the operation. Note that sort names are underlined and that operation names are generally capitalized.

Automata provide us with a familiar class of algebras. Here $S = \{\underline{\text{input}}, \underline{\text{state}}\}$, and the operations are as indicated by Figure 5.2.2. Thus, M is the transition function and q_0 is the initial state of a (Moore) automaton.

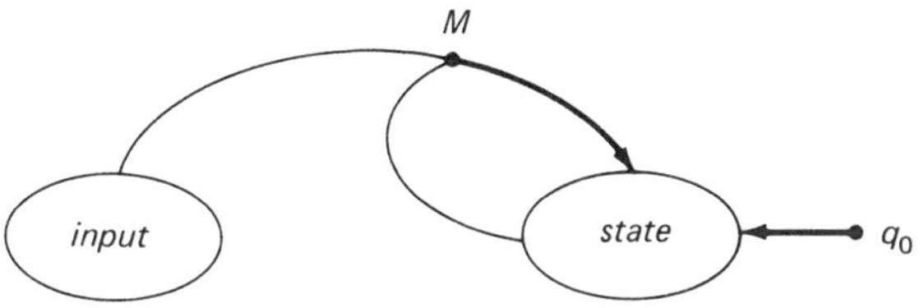

Figure 5.2.2

Following ADJ (1973), given the set S of *sorts*, we have

> **Definition 1.** An S-sorted *signature*[4] or *operator domain* Σ is a family $\Sigma_{w,s}$ of sets, for $s \in S$ and $w \in S^*$ (where S^* is the set of all finite strings from S, including the empty string λ). Call $F \in \Sigma_{w,s}$ an *operation symbol* of *rank* w, s, of *arity* w, and of *sort* s.

Thus diagrams like those above describe many-sorted signatures: An operation symbol $F \in \Sigma_{w,s}$ for $w = s_1 \ldots s_n$ corresponds to a *polyadic edge*[5] (see Figure 5.2.3)

[4]This is meant in the same sense as signature in "key signature" in music.

[5]*Polyadic graphs*, consisting of a set S of *nodes*, a set E of (polyadic) *edges*, and *source* and *target functions* mapping E to S^* and S, respectively, occur in various disguises in (for example) Burstall (1972), Landin (1970), and Rutledge (1973).

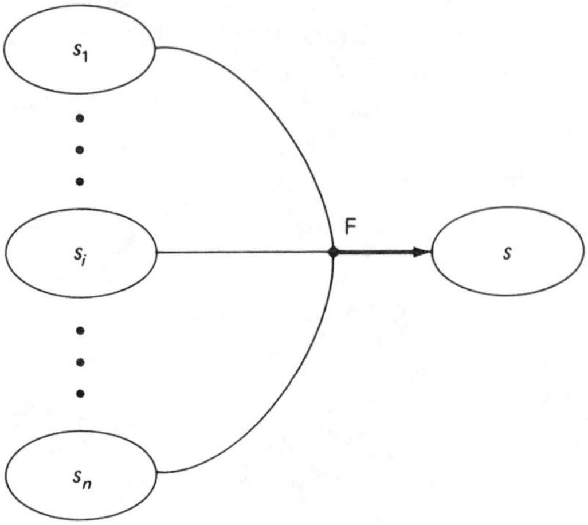

Figure 5.2.3

with *source* (or origin) $s_1 \ldots s_n$ and *target* (or terminus) s. If S is finite, if there are only a finite number of nonempty $\Sigma_{w,s}$, and if each of these is finite, the graphical notation is applicable. For automata (Figure 5.2.2), $\Sigma_{\underline{\text{input}}\ \underline{\text{state}},\ \underline{\text{state}}} = \{M\}, \Sigma_{\lambda,\underline{\text{state}}} = \{q_0\}$, and $\Sigma_{w,s} = \varnothing$ otherwise. From Figure 5.2.1, $\Sigma_{\underline{\text{bool}}\ \underline{\text{real}}\ \underline{\text{real}},\ \underline{\text{real}}} = \{\text{COND}\}$, $\Sigma_{\underline{\text{real}}\ \underline{\text{int}},\ \underline{\text{int}}} = \{\text{EXP}\}$, and $\Sigma_{w,s} = \varnothing$ otherwise.

We shall now give a precise definition of a many-sorted algebra.

Definition 2. Let Σ be an S-sorted signature. Then a Σ-*algebra* A consists of a set A_s for each $s \in S$ (called the *carrier of* A *of sort* s) and a function

$$\sigma_A \colon A_{s_1} \times A_{s_2} \times \cdots \times A_{s_n} \longrightarrow A_s$$

for each $\sigma \in \Sigma_{w,s}$ with $w = s_1 s_2 \ldots s_n$ (called the *operation of* A *named by* σ). For $\sigma \in \Sigma_{\lambda,s}$ we have $\sigma_A \in A_s$ (also written $\sigma_A \colon \longrightarrow A_s$); that is, $\Sigma_{\lambda,s}$ is the set of (names of) constants of A of sort s.

If S has just one element (say $S = \{s\}$), then in any Σ-algebra A, all operations σ_A are defined on A_s^n for some $n \geq 0$, the *rank* of σ, taking values in the single carrier, A_s. In this case it is easier to describe Σ as a *graded set* or *ranked alphabet*, that is, a family Σ_n of sets (for $n \geq 0$) of operator symbols. (Σ_n here corresponds to $\Sigma_{s^n,s}$ in the other notation, and $\sigma \in \Sigma_n$ has *rank* or *arity* n.)

Perhaps surprisingly, it is only a little more difficult to handle many-sorted algebras than one-sorted algebras if we use conventions and notations carefully. For example, $a \in A$ will mean (i.e., is short for) $a \in A_s$ for some $s \in S$. The main idea is that the carriers of S-sorted algebras are just S-indexed families of sets, that is, $A = \langle A_s \rangle_{s \in S}$, so that notation, terminology, and even results familiar for ordinary sets, extended naturally to S-indexed families, apply to S-sorted algebras. For example, we write $A \subseteq B$ to mean that $A_s \subseteq B_s$ for all $s \in S$; $f \colon A \longrightarrow B$ means a family of functions $\langle f_s\colon A_s \longrightarrow B_s\rangle_{s\in S}$, etc. In the same way, when A and B are Σ-algebras, $A \subseteq B$ (A is a *subalgebra* of B) means that $A \subseteq B$ (for their carriers) and that each operation, named by $\sigma \in \Sigma_{s_1\ldots s_n, s}$, in A is exactly that in B, restricted to the carrier of A; i.e., for all $a_i \in A_{s_i}$, for $i = 1, \ldots, n$,

$$\sigma_A(a_1, \ldots, a_n) = \sigma_B(a_1, \ldots, a_n).$$

The following is another illustration of this principle.

Definition 3. If A and B are both Σ-algebras, a Σ-*homomorphism* $h\colon A \longrightarrow B$ is a family of functions $\langle h_s\colon A_s \longrightarrow B_s\rangle_{s\in S}$ that preserve the operations, i.e., that satisfy

(h0) If $\sigma \in \Sigma_{\lambda, s}$, then $h_s(\sigma_A) = \sigma_B$;

(h1) If $\sigma \in \Sigma_{s_1\ldots s_n, s}$ and $\langle a_1, \ldots, a_n\rangle \in A_{s_1} \times \cdots \times A_{s_n}$, then $h_s[\sigma_A(a_1, \ldots, a_n)] = \sigma_B[h_{s_1}(a_1), \ldots, h_{s_n}(a_n)]$.

A *category* **C** of Σ-*algebras* consists of a class $|\mathbf{C}|$ of Σ-algebras which are called the *objects* of **C** together with *all* Σ-homomorphisms between the algebras. The homomorphisms are often called *morphisms* of **C**.

The composite of homomorphisms is again a homomorphism; composition of homomorphisms is an associative operation; and for each algebra A in **C**, the identity function 1_A on the carrier of A is a Σ-homomorphism which is the identity for composition; i.e., given $h\colon A \longrightarrow B$, $h1_A = 1_B h = h$. A homomorphism $h\colon A \longrightarrow A'$ is an *isomorphism* iff there exists $g\colon A' \longrightarrow A$ such that $gh = 1_A$ and $hg = 1_{A'}$; g is called the *inverse* of h.

The following is the key concept of this chapter.

Definition 4. An algebra A is *initial* in a category **C** of Σ-algebras iff for every algebra B in **C** there exists a *unique* homomorphism $h\colon A \longrightarrow B$.

The tremendous usefulness of this concept is embodied in the following result.

Proposition 1

If algebras A and A' are both initial in a category **C** of Σ-algebras, then A and A' are isomorphic. If an algebra A'' in **C** is isomorphic to an algebra A which is initial in **C**, then A'' is also initial.

It is standard practice in abstract algebra to "identify" isomorphic objects, that is, to treat them as identical. Thus, one speaks of "*the* real n-dimensional vector space," "*the* free group on n generators," and so on. Similarly, in the light of Proposition 1, we may speak of "*the* initial algebra" in a category **C** of Σ-algebras (the above two examples from abstract algebra are actually special cases of this): for any two initial objects are isomorphic, and, in fact, there is a unique isomorphism from one to the other. The wonderful thing about initiality is that it characterizes uniquely up to isomorphism; that is, it characterizes the isomorphism class of an object; in view of the discussion in the introduction, this means it characterizes an object "abstractly," that is, independent of representation or only in terms of its structure. This is, of course, just what is wanted for abstract data types, and so we offer the following:

> **Definition 5.** An *abstract data type* is the isomorphism class of an initial algebra in a category[6] **C** of Σ-algebras.

Thus, we can speak of *an* initial algebra A in **C** as *being the* abstract data type. The point is that initiality provides an *abstract* characterization, up to isomorphism.

The remainder of this chapter will amply demonstrate that what we generally think of as data types fit nicely into the framework of Definition 5. However, this definition can be both broadened and narrowed in interesting ways, and, in fact, it represents an artful compromise among various alternatives explored in this chapter and in the literature and as yet unexplored in print.

Clearly we are not really interested in *all* the categories **C** of Σ-algebras: Because we are only interested in abstract data types which are (finitely) describable, we are only interested in categories **C** which are (finitely) describable, but most[7] categories of Σ-algebras will be "indescribable." In this chapter we shall be particularly concerned with categories **C** having as objects all Σ-algebras satisfying some set $\mathcal{E}$ of equations.[8] This is brought out explicitly in later definitions. However, we do not wish to exclude other possibilities. For example, Zilles (1974, 1975) has considered "conditional equations," and more generally still, one might want to consider categories **C** of algebras satisfying some set of *Horn sentences* [see Cohn (1965)]. The subject of abstract data type specification is still in its infancy, and we just do not yet know what all the possibilities are or what their uses might be. It is therefore unwise to limit the scope of inquiry in the basic definition. However, we do show in this chapter that a surprising amount can be done within the classical framework of purely equational specification.

Turning now to senses in which Definition 5 may be too restrictive, there are good reasons to consider "categories" **C** in a more general sense, whose objects are not just Σ-algebras; for example, to capture Scott's (1972) "data types as lattices," we have considered (in as yet unpublished collaboration with J. B. Wright) initial objects in certain specialized categories of "solutions." We expect that there will be a number of uses for categories of "order-enriched algebras." In particular, this seems to be the proper domain for considering *abstract control structures*.

One further point about Definition 5. Both Guttag (1975) and Zilles (1974, 1975) single out one type; Guttag calls it the "type of interest." We have not done so, for

[6]Recall from Definition 3 that a category of Σ-algebras, in this chapter, includes *all* the Σ-homomorphisms between its objects. (In more technical language we are considering only *full* subcategories of the category of all Σ-algebras.)

[7]We do not think it is worthwhile to be completely formal about this point, since it is used only by way of discussion. The idea is that there can be only a countable number of "descriptions" in any given formal language, whereas there are far more than an uncountable number of choices for **C** (in fact, there are so many that a cardinality can't even be assigned.)

[8]The class of all Σ-algebras satisfying some set of equations is classically called a *variety* and as such has been considered by Tarski, Birkhoff, and many others in "universal" algebra.

two reasons. First, there is often not a single type of interest but two or more which must be considered together, in the sense that each should have access to the others' data representation in the implementation. This is easy to handle by distinguishing ing a nonsingleton subset of the sort set S. However, this is an inadequate representation of the relationships which actually exist among the sorts in a data type. As we shall see in Section 5.3, some may enter as parameters for which any suitable data type can be substituted [as $\underline{d}$ in $\underline{\text{stack}}(\underline{d})$], others enter as auxiliary or "helper" types (often $\underline{\text{bool}}$ or $\underline{\text{nat}}$ play this role), while others are being defined. Things can get even more involved, as in $\underline{\text{stack}}(\underline{\text{list}}(\underline{d}))$.

In this chapter, as indicated, we are primarily concerned with abstract data types which are specified by equations, also called *laws* or *identities*. This section is intended to present the mathematics needed to do that. There are two main theorems, each of which asserts the existence of initial Σ-algebras in certain categories of Σ-algebras. The first theorem asserts that there is an initial Σ-algebra in the category $\mathbf{Alg}_\Sigma$ of *all* Σ-algebras, while the second covers the category $\mathbf{Alg}_{\Sigma,\mathcal{E}}$ of all Σ-algebras satisfying some set $\mathcal{E}$ of equations. (The first is then a special case with $\mathcal{E} = \varnothing$.) We shall now give several illustrations of abstract data types which are initial in a category $\mathbf{Alg}_\Sigma$ of all Σ-algebras. These seem to correspond to particularly fundamental structures of the kind generally taken as basic in programming languages and in mathematics.

Example 1

A most venerable data type, natural number, here denoted $\underline{\text{nat}}$, has been characterized by Lawvere [see pp. 67–70 of MacLane and Birkhoff (1967) for more details] as the initial Σ-algebra in the category of *all* Σ-algebras with Σ as indicated by Figure 5.2.4 (i.e., $S = \{\underline{\text{nat}}\}$, $\Sigma_{\lambda,\underline{\text{nat}}} = \{0\}$, $\Sigma_{\underline{\text{nat}},\underline{\text{nat}}} = \{\text{SUCC}\}$, and $\Sigma_{w,s} = \varnothing$ otherwise; this is a one-sorted type, though expressed in the many-sorted notation).

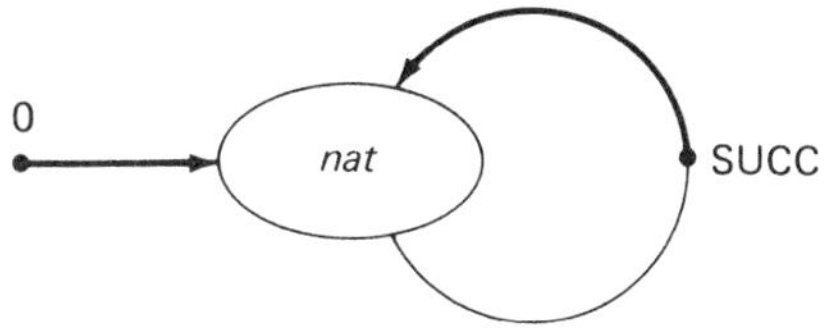

Figure 5.2.4

The basic idea is that every natural number and all further operations of interest upon natural numbers can be expressed in terms of just the two basic ones, SUCC and 0: Thus, n is expressed as n applications of SUCC to 0; recursive formulations of addition and so on will be given in later examples. Initiality provides the key to unique characterization. In many ways, this is a more satisfactory axiomatic formulation of the notion of natural number than the usual second-order predicate calculus formulation (Peano's axioms): Our language (first-order universally quantified equations, to put it in the terminology of logic) is simpler, and so are most proofs. A property which the algebraic approach shares with all abstract or axiomatic characterizations is independence of representation. That is, we are not committed to thinking of integers as strings of decimal, or binary, or Roman characters. This is, of course, crucial to being able to prove correctness of data representations. We can, therefore, and perhaps should, go so far as to *define* a *natural number* to be an element of the carrier of an initial Σ-algebra, for the above Σ.

Example 2

In the same manner, if Σ is any ranked alphabet, *define* a Σ*-tree* to be an element of the carrier of an initial Σ-algebra in the category of all Σ-algebras. In this way we are not tied to any particular representation of trees (Polish notation, infix terms, prefix parenthesized terms, functions defined on tree domains, or certain directed ordered labeled graphs). This data type is basic to the developments of this chapter and is therefore discussed in a number of places below. In particular, we shall show in succeeding examples how some other well-known data types are special cases of this one, and we shall also give in detail a particular mathematical representation of Σ-trees, the Σ-terms, that is, a particular algebra which is initial in $\mathbf{Alg}_\Sigma$.

Before continuing, note the immediate generalization to many-sorted Σ-trees obtained by permitting arbitrary many-sorted signatures. The intuitive idea here is that Σ-trees and all operations of interest upon them are characterized just by Σ and initiality: To know a Σ-tree, one need only know the operations occurring in it and how they are combined, and as with natural numbers, further operations are obtained by recursive definitions, expressed algebraically with equations, and based on initiality.

Example 3

A simple special case of the above is *string* from an alphabet A (any set). Here (in one-sorted notation) $\Sigma_0 = \{\Lambda\}$, $\Sigma_1 = A$, and $\Sigma_n = \varnothing$ for $n \geq 2$. Thus the Σ-tree for the string $a_1a_2a_3$ looks (as a Σ-term, see below) like $a_3(a_2(a_1(\Lambda)))$.

Example 4

An even simpler special case is that of the Boolean truth values, with the sort set $S = \{\underline{\text{bool}}\}$ to be explicit. Then $\Sigma_{\lambda,\underline{\text{bool}}} = \{T, F\}$, and $\Sigma_{w,s} = \varnothing$ otherwise. Note that $A_{\underline{\text{bool}}} = \{T, F\}$, with the constants T and F "named by themselves," is in fact a Σ-algebra; indeed it is initial.

One thing we obviously need is a general existence theorem for initial algebras; we want to know that these objects exist and something about what they look like. We shall now give an S-sorted *word algebra* (or *Herbrand universe*) construction for an initial Σ-algebra T_Σ by mutual recursion among sets $T_{\Sigma,s}$ of Σ-terms (also called well-formed expressions, or formulas, or sometimes even trees) as sorts as follows.

Let Σ (ambiguously) denote the set of all operator symbols in the S-sorted signature Σ, i.e., $\bigcup_{w \in S^*, s \in S} \Sigma_{w,s}$. Now let $\langle T_{\Sigma,s} \rangle_{s \in S}$ be the smallest family of sets of strings contained in $(\Sigma \cup \{\underline{(},\underline{)}\})^*$ satisfying the following two conditions (here $\{\underline{(},\underline{)}\}$ is a two-element set disjoint from Σ, but be warned that later we shall omit the underlines):

(T0) $\Sigma_{\lambda,s} \subseteq T_{\Sigma,s}$;

(T1) If $\sigma \in \Sigma_{w,s}$, $w = s_1 \ldots s_n$ and $t_i \in T_{\Sigma,s_i}$, then $\sigma\underline{(}t_1 \ldots t_n\underline{)} \in T_{\Sigma,s}$.

Then make the family $\langle T_{\Sigma,s} \rangle$ into a Σ-algebra by defining the operations (we use σ_T instead of the typographically burdensome σ_{T_Σ} for the operation in T_Σ named by σ)

(0) For $\sigma \in \Sigma_{\lambda,s}$, $\sigma_T = \sigma \in T_{\Sigma,s}$;

(1) For $\sigma \in \Sigma_{w,s}$, $w = s_1 \ldots s_n$ and $t_i \in T_{\Sigma,s_i}$, $\sigma_T(t_1, \ldots, t_n) = \sigma\underline{(}t_1 \ldots t_n\underline{)} \in T_{\Sigma,s}$.

The essential result [which is proved in the appendix (Section 5.6)] is as follows:

Theorem 2

T_Σ is an initial algebra in the category $\mathbf{Alg}_\Sigma$ of *all* Σ-algebras.

The theorem is very well known; its one-sorted version dates back to Birkhoff (1938), and with some formulational (and significant notational) differences, the many-sorted version is in Higgins (1963), Benabou (1966), and Birkhoff and Lipson (1970).

Of course, it is important for us because we need to know that initial Σ-algebras exist in order for our principal definition to be of any use at all. But not only do we know that they exist, we know what they look like; any Σ-algebra which is initial in $\mathbf{Alg}_\Sigma$ is (uniquely) isomorphic to the algebra of Σ-terms described above (Proposition 1, again). Furthermore, the carriers of initial Σ-algebras, in categories of algebras satisfying certain identities, will consist of equivalence classes of Σ-terms (i.e., they will be *quotients* of T_Σ), and familiar methods of algebra (substitution of equals for equals, replacement, reduction, and the like) are crucial for our proofs of correctness of data type specifications and for our ideas about automatic implementation of data types from their specifications.

For the data type nat (natural number; see Example 1), T_Σ is isomorphic to the set $\omega = \{0, 1, 2, \ldots\}$ of nonnegative integers by the correspondence of n with $\mathrm{SUCC}^n\underline{(}0\underline{)}$, where $\mathrm{SUCC}^n\underline{(}0\underline{)}$ abbreviates the Σ-term

$$\underbrace{\mathrm{SUCC}\underline{(}\mathrm{SUCC}\underline{(}\ \ldots\ \mathrm{SUCC}\underline{(}0\underline{)}}_{n}\ \ldots\ \underline{)}\underline{)}.$$

For Example 2, we take the correspondence between Σ-terms and Σ-trees as being well known. For Example 3, the string $a_1 a_2 \ldots a_n$ corresponds to the term $a_n\underline{(}\ \ldots\ a_2\underline{(}a_1\underline{(}\Lambda\underline{)}\underline{)}\ \ldots\ \underline{)}$.

The initial algebra in the category $\mathbf{Alg}_\Sigma$ of all Σ-algebras is sometimes called the *anarchic* Σ-algebra, since it obeys no laws at all. It provides only a beginning point, since, as we have said, we want to consider initial (and free) algebras in categories of algebras which are constrained to satisfy certain "laws" or "axioms" or "equations."

For example, we might require a binary (one-sorted) operation TIMES (in Σ_2) to be associative, i.e., to "satisfy"

$$\mathrm{TIMES}\underline{(}x_1\underline{(}\mathrm{TIMES}\underline{(}x_2x_3\underline{)}\underline{)} = \mathrm{TIMES}\underline{(}\mathrm{TIMES}\underline{(}x_1x_2\underline{)}x_3\underline{)}.$$

For a computer-science-oriented example, we might have $S = \{\underline{\text{data}}, \underline{\text{stack}}, \underline{\text{bool}}\}$ for sorts, with Σ as shown in Figure 5.2.5 (this example is treated in detail as Example 18 in Section 5.3). A typical equation which we shall want to see satisfied is

$$\mathrm{TOP}\underline{(}\mathrm{PUSH}\underline{(}\mathrm{D}\ S\underline{)}\underline{)} = D.$$

To make precise the ideas of "equation" and "satisfaction" requires a somewhat elaborate preparation, upon which we shall now embark.

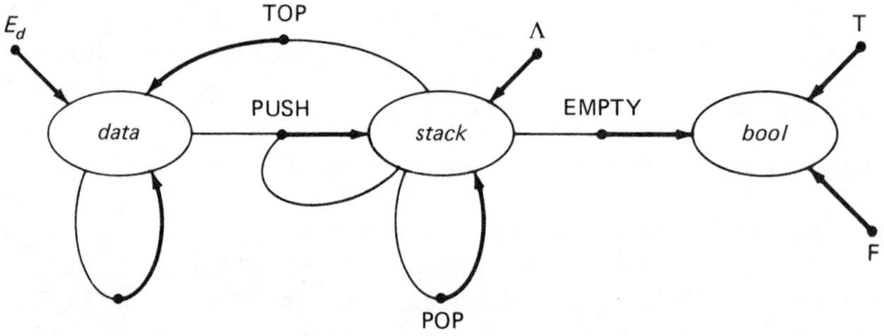

Figure 5.2.5

First, to make Σ-terms more conveniently usable, we shall from now on feel free to drop the underlines on parentheses and to add commas between arguments. Thus, the left-hand side of the above equation would be written

$$\mathrm{TOP}(\mathrm{PUSH}(D, S)).$$

This is to be regarded as mere notational convenience.

Next, the status of *variables* (D and S above) has to be clarified. The basic idea is that for each possible sort there should be an inexhaustible supply of special symbols disjoint from any signature. For mathematical purposes it is convenient to fix these symbols once and for all and to agree that they shall not be used in signatures. Thus, given S and $s \in S$, let $X_s = \{x_{s,n} \mid n \in \omega\}$ be a set of symbols disjoint from $X_{s'}$ for $s' \neq s$ and from the S-sorted signature Σ. We shall call elements of X_s *variables of sort* s. However, for practical notational purposes, we shall use capital letters which suggest the sorts, adding subscripts, primes, etc., as needed. Thus, D, D_1, D', D'', etc., can be thought of as notation for elements of $X_{\underline{\text{data}}}$.

Now what we need is a way of getting these symbols in X_s into Σ-terms, so that they can function as "variables": This can be accomplished by simply treating them as constants of sort s in an enlarged signature $\Sigma(X)$; then $\Sigma(X)$-terms look precisely as desired. Proceeding formally now, for any S-indexed family $Y = \langle Y_s \rangle_{s \in S}$, with

$Y_s \subseteq X_s$, let us define $\Sigma(Y)$ to be the S-sorted signature with $\Sigma(Y)_{\lambda,s} = \Sigma_{\lambda,s} \cup Y_s$ for $s \in S$ and with $\Sigma(Y)_{w,s} = \Sigma_{w,s}$ for $w \neq \lambda$. (We shall need families Y other than X later.)

Using the notational conventions developed above, a typical element of $T_{\Sigma(X),\underline{\text{stack}}}$ (for Σ as in Figure 5.2.5) is

$$\text{POP(PUSH(FN}(D)\text{), PUSH}(D', S)\text{))},$$

which might appear in its unretouched form as

$$\underline{\text{POP}}\underline{(}\underline{\text{PUSH}}\underline{(}\underline{\text{FN}}\underline{(}x_{\underline{\text{data}},0}\underline{)}\underline{\text{PUSH}}\underline{(}x_{\underline{\text{data}},1}x_{\underline{\text{stack}},0}\underline{)}\underline{)}\underline{)}.$$

In $\Sigma(X)$, the elements of X have been added as zero-ary terms, or to put it perhaps confusingly but prophetically, as names for constants. It is how we use them that makes them variables.

Now there are two problems with $T_{\Sigma(X)}$. One is that it has more variable symbols than we shall need for most purposes. This is easily solved by choosing a smaller collection of variables. Thus, if $Y \subseteq X$ (this means, as usual, $Y_s \subseteq X_s$ for all $s \in S$), we can form $T_{\Sigma(Y)}$. If $t \in T_{\Sigma(X)}$, let var(t) be the (S-indexed) family of variable symbols which occur in t (because t is just a string, "x occurs in t" has the usual meaning, $t = uxv$, for u and v strings); then for $Y =$ var(t), we have $t \in T_{\Sigma(Y)}$.

The second problem is that we really want to think of $T_{\Sigma(Y)}$ as a Σ-algebra, whereas it has $\Sigma(Y)$ as signature. However, this merely involves "forgetting" that the variables' names are in the signature; that is, we can regard the carriers of $T_{\Sigma(Y)}$ with operations in Σ as a Σ-algebra; being so regarded, let it be denoted $T_\Sigma(Y)$. Removing the variables from the signature is the first step toward letting them "vary."

For any S-sorted Σ-algebra A and S-indexed family $Y \subseteq X$, call $\theta: Y \longrightarrow A$ (that is, $\langle \theta_s: Y_s \longrightarrow A_s \rangle$) an *interpretation* or *assignment* of values of sort s in A to variables of sort s in Y. The idea is that any such assignment θ uniquely determines a value $\bar{\theta}(t)$ in A_s for each $t \in T_\Sigma(Y)_s$; it is the familiar process of *evaluating* an expression, given values for the variables. We make this precise with the following result that $T_\Sigma(Y)$ is the Σ-algebra *freely generated by* Y.

Proposition 3

Let A be a Σ-algebra and $\theta: Y \longrightarrow A$ an assignment. Then there exists a unique Σ-homomorphism $\bar{\theta}: T_\Sigma(Y) \longrightarrow A$ that extends θ in the sense that $\bar{\theta}_s(x) = \theta_s(x)$ for all $s \in S$ and $x \in Y_s$.

It should be particularly emphasized that despite all the notation, what we are talking about is intuitively very familiar. Here $t \in T_\Sigma(Y)$ is an expression involving variables in Y, and θ is an assignment of values in an algebra A to these variables (the fact that A is a Σ-algebra means that the symbols from Σ in t already have meanings in A); then $\bar{\theta}(t)$ *evaluates* t to get a unique value in A. Thus $\bar{\theta}$ is the process of evaluating terms with the values of the variables given by θ.

A particularly interesting case of evaluation arises when the target of the assignment is the free Σ-algebra $T_\Sigma(Z)$ for some possibly different family of variables $Z \subseteq X$.

Then $\theta\colon Y \longrightarrow T_\Sigma(Z)$ is called a *substitution*, and evaluation $\bar{\theta}(t)$ is the operation of substituting $\theta(x)$ for each occurrence of the variable x in the term t.

Definition 6. A Σ-*equation* is a pair $e = \langle L, R\rangle$, where $L, R \in T_\Sigma(X)_s$ for some s. Let $\text{var}(e) = \text{var}(L) \cup \text{var}(R)$ (union as S-indexed families). A Σ-algebra A *satisfies* e iff $\bar{\theta}(L) = \bar{\theta}(R)$ for *all* assignments $\theta\colon Y \longrightarrow A$, where $Y = \text{var}(e)$. If $\mathcal{E}$ is a set of Σ-equations, then A *satisfies* $\mathcal{E}$ iff A satisfies every $e \in \mathcal{E}$. Such a set of equations is called a Σ-*presentation*, an algebra satisfying $\mathcal{E}$ is called a $(\Sigma, \mathcal{E})$-algebra, and the category of $(\Sigma, \mathcal{E})$-algebras (with all Σ-homomorphisms between them) is denoted $\mathbf{Alg}_{\Sigma,\mathcal{E}}$.

It is convenient to write an equation $\langle L, R\rangle$ in the usual notation, $L = R$, rather than as an ordered pair. This notation is conventional and suggestive since in an algebra A satisfying $\langle L, R\rangle$, L indeed does equal R for any choice of values in A of the variables in $\langle L, R\rangle$. For some purposes, it is convenient to regard $\mathcal{E}$ as an S-indexed family, rather than just a set: $\mathcal{E}_s \subseteq T_\Sigma(X)_s \times T_\Sigma(X)_s$ is the set of pairs $\langle L, R\rangle$ with both L, R of sort s.

We have indicated above that $\mathbf{Alg}_{\Sigma,\mathcal{E}}$ also has an initial algebra, to be denoted $T_{\Sigma,\mathcal{E}}$. We shall say that $T_{\Sigma,\mathcal{E}}$, and thus the corresponding abstract data type, is *presented* by $\mathcal{E}$. The construction of $T_{\Sigma,\mathcal{E}}$ requires some further machinery.

Definition 7. A Σ-*congruence* $\equiv$ on a Σ-algebra A is a family $\langle \equiv_s\rangle_{s\in S}$ of equivalence relations, $\equiv_s$ on A_s for $s \in S$, such that if $\sigma \in \Sigma_{s_1\ldots s_n, s}$, if $a_i, a_i' \in A_{s_i}$, and if $a_i \equiv_{s_i} a_i'$ for $i = 1, \ldots, n$, then $\sigma_A(a_1, \ldots, a_n) \equiv_s \sigma_A(a_1', \ldots, a_n')$.

If A is a Σ-algebra and $\equiv$ is a Σ-congruence on A, let $(A/{\equiv})_s = A_s/{\equiv_s}$ be the set of $\equiv_s$-equivalence classes of A_s. For $a \in A_s$, let $[a]_s$ (or just $[a]$) denote the $\equiv_s$-class containing a. Note that each element of $A_s/{\equiv_s}$ is of the form $[a]_s$, but of course the choice of $a \in A_s$ is not uniquely determined. We now make the S-indexed family $A/{\equiv}$ into a Σ-algebra by defining the operations $\sigma_{A/\equiv}$ as follows:

(q0) If $\sigma \in \Sigma_{\lambda, s}$, then $\sigma_{A/\equiv} = [\sigma_A]$;

(q1) If $\sigma \in \Sigma_{s_1\ldots s_n, s}$ and $[a_i] \in (A/{\equiv})_{s_i}$, then $\sigma_{A/\equiv}([a_1], \ldots, [a_n]) = [\sigma_A(a_1, \ldots, a_n)]$.

Proposition 4

If A is a Σ-algebra and $\equiv$ is a Σ-congruence on A, then $A/{\equiv}$, as defined above, is a Σ-algebra, called the *quotient* of A by $\equiv$.

Proof: We have to show that the definitions of $\sigma_{A/\equiv}$ given by (q0) and (q1) above are independent of choices of representatives from equivalence classes. But this is just what the congruence property (substitution property) guarantees: If

$[a_i] = [a'_i]$ for $i = 1, \ldots, n$, then $a_i \equiv_{s_i} a'_i$ so that $\sigma_A(a_1, \ldots, a_n) \equiv_s \sigma_A(a'_1, \ldots, a'_n)$; i.e., $[\sigma_A(a_1, \ldots, a_n)] = [\sigma_A(a'_1, \ldots, a'_n)]$.

The initial algebra $T_{\Sigma,\mathcal{E}}$, in the category of all Σ-algebras satisfying $\mathcal{E}$, is, as we have said, a quotient of T_Σ by a congruence relation obtained from $\mathcal{E}$. To make this precise, we first define the "congruence relation generated by an (arbitrary) relation" on an algebra A; we then apply this to the relation on T_Σ of all *substitution instances* of $\mathcal{E}$, that is, of all pairs $\langle t, t' \rangle$ in T_Σ^2 which result from substituting (constant) terms of corresponding sorts for variables occurring in equations of $\mathcal{E}$.

Proposition 5

Let A be a Σ-algebra, and let R be a relation on A (i.e., as usual, $R = \langle R_s \rangle_{s \in S}$ for $R_s \subseteq A_s \times A_s$). Then there is a least Σ-congruence relation on A containing R; it is called the *congruence relation generated by* R on A.

As usual, the proof is in the appendix (Section 5.6). It is highly nonconstructive and gives no hint about how to determine whether some pair $\langle a, a' \rangle$ is in the congruence.

We now come to the final step of going from a Σ-presentation to a quotient. A Σ-presentation $\mathcal{E}$ determines a relation $\mathcal{E}(A)$ on any Σ-algebra A in which $\mathcal{E}(A)_s$ is the set of all pairs $\langle \bar{\theta}_s(L), \bar{\theta}_s(R) \rangle$ such that $e = \langle L, R \rangle$ is in $\mathcal{E}_s$ and θ: var$(e) \longrightarrow A$ is an assignment. Thus $\mathcal{E}(A)_s$ is the set of pairs of elements of the carrier A_s that $\mathcal{E}$ "requires" to be equal or identified. But to get a congruence we may need some further identification; for example, if $\langle a_1, a'_1 \rangle$ and $\langle a_2, a'_2 \rangle$ are in $\mathcal{E}(A)$ and if $\sigma \in \Sigma_2$ (in a one-sorted case), then $\langle \sigma_A(a_1, a_2), \sigma_A(a'_1, a'_2) \rangle$ must be in the congruence generated by $\mathcal{E}$. This is what the construction of Proposition 5 gives us from $\mathcal{E}(A)$.

The generalization of Theorem 2 toward which we have been working can now be stated; it applies the above machinery to the algebra $A = T_\Sigma$.

Theorem 6

Let $\mathcal{E}$ be a Σ-presentation, and let $\equiv_{\mathcal{E}}$ be the Σ-congruence on T_Σ generated by $\mathcal{E}(T_\Sigma)$. Then $T_\Sigma/{\equiv_{\mathcal{E}}}$, the quotient of T_Σ by $\equiv_{\mathcal{E}}$, hereafter denoted $T_{\Sigma,\mathcal{E}}$, is the initial algebra in the category $\mathbf{Alg}_{\Sigma,\mathcal{E}}$ of all Σ-algebras satisfying $\mathcal{E}$.

This theorem concludes the general results from *universal algebra* that we shall be using. As we have mentioned, the fundamental ideas for one-sorted algebras go back to Birkhoff (1938). More recent texts include Cohn (1965) and Graetzer (1968); Birkhoff's (1948) preface on universal algebra (a chapter in revised editions) is a succinct treatment of this material. Many of the ideas in this chapter may be viewed more satisfactorily using many-sorted algebraic theories, as discussed in Goguen (1976). The notions of many-sorted algebra and many-sorted theory are traceable to Higgins (1963), Benabou (1966), and Birkhoff and Lipson (1970). We have been following the notationally simpler approach of ADJ (1973).

5.3. SPECIFICATION OF ABSTRACT DATA TYPES

In the previous section we introduced four fundamental abstract data types; these have no equations in their specifications and rely upon Theorem 2 to give an initial algebra for the abstract type. In this section we shall give a number of additional specifications in which the set $\mathcal{E}$ of equations is nonempty; these therefore rely upon Theorem 6 to give the abstract type as (the isomorphism class of) $T_{\Sigma,\mathcal{E}}$. Not only shall we give some examples of specifications for familiar data types along with discussion of their particular features and intuitive significance, but we shall use them to illustrate a variety of specification techniques. The goal is to give enough examples and techniques so that the reader can write specifications on her own.

The reader might doubt some of the specifications given here, in part because the traditional fuzzy use of terms such as "stack," "structure," and "array" in computer science fits a variety of types and also varies from user to user, whereas we specify one particular structure, $T_{\Sigma,\mathcal{E}}$. If the one we give isn't just what the reader has in mind, we hope he can juggle the equations (or even the signature) to get an exact fit.

In Section 5.4 we shall provide methods for proving correctness of specifications, and some of the examples given here are proven correct. But there might be errors in some other specifications, as we have not carried out mathematical correctness proofs for all of them; there certainly were errors in some earlier versions. Since algebraic specifications are halfway between our intuitive sense of what we want and actual computer code, both of which are error prone, it is only to be expected that the abstract specifications are going to have to undergo debugging too. It will take time and experience to build up a good library (or dictionary) of specifications for data types; we invite the reader to participate in this process.

5.3.1. Specification

Initial algebras are generally infinite objects; we therefore need convenient ways to describe them in finite terms if we are going to use them for abstract data types. This is the purpose of specifications, for which we shall now give a formal definition.

> **Definition 8.** A *specification* (*of d*) is a triple $\langle S, \Sigma, \mathcal{E}\rangle$ (where $d \in S$), where Σ is an S-sorted signature and $\mathcal{E}$ is a set of Σ-equations. As a matter of notational convenience, we shall often delete S from specifications, thus getting pairs $\langle \Sigma, \mathcal{E}\rangle$.

There are cases where we want to specify a number of sorts $d_1, \ldots, d_n$; Definition 8 is easily modified to cover this, but as there are not examples of this kind in this chapter, we shall not belabor the point.

The fundamental idea, as we have already often hinted, is that $\langle S, \Sigma, \mathcal{E}\rangle$ specifies an abstract data type by defining $T_{\Sigma,\mathcal{E}}$ (as a representative for the isomorphism class of Σ-algebras).

For complicated types we may not want to give the entire specification at once: We may well find it easier to modify and/or combine existing types. Indeed, the examples given later in this section provide a collection of types to use in this way. At least as importantly, they illustrate a number of techniques for modifying and/or combining already given types. The examples are presented in accordance with the following somewhat tentative classification scheme of techniques:

1. *Fundamental* types have the empty set of equations in their specification. Examples have been given already in Section 5.2. Such abstract types are fundamental not in the sense that they are traditionally so used in programming languages (such as real and int) but in a more basic mathematical sense.

2. Some specifications seem to be most naturally viewed as imposing equations on Σ-terms. This is of course the prototypical case, but sometimes it has particular intuitive significance. Section 5.3.2 contains some examples of imposing equations on fundamental types. Somewhat more generally, we might want to impose further equations on an existing type, going from $T_{\Sigma,\mathcal{E}}$ to $T_{\Sigma,\mathcal{E}\cup\mathcal{E}'}$, so that the new type is a *quotient* of the old. For example, bag can be viewed as a quotient of string and set as a quotient of bag. (These are not illustrated in Section 5.3.3 since they are not yet defined.)

3. Sometimes we want to *enrich* an existing data type with new operations (having corresponding equations) without upsetting the existing carriers or operations. More precisely, given a specification $\langle S, \Sigma, \mathcal{E}\rangle$, let Σ' be an S-sorted signature disjoint from Σ, and let $\mathcal{E}'$ be a set of $\Sigma \cup \Sigma'$-equations. Then we shall say that the specification $\langle S, \Sigma \cup \Sigma', \mathcal{E} \cup \mathcal{E}'\rangle$ is an *enrichment* of $\langle S, \Sigma, \mathcal{E}\rangle$ provided that $T_{\Sigma,\mathcal{E}} \cong T_{\Sigma\cup\Sigma',\mathcal{E}\cup\mathcal{E}'}$ as Σ-algebras, where $T_{\Sigma\cup\Sigma',\mathcal{E}\cup\mathcal{E}'}$ is regarded as a Σ-algebra by "forgetting" its operations in Σ'; we may regard the elements of $\mathcal{E}'$ as "defining equations" for operations in Σ'. In Section 5.3.3 we shall illustrate this by adding the usual arithmetic operations to nat and int.

A special kind of enrichment occurs when elements of Σ' are *derived operators* out of T_Σ; this means that each element of $\mathcal{E}'$ is of the form $\langle\sigma(y_1, \ldots, y_n), t\rangle$ with $\sigma \in \Sigma'_{s_1\ldots s_n, s}$, $t \in T_\Sigma(y_1, \ldots, y_n)$, and y_i of sort s_i; there should be exactly one such equation for each $\sigma \in \Sigma'$. This is illustrated in Section 5.3.3 by adding some derived operators to bool.

There are also cases in which we want to add operations which require new sorts. For one class of examples, we may want to add *predicates* (which we view as elements in $\Sigma'_{d,\text{bool}}$), *conditionals* (in $\Sigma'_{\text{bool}\ dd,d}$; see Figure 5.2.1), or *relations* (in $\Sigma'_{dd,\text{bool}}$) to an existing type which does not have bool. But we can always add bool, with its operations and equations, to the specification if it isn't there and then enrich the result. This yields a specification which extends (both bool and) all the old sorts, which we shall say are therefore *protected.* This is made precise in

Definition 9. Let $\langle S, \Sigma, \mathcal{E}\rangle$ be a specification, and let $\langle S \cup S', \Sigma \cup \Sigma', \mathcal{E}'\rangle$ be another, with both S and S' and Σ and Σ' disjoint. Let $\bar{S} = S \cup S'$, $\bar{\Sigma} = \Sigma \cup \Sigma'$, and $\bar{\mathcal{E}} = \mathcal{E} \cup \mathcal{E}'$. We shall say that $\langle \bar{S}, \bar{\Sigma}, \bar{\mathcal{E}}\rangle$ is an *extension* of $\langle S, \Sigma, \mathcal{E}\rangle$ if $T_{\Sigma,\mathcal{E}} \cong T_{\bar{\Sigma},\bar{\mathcal{E}}}$ as S-sorted Σ-algebras (forget the sorts in S' and the operators in Σ'). If $S' = \varnothing$, we call $\langle S, \bar{\Sigma}, \bar{\mathcal{E}}\rangle$ an *enrichment* of $\langle S, \Sigma, \mathcal{E}\rangle$.

When we use a sort symbol d (e.g., bool or int) as an abbreviation for a specific specification $\langle S, \Sigma, \mathcal{E}\rangle$ for d, we shall say that "d is *protected* in (a specification) $\langle \bar{S}, \bar{\Sigma}, \bar{\mathcal{E}}\rangle$" if $\langle \bar{S}, \bar{\Sigma}, \bar{\mathcal{E}}\rangle$ is an extension of $\langle S, \Sigma, \mathcal{E}\rangle$.

4. In some cases, we are not merely adding operations among types thought of as previously existing but are interested in creating new structures using old ones. One special case is when things of the new sort are pairs, or more generally n-tuples, of things of previously given types, and the new operations are defined from ones given on the components. We call this *tupling* of types; generally we shall want to enrich after tupling. Another example is string(int), which uses both int and bool. Here, too, we shall want the old sorts to be protected, but it doesn't make sense for the sort string to be protected, because there is nothing to compare it to. In Section 5.3.4 we shall give some examples of extensions.

5. Often, given a specification $\langle S, \Sigma, \mathcal{E}\rangle$ of a data type $d \in S$, we extend it by adding a single new sort t and additional operators Σ' and equations $\mathcal{E}'$. In many important cases Σ' and $\mathcal{E}'$ can be used to extend a variety of specifications $\langle S, \Sigma, \mathcal{E}\rangle$ for different data types d. When this is the case we can look at the specification $\langle S \cup \{t\}, \bar{\Sigma}, \bar{\mathcal{E}}\rangle$ as having d as a parameter and as defining a new type $t(d)$ for each choice of (a specification for) d. A prototypical example is string(d), which extends a specification for type d to a specification which includes a new sort whose carrier is the set of all strings on the carrier of sort d. When specifications are used in this manner we call them *parameterized* specifications. Examples are given in Section 5.3.6.

Both techniques 4 and 5 can run into the need for operations which are either partially defined or produce *error messages*. This may not seem like much of a problem, but as will be seen, it is difficult to handle in a concise and accurate manner. As a preview, let's just say that once error messages are introduced into the abstract type, the original axioms are made *conditional* on the operands not being errors.

We now proceed with the promised examples of abstract data type specifications.

5.3.2. Quotients

Recall that these are cases in which it is convenient to view the type being defined as a quotient of an existing type. In this section we shall give some examples of quotients of fundamental types for the sake of simplicity. However, as noted before, there are other examples, such as bag as a quotient of string or set as a quotient of bag.

Example 5

The data type int is specified by the signature of Figure 5.3.1 and equations making predecessor (PRED) and successor (SUCC) inverses of one another:

int-1 PRED(SUCC(X)) = X

int-2 SUCC(PRED(X)) = X.

The type of which this is a quotient has a single constant 0 and two unary operators, SUCC and PRED. The reader may be convinced that the terms PRED^n(0),

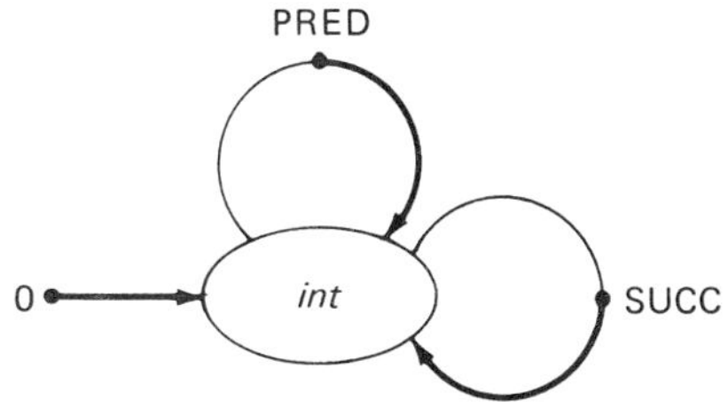

Figure 5.3.1

0, and $SUCC^n(0)$ for $n > 0$ are representatives of distinct equivalence classes in the quotient, corresponding to $-n$, 0, and n, respectively.

Example 6

Let $A = \{a_1, a_2, \ldots, a_n\}$ be a set (for example, of characters). The abstract data type string-of-A is specified by the signature of Figure 5.3.2 and the equations

string-1 $\quad CONCAT(CONCAT(S, S'), S'') = CONCAT(S, CONCAT(S', S''))$

string-2 $\quad CONCAT(S, \lambda) = CONCAT(\lambda, S) = S.$

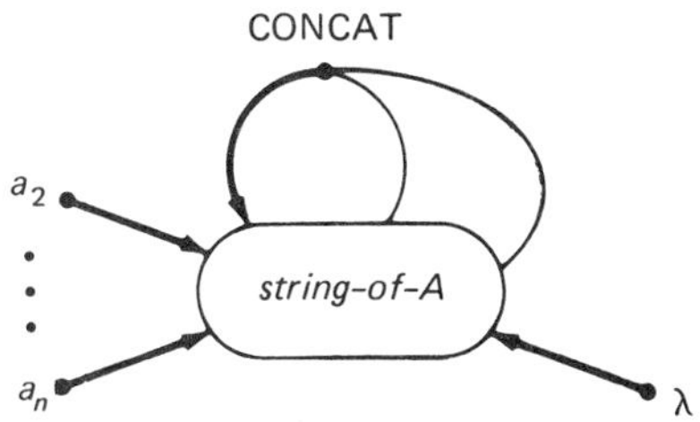

Figure 5.3.2

These are just the axioms for a monoid, and the initial $(\Sigma, \mathcal{E})$-algebra in this case is the free monoid generated by $A = \{a_1, \ldots, a_n\}$. It is a quotient of T_Σ, of course.

5.3.3. Enrichments

In this section we shall give some examples of adding new operations to an existing type without disturbing it, including a general discussion of derived operators. (See Definition 9 for a review of terminology.)

Example 7

The well-known and extremely important data type bool had a signature containing only the two truth values in Example 4. Now we add two Boolean operations and their defining equations:

bool-1	$\neg T = F$
bool-2	$\neg(\neg B) = B$
bool-3	$T \wedge B = B$
bool-4	$F \wedge B = F$
bool-5	$B \wedge B' = B' \wedge B.$

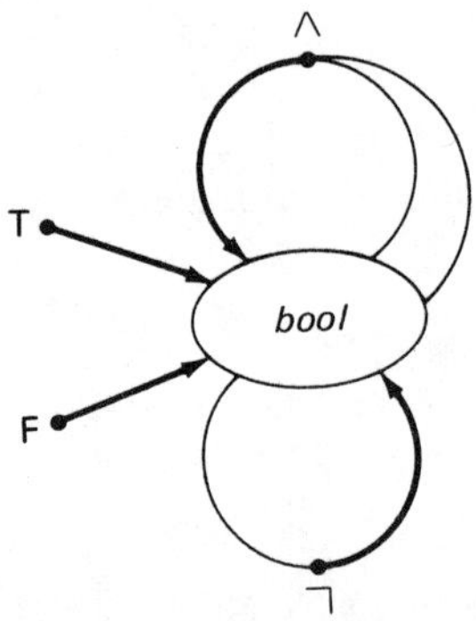

Figure 5.3.3

The correctness proof of this specification shows that every term in T_Σ (for Σ of Figure 5.3.3) is equivalent to T or F under these equations *and* that T and F do not become congruent. That is, the original specification of bool (Example 4) is protected.

Example 8

Here we add arithmetic operations to the fundamental data type nat of Example 1, as shown in Figure 5.3.4, using equations which are primitive recursive definitions[9]:

nat-1	$\text{PRED}(0) = 0$
nat-2	$\text{PRED}(\text{SUCC}(N)) = N$
nat-3	$N \dot{-} 0 = N$
nat-4	$N \dot{-} \text{SUCC}(N') = \text{PRED}(N \dot{-} N')$
nat-5	$N + 0 = N$
nat-6	$N + \text{SUCC}(N') = \text{SUCC}(N + N')$
nat-7	$N * 0 = 0$
nat-8	$N * \text{SUCC}(N') = N + (N * N').$

[9]It should be possible to prove that any such *primitive recursive* extension of a fundamental type does what it is supposed to, but this is far beyond the scope of this chapter.

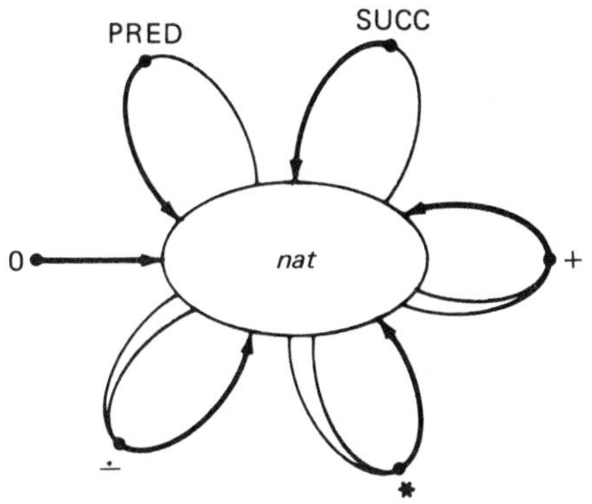

Figure 5.3.4

Example 9

Here we enrich int in a way similar to that in Example 8 for nat as shown in Figure 5.3.5. Note that the original data type is not fundamental, as was nat.

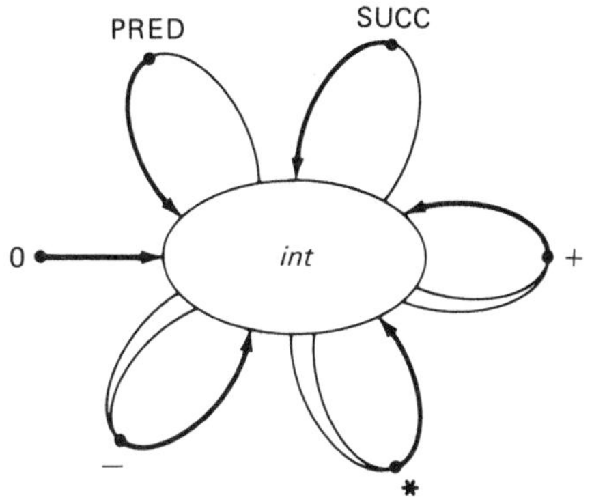

Figure 5.3.5

int-3	$N + 0 = N$
int-4	$N + \text{SUCC}(N') = \text{SUCC}(N + N')$
int-5	$N + \text{PRED}(N') = \text{PRED}(N + N')$
int-6	$N - 0 = N$
int-7	$N - \text{SUCC}(N') = \text{PRED}(N - N')$
int-8	$N - \text{PRED}(N') = \text{SUCC}(N - N')$
int-9	$N * 0 = 0$
int-10	$N * \text{SUCC}(N') = (N * N') + N$
int-11	$N * \text{PRED}(N') = (N * N') - N.$

A Σ-algebra has available not only the operations σ_A for each $\sigma \in \Sigma$ but also the *derived operations* t_A for each $t \in T_\Sigma(X)$. (Recall from Section 5.2 that X is our inexhaustible supply of variables, $\{x_{s,i} \mid s \in S \text{ and } i \in \omega\}$.) The intuition here is very simple: A Σ-term t in variables $y_1, \ldots, y_n$ (of sorts $s_1, \ldots, s_n$) defines an actual function t_A on any Σ-algebra A by just substituting a value a_i (of sort s_i) for each variable y_i and "evaluating" the whole thing in A. The precise version relies on applying Proposition 3 (with a possibly confusing reversal of notation), but the intuition will do for reading the rest of this section.

We now turn to the formal development. Given $t \in T_\Sigma(X)_s$, let $\text{var}(t) = Y = \{y_1, \ldots, y_n\}$, and let y_i be a variable of sort s_i; note that $t \in T_\Sigma(Y)_s$. Now given $\theta\colon Y \longrightarrow A$, we get $\bar{\theta}(t) \in A_s$ from Proposition 3. If t is fixed and θ is permitted to vary (note that this is the reverse of the point of view originally implied in Proposition 3), then we get a function $t_A\colon A_{s_1} \times \cdots \times A_{s_n} \longrightarrow A_s$, which is called the *derived operation*[10] of t in A: If $\theta(y_i) = a_i \in A_{s_i}$, then $t_A(a_1, \ldots, a_n) = \bar{\theta}(t) \in A_s$.

The reason for bringing this up here is that adding derived operations to an existing type clearly leaves it protected; thus derived operators provide a generally valid method for enrichment. More precisely now, given $\langle \Sigma, \mathcal{E} \rangle$, let t be an s-sorted Σ-term, with $\text{var}(t) = \{y_1, \ldots, y_n\}$ and y_i of sort s_i as above; let $w = s_1 \ldots s_n$ and let τ be a symbol not in Σ; let $\bar{\Sigma}_{w,s} = \Sigma_{w,s} \cup \{\tau\}$ and $\bar{\mathcal{E}} = \mathcal{E} \cup \{\tau(y_1, \ldots, y_n) = t\}$. That is, $\langle \bar{\Sigma}, \bar{\mathcal{E}} \rangle$ contains τ as a new operation symbol of rank $\langle w, s \rangle$ and defined by t. Then $T_{\bar{\Sigma},\bar{\mathcal{E}}}$ regarded as a Σ-algebra is isomorphic to $T_{\Sigma,\mathcal{E}}$. In the same way, we can add any number of derived operations all at once.

The data type <u>bool</u> provides a nice illustration of this.

Example 7 (continued)

It is easy (and quite standard) to define further logical operations in terms of $\wedge$ and $\neg$:

$$B \vee B' = \neg(\neg(B) \wedge \neg(B'));$$

$$B \Rightarrow B' = \neg(B) \vee B';$$

$$B \Leftrightarrow B' = (B \Rightarrow B') \wedge (B' \Rightarrow B).$$

Conjunctions and disjunctions with $n \geq 0$ arguments are convenient in some specifications; these operations are denoted $\wedge_{i=1}^{n}$ and $\vee_{i=1}^{n}$, respectively, and are defined by

$$\wedge_{i=1}^{0} = T \qquad \wedge_{i=1}^{1} B = B$$

$$\wedge_{i=1}^{n+1} B_i = (\wedge_{i=1}^{n} B_i) \wedge B_{n+1}$$

$$\vee_{i=1}^{0} = F \qquad \vee_{i=1}^{1} B = B$$

$$\vee_{i=1}^{n+1} B_i = (\vee_{i=1}^{n} B_i) \vee B_{n+1}.$$

[10] If we want to assign a rank to t, here is one specific way to do so: Let $y_1, \ldots, y_n$ be the distinct variables occurring in t; if y_i is of sort s_i, then we shall take the *arity* of t to be $w = s_1 \ldots s_n$. Of course, the *sort* of t is s, and the *rank* of t is $\langle w, s \rangle$.

For each $n \geq 0$, these equations define a perfectly ordinary n-ary-derived operator; thus, the equations are not part of the enriched specification but tell how to define the things which are. For example, the equation for $\bigwedge_{i=1}^{3}(B_1, B_2, B_3)$ is

$$\bigwedge_{i=1}^{3}(B_1, B_2, B_3) = (B_1 \wedge B_2) \wedge B_3.$$

There is no difficulty in principle with adding an infinite number of operator symbols and equations, but in practice one might want to think of only those derived operators being added which are actually being used.

In the specifications that follow, we shall not always bother to include derived operators; they can be defined and used as needed.

Similarly, if $\langle S, \Sigma, \mathcal{E}\rangle$ is any specification with $\underline{\text{bool}} \in S$, we can define *conditionals* of sort s for each $s \in S$, $\text{IF}_s \in \Sigma'_{\underline{\text{bool}}\ s\ s,\ s}$, by the equations

$$\text{IF}_s(T, S, S') = S$$
$$\text{IF}_s(F, S, S') = S'.$$

If $\underline{\text{bool}}$ is protected, this is always an enrichment; thus we shall feel free to use these operations as derived operations, adding them without warning or worry. These operations, and their cousins, play a particularly important role, since they permit us to write conditional equations without departing from the framework of standard algebra.

5.3.4. Extensions

We shall now consider cases in which new sorts, as well as new operations and equations, are added to an existing type; recall that the notion of *extension* has been defined in Section 5.3.1 (see Definition 9).

Example 10

We add the predicate LE (less than or equal) to the combination of $\underline{\text{nat}}$ and $\underline{\text{bool}}$. Note that the signature (in Figure 5.3.6) only indicates the new operations, those

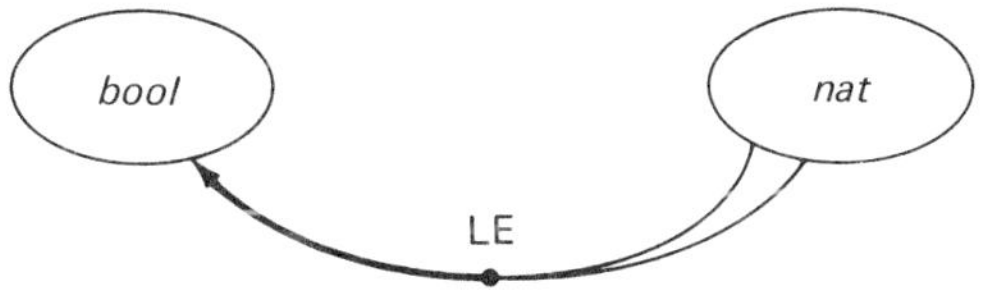

Figure 5.3.6

in Σ'. The equations are as follows:

$\underline{\text{natle-1}}$	$\text{LE}(0, N) = T$
$\underline{\text{natle-2}}$	$\text{LE}(\text{SUCC}(N), 0) = F$
$\underline{\text{natle-3}}$	$\text{LE}(\text{SUCC}(N), \text{SUCC}(N')) = \text{LE}(N, N')$.

With this presentation "equals" becomes a derived operator:

$$\text{EQ}(N, N') = \text{LE}(N, N') \wedge \text{LE}(N', N).$$

Example 11

In defining "equals" (EQ) for the data type string-of-A, we use families of equations which are indexed by $a \in A$ as shown in Figure 5.3.7:

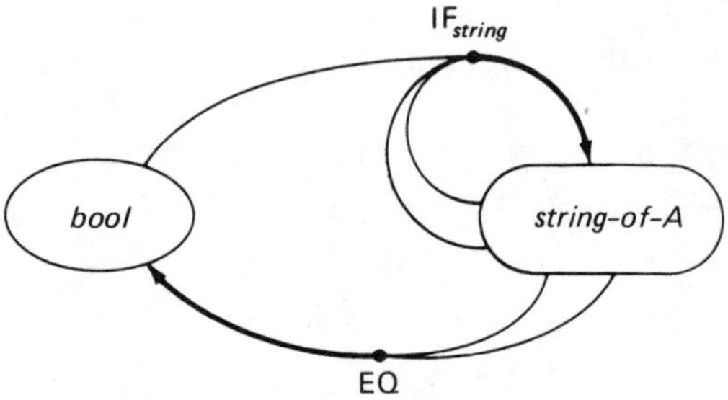

Figure 5.3.7

string eq-1	$\text{EQ}(\lambda, \lambda) = T$	
string eq-2	$\text{EQ}(a, a) = T$	for $a \in A$
string eq-3	$\text{EQ}(a, \lambda) = \text{EQ}(\lambda, a) = F$	for $a \in A$
string eq-4	$\text{EQ}(\text{CONCAT}(a, s), \text{CONCAT}(a, s'))$ $= \text{EQ}(s, s')$	for $a \in A$
string eq-5	$\text{EQ}(\text{CONCAT}(a, s), \text{CONCAT}(a', s'))$ $= F$	for $a, a' \in A$ and $a \neq a'$.

These equations could be somewhat simplified and clarified by making use of an EQ predicate on A.

Example 12

As an example of extending with something besides bool, we present equations for the length function on strings as in Figure 5.3.8:

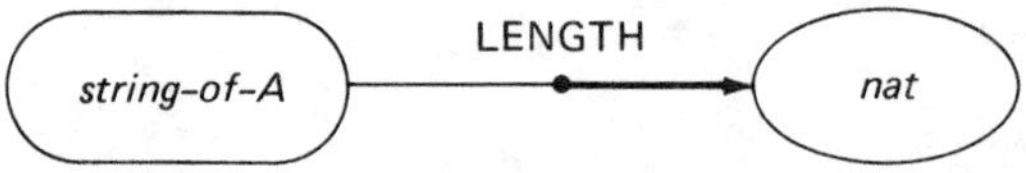

Figure 5.3.8

length-1	$\text{LENGTH}(\lambda) = 0$	
length-2	$\text{LENGTH}(a) = \text{SUCC}(0)$	for $a \in A$
length-3	$\text{LENGTH}(\text{CONCAT}(S, S')) = \text{LENGTH}(S) + \text{LENGTH}(S')$.	

Let us now consider some extensions in which the things of the new sort are tuples of things of given sorts.

Example 13

One of the simplest and most familiar examples is *complex numbers*. For illustration we look at complex integers defined in Figure 5.3.9. The MAKE function takes a pair $\langle a, b \rangle$ of integers as arguments; the result can be thought of as $a + bi$. For each complex integer C we can retrieve its real part RE(C) and its imaginary part IM(C):

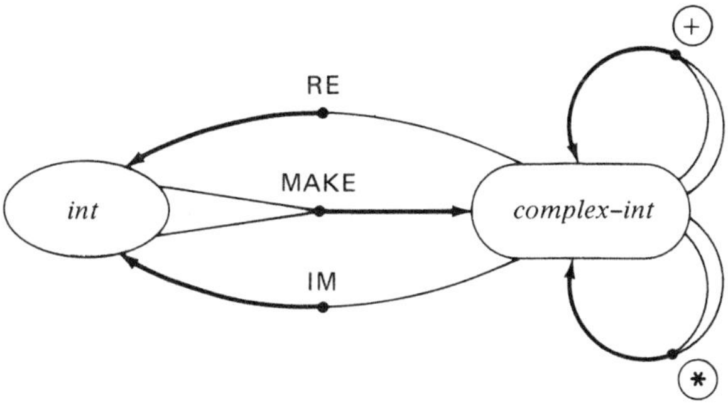

Figure 5.3.9

complex-1	$\text{MAKE}(\text{RE}(C), \text{IM}(C)) = C$
complex-2	$\text{RE}(\text{MAKE}(N, N')) = N$
complex-3	$\text{IM}(\text{MAKE}(N, N')) = N'$
complex-4	$\text{MAKE}(N, N') \oplus \text{MAKE}(M, M') = \text{MAKE}(N + M, N' + M')$
complex-5	$\text{MAKE}(N, N') \circledast \text{MAKE}(M, M') = \text{MAKE}((N * M) - (N' * M'), (N * M') + (N' * M))$.

Example 14

Another example, given by Figure 5.3.10, using pairs of objects is the common implementation of "the integers" as sign-number pairs. For convenience we shall use the data type bool for the signs (T for "positive," F for "negative"):

signat-1	$\langle \lvert S \rvert, \text{SGN}(S) \rangle = S$
signat-2	$\lvert \langle N, B \rangle \rvert = N$
signat-3	$\text{SGN}(\langle N, B \rangle) = B$
signat-4	$S \oplus S' = \text{IF}(\text{SGN}(S) \Leftrightarrow \text{SGN}(S'), \langle \lvert S \rvert + \lvert S' \rvert, \text{SGN}(S) \rangle, \text{IF}(\text{LE}(\lvert S \rvert, \lvert S' \rvert), \langle \lvert S' \rvert \dot{-} \lvert S \rvert, \text{SGN}(S') \rangle, \langle \lvert S \rvert \dot{-} \lvert S' \rvert, \text{SGN}(S) \rangle))$
signat-5	$S \circledast S' = \langle \lvert S \rvert * \lvert S' \rvert, (\text{SGN}(S) \Leftrightarrow \text{SGN}(S')) \rangle$.

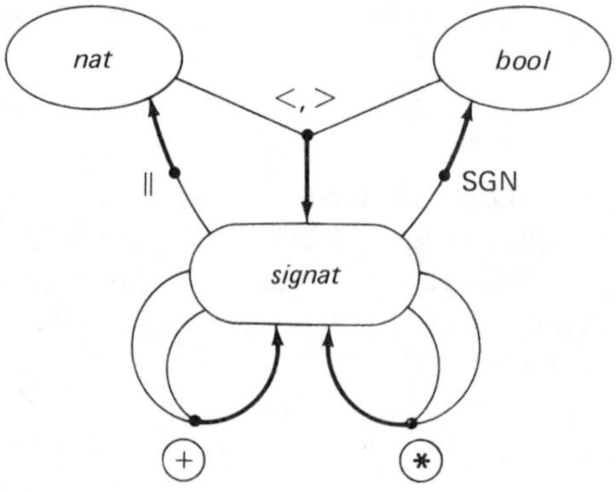

Figure 5.3.10

The data type signat differs from the int of Example 9 in having two zeros ($\langle 0, T\rangle$ and $\langle 0, F\rangle$), while int has only one. Actually, signat is a commonly implemented data type.

5.3.5. Errors

The fact is that the problem of errors is a great deal more subtle than has been generally recognized, and the usual ways to treat errors in abstract data types just are not mathematically sound. For example, if one writes, as in Guttag et al. (1976),

$$\text{TOP(NEWSTACK)} = \text{UNDEFINED}$$

for TOP: $\underline{\text{stack}} \to \underline{\text{data}} \cup \{\text{UNDEFINED}\}$, then one must give some account of what the operations on the data do to UNDEFINED or else abandon the convenience of working with algebras in the straightforward way. If the second option is chosen, one is mathematically obliged to give an account of what one is doing: For example, is UNDEFINED a value, or is TOP a partially defined function? Both possibilities lead to further difficulties: If UNDEFINED is a value, in what carrier? And if not, then the theory of partial algebras must be used.

No doubt such difficulties can be overcome in a variety of ways; the problem is that they have not previously even been explicitly recognized as difficulties. Our purpose in this section is to develop the idea that there are genuine mathematical difficulties here and to suggest some possible ways of approaching them. This will be done primarily through the careful consideration of examples. We shall start rather gently with an example which earlier caused us some difficulty [ADJ (1975a)].

Example 15

In Example 6 we considered string-of-A for a set A; now we consider string(int), strings of integers, to be formed from int (and bool) in such a way as to protect them. Rather than have all the integers as constants, we introduce a function MAKE which makes a string of length 1 from an integer. Then the axioms of

Example 6 (string-1, 2) suffice, in the sense that the string(int) carrier of $T_{\Sigma,\mathcal{E}}$ (Σ as in Figure 5.3.11 and $\mathcal{E}$ consisting of int-1, 2 and string-1, 2) is isomorphic to the free monoid generated by the integers.

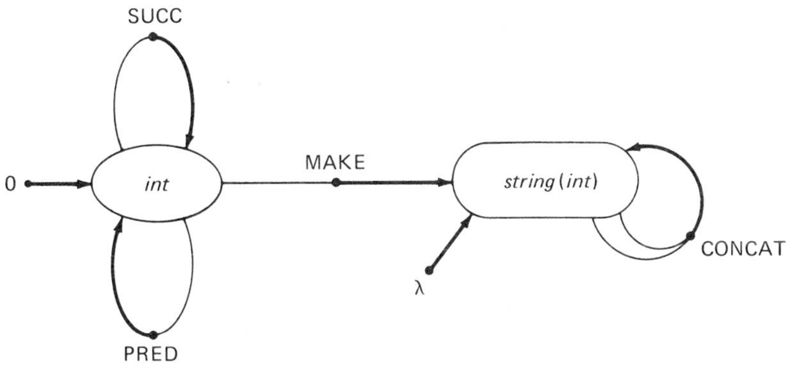

Figure 5.3.11

This specification excludes many interesting operations on strings, such as HEAD and TAIL, whose values should be of sort int but which are "sometimes undefined"—or, better put, should return *error messages* under certain conditions. These are the kinds of operations which lead to difficulties. Thus, let us consider the signature of Figure 5.3.12 and some expected axioms:

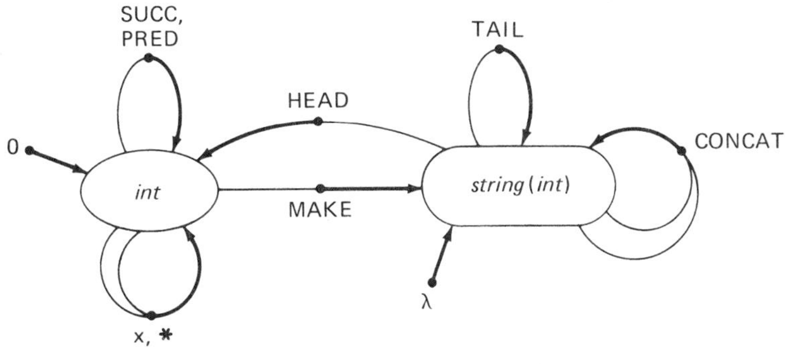

Figure 5.3.12

string-1, 2	
int-1, 2, 3, 4, 9, 10, 11	
string-3	HEAD(CONCAT(MAKE(N), S)) $=$ N
string-4	TAIL(CONCAT(MAKE(N), S)) $=$ S
string-5	CONCAT(HEAD(S), TAILS(S)) $=$ S
string-6	TAIL(λ) $=$ λ.

The trouble with this specification is that int is not protected: The resulting data type has a lot of strange things of sort int in it, such as HEAD(λ) and SUCC(SUCC(HEAD(λ))), and furthermore, these lead to some strange things of sort string(int), such as MAKE(SUCC(SUCC(HEAD(λ)))).

We might well try to get out of this by forcing HEAD(λ) to be some integer, say 0, by adding to the specification an axiom like

$$\text{HEAD}(\lambda) = 0.$$

But this won't work, because then

$$\lambda = \text{CONCAT}(\text{MAKE}(\text{HEAD}(\lambda)), \text{TAIL}(\lambda)) = \text{CONCAT}(\text{MAKE}(0),\lambda) = \text{MAKE}(0),$$

so that the string corresponding to 0 is the empty string, which we really don't want.[11]

From the intuitive point of view, the empty string doesn't have a "first symbol" and any attempt to compute it should result in an error message telling us that we are trying to do the impossible.

This suggests then that we modify the specification of int to include an error message. That is, we want to add an element E_{int} to the set of integers without disturbing anything else. If this is done, the problem with HEAD(λ) can be resolved by adding the axiom

$$\text{string-7} \qquad \text{HEAD}(\lambda) = E_{\text{int}}.$$

But in adding E_{int} to sort int, we have to take care of all the new terms created, such as MAKE(E_{int}) and PRED($E_{\text{int}} + 0$).

We can take care of MAKE(E_{int}) by adding an error message to string, i.e., by adding an element E_{string} to $\Sigma_{\lambda,\text{string}}$ and another axiom:

$$\text{MAKE}(E_{\text{int}}) = E_{\text{string}}.$$

This is reasonable since if we get an error, any operation on it also yields an error. On the other hand, adding E_{string} also results in an infinitude of terms using it, such as CONCAT(MAKE(0), E_{string}). However, these terms are not difficult to handle with the philosophy that once an error occurs it is propagated, i.e., that if any argument of an operator is an error, then its value is an error. This can be done by adding to the specification special *error axioms*:

$\text{SUCC}(E_{\text{int}}) = E_{\text{int}}$	$E_{\text{int}} * N = E_{\text{int}}$
$E_{\text{int}} + N = E_{\text{int}}$	$N * E_{\text{int}} = E_{\text{int}}$
$\text{CONCAT}(S, E_{\text{string}}) = E_{\text{string}}$	$\text{PRED}(E_{\text{int}}) = E_{\text{int}}$
$\text{TAIL}(E_{\text{string}}) = E_{\text{string}}$	$N + E_{\text{int}} = E_{\text{int}}$
$\text{HEAD}(E_{\text{string}}) = E_{\text{int}}$	$\text{CONCAT}(E_{\text{string}}, S) = E_{\text{string}}.$

[11]Actually we can write a specification for *string*(*int*) which omits *string*-5, but since our objective here is to show the kind of difficulties which can arise, we don't want to side-step them.

[Note that among these axioms would be MAKE($\underline{E_{\text{int}}}$) = $\underline{E_{\text{string}}}$, but we omit it since it was already listed.]

These error axioms reduce any term containing an error message to the error message of the appropriate sort, thus eliminating unwanted elements of the carrier. Unfortunately they also collapse the carrier of sort int, so that we don't have the wanted elements either! Consider the following deductions,

$$
\begin{aligned}
0 &= E_{\underline{\text{int}}} * 0 && \text{by int-9} \\
&= E_{\underline{\text{int}}} && \text{by error axioms} \\
N &= N + 0 && \text{by int-3} \\
& \quad N + E_{\underline{\text{int}}} && \text{by the above} \\
&= E_{\underline{\text{int}}} && \text{by the error axioms,}
\end{aligned}
$$

which show that for every N of sort int, $N = E_{\underline{\text{int}}}$. Thus we have collapsed the denumerable set of integers $\{0, \pm 1, \pm 2, \ldots\}$ down to the one-element set $\{E_{\underline{\text{int}}}\}$.

This sorry state of affairs arises from having two axioms (int-9 and an error axiom) that apply to the term $E_{\underline{\text{int}}} * 0$. Obviously we do not want $E_{\underline{\text{int}}} * 0 = 0$, but rather $E_{\underline{\text{int}}} * 0 = E_{\underline{\text{int}}}$; that is, we only want to apply $N * 0 = 0$ when $N \neq E_{\underline{\text{int}}}$. This suggests using *conditional error axioms*; for example, replace int-9 by

"If $N \neq E_{\underline{\text{int}}}$, then $N * 0 = 0$."

What may seem surprising is that this can be done entirely in the initial algebra framework: These conditional error axioms can be given by appropriate specifications.

We apologize for leaving this example momentarily unresolved, but in order to treat axioms which are conditioned by the nonoccurrence of errors, as was suggested by the discussion of the example, it is first necessary to develop some special machinery.

Because the abstract data type bool with a single error message plays a central role in all other error specifications, we shall develop it as a special case first.

Example 7E

The main point is to add to the specification of Example 7 a new constant $E_{\underline{\text{bool}}}$; it is also necessary to add a new unary operator $\text{OK}_{\underline{\text{bool}}}$ which tells (as a predicate) when an argument is not an error—and, of course, we add some equations. As mentioned above, the old equations will be *conditioned* on their arguments not being errors; this is accomplished by using an IF on the extended bool, of rank ⟨bool bool bool, bool⟩, denoted IFE. We shall denote this extended type boole when it is desirable to distinguish it from bool; sometimes we shall not bother to make the distinction. The signature therefore is that in Figure 5.3.13 with subscripts bool omitted for convenience, as we shall also do in the equa-

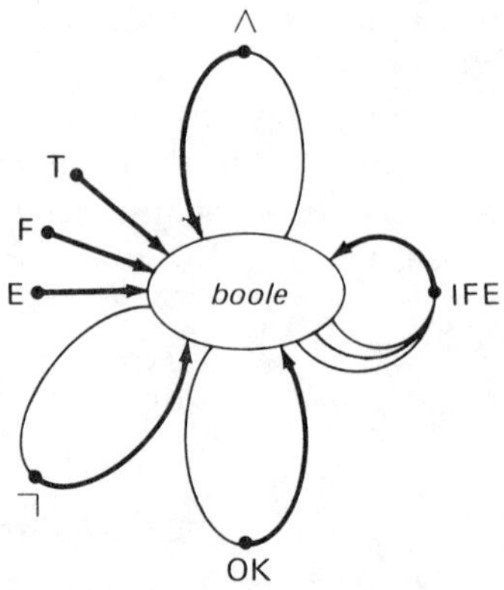

Figure 5.3.13

tions. These will be given in groups with an explanation of their significance, starting with those for the extended conditional:

$$\mathrm{IFE}(T, B, B') = B$$
$$\mathrm{IFE}(F, B, B') = B'$$
$$\mathrm{IFE}(E, B, B') = E.$$

Next, we define the predicate OK on the constants

$$\mathrm{OK}(T) = T$$
$$\mathrm{OK}(F) = T$$
$$\mathrm{OK}(E) = F$$

and then move on to equations which ensure it works as we intend on compound terms:

$$\mathrm{OK}(\neg B) = \mathrm{OK}(B)$$
$$\mathrm{OK}(B \wedge B') = \mathrm{OK}(B) \wedge \mathrm{OK}(B').$$

Also, we had better be sure that compound terms involving errors give errors as values ("errors propagate"):

$$\neg E = E$$
$$E \wedge B = B \wedge E = E.$$

We now begin preparation for the conditioned forms of the original equations. If an equation involves $n > 0$ arguments, it is convenient to have a derived operator expressing that all of them are "ok," defined by

$$\mathrm{OK}_n(B_1, \ldots, B_n) = \wedge_{i=1}^{n} \mathrm{OK}(B_i).$$

Next, we have a derived conditional using the above,

$$\mathrm{IFOK}_n(B_1, \ldots, B_n, B) = \mathrm{IFE}(\mathrm{OK}_n(B_1, \ldots, B_n), B, E)$$

whose value is B if all arguments are ok and otherwise E. Note that $\bigwedge_{i=1}^{0}$ is by convention T. Now we are ready for the axioms, which are conditioned versions of those of Example 7 (because the first equation involves no variables, the conditioning has no effect; we therefore write it in unconditioned form):

boole-1	$\neg T = F$
boole-2	$\mathrm{IFOK}_1(B, \neg(\neg B)) = \mathrm{IFOK}_1(B, B)$
boole-3	$\mathrm{IFOK}_1(B, T \wedge B) = \mathrm{IFOK}_1(B, B)$
boole-4	$\mathrm{IFOK}_1(B, F \wedge B) = \mathrm{IFOK}_1(B, F)$
boole-5	$\mathrm{IFOK}_2(B, B', B \wedge B') = \mathrm{IFOK}_2(B, B', B' \wedge B)$.

We shall soon show that all the error axioms arise in a perfectly standarized way. The tricky thing is to show that the original algebra for bool has been preserved as a subalgebra (of the initial algebra) in the new specification, which differs only by $E_{\underline{\mathrm{bool}}}$; see Section 5.4.

We shall give one more example before the general error message adding recipe, but first, we shall generalize the notation of the above example to the many-sorted case. This will be used in both the example and the recipe.

For each $s \in S$, we define a special conditional of sort s which is sensitive to Boolean errors by

$\underline{\mathrm{ife}_s}$-1	$\mathrm{IFE}_s(T, S, S') = S$
$\underline{\mathrm{ife}_s}$-2	$\mathrm{IFE}_s(F, S, S') = S'$
$\underline{\mathrm{ife}_s}$-3	$\mathrm{IFE}_s(E_{\underline{\mathrm{bool}}}, S, S') = E_s$,

assuming that each sort s has an error E_s.

Now assuming each sort $s \in S$ has had the predicate OK_s added to the signature, define derived operators, for $w = s_1 \ldots s_n \in S^*$, y_i a variable of sort s_i and x of sort s, by

$$\mathrm{OK}_w(y_1, \ldots, y_n) = \bigwedge_{i=1}^{n} \mathrm{OK}_{s_i}(y_i)$$

and

$$\mathrm{IFOK}_{w,s}(y_1, \ldots, y_n, x) = \mathrm{IFE}_s(\mathrm{OK}_w(y_1, \ldots, y_n), x, E_s).$$

These will be used to condition equations to hold only for "ok" arguments.

If $e = \langle L, R \rangle$ is a Σ-equation, if $y_1, \ldots, y_n$ are the distinct variables occurring in L and R, and if y_i is of sort s_i, then we shall say that the *arity* of e is $w = s_1 \ldots s_n$ and write $w = \mathrm{arity}(e)$.

Example 9E

We indicate in Figure 5.3.14 only the additions to the signature of Example 9 (Figure 5.3.5). Note that we may or may not add the letter e to the sort names, as seems convenient. For equations, we take all equations in Example 7E (in the new notation) plus

$$\mathrm{OK}_{\underline{\mathrm{int}}}(0) = T$$

$$\mathrm{OK}_{\underline{\mathrm{int}}}(E_{\underline{\mathrm{int}}}) = F$$

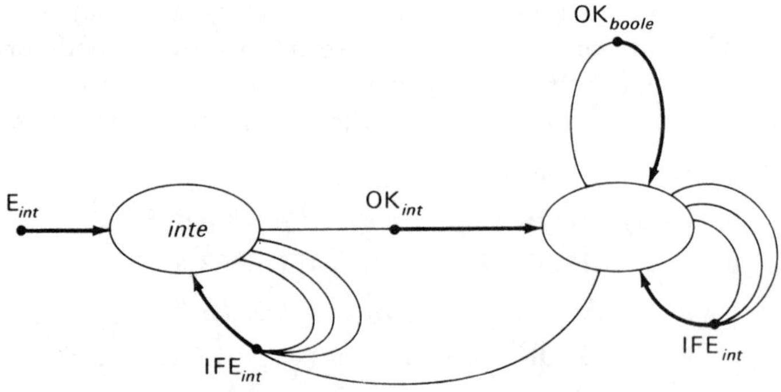

Figure 5.3.14

to handle constants of sort int, and

$$\mathrm{OK}_{\underline{\mathrm{int}}}(\mathrm{SUCC}(N)) = \mathrm{OK}_{\underline{\mathrm{int}}}(N)$$
$$\mathrm{OK}_{\underline{\mathrm{ini}}}(\mathrm{PRED}(N)) = \mathrm{OK}_{\underline{\mathrm{int}}}(N)$$
$$\mathrm{OK}_{\underline{\mathrm{int}}}(N + N') = \mathrm{OK}_{\underline{\mathrm{int}}}(N) \wedge \mathrm{OK}_{\underline{\mathrm{int}}}(N')$$
$$\mathrm{OK}_{\underline{\mathrm{int}}}(N * N') = \mathrm{OK}_{\underline{\mathrm{int}}}(N) \wedge \mathrm{OK}_{\underline{\mathrm{int}}}(N')$$
$$\mathrm{OK}_{\underline{\mathrm{int}}}(N - N') = \mathrm{OK}_{\underline{\mathrm{int}}}(N) \wedge \mathrm{OK}_{\underline{\mathrm{int}}}(N')$$

to be sure that $\mathrm{OK}_{\underline{\mathrm{int}}}$ is "ok" on compound terms. Next, we want to be sure that errors propagate through compound terms, so (patiently, now)

$$\begin{aligned}
\mathrm{SUCC}(E_{\underline{\mathrm{int}}}) &= E_{\underline{\mathrm{int}}}\\
\mathrm{PRED}(E_{\underline{\mathrm{int}}}) &= E_{\underline{\mathrm{int}}}\\
E_{\underline{\mathrm{int}}} + N &= E_{\underline{\mathrm{int}}}\\
N + E_{\underline{\mathrm{int}}} &= E_{\underline{\mathrm{int}}}\\
E_{\underline{\mathrm{int}}} * N &= E_{\underline{\mathrm{int}}}\\
N * E_{\underline{\mathrm{int}}} &= E_{\underline{\mathrm{int}}}\\
E_{\underline{\mathrm{int}}} - N &= E_{\underline{\mathrm{int}}}\\
N - E_{\underline{\mathrm{int}}} &= E_{\underline{\mathrm{int}}}.
\end{aligned}$$

(Actually, not all these equations are necessary.) Last, we must take the 11 equations of Example 9 (elements of $\mathcal{E}_{\underline{\mathrm{int}}}$) and condition them. It will be easier to anticipate the general method; thus we add the equation

$$\mathrm{IFOK}_{w,\underline{\mathrm{int}}}(y_1, \ldots, y_n, L) = \mathrm{IFOK}_{w,\underline{\mathrm{int}}}(y_1, \ldots, y_n, R)$$

for each $e = \langle L, R \rangle \in \mathcal{E}_{\underline{\mathrm{int}}}$, where $w = \mathrm{rank}(e)$ and $y_1, \ldots, y_n$ are the variables in e.

Now assume we are given a specification $\langle S, \Sigma, \mathcal{E} \rangle$ with $\underline{\mathrm{bool}} \in S$ protected (if $\underline{\mathrm{bool}} \notin S$, let it be added with the specification of Example 7). We define a specification

$\langle S, \bar{\Sigma}, \bar{\mathcal{E}}\rangle$. First $\bar{\Sigma}$ differs from Σ by the addition, for each $s \in S$, of

$$E_s \quad \text{to } \Sigma_{\lambda, s}$$
$$\text{OK}_s \quad \text{to } \Sigma_{s, \underline{\text{bool}}}$$
$$\text{IFE}_s \quad \text{to } \Sigma_{\underline{\text{bool}}\, ss, s}$$

plus the derived IFOK operators. Now we let $\bar{\mathcal{E}}$ contain the equations ($\underline{\text{ife}_s}$) for IFE_s as given above, plus

$\underline{\text{ok}_s}$ $\quad \text{OK}_s(E_s) = F \quad$ for each $s \in S$

$\underline{\text{ok}_\sigma}$ $\quad \text{OK}_s(\sigma(y_1, \ldots, y_n)) = \text{OK}_w(y_1, \ldots, y_w) \quad$ for each $\sigma \in \Sigma_{w,s}$.

Note that ok_σ includes, for the special case $w = \lambda$, the equations

$$\text{OK}_s(\sigma) = T \qquad \text{for each } \sigma \in \Sigma_{\lambda, s}, \qquad s \in S$$

$\underline{\text{error-prop}_{\sigma,i}}$ $\quad \sigma(y_1, \ldots, E_{si}, \ldots, y_n) = E_s$

for each $\sigma \in \Sigma_{w,s}$ and $1 \le i \le n$

$\underline{\text{ifok}_e}$ $\quad \text{IFOK}_{w,s}(L) = \text{IFOK}_{w,s}(R)$

for each $e = \langle L, R\rangle \in \mathcal{E}_s$, $s \in S$, $w = \text{arity}(e)$.

(The omission of y's in $\underline{\text{ifok}_e}$ is just notational convenience.)

We are now ready to state

Proposition 7

Let $\langle S, \Sigma, \mathcal{E}\rangle$ be a specification with $\underline{\text{bool}} \in S$ protected, and define $\langle S, \bar{\Sigma}, \bar{\mathcal{E}}\rangle$ as above. Let $A_s = (T_{\Sigma,\mathcal{E}})_s \cup \{E_s\}$ for $s \in S$, and for $\sigma \in \Sigma_{w,s}$, $w = s_1 \ldots s_n$, $t_i \in A_{s_i}$, define

$$\sigma_A(t_1, \ldots, t_n) = \begin{cases} E_s & \text{if any } t_i = E_{s_i} \\ \sigma_T(t_1, \ldots, t_n) & \text{otherwise} \end{cases}$$

(where σ_T is σ in $T_{\Sigma,\mathcal{E}}$); for $s \in S$, $t \in A_s$,

$$\text{OK}_{s,A}(t) = \begin{cases} F & \text{if } t = E_s \\ T & \text{otherwise;} \end{cases}$$

and for $b \in A_{\underline{\text{bool}}} = \{T, F, E_{\underline{\text{bool}}}\}$ (the equality holds since $\underline{\text{bool}}$ is protected) and $t_1, t_2 \in A_s$,

$$\text{IFE}_{s,A}(b, t_1, t_2) = \begin{cases} t_1 & \text{if } b = T \\ t_2 & \text{if } b = F \\ E_s & \text{if } b = E_{\underline{\text{bool}}}. \end{cases}$$

Then A is an initial $(\bar{\Sigma}, \bar{\mathcal{E}})$-algebra (i.e., is isomorphic to $T_{\bar{\Sigma},\bar{\mathcal{E}}}$).

Things get more interesting when the type being specified generates error messages, as it is necessary to properly coordinate the general error axioms with those special to the specification at hand. We shall illustrate this with

Example 16

We specify stack(int), a pushdown stack for integers, such that if one asks for the TOP of the empty stack (denoted λ), one gets the error message $E_{\underline{\text{int}}}$. Thus, we need inte as in Example 9E, and of course boole, upon which inte relies. The signature, showing only the operations not already included in Examples 9 or 9E, is in Figure 5.3.15 [in which $\underline{st}$ abbreviates stack(int) and e's are added to int

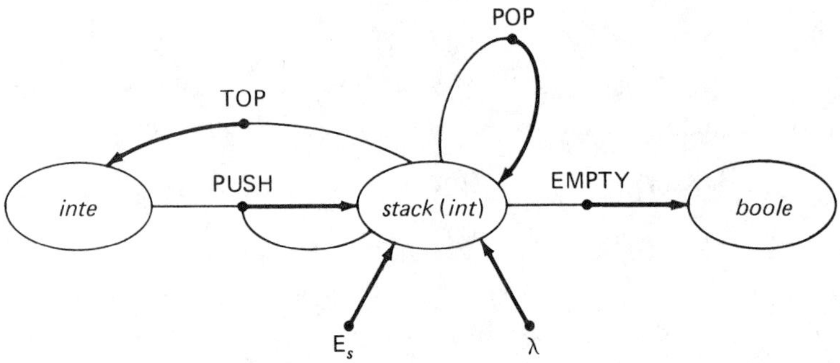

Figure 5.3.15

and bool for emphasis]. [Incidentally, stack(int) is *not* intended to permit stacking errors of sort int and has only its single error message $E_{\underline{st}}$.] We shall be working with the signature $\bar{\Sigma}$, which includes all the above, everything in Examples 9 and 9E, plus $OK_{\underline{st}}$, $IFE_{\underline{st}}$, and whatever derived operators are needed.

We first give the "usual" axioms for a stack, but in error-conditioned form (omitting subscripts on the IFOK's):

stack-1 $\quad \text{IFOK}(I, S, \text{TOP}(\text{PUSH}(I, S))) = \text{IFOK}(I, S, I)$

stack-2 $\quad \text{IFOK}(I, S, \text{POP}(\text{PUSH}(I, S))) = \text{IFOK}(I, S, S)$

stack-3 $\quad \text{EMPTY}(\lambda) = T$

stack-4 $\quad \text{IFOK}(I, S, \text{EMPTY}(\text{PUSH}(I, S))) = \text{IFOK}(I, S, F)$

stack-5 $\quad \text{POP}(\lambda) = \lambda$

stack-6 $\quad \text{TOP}(\lambda) = E_{\underline{\text{int}}}.$

We shall also accept all the error axioms given in Example 9E, but if we were to accept all those delivered by the general construction of Proposition 7, among them would be

$$(*) \qquad OK_{\underline{\text{int}}}(\text{TOP}(S)) = OK_{\underline{st}}(S),$$

which is in blatant conflict with stack-6, in that they could together violate protection of bool, since

$$\text{OK}(\text{TOP}(\lambda)) = \text{OK}(\lambda) = T \qquad \text{by } (*)$$

while

$$\text{OK}(\text{TOP}(\lambda)) = \text{OK}(E_{\underline{\text{int}}}) = F \qquad \text{by stack-6}$$

so that

$$T = F.$$

Actually, *all* the other axioms delivered by the general construction are desirable; for completeness, we list those not already in Example 9E, starting with

$$\mathrm{OK}_{\underline{st}}(E_{\underline{st}}) = F$$
$$\mathrm{OK}_{\underline{st}}(\lambda) = T$$
$$\mathrm{OK}_{\underline{st}}(\mathrm{PUSH}(I, S)) = \mathrm{OK}_{\underline{\mathrm{int}}}(I) \wedge \mathrm{OK}_{\underline{st}}(S)$$
$$\mathrm{OK}_{\underline{st}}(\mathrm{POP}(S)) = \mathrm{OK}_{\underline{st}}(S)$$
$$\mathrm{OK}_{\underline{\mathrm{bool}}}(\mathrm{EMPTY}(S)) = \mathrm{OK}_{\underline{st}}(S)$$

for "ok propagation." Next, the "error-propagation" axioms:

$$\mathrm{PUSH}(E_{\underline{\mathrm{int}}}, S) = E_{\underline{st}}$$
$$\mathrm{PUSH}(I, E_{\underline{st}}) = E_{\underline{st}}$$
$$\mathrm{POP}(E_{\underline{st}}) = E_{\underline{st}}$$
$$\mathrm{TOP}(E_{\underline{st}}) = E_{\underline{\mathrm{int}}}$$
$$\mathrm{EMPTY}(E_{\underline{st}}) = E_{\underline{\mathrm{bool}}}.$$

There are some interesting—and perhaps surprising—points about this specification. First, one might worry that without the unfortunate equation (*), bool will be polluted with a lot of new terms of the form OK(TOP(S)). However, this is not the case, since every term of the form TOP(S) is either $E_{\underline{\mathrm{int}}}$ (when $S = \lambda$) or else of the form I [when $S = \mathrm{PUSH}(I, S')$ and $S' \neq E_{\underline{st}}$]. Second, one might well think that some (conditioned) form of the equation

$$\mathrm{PUSH}(\mathrm{TOP}(S), \mathrm{POP}(S)) = S$$

is needed. However, the correct value of the left-hand side can always be found from other equations already in the specification, so this troublesome creature is not needed after all.

Next, one might perfectly well replace stack-5 by the equation

$$\underline{\text{stack}}\text{-7} \qquad \mathrm{POP}(\lambda) = E_{\underline{st}},$$

which would conflict with the error equation

$$(**) \qquad \mathrm{OK}(\mathrm{POP}(S)) = \mathrm{OK}(S)$$

(giving, as before, $T = F$ in violation of bool for $S = \lambda$). And once again, the answer is just to drop (**) iff stack-7 is added; this works because every term of the form POP(S) is either E_s (for $S = \lambda$ or $E_{\underline{st}}$), or λ [for $S = \mathrm{PUSH}(/I, \lambda)$], or else $\mathrm{PUSH}(I', S')$ [for $S = \mathrm{PUSH}(I, \mathrm{PUSH}(I', S'))$ and $S' \neq E_{\underline{st}}$]. These points will (presumably) be clearer in the light of the correctness proof to be given in Section 5.4.

Note the minor difference of this form of stack from the "usual," which performs TOP and POP simultaneously; i.e., it has an operation $\underline{\text{stack}} \longrightarrow \underline{\text{stack}}$

int, which we have instead taken as separate components, designated POP and TOP. Actually, there is no difficulty in permitting tuple-valued operations in our formalism if we want to, but it is more convenient to develop this in the context of "algebraic theories" [cf. Goguen (1976)] than to employ signatures of the form $\Sigma = \langle \Sigma_{w,w'} \rangle_{w,w' \in S^* \times S^+}$, though this certainly could be done.

It will probably not have escaped the reader's attention that the resulting total specification in Example 9E is unbelievably complicated. It is also unnecessarily complicated. But please remember that our point has been to discuss the kinds of difficulties which arise in a rigorous treatment of errors. We give a much more satisfactory treatment of this example in Goguen (1977), plus several others, using the notion of an error algebra, thus demonstrating that the quagmire exposed in this section can in fact be escaped.

5.3.6. Parameterized Specifications

The most important technique for creating new types from old is what we call *parameterized specifications*. The idea is to generalize constructions like those of Section 5.3.4 so that, for example, one specifies string(d) independently of how d is specified. The general theory required for this cannot be included here; we shall confine ourselves to examples but hope to give the subject the treatment it deserves elsewhere.

Example 17

Assume that we are given a specification $\langle S, \Sigma, \mathcal{E} \rangle$ with $\underline{\text{bool}} \in S$ protected, $d \in S$, and EQ $\in \Sigma_{dd,\underline{\text{bool}}}$ equality, and not involving errors. We now specify $\underline{\text{set}}(d)$, the abstract data type of finite sets of elements from d. The signature adds to $\langle S, \Sigma, \mathcal{E} \rangle$ the operations of Figure 5.3.16. We shall use the usual infix notation for union, that is, $S \cup S'$ instead of $\cup(S, S')$. Similarly, we shall use the

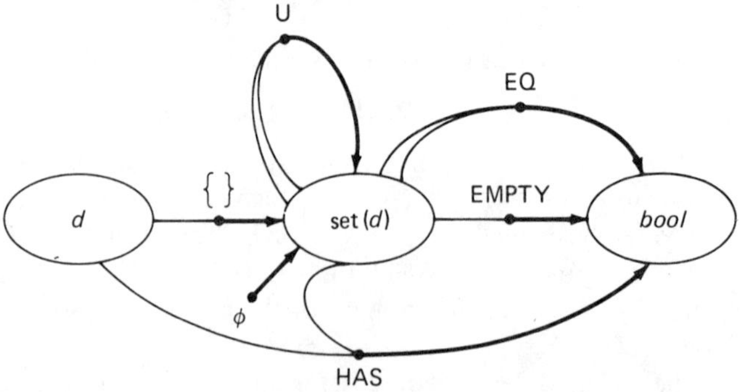

Figure 5.3.16

usual *outfix* notation for singleton, that is, $\{D\}$ instead of $\{\ \}(D)$. Then the equations are

set-1	$\varnothing \cup S = S$
set-2	$(S \cup S') \cup S'' = S \cup (S' \cup S'')$
set-3	$S \cup S' = S' \cup S$
set-4	$S \cup S = S$
set-5	$\text{EMPTY}(\varnothing) = T$
set-6	$\text{EMPTY}(\{D\} \cup S) = F$
set-7	$\text{HAS}(D, \varnothing) = F$
set-8	$\text{HAS}(D, \{D'\} \cup S) = \text{HAS}(D, S) \vee \text{EQ}(D, D')$
set-9	$\text{EQ}(S, S) = T$
set-10	$\text{EQ}(S, S') = \text{EQ}(S', S)$
set-11	$\text{EQ}(\{D\} \cup S, S') = \text{IF HAS}(D, S') \text{ THEN EQ}(\{D\} \cup S, S') \text{ ELSE } F.$

The conditional in set-11 is the usual one, but the definition of equality is a bit tricky; in particular, set-11 really says nothing at all if HAS(D, S') is true. Note that set-8 uses EQ on d; EQ $\in \Sigma_{dd,\text{bool}}$ is an equality iff for all $D, D' \in T_\Sigma$, $\text{EQ}(D, D') \equiv_{\mathcal{E}} T$ if $D \equiv_{\mathcal{E}} D'$ in T_Σ, and $\text{EQ}(D, D') \equiv_{\mathcal{E}} F$ otherwise. Because of this last (completeness) requirement, it is not always possible to specify an equality predicate on an abstract data type.

Now we have a parameterized specification which does involve error messages.

Example 18

We assume we are given a specification $\langle S, \Sigma, \mathcal{E}\rangle$ of $d \in S$, with boole $\in S$ protected and with error messages E_s, error conditions IFE$_s$, and error predicates OK$_s$ in Σ for each sort $s \in S$; if they aren't there, add them using Proposition 7. We specify stack(d). The signature $\bar{\Sigma}$ is as given in Figure 5.3.17 plus Σ,

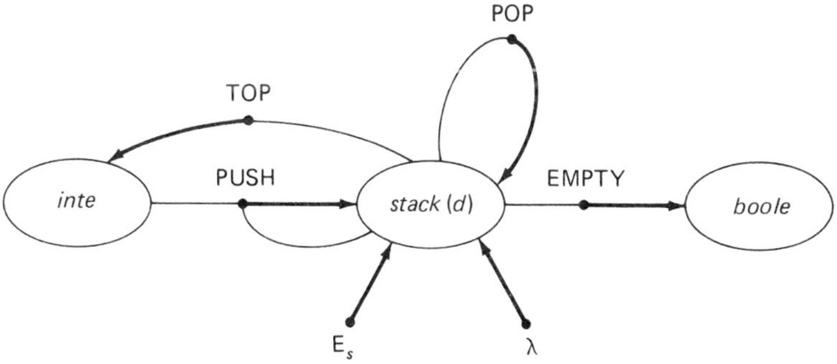

Figure 5.3.17

and the equations in $\bar{\mathcal{E}}$ are the following: those in $\mathcal{E}$; error-conditioned versions of the axioms stack-1, 2, 3, 4, 5, 6 of Example 16; plus exactly the ok-propagation and error-propagation axioms given in Example 16 but with int systematically replaced by d. In fact, the only significant difference between this example and that is in the setting up, which assumes that d is already specified and that errors have already been handled for it, so that we can just toss its specification into that of stack(d) without worrying. (In case you are still worrying, we shall give a proof that this works in Section 5.4.)

Actually, there are points of view from which it is more profitable to view parameterized types as functors on appropriate categories of many-sorted theories [see Goguen (1976) for some discussion], but we are unable to pursue this topic here.

5.4. CORRECTNESS OF SPECIFICATIONS

Sometimes there is a previously existing standard mathematical model for an abstract data type, for example, integer, set, and string. Some other data types were first defined by computer scientists, often intuitively or in terms of an implementation; among these are stack, S-expression, deque, and symbol table. For such examples, there may be a more or less acceptable mathematical model. In other cases, to produce such a model might be a major undertaking. In still other cases, the type is highly specialized and is being defined by the user specifically for his program, e.g., gas-station.

When there is an existing mathematical standard for an abstract data type, a rigorous proof of the correctness of the algebraic specification is possible and necessary. When the mathematical model is not entirely well defined, it can be clarified in the process of validating an algebraic specification. For highly specialized or complex types particularly—but also for simpler ones[12]—the problem of validating the specification itself is of paramount importance. In simulation problems (such as were particularly addressed by SIMULA 67) details of the specification are sensitive, since the program behavior is often unknown; indeed, it is what one wrote the program to find out!

Our purpose in this section is to show how ordinary mathematical methods can be applied to show correctness of specifications which already have accepted mathematical models. The basic idea is that a specification $(\Sigma, \mathcal{E})$ is correct if $T_{\Sigma,\mathcal{E}}$ is isomorphic to the mathematical model. We shall illustrate this in several examples from the previous sections.

The correctness proofs can be viewed the other way around. That is, we can assume that $(\Sigma, \mathcal{E})$ is correct and then prove a model is correct by showing it is isomorphic to $T_{\Sigma,\mathcal{E}}$.

[12]ADJ, as embarrassingly pointed out by Zilles (1975, 1977), has been responsible for errors even for seemingly simple types.

To make these ideas clearer, we shall first prove the correctness of nat (Example 1). This special case does not require the machinery developed in the next subsection.

Example 1C

In Section 5.2 we claimed that the signature $\Sigma = \{0\}, \{\text{SUCC}\}, \varnothing, \ldots, \varnothing, \ldots$ with $\mathcal{E} = \varnothing$ specifies the natural numbers (with successor); that is, letting ω denote the set $\{0, 1, 2, \ldots\}$ of natural numbers we claimed that the Σ-algebra A with carrier ω, $0_A = 0$, and $\text{SUCC}_A\colon n \mapsto n + 1$ is an initial Σ-algebra.

We shall give two proofs of this. The first seems somewhat informal in that it depends on familiarity with the natural numbers and successor. The second is closer to the mathematical foundations in that it shows that an alternative characterization of the natural numbers (Peano's axioms) defines the same isomorphism class of algebras (the same abstract data type).

Proof 1: A is clearly a Σ-algebra; thus there exists a (unique) homomorphism $h\colon T_\Sigma \longrightarrow A$. We claim that for each $n \in \omega$, $h(\text{SUCC}^n(0)) = n$ [where $\text{SUCC}^0(0) = 0$ and $\text{SUCC}^{n+1}(0) = \text{SUCC}(\text{SUCC}^n(0))$]. This follows by mathematical induction: Since h is a homorphism, we have $h(0) = 0_A = 0$, and if $h(\text{SUCC}^n(0)) = n$, then $h(\text{SUCC}^{n+1}(0)) = h(\text{SUCC}(\text{SUCC}^n(0))) = \text{SUCC}_A(h(\text{SUCC}^n(0))) = \text{SUCC}_A(n) = n + 1$. Thus we know h is onto; it is one to one since $n = p$ implies $\text{SUCC}^n(0) = \text{SUCC}^p(0)$. Thus h is an isomorphism.

The reader may well want to skip the following proof, which is much more specific in its assumptions about ω and successor.

Proof 2: In fact, let us assume[13]

P.1. SUCC_A is a function; i.e., for each $n \in \omega$, $n + 1$ is uniquely determined.

P.2. $0 \in \omega$, and for all $n \in \omega$, $n + 1 \neq 0$.

P.3. $n + 1 = p + 1$ implies $n = p$.

P.4. For any $M \subseteq \omega$, if $0 \in M$ and $n \in M$ imply $n + 1 \in M$, then $M = \omega$.

Now for the proof. Because SUCC_A is a function (P.1) and $0 \in \omega$ (P.2), we see that A is a Σ-algebra. And since T_Σ is initial, there exists a (unique) Σ-homomorphism $h\colon T_\Sigma \longrightarrow A$, by Theorem 2. What we must show is that h is one-to-one and onto.

To see that h is onto, let $M \subseteq \omega$ be the image of h, $M = \{h(t) \mid t \in T_\Sigma\}$. Then h is onto iff $M = \omega$. Since h is a Σ-homomorphism, $h(0) = 0_A = 0$; thus $0 \in M$. On the other hand, if $n \in M$ and $h(t) = n$, then

$$\begin{aligned} h(\text{SUCC}(t)) &= \text{SUCC}_A(h(t)) && \text{def. homomorphism} \\ &= \text{SUCC}_A(n) && \text{assumption} \\ &= n + 1 && \text{def. } \text{SUCC}_A. \end{aligned}$$

[13] The reader may recognize that P.1–P.4 are Peano's axioms for the natural numbers.

Thus $n \in M$ implies $n + 1 \in M$; therefore $M = \omega$ by P.4.

To see that h is one-to-one, let M be the set of all $n \in \omega$ such that there *do not* exist $t, t' \in T_\Sigma$ such that $t \neq t'$ but $h(t) = h(t') = n$. Then h is one-to-one iff $M = \omega$. We show $M = \omega$ by induction (P.4).

To show that $0 \in M$, assume the contrary, that $0 \notin M$. Then there exist $t, t' \in T_\Sigma$ such that $t \neq t'$ but $h(t) = h(t') = 0$. Since $h(0) = 0$, we can assume $t = 0$. Then, $t' \neq 0$, so it must be of the form SUCC(t'') for some $t'' \in T_\Sigma$. But then

$$0 = h(t') = h(\text{SUCC}(t'')) = \text{SUCC}_A(h(t'')) = h(t'') + 1,$$

so $0 = h(t'') + 1$, contradicting P.2; thus $0 \in M$.

Now assume $n \in M$. If $n + 1 \notin M$, there must exist $t, t' \in T_\Sigma$ such that $h(t) = h(t') = n + 1$. But $t, t' \neq 0$ [since $h(0) = 0 \neq n + 1$ by P.2], so there must exist $t_1, t_1' \in T_\Sigma$ with $t_1 \neq t_1'$ and such that $t = \text{SUCC}(t_1)$ and $t' = \text{SUCC}(t_1')$. This gives us

$$\begin{aligned} h(t_1) + 1 &= h(\text{SUCC}(t_1)) = h(t) \\ &= n + 1 = h(t') = h(\text{SUCC}(t_1')) = h(t_1') + 1. \end{aligned}$$

Therefore $h(t_1) + 1 = n + 1 = h(t') + 1$, which yields $h(t_1) = n = h(t_1')$ by P.3, contradicting $n \in M$. Thus $0 \in M$, and $n \in M$ implies $n + 1 \in M$. Finally, $M = \omega$ by P.4, and the proof is complete.

5.4.1. Canonical Term Algebras

The first proof of the correctness of nat exhibited an isomorphism between an algebra of terms and a known mathematical structure. In that case there were no equations so the term algebra we used was just T_Σ.

To prove correctness of some more complicated specifications, we shall develop some special methods for treating canonical representatives of equivalence classes of terms (that is, elements of $T_{\Sigma,\mathcal{E}}$). The idea is to get one concrete $(\Sigma, \mathcal{E})$-algebra C whose carriers consist of *canonical terms* and then to show that C is isomorphic to the mathematical model A. Since (by the result to be given) $C \cong T_{\Sigma,\mathcal{E}}$, we conclude that $A \cong T_{\Sigma,\mathcal{E}}$, as desired. Note also that since we know C satisfies $\mathcal{E}$, we do not have to verify that A does if $A \cong C$ is a Σ-isomorphism.

Of course, this may not be the only way to prove correctness of specifications, but it is heavily used in what follows.

If $\langle S, \Sigma, \mathcal{E} \rangle$ is a specification, then there always exists an initial $(\Sigma, \mathcal{E})$-algebra A whose carriers are Σ-terms; one need only choose a single representative t^* of each equivalence class $[t]$ in $T_{\Sigma,\mathcal{E}}$ and define the operations by $\sigma_A(t_1^*, \ldots, t_n^*) = (\sigma(t_1 \ldots t_n))^*$ In principle, the choice of representatives is totally arbitrary, but in practice one needs to make the selection in some disciplined way so that the structure of the terms can be exploited in proofs. The following definition provides such a discipline.

Definition 10. We say that a Σ-algebra C is a *canonical Σ-term algebra* if $C_s \subseteq T_{\Sigma,s}$ for each $s \in S$, and if $\sigma(t_1 \ldots t_n) \in C$, then $t_i \in C$ and $\sigma_C(t_1, \ldots, t_n) = \sigma(t_1 \ldots t_n)$.

When tackling a given specification one naturally tends to select a canonical term algebra as a candidate for an initial algebra; what is perhaps surprising is that one always exists.

Theorem 8

Let $\langle S, \Sigma, \mathcal{E} \rangle$ be a specification; then there exists an initial $(\Sigma, \mathcal{E})$-algebra C which is a canonical term algebra.

The proof of Theorem 8 [see the appendix (Section 5.6)] gives no prescription for constructing a canonical term algebra. In correctness proofs one generally has a good idea what kind of terms should serve as representatives, and the following result is the key for checking that the proposed term algebra is initial.

Theorem 9

Let $\langle S, \Sigma, \mathcal{E} \rangle$ be a specification, and let C be a canonical Σ-term algebra. Then $C \cong T_{\Sigma,\mathcal{E}}$ iff

(1) C satisfies $\mathcal{E}$, and

(2) For each $\sigma \in \Sigma_{s_1 \ldots s_n, s}$ and $t_i \in C_{s_i}$,

$$\sigma(t_1 \ldots t_n) \equiv_{\mathcal{E}} \sigma_C(t_1, \ldots, t_n).$$

Again, the proof is in the appendix, but some discussion may help clarify applications of Theorem 9 to correctness proofs. It is usually quite clear how to construct a canonical term algebra C which satisfies $\mathcal{E}$; most of the work comes in verifying condition (2) of Theorem 9 to show that C is initial. Let $h: T_\Sigma \longrightarrow C$ be the unique homomorphism guaranteed by Theorem 2. Then an argument by structural induction on Σ-terms with condition (2) shows that for all $t \in T_\Sigma$, $t \equiv_{\mathcal{E}} h(t)$; that is, t is in fact congruent to its intended canonical representative. So verification of (2) amounts to showing that the canonical terms *represent* $\equiv_{\mathcal{E}}$-classes. We call (2) the *representation condition.*

Whereas Theorem 9 provides a general methodology for proving initiality (thus correctness), the following corollary is useful for the case of enrichments.

Corollary 10

Let $\langle S, \Sigma, \mathcal{E} \rangle$ be a specification, let $\langle S, \bar{\Sigma}, \bar{\mathcal{E}} \rangle$ be a specification such that $\Sigma \subseteq \bar{\Sigma}$ and $\mathcal{E} \subseteq \bar{\mathcal{E}}$, and let A be an initial $(\Sigma, \mathcal{E})$-algebra of canonical terms. Then a $\bar{\Sigma}$-algebra $\bar{A}$ such that

(a) $\bar{A}_s = A_s$ for each $s \in S$, and

(b) $\sigma_{\bar{A}} = \sigma_A$ for each $\sigma \in \Sigma$

is an initial $(\bar{\Sigma}, \bar{\mathcal{E}})$-algebra, and $\langle S, \bar{\Sigma}, \bar{\mathcal{E}}\rangle$ is an enrichment of $\langle S, \Sigma, \mathcal{E}\rangle$ if

(1) $\bar{A}$ satisfies $\bar{\mathcal{E}} - \mathcal{E}$, and

(2) For each $\sigma \in (\bar{\Sigma}_{s_1 \ldots s_n, s} - \Sigma_{s_1 \ldots s_n, s})$ and all $t_i \in A_{s_i}$,

$$\sigma(t_1 \ldots t_n) \equiv_{\bar{\mathcal{E}}} \sigma_{\bar{A}}(t_1, \ldots, t_n).$$

The idea behind using Corollary 10 is that you have an initial algebra A of canonical Σ-terms and make it into a $\bar{\Sigma}$ algebra by defining the operations corresponding to new operator symbols in $\bar{\Sigma} - \Sigma$. If you do this in such a way that (1) and (2) are satisfied, then Corollary 10 says that the algebra so constructed is an initial $(\bar{\Sigma}, \bar{\mathcal{E}})$-algebra.

5.4.2. Examples without Errors[14]

We shall now exploit the results of the previous subsection for a number of the less complicated examples from Section 5.3. In the process, a number of interesting points about the method of canonical terms are illustrated.

Example 6C

The correctness proof for the data type string-of-A depends heavily on how one conceives of strings. Informally, the algebra M in question has carrier A^* (the set of strings on A); one constant, λ_M (the empty string); and one operation, CONCAT_M (concatenation of strings).

Some authors define A^* as the carrier of the free monoid generated by A, CONCAT_M as the operation of that monoid, and λ_M as the unit of the monoid. In this case there is nothing to prove, since $T_{\Sigma,\mathcal{E}}$ *is* the free monoid generated by A.

On the other hand, using an intuitive view of A^*, we can identify each element m of A^* with a *canonical representative* $\rho(m)$ in T_Σ as follows:

I-1 $\rho(\lambda) = \lambda$

I-2 $\rho(a) = a$

I-3 $\rho(aw) = \text{CONCAT}(a, \rho(w))$,

so that $\rho(a_1 \ldots a_n) = \text{CONCAT}(a_1, \text{CONCAT}(a_2, \ldots \text{CONCAT}(a_{n-1}, a_n) \ldots))$. We then make the set $\{\rho(m) \mid m \in A^*\}$ of representatives into a Σ-algebra C by

C-1 $\lambda_C = \rho(\lambda) = \lambda$

C-2 $a_C = \rho(a) = a$

C-3 $\text{CONCAT}_C(\rho(m), \rho(m')) = \rho(mm')$.

Now the function ρ is surjective by definition, is obviously injective, and is a

[14]Hopefully!

homomorphism by C-1, 2, 3. Thus A^* and C are isomorphic Σ-algebras, and because A^* satisfies the equations in $\mathcal{E}$, so does C. Moreover, C is a canonical Σ-term algebra, because

$$\lambda_C = \lambda;\ a_C = a;$$

and for CONCAT$(a, \rho(w))$, $a \in C$, $\rho(w) \in C$, and

$$\text{CONCAT}_C(a, \rho(w)) = \text{CONCAT}_C(\rho(a), \rho(w)) = \rho(aw) = \text{CONCAT}(a, \rho(w)).$$

To apply Theorem 9, we have to show that condition (2) of its hypothesis holds. But $\lambda_C = \lambda$ and $a_C = a$, so $\lambda_C \equiv \lambda$ and $a_C \equiv a$. Now, for concatenation, we show $\text{CONCAT}(\rho(w_1), \rho(w_2)) \equiv \text{CONCAT}_C(\rho(w_1), \rho(w_2))$ by induction on the length of w_1:

$$\begin{array}{rlr}
\text{CONCAT}(\rho(\lambda), \rho(w_2)) & = \text{CONCAT}(\lambda, \rho(w_2)) & \text{I-1} \\
& \equiv \rho(w_2) & \text{string-1} \\
& = \text{CONCAT}_C(\rho(\lambda), \rho(w_2)) & \text{C-3} \\
\text{CONCAT}(\rho(a), \rho(w_2)) & = \text{CONCAT}(a, \rho(w_2)) & \text{I-2} \\
& = \rho(aw_2) & \text{I-3} \\
& = \text{CONCAT}_C(\rho(a), \rho(w_2)) & \text{C-3} \\
\text{CONCAT}(\rho(aw_1), \rho(w_2)) & = \text{CONCAT}(\text{CONCAT}(a, \rho(w_1)), \rho(w_2)) & \text{I-3} \\
& \equiv \text{CONCAT}(a, \text{CONCAT}(\rho(w_1), \rho(w_2))) & \text{string-2} \\
& \equiv \text{CONCAT}(a, \text{CONCAT}_C(\rho(w_1), \rho(w_2)) & \text{induction} \\
& = \text{CONCAT}(a, \rho(w_1 w_2)) & \text{C-3} \\
& = \rho(aw_1 w_2) & \text{I-3} \\
& = \text{CONCAT}_C(\rho(aw_1), \rho(w_2)) & \text{C-3.}
\end{array}$$

Thus the hypotheses of Theorem 9 are met, and C (and thus A^*) is initial; thus the specification is correct.

Example 7C

To show bool correct, we use Corollary 10, by making the canonical Σ-term algebra T_Σ (of Example 4) into a $\bar{\Sigma}$-algebra ($\bar{\Sigma} = \{T, F\}, \{\neg\}, \{\wedge\}, \varnothing, \ldots$), calling it C.

B	$\neg_C B$
T	F
F	T

B	B'	$B \wedge_C B'$
T	T	T
T	F	F
F	T	F
F	F	F

Recall that the equations $\bar{\mathcal{E}}$ for bool (with operations) are

bool-1	$\neg T = F$
bool-2	$\neg(\neg B) = B$
bool-3	$T \wedge B = B$
bool-4	$F \wedge B = F$
bool-5	$B \wedge B' = B' \wedge B.$

C clearly satisfies $\bar{\mathcal{E}}$. We need to verify the representation condition:

$\neg T \equiv F = \neg_C(T)$	bool-1
$\neg F \equiv \neg(\neg T) \equiv T \neg_C(F)$	bool-1, 2
$T \wedge T \equiv T = T \wedge_C T$	bool-3
$T \wedge F \equiv F = T \wedge_C F$	bool-3
$F \wedge B \equiv F = F \wedge_C B$	bool-4

By Corollary 10, C is the initial $(\bar{\Sigma}, \bar{\mathcal{E}})$-algebra, and since this is (isomorphic to) our intended algebra, the specification of bool is correct. Note that bool-5 is not used and therefore is not needed in the specification.

Example 8C

We know nat is correct (Example 1C), and we intend the specification of Example 8 to be an enrichment of nat by various arithmetic operations. We'll prove the correctness of the specification for $+$ and $*$ (leaving the others to the reader) by defining the operations on canonical terms and using Corollary 10.

As in Example 6C, we use the method of explicitly describing the canonical representative $\rho(n)$ of each natural number n:

I-1	$\rho(0) = 0$
I-2	$\rho(n+1) = \mathrm{SUCC}(\rho(n)).$

Then we feel free to use what we know about arithmetic to define the operations on canonical terms:

C-0	$0_C = \rho(0)$
C-1	$\mathrm{SUCC}_C(\rho(n)) = \rho(n+1)$
C-2	$\rho(n) +_C \rho(n') = \rho(n+n')$
C-3	$\rho(n) *_C \rho(n') = \rho(n * n').$

The equations for nat (with $+$ and $*$) are

nat-5	$N + 0 = N$
nat-6	$N + \mathrm{SUCC}(N') = \mathrm{SUCC}(N + N')$
nat-7	$N * 0 = 0$
nat-8	$N * \mathrm{SUCC}(N') = N + (N * N')$

Again it is clear that the operations $+_C$ and $*_C$ satisfy these equations. For the representation condition, we need to prove

$$(*) \qquad \rho(n) + \rho(n') \equiv \rho(n) +_C \rho(n')$$

and

$$(**) \qquad \rho(n) * \rho(n') \equiv \rho(n) *_C \rho(n')$$

for all $n, n' \in \omega$. This we do by induction (which we are also free to use) on n', first for $(*)$, and $n' = 0$:

$$\begin{aligned} \rho(n) + \rho(0) &= \rho(n) + 0 && \text{I-1} \\ &\equiv \rho(n) && \underline{\text{nat}}\text{-5} \\ &= \rho(n + 0) && \text{arithmetic} \\ &= \rho(n) +_C \rho(0) && \text{C-2.} \end{aligned}$$

Assuming $(*)$ for n', we consider $n' + 1$:

$$\begin{aligned} \rho(n) + \rho(n' + 1) &= \rho(n) + \text{SUCC}(\rho(n')) && \text{I-2} \\ &\equiv \text{SUCC}(\rho(n) + \rho(n')) && \underline{\text{nat}}\text{-6} \\ &\equiv \text{SUCC}(\rho(n) +_C \rho(n')) && \text{induction} \\ &= \text{SUCC}(\rho(n + n')) && \text{C-2} \\ &= \rho(n + n' + 1) && \text{I-2} \\ &= \rho(n) +_C \rho(n' + 1) && \text{C-2.} \end{aligned}$$

This completes the induction for plus; for times we do the same thing but we need to use $(*)$ in the proof:

$$\begin{aligned} \rho(n) * \rho(0) &= \rho(n) * 0 && \text{I-1} \\ &\equiv 0 && \underline{\text{nat}}\text{-7} \\ &= \rho(n * 0) && \text{I-1} \\ &= \rho(n) *_C \rho(0) && \text{C-3.} \end{aligned}$$

And now the inductive step:

$$\begin{aligned} \rho(n) * \rho(n' + 1) &= \rho(n) * \text{SUCC}(\rho(n')) && \text{I-2} \\ &\equiv \rho(n) + (\rho(n) * \rho(n')) && \underline{\text{nat}}\text{-8} \\ &\equiv \rho(n) + (\rho(n) *_C \rho(n')) && \text{induction} \\ &= \rho(n) + \rho(n * n') && \text{C-3} \\ &\equiv \rho(n) +_C \rho(n + n') && (*) \\ &= \rho(n + n * n') && \text{C-2} \\ &= \rho(n * (n' + 1)) && \text{arithmetic} \\ &= \rho(n) *_C \rho(n' + 1) && \text{C-2.} \end{aligned}$$

This completes the second induction and the proof of (**); thus Corollary 10 applies and C is an initial $(\Sigma, \mathcal{E})$-algebra; it is isomorphic to the natural numbers under $+$, $*$ by construction.

Example 10C

We want to show that the specification of the predicate LE (less-than-or-equal) of Example 10 is correct. For this we use the canonical term algebras for nat and bool and the isomorphism ρ of the previous correctness proof, defining the predicate LE_C on nat in the blatently obvious way:

$$\text{C-4} \qquad \text{LE}_C(\rho(n), \rho(n')) = \begin{cases} T & \text{if } n \leq n' \\ F & \text{otherwise.} \end{cases}$$

Then, because this predicate obviously satisfies the equations, application of Corollary 10 rests on checking the representation condition,

$$(*) \qquad \text{LE}(\rho(n), \rho(n')) \equiv \text{LE}_C(\rho(n), \rho(n'))$$

for all n, n' in ω, where now $\mathcal{E}$ is

natle-1	$\text{LE}(0, N) = T$
natle-2	$\text{LE}(\text{SUCC}(N), 0) = F$
natle-3	$\text{LE}(\text{SUCC}(N), \text{SUCC}(N')) = \text{LE}(N, N')$.

The proof of (*) requires a double mathematical induction; that is, we prove (*) for $(0, n')$ and for $(n + 1, 0)$, and we prove that (*) for (n, n') implies (*) for $(n + 1, n' + 1)$. From this it follows, by mathematical induction, that (*) is true for all n and n':

$\text{LE}(\rho(0), \rho(n')) = \text{LE}(0, \rho(n'))$	I-1
$\equiv T$	natle-1
$= \text{LE}_C(0, \rho(n'))$	C-4
$\text{LE}(\rho(n+1), \rho(0)) = \text{LE}(\text{SUCC}(\rho(n)), 0)$	I-1, 2
$\equiv F$	natle-2
$= \text{LE}_C(\rho(n+1), \rho(0))$	C-4
$\text{LE}(\rho(n+1), \rho'(n+1)) = \text{LE}(\text{SUCC}(\rho(n)), \text{SUCC}(\rho(n')))$	I-2
$\equiv \text{LE}(\rho(n), \rho(n'))$	natle-3
$\equiv \text{LE}_C(\rho(n), \rho(n'))$	induction
$= \text{LE}_C(\rho(n+1), \rho(n'+1))$	C-4

Again Corollary 10 gives us that the term algebra with LE_C is initial, and by its definition, LE_C is the intended predicate.

5.4.3. Examples with Errors[15]

We have given, in Proposition 7 (Section 5.3) a general method for inserting error messages in already specified data types. The proof of Proposition 7, which is in the appendix (Section 5.6), is actually a general correctness of specification proof, but it needs the correctness of boole as a lemma because of its dependence on predicates and conditional equations. Therefore, both as an example and a requirement for the proof of Proposition 7, we shall tackle the correctness of boole.

The key to specifying the addition of error messages is the use of the conditionals IFE_s, the non-error tests, OK_s, and the associated derived operators, $\text{IFOK}_{w,s}$ and OK_w. The following equational version of the modus ponens rule of inference indicates that these operations are working as they should and greatly simplifies subsequent proofs.

Lemma 11

Let $\mathcal{E}$ be a set of equations containing the IFE-axiom,

$$\underline{\text{ife}}\text{-1} \qquad \text{IFE}(T, S, S') = S,$$

and a conditioned equation,

$$(*) \qquad \text{IFOK}_{w,s}(y_1, \ldots, y_n, L) = \text{IFOK}_{w,s}(y_1, \ldots, y_n, R),$$

where $\langle L, R \rangle$ is an equation of sort s with distinct variables $y_1, \ldots, y_n$ of sorts $w = s_1 \ldots s_n$, and

$$\underline{\text{ifok}_{w,s}} \qquad \text{IFOK}_{w,s}(y_1, \ldots, y_n, x) = \text{IFE}_s(\text{OK}_w(y_1, \ldots, y_n), x, E_s).$$

Then for any terms t_i of sort s_i, if

$$(**) \qquad \text{OK}_w(t_1, \ldots, t_n) \equiv T,$$

it follows that $L(t_1, \ldots, t_n) \equiv R(t_1, \ldots, t_n)$.

Proof: The proof amounts to just unfolding the derived operators and applying the simple IFE-equation:

$$\begin{aligned}
L(t_1, \ldots, t_n) &\equiv \text{IFE}_s(T, L(t_1, \ldots, t_n), E_s) && \underline{\text{ife}}\text{-1}\\
&\equiv \text{IFE}_s(\text{OK}_w(t_1, \ldots, t_n), L(t_1, \ldots, t_n), E_s) && (**)\\
&\equiv \text{IFOK}_{w,s}(t_1, \ldots, t_n, L(t_1, \ldots, t_n)) && \underline{\text{ifok}_{w,s}}\\
&\equiv \text{IFOK}_{w,s}(t_1, \ldots, t_n, R(t_1, \ldots, t_n)) && (*)\\
&\equiv \text{IFE}_s(\text{OK}_w(t_1, \ldots, t_n), R(t_1, \ldots, t_n), E_s) && \underline{\text{ifok}_{w,s}}\\
&\equiv \text{IFE}_s(T, R(t_1, \ldots, t_n), E_s) && (**)\\
&\equiv R(t_1, \ldots, t_n) && \underline{\text{ife}}\text{-1}.
\end{aligned}$$

[15] Let the reader beware!

Example 7EC

We want to show that the specification of boole is correct, that is, that it captures the idea of inserting an error message E into bool in such a way that the old operators, $\neg$ and $\wedge$, act as before on T and F.

Let $(\Sigma, \mathcal{E})$ be the specification for bool (as in Example 7) with $\Sigma = \{T, F\}, \{\neg\}, \{\wedge\}, \varnothing, \ldots$, and let A denote the initial $(\Sigma, \mathcal{E})$-algebra.

Let $(\bar{\Sigma}, \bar{\mathcal{E}})$ be the specification for boole; recall that

$$\bar{\Sigma} = \{T, F, E\}, \{\neg, \mathrm{OK}\}, \{\wedge\}, \{\mathrm{IFE}\}, \ldots$$

($\bar{\mathcal{E}}$ is given below). What we want to show is that the $\bar{\Sigma}$-algebra $\bar{A}$ with carrier $\bar{A} = \{T, F, E\}$ and

$$\bar{A}\text{-}0 \qquad T_{\bar{A}} = T, \qquad F_{\bar{A}} = F, \qquad E_{\bar{A}} = E$$

$$\bar{A}\text{-}1 \qquad \neg_{\bar{A}}(B) = \begin{cases} \neg_A(B) & \text{if } B = T \text{ or } F \\ E & \text{if } B = E \end{cases}$$

$$\bar{A}\text{-}2 \qquad B \wedge_{\bar{A}} B' = \begin{cases} B \wedge_A B' & \text{if } B, B' \in \{T, F\} \\ E & \text{if either } B = E \text{ or } B' = E \end{cases}$$

$$\bar{A}\text{-}3 \qquad \mathrm{OK}_{\bar{A}}(B) = \begin{cases} T & \text{if } B \in \{T, F\} \\ F & \text{if } B = E \end{cases}$$

$$\bar{A}\text{-}4 \qquad \mathrm{IFE}_{\bar{A}}(B, B', B'') = \begin{cases} B' & \text{if } B = T \\ B'' & \text{if } B = F \\ E & \text{if } B = E \end{cases}$$

is the initial $(\bar{\Sigma}, \bar{\mathcal{E}})$-algebra.

Since $\bar{A} \subseteq T_{\bar{\Sigma}}$, we can employ Theorem 9. That $\bar{A}$ is a canonical $\bar{\Sigma}$-term algebra is immediate. Now $\bar{\mathcal{E}}$ consists of the following equations:

ife-1	$\mathrm{IFE}(T, B, B') = B$
ife-2	$\mathrm{IFE}(F, B, B') = B'$
ife-3	$\mathrm{IFE}(E, B, B') = E$
ok-1	$\mathrm{OK}(T) = T$
ok-2	$\mathrm{OK}(F) = T$
ok-3	$\mathrm{OK}(E) = F$
ok-4	$\mathrm{OK}(\neg B) = \mathrm{OK}(B)$
ok-5	$\mathrm{OK}(B \wedge B') = \mathrm{OK}(B) \wedge \mathrm{OK}(B')$
er-1	$\neg(E) = E$
er-2	$E \wedge B = B \wedge E = E$
boole-1	$\neg T = F$
boole-2	$\mathrm{IFOK}_1(B, \neg(\neg B)) = \mathrm{IFOK}_1(B, B)$

boole-3 $\text{IFOK}_1(B, T \wedge B) = \text{IFOK}_1(B, B)$

boole-4 $\text{IFOK}_1(B, F \wedge B) = \text{IFOK}_1(B, F)$

boole-5 $\text{IFOK}_2(B, B', B \wedge B') = \text{IFOK}_2(B, B', B' \wedge B)$

ifok-1 $\text{IFOK}_1(B, B') = \text{IFE}(\text{OK}(B), B', E)$

ifok-2 $\text{IFOK}_2(B, B', B'') = \text{IFE}(\text{OK}(B) \wedge \text{OK}(B'), B'', E)$.

It is easy, though tedious, to check that $\bar{A}$ satisfies $\bar{\mathcal{E}}$. All that remains then is to show for each $\sigma \in \bar{\Sigma}_n$ and $B_1, \ldots, B_n \in \bar{A}$ that

$$(*) \qquad \sigma(B_1 \ldots B_n) \equiv \sigma_{\bar{A}}(B_1, \ldots, B_n).$$

For $\sigma = T$, F, or E this is immediate, since $\sigma_A = \sigma$. For $\sigma = \text{OK}$, the result follows by ok-1, 2, 3. For $\sigma = \text{IFE}$, it follows from ife-1, 2, 3.

We now come to the more interesting cases. For $\sigma = \neg$, we have directly that $\neg(T) \equiv F = \neg_{\bar{A}}(T)$ by boole-1 and $\bar{\text{A}}$-1. By boole-1, we have $\neg F \equiv \neg(\neg T)$. Since $\text{OK}(F) \equiv T$ by ok-2, Lemma 11 and boole-2 give $\neg(\neg T) \equiv T$. So $\neg F \equiv T = \neg_{\bar{A}}(F)$, as required. The last case for negation is $\neg(E)$, but $\neg(E) \equiv \neg_{\bar{A}}(E)$ by er-1 and $\bar{\text{A}}$-1.

The proofs for $\wedge$ are just the same except there are nine cases. $\text{OK}(T) \equiv T$ by ok-1, so Lemma 11 and boole-3 give $T \wedge T \equiv T = T \wedge_{\bar{A}} T$. The other four nonerror cases work the same way. The five cases with errors are handled by er-2, e.g., $E \wedge T \equiv E = E \wedge_{\bar{A}} T$.

Example 16C

We shall prove the correctness of stack(int), and we shall carry it out in more detail than in some of the previous examples. The point is to see that *this* proof is in fact a proof of stack(d) for d a suitably specified type.

The "usual" model A for stack(int) has carriers $A_{\text{inte}} = Z \cup E_{\text{int}}$, $A_{\text{boole}} = \{T, F, E_{\text{bool}}\}$, and $A_{\text{stack}} = Z^* \cup E_{st}$. That is, an object of type stack is either the error message E_{st} of type stack, or it is a string of integers $n_1 \ldots n_p$ corresponding, intuitively, to the contents of the stack (with n_1 being at the top and n_p being at the bottom of the stack). Now, (forgetting the operations for the time being), we want to describe a corresponding canonical term algebra. We assume we know the canonical term algebra for inte consisting of E_{int} and $\rho(n)$ for each integer n and also that for boole, consisting of $\{T, F, E_{\text{bool}}\}$. Then our purpose is to construct a canonical term carrier for stack consisting of E_{st} and $\bar{\rho}(w)$, where w is a string of integers; $\bar{\rho}(w)$ is defined inductively by

I-1 $\bar{\rho}(\lambda) = \lambda$

I-2 $\bar{\rho}(nw) = \text{PUSH}(\rho(n), \bar{\rho}(w))$.

Thus the terms in the carrier stack are E_{st}, λ, $\text{PUSH}(\rho(n), \lambda)$, $\text{PUSH}(\rho(n'), \text{PUSH}(\rho(n), \lambda))$, etc. We now need to define the new operations, i.e., those taking arguments or values in stack to make C into a Σ-algebra. Note that subscripts (stack, int, bool) on E, OK, IFE, and the like will be clear from context and are thus omitted. Those operations are given as follows:

C-0: $E_C = E \qquad \lambda_C = \lambda$

C-1:

I \ S	E	$\bar{\rho}(\omega)$
E	E	E
$\rho(n)$	E	$\bar{\rho}(nw)$

$\text{PUSH}_C(I, S)$

C-2:

S	$\text{OK}_C(S)$
E	F
$\bar{\rho}(w)$	T

C-3:

B	$\text{IFE}_C(B, S, S')$
T	S
F	S'
E	E

C-4:

S	$\text{POP}_C(S)$
E	E
λ	λ
$\bar{\rho}(nw)$	$\bar{\rho}(w)$

C-5:

S	$\text{TOP}_C(S)$
E	E
λ	E
$\bar{\rho}(nw)$	$\rho(n)$

C-6:

S	$\text{EMPTY}_C(S)$
E	E
λ	T
$\bar{\rho}(nw)$	F

This description yields a canonical term algebra because the only terms are the constants λ, E and $\lambda_C = \lambda$, $E_C = E$, and $\bar{\rho}(nw)$ for n an integer and w a string of integers. But $\bar{\rho}(nw) = \text{PUSH}(\rho(n), \bar{\rho}(w))$, and $\rho(n)$ and $\bar{\rho}(w)$ are in their respective canonical carriers; further, by C-1, $\text{PUSH}_C(\rho(n), \bar{\rho}w)) = \bar{\rho}(nw)$, so the conditions for a canonical term algebra are met.

We must check that this algebra, which we are calling C, satisfies the axioms and that the representation condition of Theorem 9 holds. For reference, we repeat the axioms:

stack-1	$\text{IFOK}(I, S, \text{TOP}(\text{PUSH}(I, S))) = \text{IFOK}(I, S, I)$
stack-2	$\text{IFOK}(I, S, \text{POP}(\text{PUSH}(I, S))) = \text{IFOK}(I, S, S)$
stack-3	$\text{EMPTY}(\lambda) = T$
stack-4	$\text{IFOK}(I, S, \text{EMPTY}(\text{PUSH}(I, S))) = \text{IFOK}(I, S, F)$
stack-5	$\text{POP}(\lambda) = \lambda$
stack-6	$\text{TOP}(\lambda) = E$
ife-1	$\text{IFE}(T, S, S') = S$
ife-2	$\text{IFE}(F, S, S') = S'$
ife-3	$\text{IFE}(E, S, S') = E$
ok-1	$\text{OK}(E) = F$
ok-2	$\text{OK}(\lambda) = T$
ok-3	$\text{OK}(\text{PUSH}(I, S)) = \text{OK}(I) \wedge \text{OK}(S)$
er-1	$\text{PUSH}(E, S) = E$
er-2	$\text{PUSH}(I, E) = E$
er-3	$\text{POP}(E) = E$
er-4	$\text{TOP}(E) = E$
er-5	$\text{EMPTY}(E) = E.$

We have, in previous proofs, avoided the explicit verification that the canonical term algebra satisfied the equations. This may not be quite so obvious here. But for stack-3, 5, 6, ife-1, 2, 3, ok-1, 2, 3, and er-1, 2, 3, 4, 5, the agreement between axioms and operations can be read directly from the tables defining those operations. For the others (stack-1, 2, 4), stack-1 is typical. Expanding the derived operators, we want to check

$$\text{IFE}_C(\text{OK}_C(I) \wedge \text{OK}_C(S), \text{TOP}_C(\text{PUSH}_C(I, S)), E)$$
$$= \text{IFE}_C(\text{OK}_C(I) \wedge \text{OK}_C(S), I, E)$$

for all I in inte and S in stack. If either I or S is E, then $\text{OK}_C(I) \wedge \text{OK}_C(S) = F$ by C-2 and both sides are E by C-3. Otherwise $I = \rho(n)$ and $S = \bar{\rho}(w)$, in which case $\text{OK}_C(I) \wedge \text{OK}_C(S) = T$; by C-3 the left side becomes

$$\text{TOP}_C(\text{PUSH}_C(\rho(n), \bar{\rho}(w))) = \text{TOP}_C(\bar{\rho}(nw)) \qquad \text{C-1}$$
$$= \rho(n) \qquad \text{C-5}$$

and the right side is also $\rho(n)$.

For our intended application of Theorem 9, we now turn to the representation condition, i.e.,

$$\sigma(t_1, \ldots, t_n) \equiv \sigma_C(t_1, \ldots, t_n),$$

and consider each of the operations separately.

For PUSH(I, S), if either I or S is E, then PUSH(I, S) $\equiv E =$ PUSH$_C$(I, S) by er-1, 2 and C-1. If neither I nor S is error, then PUSH($\rho(n)$, $\bar{\rho}(w)$) $= \bar{\rho}(nw)$ $=$ PUSH$_C$($\rho(n)$, $\bar{\rho}(w)$) by I-2 and C-1. Thus for the first operation, we have

$$\text{PUSH}(I, S) \equiv \text{PUSH}_C(I, S).$$

For IFE, IFE(B, S, S') $\equiv$ IFE$_C$(B, S, S') directly from ife-1, 2, 3 for the three cases $B = T, F, E$. Now for OK:

$$\begin{array}{rll}
\text{OK}(E) \equiv F & = \text{OK}_C(E) & \text{ok-1, C-2} \\
\text{OK}(\lambda) \equiv T & = \text{OK}_C(\lambda) & \text{ok-2, C-2} \\
\text{OK}(\bar{\rho}(nw)) & = \text{OK}(\text{PUSH}(\rho(n), \bar{\rho}(w)) & \text{I-2} \\
 & \equiv \text{OK}(\rho(n)) \wedge \text{OK}(\bar{\rho}(w)) & \text{ok-3} \\
 & \equiv T \wedge T & \text{inte, induction} \\
 & \equiv T & \text{boole} \\
 & = \text{OK}_C(\bar{\rho}(nw)) & \text{C-2.}
\end{array}$$

The justification "inte" in the fifth line is based on our assumption that OK is correct in inte, and similarly that $T \wedge T \equiv T$ assumes boole to be correct. From this proof we have

$$(*) \qquad \text{OK}(\rho(n), \bar{\rho}(w)) \equiv T,$$

where, consistent with the presentation, we omit the subscript on the derived operator, OK$_{\text{int } st}$.

$$\begin{array}{rll}
\text{POP}(E) \equiv E & = \text{POP}_C(E) & \text{er-3, C-4} \\
\text{POP}(\lambda) \equiv \lambda & = \text{POP}_C(\lambda) & \text{stack-5, C-4} \\
\text{POP}(\bar{\rho}(nw)) & = \text{POP}(\text{PUSH}(\rho(n), \bar{\rho}(w))) & \text{I-2} \\
 & \equiv \bar{\rho}(w) & (*)\text{, stack-2, Lemma 11} \\
 & = \text{POP}_C(\bar{\rho}(nw)) & \text{C-4}
\end{array}$$

Exactly the same argument applies to TOP using C-5, er-4, stack-6, and stack-1.

$$\begin{array}{rll}
\text{EMPTY}(E) \equiv E & = \text{EMPTY}_C(E) & \text{er-5, C-6} \\
\text{EMPTY}(\lambda) \equiv T & = \text{EMPTY}_C(\lambda) & \text{stack-3, C-6} \\
\text{EMPTY}(\bar{\rho}(nw)) & = \text{EMPTY}(\text{PUSH}(\rho(n), \rho(w))) & \text{I-2} \\
 & \equiv F & (*)\text{, stack-4, Lemma 11} \\
 & = \text{EMPTY}_C(\bar{\rho}(nw)) & \text{C-6.}
\end{array}$$

This completes the correctness proof of stack(int) because the conditions of Theorem 9 are met and our canonical term algebra is initial, and that term algebra is (isomorphic to) the intended model.

Example 18C

The correctness proof for stack(d) follows that of stack(int) almost to the letter. Here we assume d specified by $(S, \Sigma, \mathcal{E})$ with a canonical term algebra C for $(S, \Sigma, \mathcal{E})$. It is stacks of $C_d - \{E_d\}$ that are of interest, so the canonical terms of sort stack are now defined from strings over $C_d - \{E_d\}$; ρ maps $(C_d - \{E_d\})^*$ into the appropriate terms:

$$\text{I-1} \qquad \bar{\rho}(\lambda) = \lambda$$

$$\text{I-2} \qquad \bar{\rho}(tw) = \text{PUSH}(t, \bar{\rho}(w)) \qquad \text{for } t \neq E_d.$$

Then the image of ρ consists of terms over Σ together with λ and PUSH. The operations on this new algebra are defined exactly as in Example 16C with $t \in C_d$ $(t \neq E_d)$ replacing each and every occurrence of $\rho(n)$. [Of course, $\rho(n)$ was a canonical term for the integer n.] For example,

C-1 $\text{PUSH}_C(D, S)$

D \ S	E	$\bar{\rho}(w)$
E	E	E
t	E	$\bar{\rho}(tw)$

That these operations (so modified) satisfy the axioms is argued just as in Example 16C. In the proofs of the representation conditions, which are carried out quite carefully in Example 16C, the only references to int concern either checking the condition $\text{OK}_{\underline{\text{int}}}(n) \equiv T$ for $n \neq E_{\underline{\text{int}}}$ or that $\text{IFE}_{\underline{\text{int}}}(T, n, n') \equiv n$. That is, no special properties of int are used other than those which are assumed for d in specification of stack(d). Similarly, the assumption that boole is protected $\langle S, \Sigma, \mathcal{E} \rangle$ ensures that the properties of $\text{OK}_{\underline{\text{boole}}}$ and $\text{IFE}_{\underline{\text{bool}}}$ used in the proof of Example 16C are again available here.

5.5. IMPLEMENTATIONS

It is crucial for applications to have a notion of implementation for abstract data types; only then can we test existing software against mathematical standards. The notion turns out to be more subtle than one might have hoped, but also more interesting.

An implementation is necessarily made within a specific framework, such as a particular programming language or machine. Our precise definition of *implementation* will need to represent such a framework. The most obvious, and probably best, approach is to model an implementation framework as an algebra, with the elements of the carrier(s) being concrete data representations (machine states, primitive data types) and its operations the given basic operations (machine operations, basic instructions, programs) on these data representations.

Thus we shall assume we are given an *implementation algebra.* One issue is its level of abstraction. We contend that a variety of levels should be permitted. For example, a general method of implementation might be shown to be correct and then a particular instance shown correct relative to that. Thus, one might show the pointer-array implementation for stacks correct on a rather abstract level and then show that a particular program correctly implements the pointer-array model. As a rule it will probably be easier to specify the more abstract implementation algebra. For example, the pointer-array model is easily described as an abstract data type, and the corresponding initial algebra (or some convenient canonical term algebra for it) can then be taken as an implementation algebra. But if we have to describe an implementation algebra for some ordinary programming language, we probably have a major job on our hands. To begin with, the language has to have a rigorous semantics.

A rather annoying, but hopefully unimportant, problem is that the mathematical models, including both our specifications and standard approaches to programming language semantics, make certain idealization assumptions—for example, that *all* the integers are available; clearly no real machine has the storage capacity for arbitrarily large numbers. But different machines have different capacities, which may in fact vary with time (the limit of multiple precision arithmetic in a time-shared environment will depend on what other users are doing, and of course, auxiliary storage devices often come and go, albeit over a longer time period). It would be most inconvenient to have to take into account such factors in designing data structures; the simplest approach is just to idealize, to assume infinite storage. It is also possible to axiomatize finite structures, with particular size bounds, using the methods of this chapter, but it seems that the more standard idealized structures illustrate our approach at least as well and are a bit simpler. In any case, we believe questions of degree of numerical approximation and so on belong to a domain which can be considered separately from abstract data types.

To return to the main point, we shall deal with implementation algebras in which operations are expressed set-theoretically rather than in some programming language. This can protect us from having to consider distracting details (such as storage size) while still permitting us to prove correctness of essential implementation features, such as linking. Sometimes the phrase "abstract implementation" is used in this connection, but as we have argued in the introduction, this use of the word *abstract* is different from that in the title of the chapter and is therefore not used, to avoid perpetuating confusion.

Let B denote the implementation algebra and let Ω be its signature. Let $\langle S, \Sigma, \mathcal{E}\rangle$ be a specification for the *specification algebra* $T_{\Sigma,\mathcal{E}}$. The question now is, What relationship between $T_{\Sigma,\mathcal{E}}$ and B constitutes an *implementation*?

A first approximation might be isomorphism, that is, $T_{\Sigma,\mathcal{E}} \cong B$. This certainly captures the idea of taking a specific $\langle S, \Sigma, \mathcal{E}\rangle$-algebra as an implementation of the data type specified by $\langle S, \Sigma, \mathcal{E}\rangle$. But isomorphism is not enough to cover the cases which actually come up (see later for an example).

First, we need not have $\Omega = \Sigma$. Indeed, the general idea is to express the "sophisticated" operations in Σ in terms of the "more basic" operations in Ω. The appropriate mathematical concept, explained below, is that of a derived Σ-algebra dB of the Ω-algebra B.

Definition 11. Let Σ be an S-sorted operator domain, and let Ω be an S'-sorted operator domain. Then a *derivor* from Σ to Ω is a function[16] $f: S \longrightarrow S'$ and a family $d_{w,s}: \Sigma_{w,s} \longrightarrow (T_\Omega)_{f(w),f(s)}$, where $f(s_1 \ldots s_n) = f(s_1) \ldots f(s_n)$ and where $(T_\Omega)_{f(w),f(s)}$ denotes the set of all Ω-terms of sort $f(s)$ using variables $\{y_1, \ldots, y_n\}$ with y_i of sort $f(s_i)$. (Each operation symbol $\sigma \in \Sigma_{w,s}$ is expressed using a derived operation $d_{w,s}(\sigma)$ of the appropriate arity.) We shall generally let just d denote a derivor $\langle f, d\rangle$. Now let B be an Ω-algebra. Then the *d-derived algebra dB* of B is the Σ-algebra, with σ_{dB} (for $\sigma \in \Sigma$) defined to be $(d(\sigma))_B$, the derived operator of the Ω-term $d(\sigma)$.

A very special case of d-derived algebra has been called *reduct* in universal algebra. There, $\Sigma \subseteq \Omega$, f is the identity, and $d_{w,s}$ sends each $\sigma \in \Sigma_{w,s}$ to the primitive term $\sigma(y_1, \ldots, y_n)$ (here $w = s_1 \ldots s_n$, and y_i is of sort s_i). Then a d-derived algebra dB is the Σ-reduct of the Ω-algebra B.

These ideas intimately depend on the concept of a derived operator as defined in Section 5.3. By means of the obvious derivor, we can implement $\underline{\text{bool}}$ with operators $\wedge, \neg, \vee, \Rightarrow$, and $\Leftrightarrow$ in (an initial algebra corresponding to) $\underline{\text{bool}}$ with only operators $\wedge$ and $\neg$. Similarly, we can implement $\underline{\text{complex}}$-$\underline{\text{int}}$ (Example 13) in its "sub-data-type" whose specification just contains the operator RE, MAKE, and IM (plus those of $\underline{\text{int}}$) and the first three axioms for $\underline{\text{complex}}$-$\underline{\text{int}}$.

In both these cases we get $T_{\Sigma,\mathcal{E}} \cong dB$. However, other examples suggest that $T_{\Sigma,\mathcal{E}} \lesssim dB$ (meaning isomorphic to a subalgebra of) would be a better definition of implementation.

In particular, it seems natural to say that we can implement $\underline{\text{nat}}$ (with operators 0, +, *, and SUCC) in the algebra B whose carrier is all integers (with the operations 0, +, *, and SUCC) using the identity derivor [$d(+) = +$, etc]. But here we do not have $T_{\Sigma,\mathcal{E}} \cong dB$, because dB has all the negative integers in its carrier. However, d induces a homomorphism $h: T_\Sigma \longrightarrow dB$, and $T_{\Sigma,\mathcal{E}}$ is isomorphic to the image of this homomorphism.

Even this doesn't quite cover all the cases that come up, because it is often the case that a single element of $T_{\Sigma,\mathcal{E}}$ is represented by a number of different elements of the implementation algebra. For example, a given string $a_1a_2a_3$ can be represented by a large number of linear linked lists, differing in the addresses at which the items a_1, a_2, a_3 are stored. These different representations are, of course, equivalent, and this equivalence relation is actually a Σ-congruence on the (derived) implementation algebra. One subtle point, however, is that this relation is not, in general, describable purely in terms of the derived operations but requires use of the more basic operations (in Ω).

[16]Actually, there is no difficulty in letting $f: S \longrightarrow S'^*$; although there are cases where this comes up, we opt here for the simpler case, primarily for clarity.

Pulling all this together suggests the following concept:

> **Definition 12.** Let $P = \langle S, \Sigma, \mathcal{E}\rangle$ be a specification. Then an *implementation* of P is a triple $\langle B, d, \equiv\rangle$, where B is an S'-sorted Ω-algebra, d is a derivor from Σ to Ω, and $\equiv$ is a Σ-congruence on dB, such that $T_{\Sigma,\mathcal{E}} \lesssim (dB)/\equiv$ as Σ-algebras.

Some may consider this definition too general; we feel it is quite reasonable, except that one might restrict the congruence to be effective (decidable).

On the other hand, some might argue that this notion of implementation is too restrictive. In particular, there is some motivation for "implementations" in which for selected sorts $s \in S$ the carrier of sort s is a quotient of $(T_{\Sigma,\mathcal{E}})_s$ rather than the other way around. This, in effect, allows one to write looser (and shorter) specifications. Some ideas along these lines are found in Guttag et al. (1976a) and in Giarratana et al. (1976).

We shall now present an example, which will hopefully make the above definitions seem less abstract.

Example 19

We show that $\underline{\text{signat}}$ implements $\underline{\text{int}}$, taking $\underline{\text{int}}$ as specified by $\langle S, \Sigma, \mathcal{E}\rangle$ in Example 9 (Σ contains 0, SUCC, PRED, $-$, $+$, $*$) and $\underline{\text{signat}}$ as specified by $\langle \bar{S}, \Omega, \bar{\mathcal{E}}\rangle$ in Example 14 (Ω contains $<$, $>$, $|\ |$, SGN, $\oplus$, $\circledast$, plus the usual Boolean operations). Thus $S = \{\underline{\text{int}}\}$, $\bar{S} = \{\underline{\text{nat}}, \underline{\text{bool}}, \underline{\text{signat}}\}$, and, of course, $f(\underline{\text{int}}) = \underline{\text{signat}}$. An appropriate derivor $d_{\underline{\text{nat}}^n,\underline{\text{nat}}}\colon \Sigma_{\underline{\text{nat}}^n,\underline{\text{nat}}} \longrightarrow (T_\Omega)_{\underline{\text{signat}}^n,\underline{\text{signat}}}$ is defined as follows:

$$
\begin{aligned}
d(0) &= \langle 0, T\rangle\\
d(\text{SUCC}) &= S \oplus \langle \text{SUCC}(0), T\rangle\\
d(\text{PRED}) &= S \oplus \langle \text{SUCC}(0), F\rangle\\
d(-) &= S \oplus \langle |S'|, \neg\text{SGN}(S')\rangle\\
d(+) &= S \oplus S'\\
d(*) &= S \circledast S'.
\end{aligned}
$$

This is just the "usual" way of expressing integers as signed natural numbers. Thus, we get the derived Σ-algebra $dT_{\Omega,\bar{\mathcal{E}}}$ from the Ω-algebra $T_{\Omega,\bar{\mathcal{E}}}$, denoted dB and B, respectively.

It remains to give a Σ-congruence $\equiv$ on dB. We take $\equiv$ to be the Σ-congruence generated by the single equation

$$\langle 0, F\rangle = \langle 0, T\rangle,$$

which may be thought of as identifying -0 with $+0$. In fact, $\equiv$ is

$$\{\langle\langle 0, F\rangle, \langle 0, T\rangle\rangle, \langle\langle 0, T\rangle, \langle 0, F\rangle\rangle\} \cup \{\langle S, S\rangle \mid S \in (dB)\}$$

(noting that dB has just one carrier). To show this, it suffices to show that the above relation is a Σ-congruence, for if it is a Σ-congruence, it is surely the least one containing $\langle\langle 0, F\rangle, \langle 0, T\rangle\rangle$. To show it is a Σ-congruence, we verify the equations

$$\begin{aligned} d(\text{SUCC})(+0) &= d(\text{SUCC})(-0) \\ d(\text{PRED})(+0) &= d(\text{PRED})(-0) \\ d(\sigma)(+0, S') &= d(\sigma)(-0, S') \\ d(\sigma)(S, +0) &= d(\sigma)(S, -0) \end{aligned}$$

for all $\sigma \in \Sigma_2$ and $S, S' \in dB$, which is straightforward but tedious.

Next, to show that $T_{\Sigma,\mathcal{E}} \cong (dT_{\Omega,\bar{\mathcal{E}}})/\equiv$, it suffices to construct a Σ-homomorphism from dB to $T_{\Sigma,\mathcal{E}}$ and then show that its kernel is $\equiv$. For this purpose, we need to know that the terms $\langle N, B\rangle$ form a canonical term algebra for signat. We assume this result and define

$$h(\langle N, B\rangle) = \text{IF } B \text{ THEN } N \text{ ELSE } (0 - N).$$

Then clearly $h(+0) = h(-0) = 0$, and we have to show that nothing else is identified by h. Noting that N and $0 - N$ are distinct in int unless $N = 0$, we see that $h(\langle N, B\rangle) = h(\langle N', B'\rangle)$ iff $N = N'$ and $B = B'$, or else $N = N' = 0$. Thus we have an implementation.

The reader may wonder why such an apparently simple result took such labor to verify. The most immediate answer is that implementations are not nearly so simple as our intuition about them seems to suggest. This may be seen theoretically in both Definition 12 and Example 19, and it may be seen practically from one's experience in debugging data representations: It often is much harder than you would have thought. On a more encouraging note, the proof sketched in Example 19 above isn't so difficult as it might look: First, there really is no difficulty in guessing what the congruence relation and canonical term algebra must be, and second, the rather tedious algebraic manipulations required are exactly the kind of thing one can even today confidently give to an automatic theorem prover. Moreover, we believe this to be a rather typical situation: A good understanding of what he is doing will enable the programmer to come up with the proper congruence relation and canonical term algebras, and proper modularization (that is, use of parameterized types) will produce tractable algebraic manipulation problems.

It should not be thought that Example 19 is the most complicated example we can handle; it is merely a convenient illustration for present purposes. We have, in fact, elsewhere given an implementation of stack by pointer-array [see Goguen (1977)]; it is, however, unsuitable for inclusion here because of its different treatment of error messages. In fact, we may often expect that the more complex examples will involve errors in a significant way and therefore drive us out of the framework of the present chapter. It is nevertheless the case that the framework developed here gives the essential machinery which is required.

5.6. APPENDIX

This appendix contains some technical definitions and lemmas, and the proofs omitted in the body of the chapter, beginning with Section 5.2. Most results being proved are restated here for convenience of reference.

Proposition 1 *(Section 5.2.)*

If algebras A and A' are both initial in a category **C** of Σ-algebras, then A and A' are isomorphic. If an algebra A'' in **C** is isomorphic to an algebra A which is initial in **C**, then A'' is also initial.

Proof: Let $h: A \longrightarrow A'$ be the unique homomorphism guaranteed by A being initial, and let $h': A' \longrightarrow A$ be that by A'. Then $h'h: A \longrightarrow A$ and $1_A: A \longrightarrow A$ are both homomorphisms, and so by uniqueness $h'h = 1_A$. Similarly, $hh' = 1_{A'}$. Thus h is an isomorphism, so that A and A' are isomorphic.

Now let $f: A \longrightarrow A''$ be an isomorphism, with inverse $g: A'' \longrightarrow A$ and with A initial. Let A' be any algebra in **C**. Then A initial gives $h: A \longrightarrow A'$, and thus we have $h'' = hg: A'' \longrightarrow A'$, so we have one homomorphism from A'' to A'. If also $h': A'' \longrightarrow A'$, then $h'f: A \longrightarrow A'$, so that $h'f = h$. But also, $h''f = h$. Therefore $h'f = h''f$, so that $h'fg = h''fg$; i.e., $h' = h''$. Thus A'' is also initial.

The proof of Theorem 2 requires a bit of preparation. First, we ought to show that conditions (T0) and (T1) of Section 5.2 really do define something; not every recursive definition of a family of sets is actually satisfiable. The line of attack is to show that any intersection of (S-indexed families of) sets satisfying (T0), (T1) also satisfies (T0), (T1); to show that there is at least one such family of sets; and finally to define $T_\Sigma = \cap \mathfrak{F}$, where $\mathfrak{F}$ is the (nonempty) family of all (families of) sets satisfying (T0), (T1).

If $\mathfrak{F}$ is a set of S-indexed families of sets, $(\cap \mathfrak{F})_s = \cap\{A_s \mid A \in \mathfrak{F}\}$. In fact, it is pretty easily verified that, with this definition of intersection, an intersection of (families of) sets satisfying (T0) satisfies (T0) and of (families of) sets satisfying (T1) satisfies (T1). Moreover, the family A with $A_s = (\Sigma \cup \{\underline{(}, \underline{)}\})^*$ for all $s \in S$ obviously satisfies (T0) and (T1). Thus $\mathfrak{F}$ is nonempty, so that $T_\Sigma = \cap \mathfrak{F}$ exists and is thus the least family satisfying (T0), (T1), since if A satisfies (T0), (T1), then $A \in \mathfrak{F}$, so that[17] $\cap \mathfrak{F} \subseteq A$.

Thus, while the description via (T0), (T1) is easy to write, it conceals a bit of detail and moreover is not really so explicit as it appears to be. To prove initiality we shall find an explicit inductive description helpful. Thus, we shall now embark on a definition of a family W of sets. We shall give W a Σ-algebra structure, prove it initial, and finally prove it equal to T_Σ. Of course, it might have seemed simpler to let T_Σ be defined as we now define W, but unfortunately this definition is somewhat complex, and perhaps even unnatural looking.

[17]For A, B S-indexed families of sets, $A \subseteq B$ means $A_s \subseteq B_s$ for all $s \in S$.

The idea is that W is a (disjoint) union of(families of) sets $W^{(k)}$ of Σ-terms (defined as strings) of depth k, for all $k \geq 0$, where of course $(\cup_{k\geq 0} W^{(k)})_s = \cup_{k\geq 0} W_s^{(k)}$, and $W^{(k)}$ is defined (inductively) from the $W^{(j)}$ for $0 \leq j < k$. To get things started,

$$\text{(W0)} \qquad W_s^{(0)} = \Sigma_{\lambda, s} \qquad \text{for } s \in S,$$

and then the inductive step is

$$\text{(W1)} \qquad W_s^{(k)} = \{\sigma(t_1 \ldots t_n) \mid n \geq 1, \quad \sigma \in \Sigma_{s_1 \ldots s_n, s}, \quad \text{and} \quad t_i \in W_{s_i}^{(j_i)} \text{ for some } j_1, \ldots, j_n < k \text{ with } \max\{j_1, \ldots, j_n\} = k-1\}.$$

First, note that $W^{(k)} \cap W^{(m)} = \varnothing$ if $k \neq m$ (here $\varnothing$ is really the S-indexed family of empty sets); now define $W = \cup_{k\geq 0} W^{(k)}$; and, finally, give W a Σ-algebra structure as follows:

1. For $\sigma \in \Sigma_{\lambda, s}$, $\sigma_W = \sigma$ ($\sigma \in W_s^{(0)} \subseteq W_s$).
2. For $\sigma \in \Sigma_{s_1 \ldots s_n, s}$, $\sigma_W(t_1, \ldots, t_n) = \sigma(t_1 \ldots t_n)$, where if $t_i \in W_{s_i}^{(j_i)}$ for $i = 1, \ldots, n$, we have $\sigma_W(t_1, \ldots, t_n) \in W_s^{(k)}$, where $k = \max\{j_1, \ldots, j_n\} + 1$.

Lemma 2A

W is an initial Σ-algebra.

Proof: Let A be any Σ-algebra. We shall construct a Σ-homomorphism, $h: W \longrightarrow A$, piece by piece by defining $h^{(k)}: W^{(k)} \longrightarrow A$ and $h = \cup_{k\geq 0} h^{(k)}$ (think of this as a union of S-indexed families of ordered pairs). Note that h and the family $h^{(k)}$ each uniquely determine the other, because W is the disjoint union of of the $W^{(k)}$.

Let us first give a (recursive) definition of h, via the $h^{(k)}$, and show that h is a Σ-homomorphism; then later we shall show that this definition is forced by the requirement that h be a Σ-homomorphism.

Define $h^{(0)}: W^{(0)} \longrightarrow A$ by

$$\text{(hW0)} \qquad h_s^{(0)}(\sigma) = \sigma_A \qquad \text{for } \sigma \in \Sigma_{\lambda, s}.$$

Now assume that $k > 0$ and that $h^{(j)}$ is defined for $0 \leq j < k$; let $t \in W_s^{(k)}$. Then by (W1), t is of the form $\sigma(t_1 \ldots t_n)$, where $t_i \in W_{s_i}$ for $i = 1, \ldots n$, $n > 0$, $\sigma \in \Sigma_{s_1 \ldots s_n, s}$, and $k = \max\{j_1, \ldots, j_n\} + 1$. We define $h_s^{(k)}: W_s^{(k)} \longrightarrow A_s$ by

$$\text{(hW1)} \qquad h_s^{(k)}(t) = \sigma_A(h_{s_1}^{(j_1)}(t_1), \ldots, h_{s_n}^{(j_n)}(t_n)).$$

This defines $h^{(k)}: W^{(k)} \longrightarrow A$ for all $k \geq 0$ and therefore defines $h: W \longrightarrow A$.

We have to show that h is a Σ-homomorphism. Condition (h0) (in the definition of Σ-homomorphism; Section 5.2) follows directly from (hW0). As for (h1), every nonconstant term in W is of the form $\sigma(t_1 \ldots t_n) \in W^{(k)}$ for some $k > 0$, and therefore (hW1) applies, but after deleting superscripts, (hW1) is (h1).

It remains to show that this is the only possible Σ-homomorphism from W to A. For this it suffices to show that the conditions (h0), (h1) for h being a

Σ-homomorphism imply the conditions (hW0), (hW1), which we used to define h. In fact, (h0) translates directly into (hW0), and (h1) into (hW1), after adding the necessary superscripts arising from the definition of W as $\cup_{k\geq 0} W^{(k)}$ and $h^{(k)}$ as the restriction of h to $W^{(k)}$.

To complete the proof of Theorem 2, we have only to show

Lemma 2B

$$W = T_\Sigma.$$

Proof: We shall divide the proof into two parts, showing $W \subseteq T_\Sigma$ and $T_\Sigma \subseteq W$.

(A) $W \subseteq T_\Sigma$: We show that $W^{(k)} \subseteq T_\Sigma$ for all $k \geq 0$ by induction. First, $\Sigma_{\lambda,s} \subseteq T_{\Sigma,s}$ and $W_s^{(0)} = \Sigma_{\lambda,s}$, so $W^{(0)} \subseteq T_\Sigma$.

Next, assume $W^{(j)} \subseteq T_\Sigma$ for $0 \leq j < k$, and pick $t = \sigma(t_1 \ldots t_n) \in W_s^{(k)}$. Then $t_i \in W_{s_i}^{(j_i)}$ with $0 \leq j_i < k$, so that $t_i \in T_{\Sigma,s_i}$ for $i = 1, \ldots, n$. Thus by condition (T1), $t \in T_{\Sigma,s}$. Thus $W^{(k)} \subseteq T_\Sigma$.

(B) $T_\Sigma \subseteq W$: Since T_Σ is the least (family) satisfying conditions (T0), (T1), it will suffice to show that W satisfies (T0), (T1).

For (T0), $\Sigma_{\lambda,s} \subseteq W_s$ since $\Sigma_{\lambda,s} = W_s^{(0)} \subseteq W_s$.

For (T1), let $\sigma \in \Sigma_{s_1 \ldots s_n, s}$ and $t_i \in W_{s_i}$. Then for each $i = 1, \ldots, n$, $t_i \in W_{s_i}^{(j_i)}$ for a unique j_i. Let $k = \max\{j_1, \ldots, j_n\} + 1$. Then $\sigma(t_1 \ldots t_n) \in W_s^{(k)} \subseteq W_s$.

This completes the proof of Theorem 2.

Proposition 3 (Section 5.2)

Let A be a Σ-algebra, and let $\theta\colon Y \longrightarrow A$ be an assignment. Then there exists a unique Σ-homomorphism $\bar{\theta}\colon T_\Sigma(Y) \longrightarrow A$ that extends θ, in the sense that $\bar{\theta}_s(x) = \theta_s(x)$ for all $s \in S$ and $x \in Y_s$.

Proof: A is a Σ-algebra. Given $\theta\colon Y \longrightarrow A$, make A into a $\Sigma(Y)$-algebra by having x name $\theta(x)$ in A [$x_A = \theta(x)$]. By Theorem 2, there is a unique $\Sigma(Y)$-homomorphism $\bar{\theta}\colon T_{\Sigma(Y)} \longrightarrow A$, and [by clause (h0) of the definition of homomorphism] $\bar{\theta}(x_T) = \bar{\theta}(x) = x_A = \theta(x)$, so $\bar{\theta}$ extends θ. Because $\bar{\theta}$ is a $\Sigma(Y)$-homomorphism, it is immediately a Σ-homomorphism. For the uniqueness part, if $h\colon T_\Sigma(Y) \longrightarrow A$ is a Σ-homomorphism with $h(x) = \theta(x)$, then it is also a $\Sigma(Y)$-homomorphism, and thus $h = \bar{\theta}$.

Proposition 5 (Section 5.2)

Let A be a Σ-algebra, and let R be a relation on A (i.e., as usual, $R = \langle R_s \rangle_{s\in S}$, with $R_s \subseteq A_s \times A_s$). Then there exists a least Σ-congruence relation on A containing R; it is called the *congruence relation generated by* R *on* A.

Proof: Let $\mathcal{K}(R)$ be the set of all congruence relations on A that contain R. $\mathcal{K}(R) \neq \varnothing$ for the relation $U = \langle U_s = A_s \times A_s \mid s \in S \rangle$ is in $\mathcal{K}(R)$. Now let

$\equiv_R = \cap\, \mathcal{K}(R)$; i.e., for each $s \in S$, $(\equiv_R)_s = \cap\, \{K_s \mid K \in \mathcal{K}(R)\}$. Then $\equiv_R$ is a congruence relation on A for if $\sigma \in \Sigma_{s_1 \ldots s_n, s}$ and if $a_i, a_i' \in A_{s_i}$ and if $a_i \equiv_R a_i'$ for $i = 1, \ldots, n$, then this would imply $a_i K a_i'$ for each $K \in \mathcal{K}(R)$. But then by the definition of congruence, in each $K \in \mathcal{K}(R)$ we would have $\sigma(a_1, \ldots, a_n) K \sigma(a_1', \ldots, a_n')$, implying, $\sigma(a_1, \ldots, a_n) \equiv_R \sigma(a_1', \ldots, a_n')$, so $\equiv_R$ satisfies the definition of Σ-congruence.

The proof of Theorem 6 relies on some preliminary results to which we now turn.

Lemma 6A

If $h\colon B \longrightarrow A$ is a Σ-homomorphism, let $(\equiv_h)_s = \{\langle b, b'\rangle \mid b, b' \in B_s \text{ and } h_s(b) = h_s(b')\}$ for $s \in S$. Then $\equiv_h$ is a Σ-congruence on B. Conversely, if $\equiv$ is a congruence on B, then the canonical map sending $b \in B$ to $[b] \in B/\!\equiv$ is a Σ-homomorphism.

Proof: First, each $(\equiv_h)_s$ is clearly an equivalence relation. Now, let $\sigma \in \Sigma_{s_1 \ldots s_n, s}$ and assume $b_i\ (\equiv_h)_{s_i}\ b_i'$ for $i = 1, \ldots, n$. Then $h_s(\sigma_B(b_1, \ldots, b_n)) = \sigma_A(h_{s_1}(b_1), \ldots, h_{s_n}(b_n)) = \sigma_A(h_{s_1}(b_1'), \ldots, h_{s_n}(b_n')) = h_s(\sigma_B(b_1', \ldots, b_n'))$, so that $\sigma_B(b_1, \ldots, b_n)\ (\equiv_h)_s\ \sigma_B(b_1', \ldots, b_n')$. For the second part of the lemma, let $g_s(b) = [b]_s \in (B/\!\equiv)_s$. That g is a Σ-homomorphism comes directly from the definition of $B/\!\equiv$: For $\sigma \in \Sigma_{s_1 \ldots s_n, s}$ and $b_i \in B_{s_i}$, $g_s(\sigma_B(b_1, \ldots, b_n)) = [\sigma_B(b_1, \ldots, b_n)]_s = \sigma_{B/\equiv}([b_1]_{s_1}, \ldots, [b_n]_{s_n}) = \sigma_{B/\equiv}(g_{s_1}(b_1), \ldots, g_{s_n}(b_n))$.

Lemma 6B

If $\theta\colon X \longrightarrow T_\Sigma$ is a substitution[18] and $h\colon T_\Sigma \longrightarrow A$ is the unique homomorphism to a Σ-algebra A, then $h\theta$ is an assignment to the algebra A and $\overline{h\theta} = h\bar{\theta}$.

Proof: $h\bar{\theta}$ is a Σ-homomorphism and $h\bar{\theta}(x) = h\theta(x)$, so by the uniqueness part of Proposition 3, $\overline{h\theta} = h\bar{\theta}$.

Lemma 6C

Let A be a Σ-algebra satisfying $\mathcal{E}$, and let $\equiv_A$ be the Σ-congruence on T_Σ determined by the unique homomorphism $h_A\colon T_\Sigma \longrightarrow A$ via Lemma 6A. Then $\equiv_\mathcal{E}\ \subseteq\ \equiv_A$.

Proof: If we show $\mathcal{E}(T_\Sigma) \subseteq\ \equiv_A$, then we are done because $\equiv_\mathcal{E}$ is the least congruence on T_Σ containing $\mathcal{E}(T_\Sigma)$. Let $\langle\bar{\theta}(L), \bar{\theta}(R)\rangle$ be any pair in $\mathcal{E}(T_\Sigma)$: $h\bar{\theta}(L) = \overline{h\theta}(L)$ by Lemma 6B; $\overline{h\theta}(L) = \overline{h\theta}(R)$ because A satisfies $\mathcal{E}$, and $\overline{h\theta}(R) = h\bar{\theta}(R)$ by Lemma 6B again. Thus $h(\bar{\theta}(L)) = h(\bar{\theta}(R))$, so that $\bar{\theta}(L) \equiv_A \bar{\theta}(R)$ by Lemma 6A.

[18]In Section 5.2 a substitution was defined as an assignment $\theta\colon X \longrightarrow T_\Sigma(X)$; what we mean when we say "$\theta\colon X \longrightarrow T_\Sigma$ is a substitution" is that each $x \in X$ is assigned a term in which no variables occur.

Theorem 6 *(Section 5.2)*

Let $\mathcal{E}$ be a Σ-presentation, and let $\equiv_{\mathcal{E}}$ be the Σ-congruence generated by $\mathcal{E}(T_\Sigma)$. Then $T_\Sigma/\equiv_{\mathcal{E}}$, the quotient of T_Σ by $\equiv_{\mathcal{E}}$, hereafter denoted $T_{\Sigma,\mathcal{E}}$, is initial in the category $\mathbf{Alg}_{\Sigma,\mathcal{E}}$ of all Σ-algebras satisfying $\mathcal{E}$.

Proof: Let A be any Σ-algebra satisfying $\mathcal{E}$, $h_A: T_\Sigma \longrightarrow A$, and $h_{\mathcal{E}}: T_\Sigma \longrightarrow T_{\Sigma,\mathcal{E}}$ (which by Lemma 6A sends t to $[t]$). Now if there is any homomorphism $g: T_{\Sigma,\mathcal{E}} \longrightarrow A$, the composite $gh_{\mathcal{E}}: T_\Sigma \longrightarrow A$ is also a homomorphism, and by uniqueness (Theorem 2) $gh_{\mathcal{E}} = h_A$; i.e., $h_A(t) = gh_{\mathcal{E}}(t) = g([t])$. Thus we know if g exists it is unique and $g([t]) = h_A(t)$. Taking that to be the definition of g, we need to check that it is independent of representatives; i.e., if $[t] = [t']$, then $h_A(t) = h_A(t')$. This is precisely Lemma 6C. Finally, the homomorphism property for g comes directly from the definition of the quotient and the fact that h_A is a homomorphism: $g(\sigma_{T/\equiv}([t_1], \ldots, [t_n])) = g([\sigma_T(t_1, \ldots, t_n)]) = h_A(\sigma_T(t_1, \ldots, t_n)) = \sigma_A(h_A(t_1), \ldots, h_A(t_n)) = \sigma_A(g([t_1]), \ldots, g([t_n]))$.

Proposition 7 (the error-insertion result) of Section 5.3 requires results in Section 5.4 for its proof. We shall proceed with those proofs and shall conclude this appendix with the proof of Proposition 7.

The construction of a canonical term algebra for any specification is based on an induction on *depth* of terms, for which we need the following definition.

Definition 7A. Let Σ be an S-sorted signature. Given a term $t \in T_\Sigma$, the *depth* of t is defined as follows:

1. If $t \in \Sigma_{\lambda,s}$ for some $s \in S$, then depth$(t) = 0$.
2. If $t = \sigma(t_1 \ldots t_n)$, where $\sigma \in \Sigma_{s_1\ldots s_n,s}$ and $t_i \in T_{\Sigma,s_i}$, then depth$(t) = 1 + \max\{\text{depth}(t_i) \mid i = 1, \ldots, n\}$.

Theorem 8 *(Section 5.4)*

Let $\langle S, \Sigma, \mathcal{E}\rangle$ be a specification. Then there exists an initial $(\Sigma, \mathcal{E})$-algebra C which is a canonical term algebra.

Proof: Say we can find a subset $C \subseteq T_\Sigma$ such that

(a) For each equivalence class $[t] \in T_{\Sigma,\mathcal{E}}$, C contains a single element $t^* \in [t]$, and

(b) For each $\sigma \in \Sigma$, $\sigma(t_1 \ldots t_n) \in C$ implies $t_i \in C$.

Then, by (a) we can make C into a $(\Sigma, \mathcal{E})$-algebra by defining, for $t_i \in C$,

$$(*) \qquad \sigma_C(t_1, \ldots, t_n) = (\sigma(t_1 \ldots t_n))^*.$$

Then, for C to be a canonical term algebra, we also need $\sigma_C(t_1, \ldots, t_n) = \sigma(t_1 \ldots t_n)$ for $\sigma(t_1 \ldots t_n) \in C$. But with $\sigma(t_1 \ldots t_n) \in C$, (a) gives $(\sigma(t_1 \ldots t_n))^*$

$= \sigma(t_1 \ldots t_n)$, which is what is needed because $\sigma_C(t_1, \ldots, t_n) = (\sigma(t_1 \ldots t_n))^*$.

Under the above assumptions we can show that $T_{\Sigma,\mathcal{E}} \cong C$, where the isomorphism is given by the set mapping $\imath: [t] \mapsto t^*$, which is clearly a (set) isomorphism of the carriers. We must show that it is a homomorphism. Given $\sigma \in \Sigma_{s_1 \ldots s_n, s}$ and $[t_i] \in (T_{\Sigma,\mathcal{E}})_{s_i}$, we have $\imath(\sigma_T([t_1], \ldots, [t_n])) = \imath[\sigma(t_1 \ldots t_n)] = (\sigma(t_1 \ldots t_n))^* = (\sigma(t_1^* \ldots t_n^*))^*$ (because $t_i \equiv_{\mathcal{E}} t_i^*$) $= \sigma_C(t_1^*, \ldots, t_n^*) = \sigma_C(\imath[t_1], \ldots, \imath[t_n])$.

Thus, to prove the theorem it suffices to display a set C satisfying (a) and (b) above. Our approach is to define a family $\langle C_n | n \in \omega \rangle$ of subsets of T_Σ such that $C = \cup\{C_n | n \in \omega\}$ will be the desired set of representatives. We shall proceed by induction on the depth of terms to produce C_n such that

(1) If $t \in C_n$, then depth$(t) \leq n$;

(2) If $t \in T_\Sigma$ such that $[t]$ has a representative of depth $\leq n$, then there is a unique representative for $[t]$ in C_n; and

(3) If $\sigma(t_1 \ldots t_n) \in C_n$, then $t_1, \ldots, t_n \in C_{n-1}$.

Let C_0 be any subset of $\cup_s \Sigma_{\lambda,s}$ such that for each $\sigma \in \cup_s \Sigma_{\lambda,s}$ there exists a unique $\sigma^* \in C_0$ with $\sigma^* \equiv_{\mathcal{E}} \sigma$. Since the only terms of depth 0 are constants, this can clearly be done, and the conditions on C_0 are satisfied.

Assume that C_n has been defined satisfying (1), (2), and (3) above. Let T_{n+1} be the set of equivalence classes $[t]$ such that there exists $t^* \equiv_{\mathcal{E}} t$ with depth$(t^*) = n + 1$, and for all t', if $t' \equiv_{\mathcal{E}} t$, then depth$(t') \geq n + 1$. (There is a representative of depth $n + 1$, and all respresentatives have depth $n + 1$ or greater.) Let C_{n+1} be C_n together with a single representative $\sigma(t_1^* \ldots t_n^*)$ of $[t] \in T_{n+1}$, which has depth $n + 1$ and for which $t_i^* \in C_n$. This is possible since $t^* \in [t] \in T_{n+1}$ of depth $n + 1$ by definition, and $t^* = \sigma(t_1 \ldots t_n)$. But depth$(t_i) \leq n$, and thus by (2) $t_i \equiv_{\mathcal{E}} t_i^* \in C_n$, so that $\sigma(t_1^* \ldots t_n^*)$ can be chosen as the representative of $[t]$.

It follows that $C = \cup\langle C_n | n \in \omega \rangle$ contains a unique representative t^* for each $[t] \in T_{\Sigma,\mathcal{E}}$ and furthermore that $\sigma(t_1 \ldots t_n) \in C$ implies $t_1, \ldots, t_n \in C$. Thus, by the earlier remarks we are done.

Knowing that there always exists an initial canonical term algebra, the remaining results of Section 5.4 deal with checking that a proposed canonical term algebra is initial. The following simple lemma is a useful characterization for the proofs of those results.

Lemma 9A

Let $\langle S, \Sigma, \mathcal{E} \rangle$ be a specification, let A be a $(\Sigma, \mathcal{E})$-algebra, and let $\equiv_A$ be the congruence on T_Σ determined by the unique homomorphism $h_A: T_\Sigma \longrightarrow A$ (see Lemma 6C). Then $A \cong T_{\Sigma,\mathcal{E}}$ if $\equiv_A \subseteq \equiv_{\mathcal{E}}$ and h_A is surjective.

Proof: Since A satisfies $\mathcal{E}$, $\equiv_{\mathcal{E}} \subseteq \equiv_A$ by Lemma 6C. Then with the hypothesis of this lemma we have $\equiv_{\mathcal{E}} = \equiv_A$, so that $T_{\Sigma,\mathcal{E}} = T_\Sigma/\equiv_{\mathcal{E}} = T_\Sigma/\equiv_A$. The canonical map $T_\Sigma/\equiv_A \longrightarrow A$ sending $[t]$ to $h_A(t)$ is injective by the definition of $\equiv_A$, surjective by hypothesis, and a Σ-homomorphism by Lemma 6A. Thus $T_{\Sigma,\mathcal{E}} = T_\Sigma/\equiv_A \cong A$.

A crucial property of canonical Σ-term algebras immediately gives us one of the hypotheses of Lemma 9A.

Lemma 9B

If C is a canonical Σ-term algebra, then the unique homomorphism $h_C\colon T_\Sigma \longrightarrow C$ is surjective; in fact $h_C(t) = t$ for $t \in C$.

Proof: Using structural induction, if σ is in C and in $\Sigma_{\lambda,s}$ for some $s \in S$, then $h_C(\sigma) = \sigma_C = \sigma$, by Definition 11. Inductively assuming $h_C(t_i) = t_i$ for $t_i \in C$ $(i = 1, \ldots, n)$ and taking $\sigma(t_1 \ldots t_n) \in C$, we have $h_C(\sigma(t_1 \ldots t_n)) = \sigma_C(h_C(t_1), \ldots, h_C(t_n)) = \sigma_C(t_1, \ldots, t_n) = \sigma(t_1, \ldots, t_n)$, again using the definition of canonical term algebra.

Theorem 9 (*Section 5.4*)

Let $\langle S, \Sigma, \mathcal{E}\rangle$ be a specification, and let C be a canonical Σ-term algebra. Then $C \cong T_{\Sigma,\mathcal{E}}$ iff

(1) C satisfies $\mathcal{E}$.

(2) For each $\sigma \in \Sigma_{s_1 \ldots s_n, s}$ and $t_i \in C_{s_i}$, $\sigma(t_1 \ldots t_n) \equiv_{\mathcal{E}} \sigma_C(t_1, \ldots, t_n)$.

Proof: Let $h\colon T_\Sigma \longrightarrow C$ be the homomorphism given by the initiality of T_Σ.

To show that $C \cong T_{\Sigma,\mathcal{E}}$ we need, by the preceding lemma, only show that h is surjective and that $\equiv_h \subseteq \equiv_{\mathcal{E}}$. The first condition is just Lemma 9B.

To show $\equiv_h \subseteq \equiv_{\mathcal{E}}$ it suffices to prove that, for any $t \in T_\Sigma$, $t \equiv_{\mathcal{E}} h(t)$, because if $t \equiv_h t'$, then $t \equiv_{\mathcal{E}} h(t) = h(t') \equiv_{\mathcal{E}} t'$. Thus, we're showing t $\mathcal{E}$-congruent to its canonical representative.

We proceed by structural induction on t. If $t = \sigma \in \Sigma_{\lambda,s}$ for some $s \in S$, then $h(\sigma) = \sigma_C \equiv_{\mathcal{E}} \sigma$ by hypothesis. Now let $t = \sigma(t_1 \ldots t_n)$, where $\sigma \in \Sigma_{s_1 \ldots s_n, s}$ and $t_1, \ldots, t_n \in T_\Sigma$ such that $t_i \equiv_{\mathcal{E}} h(t_i)$. Then $h(\sigma(t_1 \ldots t_n)) = \sigma_C(h(t_1), \ldots, h(t_n)) \equiv_{\mathcal{E}} \sigma(h(t_1) \ldots h(t_n)) \equiv_{\mathcal{E}} \sigma(t_1 \ldots t_n)$, by the hypotheses of the theorem and the induction.

Now we have the converse, that $C \cong T_{\Sigma,\mathcal{E}}$ implies conditions (1) and (2). Trivially for C to be an initial $(\Sigma, \mathcal{E})$-algebra it must be a $(\Sigma, \mathcal{E})$-algebra and thus must satisfy $\mathcal{E}$; this takes care of (1).

Since we are assuming $C \cong T_{\Sigma,\mathcal{E}}$, it follows that $\equiv_{\mathcal{E}} = \equiv_C$, so for condition (2) we need only show $\sigma(t_1 \ldots t_n) \equiv_C \sigma_C(t_1, \ldots, t_n)$ for $t_i \in C$. But $h_C(\sigma(t_1 \ldots t_n)) = \sigma_C(h(t_1), \ldots, h(t_n)) = \sigma_C(t_1, \ldots, t_n) = h_C(\sigma_C(t_1, \ldots, t_n))$, the last two equalities from Lemma 9B.

Corollary 10 (*Section 5.4*)

Let $\langle S, \Sigma, \mathcal{E}\rangle$ be a specification, let $\langle S, \bar{\Sigma}, \bar{\mathcal{E}}\rangle$ be a specification such that $\Sigma \subseteq \bar{\Sigma}$ and $\mathcal{E} \subseteq \bar{\mathcal{E}}$, and let A be an initial $(\Sigma, \mathcal{E})$-algebra of canonical terms. Then a $\bar{\Sigma}$-algebra $\bar{A}$ such that

(a) $\bar{A}_s = A_s$ for each $s \in S$ and

(b) $\sigma_{\bar{A}} = \sigma_A$ for each $\sigma \in \Sigma$

is an initial $(\bar{\Sigma}, \bar{\mathcal{E}})$-algebra, and $\langle S, \bar{\Sigma}, \bar{\mathcal{E}}\rangle$ is an enrichment of $\langle S, \Sigma, \mathcal{E}\rangle$ if

(1) $\bar{A}$ satisfies $\bar{\mathcal{E}} - \mathcal{E}$, and

(2) For each $\sigma \in (\bar{\Sigma}_{s_1 \ldots s_n, s} - \Sigma_{s_1 \ldots s_n, s})$ and all $t_i \in A_{s_i}$, $\sigma(t_1 \ldots t_n) \equiv_{\bar{\mathcal{E}}} \sigma_{\bar{A}}(t_1, \ldots, t_n)$.

Proof: Since A is a canonical term algebra, it follows from (a) and (b) that $\bar{A}$ is a canonical term algebra. Thus all we need to do is show that $\bar{A}$ satisfies conditions (1) and (2) of Theorem 9, with respect to $\bar{\Sigma}$ and $\bar{\mathcal{E}}$.

Now since $A \cong T_{\Sigma, \mathcal{E}}$, we know that A satisfies conditions (1) and (2) of Theorem 9 with respect to Σ and $\mathcal{E}$.

Thus since $\bar{A}$ viewed as a Σ-algebra *is* A [by (a) and (b)], we know that $\bar{A}$ satisfies $\mathcal{E}$. But, by hypothesis (1), $\bar{A}$ satisfies $\bar{\mathcal{E}} - \mathcal{E}$, and so $\bar{A}$ satisfies $\bar{\mathcal{E}}$; this gives condition (1) of Theorem 9.

Since A satisfies condition (2) of Theorem 9 with respect to Σ, $\mathcal{E}$, we know that for each $\sigma \in \Sigma_{s_1 \ldots s_n, s}$ and all $t_i \in A_{s_i}$

$$(*) \qquad \sigma(t_1 \ldots t_n) \equiv_{\mathcal{E}} \sigma_A(t_1, \ldots, t_n).$$

But since $\mathcal{E} \subseteq \bar{\mathcal{E}}$, $\equiv_{\mathcal{E}} \subseteq \equiv_{\bar{\mathcal{E}}}$, and by (a) $\bar{A}_s = A_s$, and by (b) $\sigma_{\bar{A}} = \sigma_A$; thus $(*)$ implies $\sigma(t_1 \ldots t_n) \equiv_{\bar{\mathcal{E}}} \sigma_{\bar{A}}(t_1, \ldots, t_n)$ for all $\sigma \in \Sigma$, $t_i \in \bar{A}_{s_i}$. This together with hypothesis (2) then gives us condition (2) of Theorem 9 and we are done.

Proposition 7 (*Section 5.3*)

Let $\langle S, \Sigma, \mathcal{C}\rangle$ be a specification with bool $\in S$ protected, and define $\langle S, \bar{\Sigma}, \bar{\mathcal{E}}\rangle$ as follows. $\bar{\Sigma}$ differs from Σ by the addition, for each $s \in S$, of

$$E_s \quad \text{to } \Sigma_{\lambda, s}$$
$$\mathrm{OK}_s \text{ to } \Sigma_{s, \underline{\mathrm{bool}}}$$
$$\mathrm{IFE}_s \text{ to } \Sigma_{\underline{\mathrm{bool}}\, s\, s, s}.$$

Now $\bar{\mathcal{E}}$ contains the following equations, for $s \in S$, $w = s_1 \ldots s_n$, $\sigma \in \Sigma_{w,s}$, y_i of sort s_i, and $e = \langle L, R\rangle \in \mathcal{E}$ of sort s and arity w:

ife-1 $\quad \mathrm{IFE}_s(T, S, S') = S$

ife-2 $\quad \mathrm{IFE}_s(F, S, S') = S'$

ife-3	$\text{IFE}(E_{\text{bool}}, S, S') = E_s$
ok$_s$	$\text{OK}_s(E_s) = F$
ok$_\sigma$	$\text{OK}_s(\sigma(y_1, \ldots, y_n)) = \wedge_{i=1}^{n} \text{OK}_{s_i}(y_i)$
error$_{\sigma,i}$	$\sigma(y_1, \ldots, E_{s_i}, \ldots, y_n) = E_s$
ifok$_e$	$\text{IFE}_s(\wedge_{i=1}^{n} \text{OK}_{s_i}(y_i), L, E_s) = \text{IFE}_s(\wedge_{i=1}^{n} \text{OK}_{s_i}(y_i), R, E_s)$.

Let $A_s = (T_{\Sigma,\mathcal{E}})_s \cup \{E_s\}$ for $s \in S$, and for $\sigma \in \Sigma_{w,s}$, $w = s_1 \ldots s_n$, $t_i \in A_{s_i}$, define

$$\sigma_A(t_1, \ldots, t_n) = \begin{cases} E_s & \text{if any } t_i = E_{s_i} \\ \sigma_T(t_1, \ldots, t_n) & \text{otherwise} \end{cases}$$

(where σ_T is σ in $T_{\Sigma,\mathcal{E}}$). With the operations IFE_A and OK_A defined in the obvious way, A is an initial $(\bar{\Sigma}, \bar{\mathcal{E}})$-algebra (i.e., it is isomorphic to $T_{\bar{\Sigma},\bar{\mathcal{E}}}$).

Proof: Let C be a canonical term algebra for the specification $(S, \Sigma, \mathcal{E})$ (available to us by Theorem 8), and define $\bar{C}_s = C_s \cup \{E_s\}$ with operations

$$\text{C-1} \qquad \sigma_{\bar{C}}(t_1, \ldots, t_n) = \begin{cases} \sigma_C(t_1 \ldots t_n) & \text{if all } t_i \neq E_{s_i} \\ E_s & \text{otherwise.} \end{cases}$$

Where $\sigma \in \Sigma_{s_1 \ldots s_n, s}$ and $t_i \in C_{s_i}$ for $i = 1, \ldots, n$. The definitions in $\bar{C}$ of OK and IFE are

$$\text{C-2} \qquad \text{OK}_{s,\bar{C}}(t) = \begin{cases} T & \text{if } t \in C_s \\ F & \text{if } t = E_s \end{cases}$$

$$\text{C-3} \qquad \text{IFE}_{s,\bar{C}}(B, D, D') = \begin{cases} D & \text{if } B = T \\ D' & \text{if } B = F \\ E_s & \text{if } B = E_{\text{bool}}. \end{cases}$$

$\bar{C}$ is isomorphic to the algebra A described in the statement of Proposition 7, but we are talking about canonical term carriers rather than carriers of any initial algebra. The advantage is that we are in a position to apply Theorem 9 *and* that we can do structural induction on those carriers. For example we want $\text{OK}(t) \equiv T$ for $t \in C_s$. Indeed, for constant σ, $\text{OK}(\sigma) \equiv T = \text{OK}_{\bar{C}}(\sigma)$ by ok$_\sigma$ and C-2. Then for $\sigma(t_1, \ldots, t_n) \in C_s$, we know all $t_i \in C_{s_i}$ because we have a canonical term algebra, and by induction we can assume $\text{OK}(t_i) \equiv T$, whence, by the correctness of boole (Example 7EC), $\wedge_{i=1}^{n} \text{OK}(t_1) \equiv T$ and axiom ok$_\sigma$ gives

$$\text{OK}(\sigma(t_1, \ldots, t_n)) \equiv \text{OK}_w(t_1 \ldots t_n) \equiv T = \text{OK}_{\bar{C}}(\sigma(t_1 \ldots t_n)).$$

This gives the representation condition for OK; the crucial one for the operation $\sigma \in \Sigma$ depends on that for OK and is a bit more complicated. First, if one of the arguments is E, $\sigma(t_1, \ldots, E_{s_i}, \ldots, t_n) \equiv E_s = \sigma_{\bar{C}}(t_1, \ldots, E_{s_i}, \ldots, t_n)$ by error$_{\sigma,i}$ and C-1. But if no arguments are errors, we have $\sigma(t_1, \ldots, t_n)$

$\equiv_{\mathcal{E}} \sigma_C(t_1, \ldots, t_n) = \sigma_{\bar{C}}(t_1 \ldots t_n)$, because C is a canonical term algebra and because of the way $\sigma_{\bar{C}}$ is defined (C-1). We now only have to show $\equiv_{\mathcal{E}} \subseteq \equiv_{\bar{\mathcal{E}}}$ where $\bar{\mathcal{E}}$ is the family of equations above including the "conditioned" versions of $\mathcal{E}$. Recall that $\equiv_{\mathcal{E}}$ was the least congruence containing substitution instances of $\mathcal{E}$ (Theorem 6). So to establish $\equiv_{\mathcal{E}} \subseteq \equiv_{\bar{\mathcal{E}}}$ it is sufficient to show $L(t_1, \ldots, t_n) \equiv_{\bar{\mathcal{E}}} R(t_1, \ldots, t_n)$ for each $\langle L, R \rangle \in \mathcal{E}$. Having shown above $\bigwedge_{i=1}^{n} \mathrm{OK}_{s_i}(t_i) \equiv \mathrm{OK}_w(t_1, \ldots, t_n) \equiv T$, Lemma 11 (Section 5.4) gives exactly this result. This completes the proof.

CHAPTER 6

SCHEMES: A HIGH-LEVEL DATA STRUCTURING CONCEPT

JAMES G. MITCHELL
BEN WEGBREIT
Xerox Palo Alto Research Center
Palo Alto, California

Abstract

In recent years, programming languages have provided better constructs for data type definitions and have placed increasing reliance on type machinery for protection, modularization, and abstraction. In this chapter we introduce several new constructs which further these ends. Types may be defined as similar to existing types, *extended* by additional properties. *Schemes* are type-parameterized definitions. For example, symbol tables and symbol table operations can be defined as a scheme with the key and value types as parameters; an instantiation of the scheme implements a specific type of symbol table. Because new types are typically defined along with other related types, an instantiated scheme may *export* a set of new types group. A set of schemes with a common name and common external behavior can be viewed as alternative implementations of an *abstraction*. Parameter specifications associated with each scheme are used to select the appropriate implementation for each use.

6.1. INTRODUCTION

The evolution of programming languages has seen a steady development in the use of data types. Early languages provided only a fixed set of types; later ones introduced type definition facilities; more recently, types have begun to be used for program abstraction and modularization, e.g., in SIMULA 67 [Dahl (1970)]. In this chapter, we shall continue this development. We shall describe several properties desirable in a type system which are not accommodated in existing languages. We shall then describe a new program structure, the *scheme*, which provides them.

Much of the research in data types has been driven by a few sample problems which have provided a focus for programming-language research [Hoare, (1975),

Dahl (1970)]. A popular example is the notion of a list of objects: The characteristics of lists which we wish to capture are that they represent homogeneous, possibly empty sequences of objects which may grow and shrink dynamically with the insertion or deletion of objects. Since list structures generally involve the use of pointers, they are one of the more "dangerous" data structuring mechanisms in a programming language [Hoare (1975)]. One of the aims of this chapter is to present mechanisms by which the notion of "lists of objects" could be programmed once and for all and protected against misuse. We shall call a group of definitions and programs which cover a notion such as this an *implementation scheme*, or simply a *scheme*. The purpose of this work is to discuss how schemes such as "list of objects" can be added to a high-level programming language.

Other examples will involve complex numbers, the notion of a reference-counting storage allocator for any type of objects, and a family of hash table schemes. We shall first use the list example to outline a number of the properties which we desire for schemes.

6.2. PROPERTIES OF SCHEMES

6.2.1. An Example—Singly Linked Lists

The first question to be answered is, Why is it not already possible to define notions such as "list of objects" in existing languages? Suppose that an assembly-language programmer wanted to write a package of routines which could make and manipulate singly linked lists of any sort of values. He would have to establish a set of parameterized procedures to copy list cells which would either take as a parameter the number of words occupied by the datum in a cell or possibly the address of a user-supplied routine for allocating and copying those values. On this framework he could build the list processing capabilities.

This approach suffers from four drawbacks. First, if a single set of routines is to provide this capability, then many of them will have to be given extra parameters on each call to specify information such as the number of words in the datum; we would like to avoid such run-time overhead. Second, because assembly language is untyped, there are no guarantees that programs will supply such size parameters correctly, or will not attempt to make lists containing two different kinds of values; we would like the protection offered by a typed language. Third, although the list processing machinery could all be written in one physical unit, there is absolutely nothing to prevent *any* routine from maintaining its own pointers to list cells or from smashing the pointers in list cells; we would like to confine access rights for a given data structuring mechanism to textually localized regions. Fourth, in the absence of types, one cannot have common function names for similar operations on many different types of data; i.e., there can be only one procedure with a given name in a program. Hence, if one wants a function which yields the length of some object, he must name it differently for each object type; we would like a more generic naming mechanism.

To summarize, the methods of assembly-language programming require four improvements:

(R1) There should be a minimum of run-time overhead incurred by a general list processing package.

(R2) The language should be fully typed to prevent misuse of a general package.

(R3) It must be possible to confine the access to certain parts of a data structure to a specific set of routines which are held responsible for it.

(R4) It should be possible to reuse the same names for similar functions.

A high-level language does not necessarily overcome these problems. For instance, typeless languages such as BCPL [Richards (1968)] inherit the same drawbacks as assembly language. Further, BCPL imposes a language restriction that a function can return only single-word entities. Thus, any generalized implementation scheme in BCPL will require passing pointers among procedures instead of actual values. This is perfectly acceptable for the list example; for some of the other examples discussed later, it is not.

PL/I [IBM (1968)] is partially typed in that nonpointer objects have a rigid type structure, whereas pointers are effectively typeless. Thus, a technique like that suggested for BCPL can be used for the concept "list of" at the expense of giving up type protection. PL/I did, however, take a useful step forward in introducing *generic functions*, which allow a single name to be used for a number of operations, with the correct one being chosen on the basis of the types of its arguments.

In many ways, SIMULA 67 represents the most significant attempt to provide a means of associating a new set of behaviors with previously defined types. SIMULA *classes* provide several of the properties desired for schemes. A class defines a set of value *components* and operations, together called the *attributes* of the class, a terminology which we shall adopt for schemes as well. Any type in the language can be *prefixed* with a class name, meaning that it will have both the attributes of that class and those defined for the new type itself. The language is almost fully typed (there is an omission in the case of procedure variables), and much of the type checking is done at compile time. However, it lacks several other desirable features explained below:

(R5) One should be able to write *polymorphic* definitions.

(R6) One should be able to add new qualities to a given type in a more general manner than SIMULA's strict prefixing.

(R7) One should be able to deal with actual objects, not just pointers to them.

Classes in SIMULA would be truly *polymorphic* if they could have type parameters. Then one could define a class *stack*, for instance, in which the type of the objects to be the values on the stack was a parameter of the class *stack*. As it is, the ability to prefix one class with another does give a limited form of polymorphism. We would, however, like to be able to associate a number of attributes with a type in other ways than SIMULA's strict subclass capability. For instance, while it is possible in SIMULA to define a class *list* and then to use it to define lists of objects of any given type, it is not possible to define a class so that it can use the list notion twice and define objects which are simultaneously on two singly threaded lists. We would like to have a more general mechanism for associating groups of attributes with a type.

In SIMULA, one cannot create local variables of a given class, only pointers to such objects; the objects themselves must be explicitly created and are reclaimed by garbage collection. For many applications this is exactly the *right* thing to have, but it does introduce an asymmetry in the data structuring mechanisms, and it prohibits certain kinds of classes, for instance, simple, multicomponent objects such as complex numbers, which could be created as normal local variables.

The incompleteness of SIMULA's typing system was rectified in ALGOL 68. Other than this, however, ALGOL 68 [van Wijngaarden (1969)] is less suitable for our purposes than SIMULA because it has no mechanism like classes for encapsulating all the operations on the objects of some type or any means such as prefix classes for extending the behavior of previously defined types. ALGOL 68 has extended the capability for generic operations to include user-defined operators for new data types, although the programmer cannot define generic procedures.

EL1 [Wegbreit (1974)] treates types as manipulable values of the language. Types can be computed as the results of expressions, compared, and assigned to type-valued variables. One can write functions which take types as arguments and return types as their values. Such type-generating functions provide some of the facilities of schemes. For example, it is straightforward to write a function which computes "stacks of *t*" for any type argument *t*. EL1 also provides generic procedures and a partial framework for encapsulating a type and restricting access to it. It lacks a subclass mechanism such as SIMULA's, and its generic procedures are less convenient to write than the generic operators of ALGOL 68.

Other current language research efforts [Gries and Gehani (1974)], CLU [Liskov and Zilles (1974)] and ALPHARD [Wulf (1974)], deal with the notion of parameterized types, encapsulation of types, and extending built-in operators to new types. These languages provide alternative solutions to several of the problems we shall treat in this chapter.

6.2.2. Other Properties of Schemes

While reviewing the characteristics of several languages above, we outlined some of the properties which we would like schemes to have. There are some other properties which did not arise in that discussion but which we deem important:

(R8) A scheme should be able to define and export a set of related types, rather than a single type. A single type is not always sufficient to describe objects with complex behaviors.

(R9) Schemes should cascade nicely; for instance, given a scheme which can append the behavior of a reference-counted allocation scheme to any type and a scheme to implement lists of objects, one would like to be able to define a new scheme which provides lists of reference-counted objects simply by using the already existing ones without explicitly having to program their union.

(R10) It must be possible to impose constraints on the parameters to a scheme: To select one scheme from a set of schemes for symbol tables, for example, some selection on the basis of the parameters to a generic scheme is necessary.

(R11) It should be possible to completely specify the behavior of any defined type. In particular, it should be possible to specify how objects are to be initialized, how assignment and other operations are to be interpreted, and how objects are finalized and destroyed. A scheme definition should specify this behavior for a family of types.

6.2.3. An Outline of the Scheme Mechanism

Before going into detail, it will be useful to sketch the main points of the mechanism we propose. As a starting point, we take a fully typed language which has a protection mechanism to localize access authority for a type to its defining form [Morris (1973)]; for our purposes, this will be PASCAL-based [Wirth (1975)]. A *scheme* is a new language form which can be parameterized. The parameters to a scheme may be types, procedures, and other values which are known at compile time. (Such values are sometimes called "manifest.") To a rough approximation, a scheme may be regarded as a macro. Each use of a scheme is expanded during compilation to produce an *instance* of the scheme. A scheme instance is typically a type, e.g., "list of integers" or "reference-counted strings," but it can be any compile-time constant, such as a record type whose components are types, so that a single scheme can define a set of types. Schemes entail no run-time overhead because they are instantiated during compilation. Since they are parameterized, a single definition can be used to specify the behavior of a family of types. Finally, it is possible for multiple schemes to have the same name (if, for example, they represent different implementations of the same abstraction). A generic selection mechanism will be used to choose the correct scheme, based on properties of the instantiating arguments.

The remainder of this chapter is devoted to a design for schemes as an addition to the PASCAL programming language [Wirth (1975)]. We have undertaken this as an extended foray into uncharted waters. We have made little effort to be conservative; indeed, we have introduced new notation and language features whenever they seemed useful. Our aim here was not to consolidate the known but to explore the unknown. Those points where the exposition is labored often mark shoals where subsequent efforts might well be spent. Further, this is at present a paper design: No implementation has been undertaken. Our previous experience with designs for programming-language features leads us to think that errors will be discovered and changes will be made in an implementation but also that the main ideas will prove useful. Therefore, it seems appropriate to present the design in its present state.

6.3. SOME EXTENSIONS TO PASCAL

When carrying out this design, we discovered the need for several extensions to the PASCAL-type system. These extensions were required to support the scheme system but could also be used in defining individual types. They serve to facilitate definitions which would otherwise be awkward or lengthy. Because they can be presented in the context of a conventional type system and build on existing techniques [Geschke and Mitchell (1975), Wegbreit, (1974)] in a straightforward way, it will be simplest to start with them.

Suppose we wish to define the type *Rational* whose components are two integers *numerator* and *denominator*. A new *Rational* is to be initialized to zero, represented by the pair (0, 1). A procedure is to be provided for allocating *Rationals* from a free storage pool and the usual arithmetic operations are to be implemented. The definition follows; the reader is advised to skip immediately to the explanatory comments following it:

```
type Rational = record                                          (m1)
    {Rational maintains the invariant, denominator > 0}
    private var numerator, denominator: integer;                (m2)
    procedure INIT(shared p: Rational);                         (m3)
        begin
        p.numerator := 0; p.denominator := 1;                   (m4)
        end;                                                    (m5)
    function NEW returns p: Rational.ref;                       (m6)
        begin
        p.lower := new Rational.lower;                          (m7)
        INIT(p);                                                (m8)
        end;
    function PLUS(x,y: Rational) returns z: Rational;           (m9)
        begin . . . end;
    function Positive(x:Rational) returns Boolean;              (m10)
        begin
        return (x: numerator > 0);                              (m11)
        end
    . . .
    end Rational;                                               (m12)
```

The line numbers in the right margin are not part of the program; they serve as keys to the explanations given in the following sections.

6.3.1. Extensions to PASCAL Records

We have made four changes to PASCAL records. One is trivial and was added solely to enhance readability: the end for a record type may be followed by an identifier as in (m12) to say which record definition it acts as right bracket for. The second change is more consequential: The field list in a record may contain any declarations, including procedures (m3), functions (m6), constants, and types, much like modules in

MODULA [Wirth (1977)] or EUCLID (EUCLID (1977)]. The third change allows some components of a record type to be declared **private** (m2), meaning that they are not accessible from outside the record definition. The fourth generalizes the notation for referring to components of records: If a record type R defines a constant component, c, then the notation $R.c$ may be used to refer to it, since it has the same meaning in all objects of that type.

6.3.2. Changes to PASCAL Procedures and Functions

In PASCAL, parameters to procedures or functions may be passed in one of two basic ways: by value and by reference (**var**). We have changed this to the following three *parameter-passing modes*:

value: The actual parameter can be any expression (of which a simple variable is a special case); its value is copied into the parameter list for passing to the procedure or function.

const: The parameter is passed by value, just as above, but its value may not be altered in the body of the procedure or function for which it is a formal parameter.

shared: The parameter is to be passed by reference; changes to the formal parameter will change the actual parameter. The actual parameter must specify a variable and may not be a general expression.

The default parameter-passing mode is **value**. These modes are orthogonal to the types of the formal parameters.

We have expanded the possible value ranges of PASCAL functions: Here, functions may be declared to return a value of any fixed type. Also, we have altered the syntax for specifying the type of the return value to have one of the two forms

returns ⟨identifier⟩: ⟨type identifier⟩
returns ⟨type identifier⟩

and have added a return statement of the form

return ⟨expression⟩

which may appear anywhere in a function. If the result of a function is given a name (by using the first form for the **returns** specification), then a **return** statement is not necessary, and the last value assigned to that variable will be the value returned from the function. This syntax is copied directly from EUCLID [EUCLID (1977)].

6.3.3. The Lifetimes of Variables and Values

Pervading this report is a view of the lifetime of a data object, whether associated with a variable or not. This lifetime divides into three states: *nonexistent*, *space-reserved*, and *alive*. The process by which an object comes into existence, is used, and then is destroyed uses the transition operations *allocation*, *initialization*, *finalization*, and *deallocation* as shown in the *lifetime diagram* below:

```
              allocation                 initialization   finalization              deallocation
non-existent ────────► space-reserved ────────► alive ────────► space-reserved ────────► non-existent
```

A properly typed object is only accessible outside its definition when it is in the *alive* state. The four transition operations are characterized by the following:

1. *Allocation*: Space is acquired for the object. This space can come from two different kinds of storage: (a) The object can be embedded in an activation record, a record, or an array, or (b) it can be allocated separately from some free storage pool. If the former, the object's lifetime is intimately tied to the surrounding record or array, and we call it an *embedded* object. If the latter, its lifetime is strictly under program control, and we call it a *free-standing* object.
2. *Initialization*: The newly acquired space is assigned initial value(s) in order to establish some invariant property of the object. All built-in data types have an associated, system-defined initialization. All pointers are initialized to **nil**, but the initial values for integers, sets, or subrange objects are undefined.
3. *Finalization*: At the end of its useful lifetime, any housekeeping is done for the object before its space is freed for reuse. For example, the object may possess references to global objects which are to be explicitly destroyed before it can be considered finalized; if so, they would have to be finalized and deallocated as part of its finalization.
4. *Deallocation*: The object's space is freed. For an *embedded* object, this is a null operation because its storage goes away as part of deallocating the enclosing object. For a *free-standing* object, this will require a specific action to return the space to some storage pool.

This outline for each object's lifetime is reflected into our extended PASCAL as follows. Any record type may contain procedures named NEW, INIT, FINALIZE, and FREE (with suitable parameters, described below). In general, the user may supply none, some, or all four of these procedures; if he omits one, the system will supply a default meaning for it.

An *embedded* object is created when its enclosing object is. In this case, NEW and FREE of the embedded object's type are not used. However, if INIT is present, it will be invoked automatically after allocating the record or array in which the object is embedded. Before the surrounding array or record is freed, any FINALIZE procedure for that object will also be invoked automatically. This is shown in the following annotated *lifetime diagram*:

```
              enclosing                                                     deallocation
              object                                                        by an enclosing
              allocated                  INIT          FINALIZE             deallocation
non-existent ────────► space-reserved ────────► alive ────────► space-reserved ────────► non-existent
```

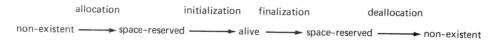

Free-standing objects are created when the program uses the **new** operator, which takes the form

new ⟨type expression⟩ ⟨parameter list⟩

This compiles into a call on the NEW function for the specified type with the additional parameters used to initialize the object. The value to be returned by the NEW function must be a reference type, pointing to the newly allocated and initialized object. In this case, the NEW function is itself responsible for initializing the new object (*otherwise, it couldn't return a pointer to a valid object*). That is, the NEW function, if provided by the programmer, is to perform the combined operations of allocation and initialization, the latter by calling INIT. The system-supplied default NEW for objects of a given type also initializes them; further, programmer-supplied initialization can be combined with system-supplied allocation by writing only an INIT procedure: If a given type specifies INIT but not NEW, the system will be responsible for allocating space for it but will call the user-supplied INIT to correctly initialize it before returning a reference value as the result of the **new** operation.

A free-standing object for which the program has a reference can be freed by using the **free** operation, which has the form

free ⟨reference value⟩

This is the dual of **new** and will compile into a call on the type's FREE procedure, if present. In parallel with the NEW function, FREE is responsible for finalizing the object (by calling FINALIZE) before deallocating its space. If no user-specified FREE is given for a type, then the system will manufacture a call on that type's FINALIZE (if present) before deallocating the object. The *lifetime diagram* is

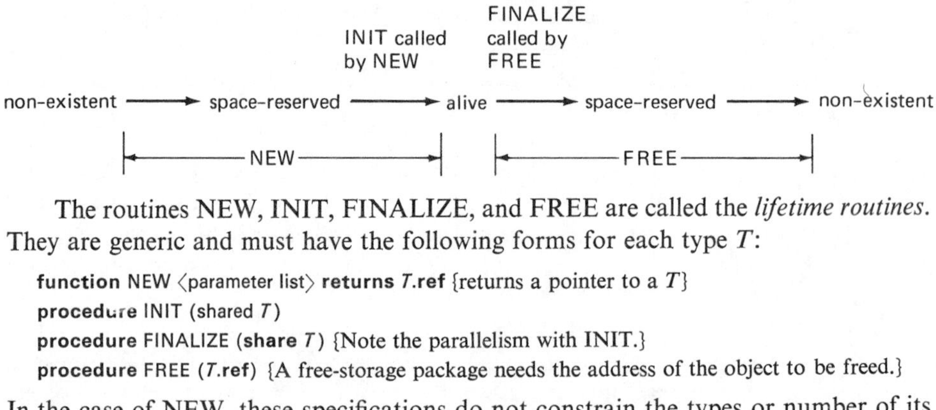

The routines NEW, INIT, FINALIZE, and FREE are called the *lifetime routines*. They are generic and must have the following forms for each type *T*:

function NEW ⟨parameter list⟩ **returns** *T*.**ref** {returns a pointer to a *T*}
procedure INIT (shared *T*)
procedure FINALIZE (**share** *T*) {Note the parallelism with INIT.}
procedure FREE (*T*.**ref**) {A free-storage package needs the address of the object to be freed.}

In the case of NEW, these specifications do not constrain the types or number of its parameters.

In the *Rational* example, both an INIT procedure and a NEW function are provided (m3 and m5), and the NEW function explicitly calls INIT (m8). The type of the result returned by NEW is specified as *Rational*.**ref**: For every type, *T*, there is an associated type *T*.**ref**, which is the type for references to objects of type *T*. We denote it as if **ref** were an attribute (a **type** attribute to be sure, but an attribute nevertheless).

It is occasionally useful to explicitly define **ref** for a record type, replacing the system-supplied attribute; in such a case, *T*.**ref** has the explicitly specified meaning. This is a way to define together a type and a special class of pointers to objects of that type. The type name then serves as a handle on both.

Conversely, for a given reference type *R*, there is an associated type, *R*.**node**, which is the type of the objects to which an *R* refers. Consequently, for any type *T*, *T*.**ref.node** = *T*.

In the example, NEW obtains storage for a *Rational* by making a **new** *Rational*.**lower**. For each record type *R* which specifies any nondefault behavior, there is an associated record type *R*.**lower** which has the same structure *but entirely standard, system-defined behavior* (i.e., no user-supplied NEW, INIT, FINALIZE, or FREE). We call this associated type the *foundation type* of *R*. To ensure type integrity the attribute **lower** cannot be applied outside the scope of *R*. The value returned from the operation **new** *Rational*.**lower** (m7) is a *Rational*.**lower.ref**, which is basically just a reference to a record of two integer components. It is assigned to *p*, which is treated as if it had type *Rational*.**lower.ref**; that *p* is to be so treated is indicated by writing *p*.**lower**.

6.3.4. Records, Procedures, and Generic Selection

There are four ways in which record attributes may be invoked:

1. With the dot notation, e.g., *Rational*.**ref**,
2. With the generic selection mechanism when triggered by an appearance of a procedure name, e.g., *Positive*,
3. With the generic selection mechanism triggered by the appearance of a language-established operation, e.g., **new** invokes NEW, ":=" invokes ASSIGN, "+" invokes PLUS, etc.
4. With the generic selection mechanism when triggered by a system action, e.g., the procedure INIT associated with object initialization.

The generic selection mechanism is invoked by the compiler when it encounters a procedure name *p* applied to arguments whose types are *t1*, . . .·, *tn* in a context requiring result type *tr*. It looks for an interpretation for *p* whose type structure agrees with *t1*, . . ., *tn*, *tr*. If a unique such meaning is found, it is used; if no meaning is found or multiple meanings are found, the expression is flagged as as error [Geschke and Mitchell (1976)]. For example, the function PLUS (m9) in *Rational* takes two *Rationals* and returns a *Rational* value; it is thus suitable for use in any expression of the form "*exp1* + *exp2*" in which *exp1* and *exp2* are both *Rational* expressions. Assignment is treated specially in one regard: If the types of the left and right sides are *L* and *R*, respectively, then an interpretation is sought in which the parameter type structure is (*L*; *R*) and *L*'s parameter-passing mode is **shared**.

Note that PLUS is allowed to access the private components of a *Rational* because it is declared within the type. This, along with generic selection, makes it possible to write binary operators dealing with the internal representation of separate values of the same type. This convention might be contrasted with that used in extensions to SIMULA 67 and various encapsulation proposals based on SIMULA classes [Palme (1976), Liskov and Zilles (1974)]. In these proposals, $x.f(y)$ can be used to invoke the f procedure defined in x's class. f has normal access to the parameter y and privileged access to x (because f is in x's class). Privileged access to y is not allowed.

We have repeatedly used the idea that each record type carries with it a set of attributes, some defined explicitly, some provided by the system as part of every record type, and some explicitly supplanting a system-provided definition. This structure serves two ends: that of providing a reasonable behavior for any defined type with minimal specification in the definition and that of allowing additional specifications to override the system defaults. One special case of overriding deserves comment: a definition which renders illegal the use of a system-defined attribute. This may be accomplished by defining an attribute with the value **Error**; use of that attribute will be detected as illegal during compilation. For example, a system-supplied attribute such as **ref** may be overriden by a declaration such as

```
type ref = Error;
```

6.3.5. Extending the Semantics of an Object

As a matter of notational convenience, it is often useful to define a new type by extending an existing one. This may be accomplished by the construction

```
type Trec = basePart: BaseType extended by ⟨field list⟩ end Trec
```

or

```
type Trec = BaseType extended by ⟨field list⟩ end Trec
```

where ⟨field list⟩ is the syntax which normally appears in the context **record** ⟨field list⟩ **end**. This is defined to be shorthand for

```
type Trec = record
    basePart: BaseType {or some unnamed BaseType component}
    ⟨field list⟩
    procedure ASSIGN (shared x. BaseType; y: Trec)
        begin x := y.basePart end;
    end Trec
```

Trec is thus defined to have a preferred *BaseType* component, additional attributes as specified, and a conversion from *Trecs* to *BaseTypes*. In this sense, *Trecs* behave as proper extensions of *BaseTypes*. The user program may supply its own ASSIGN routine in the ⟨field list⟩ to override the one supplied automatically as part of the **extended by** construction.

For example, consider extending *Rational* so that each rational keeps a count of the number of times its value is changed by assignment:

```
type TallyedRational = rat: Rational extended by
    var tally: integer;                                              (t1)
    procedure INIT(shared p: TallyedRational);                       (t2)
        begin
        p.tally := 0;
        end;
    procedure ASSIGN(shared left: TallyedRational; right: Rational); (t3)
        begin
        left.tally := left.tally+1;
        l.rat := right
        end;
    end TallyedRational
```

This defines *TallyedRational* to be like *Rational* except in three ways:

(t1) All instances have an additional component named *tally*, of type **integer**.

(t2) An INIT is supplied for *TallyedRational*.

(t3) A procedure named ASSIGN is supplied to be used when the left-hand side of an assignment is a *TallyedRational*.

6.4. EXAMPLE SCHEMES

6.4.1. An Implementation of Queues

As a first example we shall define a scheme which implements queues using a linked list of nodes which hold queue elements. Each queue has a head which contains pointers to the front and rear nodes. To make the treatment of empty and nonempty queues uniform, we shall adopt the convention that all queues end with a dummy node. Thus, the empty queue is represented by a queue head in which the front and rear pointers point to a dummy node. When a queue head is initialized, it is set to this empty state. Adding an element to a queue is accomplished by putting the element into the dummy node, allocating a new node to serve as dummy, putting it on the end of the node list, and adjusting the *rear* pointer in the queue head. Removing an element from a queue is accomplished by setting the *front* pointer in the queue head to reference the second element in the node list and returning the element found in the former first element.

The following scheme defines a record having two **type** attributes: *Head* and *Node*; also, it includes an initialization routine and the set of queue operations:

```
scheme Queue(type ItemType) = record
    type Head = record var front, rear: Node.ref end;
    type Node = item: ItemType extended by private var next: Node.ref end;
```

```
procedure INIT(shared q: Head);
{This will be invoked whenever a new Head is created.}
    begin
    q.front := new Node;
    q.rear := q.front
    end;
function Empty(q: Head) returns Boolean; {Test for the empty queue.}
    begin return (q.front = q.rear) end;
procedure Add(shared q: Head; item: ItemType);
{Add item to q, modifying q as a side effect.}
    begin
    q.rear↑.item := item;
    q.rear↑.next := new Node;
    q.rear := q.rear↑.next
    end;
function Remove(shared q: Head) returns item: ItemType;
{Remove (and return) the first item from q, modifying q as a side effect.}
    begin
    if Empty(q) then Error;
    item := q.front↑.item;
    q.front  := q.front↑.next;
    end;
end Queue;
```

To use this scheme in defining a type, we instantiate it; for example,

```
type IQ = Queue(integer);
```

defines *IQ* to be an instantiation of *Queue*. From the definition of *Queue*, it follows that *IQ* is a **record** type having attributes *Head* and *Node*, which are both types. Thus, *IQ.Head* is the data type for heads of queues which hold integers, and

```
q1: IQ.Head;
```

declares *q1* to be a variable of this type. It would, of course, be possible to contract this to the equivalent

```
q1: Queue(integer).Head;
```

Each instance of the *Queue* scheme is a separate data type which has, at least in principle, its own copy of the scheme procedures INIT, *Empty*, *Add*, and *Delete*. We consider INIT as representative. In the instance *Queue*(**integer**), the INIT procedure is defined so that *Head* in its formal parameter specification is instantiated to *Queue* (**integer**). *Head.* Thus the formal parameter *q* in INIT is passed as a **shared** parameter and has the data type

```
record
    var front, rear: Queue(integer).Node.ref
end
```

When *q1* is created, the INIT procedure will be invoked by the system. It will be seen that the types are correct. The code in INIT allocates the dummy node and links it in. If we then execute

```
Add(q1, 9)
```

the instance of *Add* in the type *Queue*(**integer**) is invoked. Similar considerations apply to the other *Queue* operations.

It is important to note that the *Queue* implementation scheme is not itself a type, but rather it serves as a template for a set of (related) data types, namely all its instantiations. There are, of course, other ways of implementing queues; they may be described by other implementation schemes.

6.4.2. Reference-Counted Objects

Next, we shall define a scheme for controlling storage allocation of objects using a reference count added to each object. The reference count keeps track of how many *pointers* refer to the object at a given time. When another pointer is made to refer to the object, its count is incremented, and when a pointer no longer refers to it, the object's count is decremented. If an object's count ever becomes zero, it is deallocated.

```
scheme ReferenceCounted(type ItemType) = item: ItemType extended by   (r1)
    var count: integer;                                               (r2)
    procedure INIT(shared p: ref);                                    (r3)
        begin p.lower := nil end;
    procedure INIT(shared rcItem: ReferenceCounted);                  (r3a)
        Error; {Creating an embedded, reference-counted object is illegal.}
    function NEW returns(newp: ref);                                  (r4)
        begin
        newp.lower := new ReferenceCounted.lower;
        newp↑.count := 1;
        end;
    procedure FINALIZE(shared p: ref );                               (r5)
        begin
        if p = nil then return
        p↑.count := p↑.count-1;
        if p↑.count = 0 then free p;                                  (r6)
        end;
    procedure ASSIGN(shared left, right: ref);                        (r7)
        begin
        if right ≠ nil then right↑.count := right↑.count+1;
        FINALIZE(left); {Finalize left side before it is smashed.}    (r8)
        left.lower := right.lower; {Smash left.}
        end;
    end of ReferenceCounted;
```

Line (r1) defines *ReferenceCounted* as a **scheme** which, given a type *ItemType*, defines a new type which extends *ItemType* with some additional attributes. The additional attributes comprise a data component, *count* (r2), and five procedures: two INIT procedures—one for references to reference counted objects and one for the objects themselves (see explanation below)—NEW, FINALIZE, and ASSIGN, all part of a single **record** added to a *ItemType*. Observe that *ReferenceCounted* is used as a type in line (r3a) within a scheme; the appearance of the scheme's name denotes the current instantiation. Similarly, **ref** denotes *ReferenceCounted*.**ref**.

We shall show how the *ReferenceCounted* scheme is used and works by explicating the following code:

```
type RCreal = ReferenceCounted(real);        (e1)
r1, r2: RCreal.ref;                          (e2)
r1 := new RCreal;                            (e3)
r2 := r1;                                    (e4)
```

Line (e1) defines a new type, *RCreal*, for reference-counted reals; this new type is the result of expanding the *ReferenceCounted* scheme with the parameter **real** supplied. In line (e2), two pointers to *RCreals*, *r1* and *r2*, are defined; their type is equivalent to *ReferenceCounted*(**real**).**ref**.

We shall follow *r1* and *r2* through their lifetimes in the execution of the program segment above. *r1* and *r2* are embedded objects, allocated as part of an enclosing frame for the current procedure activation (see Section 3.3.3). The agent who allocates that frame provides space for them. Initialization is done explicitly—by the INIT procedure beginning at line (r3), whose parameter type indicates that it initializes **refs**. We wrote this INIT to demonstrate how a scheme can control *references to objects* as well as the objects themselves. It is in fact redundant because the default initialization for **refs** sets them to **nil**.

In line (e3), a specific request is made to create a new *RCreal* object and to store a pointer to it in *r1*. Since the *ReferenceCounted* scheme has provided a suitable NEW function (r4), it will be called instead of the system-supplied NEW. NEW first invokes the NEW function for the *foundation type RCreal*.**lower** (Section 3.3.3) underlying an *RCreal*. The result of that NEW will be a *RCreal*.**lower.ref**, which will then be assigned to *newp*. The appearance of **lower** on the left-hand side causes the system ASSIGN procedure for **ref.lower** to be used. Next, the pointer *newp* is used to initialize the *count* field attached to an *ItemType* as a result of using the *ReferenceCounted* scheme. Then the pointer value is returned and will be assigned to *r1*.

Since *r1* and the value returned by *RCreal*.NEW both have type *RCreal*.**ref**, the ASSIGN procedure is invoked to do the assignment in line (e3). The actual parameters passed to it are *r1* and the newly created *RCreal*; both passed **shared** (i.e., by reference). Since the pointer returned by NEW is not **nil**, the count of the newly created *RCreal* will first be incremented to 2. The FINALIZE procedure is called with the value in *r1* as parameter [line (r8)]. Because the value of *left* is **nil**, no significant actions are performed. Next, the pointer to the new *RCreal* is stored into *r1*, and ASSIGN returns. As the last step of line (e3), the unnamed temporary holding the result of **new** *RCreal* is finalized. The FINALIZE procedure with parameter structure **shared ref** [line (r5)] is invoked: It decrements the *count* leaving it at 1.

Line (e4) is similar to (e3) and concludes with the object's reference count having the value 2, since both *r1* and *r2* point to it.

6.4.3. Linked Lists

Our next example defines linked lists. We shall provide for simple uses, e.g., singly linked homogeneous lists, as well as more complex ones, e.g., nodes with several linkage threads running through them. To obtain this generality, we define the notion of list link with some care and corresponding parameterization. A list link is a pointer to a node. Each node contains a list link as well as other information. The list link may appear anywhere in a node (for there may be many different list links), so we parameterize the procedures for accessing and changing it. Each node also contains an element which is "preferred" in the sense that the node may be considered to be a means for putting together a collection of elements; conversion from the node type to the element type is automatic in appropriate contexts (e.g., when used in a selection operation with "." or "[ ]"). Let *ItemType* be the type of the preferred element; it is a parameter to the scheme. Given a pointer *p* to a node, it should be possible to explicitly access and change that element by a qualified reference *p.item*, where *item* is the name given to the element.

In defining the *ListLink* scheme, we must observe these considerations and one other: The actual represention for list links is of no concern to the scheme, and we may well wish to use a nonstandard one; hence, the type of list link is a scheme parameter, *PtrType*. We require that *PtrType* be defined so that it has four attributes: two procedures, both named *link*, for accessing and changing the link list component in a node and two procedures, both named *item*, for accessing and changing the nonlist part of the component. The *ListLink* scheme is written so that it works properly for *PtrType*s having these properties, but not necessarily otherwise. It is desirable to state this constraint explicitly. To do so, we use the formal parameter construction

type *T* **needs attributes** (⟨field list⟩)

The **needs** construction is used to constrain the admissible values for a scheme parameter; an actual parameter which does not satisfy the specification is an illegal use of the scheme. The **needs** clause specifies that *T*, in order to be a valid argument for the scheme, must have the attributes named in the field list. *T* may have other attributes as well, but it *needs* to have at least these.

The following definition establishes that a *ListLink* is a *PtrType* extended by a set of procedures for

1. Initialization,
2. Computing the length of a list,
3. Adding a new element onto the front of a list,
4. Appending one list to another,
5. Applying a procedure to each element of a list,

6. Building up a new list by applying a procedure to each element of a list constructing a list of the results, and
7. Constructing a new list by copying a list excluding all elements equal to a given item.

```
scheme ListLink
    (
    type ItemType;
    type PtrType needs attributes
        (
        function link(ListLink) returns ListLink;
        procedure link(ListLink; ListLink);
        function item(ListLink) returns ItemType;
        procedure item(ListLink; ItemType)
        )
    )
    PtrType extended by
        function length(value p: ListLink) returns n: integer =
            begin
            n := 0;
            while p ≠ nil do begin n := n+1; p := p.link end;
            end;
        function Cons(newitem: ItemType; y: ListLink) returns p: ListLink;
            {Add newitem to the front of the list y.}
            begin
            p := new ListLink.node;                              (c1)
            p.item := newitem;                                   (c2)
            p.link := y                                          (c3)
            end;
        function Append(x,y: ListLink) returns ListLink;
            begin
            if x=nil then return y
            else return Cons(x.item, Append(x.link, y))
            end;
        procedure Map(value x: ListLink; procedure F(ItemType));
            {Apply F to each element of the list x.}
            begin
            while x ≠ nil do begin F(x.item); x := x.link end;
            end;
        function MapItem(x: ListLink; function F(ItemType) returns ItemType)
                returns ListLink;
            {Construct a new list consisting of the results of applying F to each
                element of the list x.}
            begin
            if x=nil then return nil
            else return Cons(F(x.item), MapItem(x.link, F))
            end;
```

```
function Delete(item: ItemType; x: ListLink) returns ListLink;
    begin
    if x=nil then return nil;
    if x.item=item then return Delete(item, x.link);
    return Cons(x.item, Delete(item, x.link));
    end;

. . .
end ListLink;
```

This is only part of a complete definition. To emulate all the useful properties of LISP lists, a definition would include procedures for reversing a list, for substituting one element in place of another, finding the *n*th element of a list, etc. As the above procedures illustrate the main points, we shall omit the others in the interest of brevity.

Three examples showing how this scheme is used will serve to explain the definition.

We shall first consider a simple case. *ListLink* is an implementation scheme for the linking mechanisms for singly linked lists. To use it, we need associated node and reference types. Our first example defines nodes containing integers:

```
type IntNode = record                                  (i1)
    var item: integer;                                 (i2)
    var link: ref;                                     (i3)
    type ref = ListLink (integer, ref.lower)           (i4)
    end                                                (i5)
```

IntNode has two data components, *item* and *link*, with types **integer** and **ref**, respectively. It also has a **type** attribute **ref** that overrides the system-supplied meaning; this **ref** is the result of instantiating the scheme *ListLink*.

The second parameter to *ListLink* is the *foundation type* (Section 3.3.3) for *IntNode*.**ref**. It must possess certain attributes which satisfy its **needs** clause. In particular, **ref.lower** must have associated with it four routines, two of which have the structure

```
function item (ListLink) returns integer              (Ritem)
procedure item (ListLink; integer)                     (Litem)
```

We adopt the uniform referent view in Ross (1971) and Geschke and Mitchell (1976) that every data component *d:TypeOfd* of a record type *T* implicitly defines two accessing routines

```
function d(T.ref) returns TypeOfd                      (Rd)
procedure d(T.ref, TypeOfd)                            (Ld)
```

(*Rd*) is used in right-hand contexts to access the value stored in *d*, and (*Ld*) is used in left-hand contexts to assign values to the *d* component. The form of (*Ld*) is derived in Geschke and Mitchell (1976) because *item* (*x*, *y*) is taken as an interpretation of *x.item* := *y*. In the case of *IntNode*, its component *item* is treated as implicitly defining the routines

```
function item (ref) returns integer                    (Rd')
procedure item (ref; integer)                          (Ld')
```

as attributes of *IntNode* and as attributes of **ref**. The **needs** specification of **ref**, (*Ritem*), and (*Litem*) are met by (*Rd'*) and (*Ld'*), since line (i4) establishes that **ref** is equivalent to this instance of *ListLink*. Similar considerations apply to (*Ritem*) and the two constraints on *link*.

Our second example using *ListLink* generalizes this, making a scheme from *ListLink* instead of a type. The following scheme implements a general mechanism for singly linked lists of any type of items:

```
scheme SingleListNode(ItemType: type) = item: ItemType extended by
    var link: ref;
    type ref = ListLink(ItemType, ref.lower)
    end SingleListNode;
```

A *SingleListNode* is a record consisting of an *item* of type *ItemType* and a *link* which points to the next *SingleListNode* in the list. The type of *link* is **ref**, which is defined to be the value of the *ListLink* scheme instantiated as shown. The instantiation is similar to that in *IntNode*, above. By defining the attribute **ref** in *SingleListNode* to be equal to the instantiation of *ListLink*, we override the system-defined meaning for **ref** with the procedures defined in *ListLink*.

An individual type such as *ListOfIntegers* can be defined and used:

```
type ListOfIntegers = SingleListNode(integer).ref;
ip1,ip2: ListOfIntegers;
```

ListOfIntegers is defined to be equal to the **ref** attribute of *SingleListNode*(**integer**). Thus,

```
Cons(13, ip2)
```

invokes the *Cons* routine in *ListLink* with *newitem* = 13 and y = *ip2*. The expression

```
Map(ip1, Print)
```

applies the procedure *Print* to each integer in the list *ip1*. If *Add1* is a function which takes an integer x and returns $x + 1$, then

```
ip1 := MapItem(ip2, Add1)
```

assigns to *ip1* a list in which each element is 1 greater than the corresponding element of *ip2*. Finally,

```
ip1 := Delete(13, ip2)
```

assigns to *ip1* a list which is a copy of *ip2* with all unlucky elements deleted.

Our third example using the *ListLink* scheme defines a node type which contains two list threads. Doubly threaded nodes can be used for expression nodes in an optimizing compiler [Wulf (1974)]. Each expression node is on two lists: the list of syntactically identical expressions and the list of expressions known to have the same value. It should be possible to start from such a node and follow one list thread to visit its set of nodes or to follow the other list thread and visit its set of nodes. Either thread may be regarded as defining a list to which list operations such as *Cons*, *Append*, *Map*, *MapItem*, or *Delete* may be applied. There are three classes of pointers to nodes: *LinkType1*, which defines one thread; *LinkType2*, which defines the other thread; or a simple **ref**. In the last case, the list operations are *not defined* for the pointer, and any attempt to use them is a type error. If *x* is a pointer to a node, the type of *x* determines the interpretation of expressions such as *Map*(*x*, *F*).

The *DoubleListNode* scheme defines a record type consisting of a component, *item*, of type *ItemType* and two fields to hold the list threads, *link1* and *link2*, having types *LinkType1* and *LinkType2*, respectively. To define the types *LinkType1* and *LinkType2*, the *ListLink* scheme is instantiated twice, with different arguments. The instantiations differ only in the meaning they ascribe to the attribute *link* of the scheme parameter *PtrType*. In the instantiation for *LinkType1*, *link* is tied to the component *link1*; for *LinkType2*, it is tied to *link2*.

```
scheme DoubleListNode(type ItemType) = item: ItemType extended by
    var link1: LinkType1;
    var link2: LinkType2;
    type LinkType1 =
        ListLink(ItemType, DoubleListNode.ref extended by          (n1)
            function link(x:LinkType1) returns LinkType1;          (n2)
                begin return x.link1 end;
            procedure link(x:LinkType1; q: LinkType1);             (n3)
                begin x.link1 := q end;
            end);
    type LinkType2 =
        ListLink(ItemType, DoubleListNode.ref extended by
            function link(x:LinkType2) returns LinkType2;
                begin return x.link2 end;
            procedure link(x:LinkType2; q: LinkType2);
                begin x.link2  := q end;
            end)
    end DoubleListNode
```

An instance of this scheme will aid our explanation:

```
type DLInt = DoubleListNode(integer)
```

The node type *DLInt* has three pointer types associated with it: *DLInt.LinkType1*, *DLInt.LinkType2*, and *DLInt*.**ref**—the first two are explicitly defined attributes, while the last is system-defined and not overridden. *LinkType1* and *LinkType2* are two distinct instantiations of *ListLink*, each defining a separate sort of list to which all the list operations are applicable. Consider

```
dp1: DLInt.LinkType1;            (p1)
dp2: DLInt.LinkType2;            (p2)
dpr: DLInt.ref;                  (p3)
dp1  := Cons(11, dp1);           (p4)
```

Because the type of *dp1* is *DLInt.LinkType1*, line (p4) is interpreted as follows: The *Cons* selected is the one defined in the instantiation of *ListLink* specified by the lines between (n1) and (n3). Thus, a new *DLInt* node is allocated [line (c1) of the *ListLink* scheme], the integer component is set to 11 [line (c2)], and the field *link1* is set to *dp1* [line (c3)]. That *link1* is set, rather than *link2*, occurs because the *link* procedure of the *ListLink* scheme is bound to the procedure of line (n3). The result of the *Cons* is assigned as the new value of *dp1* (its old value was **nil**). Similarly,

Map(*dp2*, *Print*)

will Print all the integers in the list defined by the second thread.

MapItem(*dpr*, *F*) constitutes a type error—*dpr* is a pointer to a *DLInt* but is not a *ListLink*, so list operations cannot be applied to it. The difficulty here is inherent in the expression—there is no way to tell which thread is to be followed by *MapItem*. Also,

dp2 := *Cons*(11, *dp1*)

is not type correct, since *Cons* in this expression returns a value of type *LinkType1* which is not *dp2*'s type.

Suppose we wished to allow expressions such as the latter, with the obvious interpretation. More generally, suppose we wish to provide a mapping from a *LinkType1*. **ref** to a *LinkType2* with the same referent. This may be accomplished by using a more complex definition of *DLInt* which has a procedure attribute *AsLink2* to perform the conversion:

```
type DLInt = DoubleListNode(integer) extended by
    function AsLink2(x: LinkType1) returns LinkType2;
        begin return x end;
    end;
```

Here we exploit a standard property of protected classes: Within a type definition, conversions from a type to its representation and conversely are legal, while outside the defining form conversion is not allowed. With this definition,

dp2 := *AsLink2*(*Cons*(11, *dp1*))

is type correct, for the function *AsLink2* invokes the conversion procedure. Similary, both *AsLink2*(*MapItem*(*dp1*, *F*)) and *MapItem*(*AsLink2*(*dp1*), *F*) are type correct, with quite different meanings. The conversion routine is, of course, bookkeeping for the type machinery—an optimizing compiler will elide it.

Note that this definition applies only to *DLInt*. Had we instead wished to provide conversion for pointers to any sort of double list node, we would have included the attribute *AsLink2* in the *DoubleListNode* scheme so that all instances of the scheme would have had it available.

6.4.4. Two-Way Lists

One particular sort of doubly threaded node sees frequent use: the *doubly linked* or *two-way* lists. In such a list, each node points to its predecessor and successor along a single chain. The two threads traverse the chain in opposite directions. If *p* points to such a node, then two invariants hold:

if $p\uparrow.link1 \neq$ **nil then** $p\uparrow.link1\uparrow.link2 = p$ (tw1)

if $p\uparrow.link2 \neq$ **nil then** $p\uparrow.link2\uparrow.link1 = p$ (tw2)

We define an implementation scheme, *TwoWayNode*, to express this notion. Structurally, such a node is identical to a *DoubleListNode*. The latter is extended in *TwoWayNode* with attributes *Unlink*, *InsertBefore*, and *Cons* (to override the one in *ListLink*), as well as some protection.

```
scheme TwoWayNode(type ItemType) = dln: DoubleListNode(ItemType)
extended by
    private link1, link2; {Make the attributes which were exported by
        DoubleListNodes, private to users of TwoWayNode.}
    procedure Unlink(p: ref);
        begin
        if p = nil then return nil;
        if p↑.link1 ≠ nil then p↑.link1↑.link2 := p↑link2;
        if p↑.link2 ≠ nil then p↑.link2↑.link1 := p↑.link1;
        p↑.link1  := nil; {to maintain (tw1)}
        p↑.link2 := nil; {to maintain (tw2)}
        end;
    function InsertBefore(p, place: ref) returns ref;
        begin
        if p = nil then return place;
        Unlink(p);
        if place = nil then return p;
        p↑.link2 := place;
        if place↑.link1 ≠ nil then
            begin place↑.link1↑.link2 := p; p↑.link1 := place↑.link1 end;
        place↑.link1 := p;
        return p
        end;
    function Cons(value: ItemType; y: ref) returns ref;
        begin
        var p: ref;
        p  := new TwoWayNode;
        p↑.dln.item := value;
        return InsertBefore(p, y);
        end;
    end TwoWayNode
```

Unlink removes a node from a list, closing up the list around the unlinked node and setting its links to **nil**. *InsertBefore* inserts a node in front of a *place* in a list, modifying the list. *Cons* overrides the procedure of the same name established in *ListLink*. As defined in *TwoWayNode*, *Cons*(*newitem*, *y*) creates a new node to hold *value*, inserts the new node in front of *y*, linking it in so that rules (tw1) and (tw2) hold. With this definition of *Cons*, the other *ListLink* procedures (e.g., *Append* and *MapItem*) work properly and construct well-formed *TwoWayNode*s. *To obtain this effect, we require that when a scheme attribute is overridden, all uses of that name obtain the new definition.*

The specification **private** makes the attributes *link1* and *link2* inaccessible outside the scheme. We claim that this ensures that all *TwoWayNodes* are well formed according to rules (tw1) and (tw2), and reason as follows: The scheme procedures are written so that their outputs satisfy rules (tw1) and (tw2) if their inputs do; the **private** specification ensures that the only modifications to the link fields are via scheme procedures; thus, it follows that all *TwoWayNodes* obey rules (tw1) and (tw2) [Wegbreit and Spitzen (1975)].

6.4.5. Lists of Reference-Counted Objects

Having defined the schemes for reference counting and lists, it is natural to ask whether the two can be combined to define schemes for lists in which the nodes are reference-counted. We answer in the affirmative and illustrate the case of reference-counted nodes having a single link field.

```
scheme RC(type ItemType) = record
    private type LinkedPart = item: ItemType extended by
        var link: ref;
        type ref = ListLink(ItemType, Node.ref.lower);
        end LinkedPart;
    type Node = ReferenceCounted(LinkedPart);
    type ref = LinkedPart.ref
    end RC;
```

The *RC* scheme defines three type attributes: *LinkedPart*, *Node*, and **ref**. *LinkedPart* is a record type consisting of two components, an *ItemType* and a **ref**. *Node* is defined by the *ReferenceCounted* scheme to be a record consisting of an **integer** *count* and a *LinkedPart*. **ref** is defined as *LinkedPart*.**ref**, which results from instantiating *ListLink*. *RC*(. . .).**ref** is the type to use for declaring pointers to reference-counted objects, e.g.,

```
type RCListOfIntegers = RC(integer).ref;
rc1, rc2: RCListOfIntegers;
```

which defines *rc1* and *rc2* to be pointers to reference-counted lists of integers.

6.4.6. Operations on Multiple Scheme Instances

In the examples so far, a scheme serves to define a set of *scheme instances*. Each instance may have procedure attributes, acting on objects of that instance type. Procedures which span instance boundaries have not yet been considered. For example, operations on lists of integers are completely disjoint from operations on lists of strings. There are cases in which it is convenient to view the instances of a scheme as being more closely related. We shall now consider schemes *C* having procedure attributes *F* such that *F*(*x*, *y*) is well defined if *x*'s and *y*'s types are instances of *C*, possibly with different scheme parameters. Further, F *has privileged access to both x and y*. In this way, a scheme serves as a higher-order encapsulation mechanism.

The following scheme for *Complex* illustrates how this is done. *Complex* takes the *FieldType* type as a scheme parameter. This would typically be **real** but might also be **integer**, *Rational*, **double precision**, or *Algebraic* (for symbolic computations). We give definitions for the structure and a few of the procedure attributes:

```
scheme Complex(type FieldType) = record
    var Re, Im: FieldType

    function Negate(x: Complex) returns z: Complex;
        begin z.Re := Negate(x.Re); z.Im := Negate(x.Im) end;

    formal type t1, t2;

    function PLUS(x: Complex(t1); y: Complex(t2))
                returns z: Complex(PLUS(t1, t2));

        begin
        z.Re := PLUS(x.Re, y.Re); z.Im := PLUS(x.Im, y.Im);
        return z;
        end;

    . . .

    end Complex
```

No INIT procedure is written, so the system will (by default) invoke the INIT for *FieldType* twice—once for the embedded *Re* component and once for *Im*. The code for *Negate* is typical of the procedures used in schemes thus far: The formal parameter *x* has type *Complex*. Each instance of the scheme *Complex* has its own *Negate* procedure in which the token *Complex* in the procedure heading is bound to that instance.

The procedure PLUS is defined to take arguments whose types are any two (possibly different) instances of *Complex*. The variables *t1* and *t2*, which are declared as formals of type **type**, serve as pattern variables in the declaration of PLUS. Such a declaration limits *t1* and *t2* to be **type** values in a pattern match. The formal type expression *Complex(t1)* will match any *Complex* instance, and, as part of the pattern matching, the formal type variable *t1* will be assigned a value. This definition of PLUS does not belong to any of the instances; rather, it is distributed across all instance pairs. More properly, it may be thought of as belonging to the scheme itself. Expressing the type returned by *Complex* PLUS also requires new notation which may be read as follows: Consider the version of PLUS which acts on values of type *t1* and *t2*,. Let *T* be the type it returns. Then PLUS returns a value of type *Complex*(*T*).

We turn now to a second example of operations on multiple scheme instances. Consider the definition of lists as provided by *ListLink* in Section 3.4.3. As written there, *MapItem* takes a list of *ItemTypes* as its argument and returns a list of *ItemTypes*. This, however, excludes taking a list of integers, applying a function that converts integers into strings, and returning a list of character string representations for the numbers. The function in such a use maps from integers to strings and is therefore not a legal second argument to *MapItem*. We are going to redefine *MapItem* to take three arguments:

1. The input,
2. A function which maps from *ItemType* to *ResultType*, and
3. The type of the result list, *RLinkType*.

The scheme for *ListLink* may be defined or extended to include this definition along with some supporting attributes:

```
formal type ResultType, t3                                              (q1)
function MapItem                                                        (q2)
    (
    x. ListLink;                                                        (q3)
    function F(ItemType) returns ResultType;
    type RLinkType needs RLinkType = ListLink(ResultType, t3)           (q4)
    ) returns RLinkType                                                 (q5)
        begin
            if x = nil then return nil                                  (q6)
            else return Cons(F(x.item), MapItem(x.link, F, RLinkType)); (q7)
        end;
```

The formal parameters to *MapItem* establish the admissible arguments for its use: *x* must be an instance of *ListLink*. *RLinkType must be the result of instantiating ListLink* with *ResultType* and some acceptable type *t3*. In fact, *t3* only serves as a place holder in the actual parameter list in that mention of *ListLink*.

The constraint on *RLinkType* extends the previous definition of needs: Here, the symbol "**needs**" is followed by a Boolean expression comparing two types. The expression must be evaluable at the time a scheme is to be instantiated, and it may involve parameters to that scheme. The earlier expression "**needs attributes**(. . .)" is a special case of this, which can only follow a **type** specification: Boolean combinations of this and other compile-time expressions are also allowed.

The role of *RLinkType* in selecting the appropriate *Cons* routine deserves explication. Together with the types of *x.link* and *F*, it determines the *MapItem* routine to be selected in line (q7); the selected *MapItem*'s result type and *F*'s result type determine the *Cons* routine to be selected.

It is interesting that most of the body of this *MapItem* routine is the same as for the earlier one. Also, observe that both routines may be defined in the same scheme, for they take different arguments, so the generic selection mechanism will choose between them.

A brief discussion of two other uses may help to demonstrate the utility of operations on multiple scheme instances.

1. It is sometimes useful in LISP to apply a function of two arguments to corresponding elements of two equal-length lists. The function that does this is called MAP2. In a language with a variety of data types and, in particular, a variety of list types, it is natural to do the same. However, the two lists need

not be of the same type. In the scheme system, MAP2 may be defined analogously to the generalized *MapItem*.

2. Consider defining a scheme for vectors which are to behave like APL arrays of rank 1. The *ItemType* is a formal parameter to the scheme. Unary operations may be defined in the obvious way. However, binary operations between vectors of *ItemType*-1 and vectors of *ItemType*-2 require the more general mechanism presented above.

6.5. ABSTRACTIONS AND SCHEMES IN PROGRAMMING

Abstractions in programming are generally acknowledged to be desirable. To what extent do schemes facilitate the use of abstractions? Viewed as a template for a set of data types, a scheme is an "abstraction" of the types in that set, for it is their generator. Stated somewhat differently, a scheme defines a notion such as "reference-counted nodes of" or "stack of" over all actual parameter types, and in this sense it may be regarded as an "abstract" data type.

A scheme may also be viewed as a parameterized implementation technique. For example, a scheme for *BinarySearchTrees* takes the key and value types as parameters; it implements a binary tree in which the keys are maintained in prefix tree order by defining the auxiliary links and the operations on the links and nodes. It does so in a manner suitable for instantiation with any (key-type, value-type) pair and is thus an "abstract" *BinarySearchTree*.

The above use of the term "abstract" should be distinguished from the idea of "abstraction" as employed in hierarchial program design [Dijkstra (1972), Parnas (1972)]. When defining and using an abstraction [Dijkstra (1972)] implemented by an information-hiding module [Parnas (1971)], one seeks different ends from those which motivate the use of schemes. As schemes and abstractions are tangentially related, an understanding of their dissimilarities and their exact relation may illuminate certain facets of the scheme system.

To review "abstractions," we shall consider the paradigm of structured programming [Dijkstra (1972)]. When writing a program at one level, one may use a set of lower-level program modules which are treated as *virtual machines*. Each virtual machine provides a set of externally available operations (and possibly objects). These machines are generally called *abstractions*. An abstraction is characterized completely by its external behavior; how it realizes this behavior is immaterial to users of that abstraction. Indeed, knowledge of the means chosen for its realization may be positively harmful [Parnas (1972)]. Several notations, e.g., Guttag et al. (1976), Wegbreit and Spitzen (1975), and Zilles (1976), have been employed for specifying module behavior in terms that are independent of its internal operation.

The purpose of such abstractions is to decouple a module's specification from its implementation. Since the only thing known about a module at a point of use is the abstract specification, the module implementor is free to choose from a variety of data and control structures when programming it. Moreover, he retains this freedom when rewriting the module at some later time as long as the external interfaces are not changed. Suppose a symbol table module is specified abstractly by stating the types of the keys and values and by expressing the relation between the set of symbol table operations—*InsertKeyValuePair*, *SearchForKey*, *DeleteKey*, etc. Then the implementor should be free to realize the symbol table abstraction by an association list, hash table, binary search tree, AVL tree, or other techniques. Conversely, a user of a symbol table module is free to switch from one realization to another to better the performance of his own program, and he should be able to do this by a simple change of declaration, not by massive program alterations.

It will be seen that abstractions and schemes are independent concepts serving different ends. *A* virtual machine *abstracts a module's specification from its possible implementations. A* scheme *abstracts an implementation technique from the data types which it implements*. What then is the relationship between schemes and abstractions? The concepts touch at two points.

One point of contact is that an abstraction might be implemented by a type produced by a particular scheme instantiation. For example, a symbol table abstraction might be implemented by a particular instantiation of an AVL-tree scheme. This is *not* to say that schemes are realizations of abstractions. Rather, an instance of a scheme *may be* a realization of an abstraction. This is not hierarchical: A scheme's instances may implement several different abstractions, while an abstraction may be implemented by several schemes.

The other point of contact lies farther afield: An abstraction might be used to good purpose to describe the admissible actual parameters corresponding to a scheme formal parameter. This construction would be desirable if a scheme were well defined only for actual parameter types satisfying certain constraints. For example, consider defining a scheme to implement a paging strategy for a parameterized type *t*. Most of the scheme definition would be concerned with storage allocation and interface to the file system. It would simplify the definition if it could ignore the issue of how the table which translates from virtual to physical addresses is implemented. One way of deferring this is to write the scheme so that is takes the *TableType* as a parameter. In such a case, it would be desirable to state in the scheme definition that *TableType* can be bound only to those types which satisfy a given abstract specification of how a *TableType* must behave. This is not to suggest that the compiler attempt to prove that a given type realizes an abstraction—such questions are undecidable in general and, with today's theorem proving technology, are intractible for any but the simplest of cases. Rather we point out the desirability of providing constructs in a programming language to

1. Specify that an actual parameter must satisfy certain abstract specifications, and

2. Assert that a given type does satisfy certain abstract specifications.

With such features, abstractions serve as part of the pattern-matching language for scheme parameter specifications.

6.6. SPECIFYING CONSTRAINTS ON PARAMETERS

In the discussion of linked lists in Sections 6.4.3 and 6.4.6, we used the notion of a *needs specification*. It was used to limit the range of acceptable types which could be used as parameters to a scheme to those having at least the attributes given in the specification. It is often useful to employ a needs specification in a somewhat different way: to choose from a set of entities (whether procedures or schemes) the one to be selected in a particular context.

The idea is simple: Extend generic selection to schemes. Several schemes may have the same name, say *S*. (This is particularly useful when the several schemes provide alternative implementation techniques for some common abstraction.) When the name appears in an instantiation, e.g.,

t: **type** = *S*(α),

the generic mechanism selects the appropriate scheme based on the actual parameters α: That **scheme** is chosen whose **needs** specification is satisfied by α. The **needs** specification serves to discriminate among generic schemes just as type structure discriminates among generic procedures: It may be any Boolean expression which can be evaluated at compile time; the form **needs attributes** (. . .) is a special case of this.

Consider the symbol table notion mentioned above. If one is to choose among a number of alternative implementations depending on, say, performance desiderata, then there must be some form of documentation to help the user choose. For instance, a hash table might be the preferred choice, depending on the key or value types and on the number of (key, value) pairs to be stored in the table. One might discriminate more finely and pick one of a number of different hash table disciplines depending on the number of items, space constraints, etc. The following three schemes all define symbol tables and have the same name; by using needs specifications, we make them all take the same number and type of parameters, with the best one for a given scheme instantiation being chosen generically:

```
scheme SymbolTable                                              (s1)
        (
        type keytype, valuetype;
        ordered: Boolean;
        maxEntries: integer needs (maxEntries in 11..1000)
        ) =
    HashTable(keytype, valuetype, maxEntries)
    end SymbolTable;
```

```
scheme SymbolTable                                              (s2)
        (
        type keytype, valuetype;
        ordered: Boolean needs ordered;
        maxEntries: integer needs (maxEntries > 1000)
        ) =
    AVLTree(keytype, valuetype)
    end SymbolTable;

scheme SymbolTable                                              (s3)
        (
        type keytype, valuetype;
        ordered: Boolean;
        maxEntries: integer needs (maxEntries in 0..10)
        ) =
    LinearSymbolTable(keytype, valuetype, maxEntries)
    end SymbolTable;
```

Scheme definition (s1) basically says the following: If you need a symbol table package in which *ordering* is not constrained and for which the maximum number of entries is in the range 11..1000, then use some *HashTable* scheme selected by the same parameters (we shall give a number of scheme definitions for *HashTable* below). Scheme (s2) says the following: If the symbol table must be ordered and there are more than 1000 items to be stored, then an AVL-tree implementation is the one of choice. Last, scheme definition (s3) says the following: Just use a simple *LinearSymbolTable* if there are only a few (less than 11) items to be stored.

Simple constraints on the range of an integer variable have previously been used in the type machinery of a number of languages such as PASCAL [Wirth (1975)], but there are two difficulties [Habermann (1973)].

1. Types are intended to be checkable at compile time, but assignment of an integer value to a restricted range variable really requires run-time checking or verification [EUCLID (1977), Suzuki and Ishihata (1977)];
2. The only way to relate type definitions is by nested definition, which forces a strict hierarchy among defined types, whereas subrange declarations can form a lattice.

We propose instead to treat such constraints separately from the type structure; thus, *maxEntries* in the above declarations is simply an integer which is constrained to a specific range in each declaration. This does not eliminate the need for run-time checks but does factor it out from type checking. In the above case, the constraints must be satisfied at scheme instantiation time, and we shall continue to assume compile-time constraint checking in this section.

The next skeletal schemes, each named *HashTable*, are intended as alternative definitions suitable for use with the *SymbolTable* scheme (s1) and will further constrain the possible values of type parameters:

```
scheme HashTable                                                    (h1)
        (
        type keytype needs keytype = string or keytype = integer;
        type valuetype;
        maxEntries: integer needs maxEntries in 11..100
        ) =
        {simple linear probe hash table}
    . . .
    end HashTable;
scheme HashTable                                                    (h2)
        (
        type keytype
            needs attributes(procedure Hash(keytype) returns 0..maxEntries-1);
        type valuetype;
        maxEntries: integer needs maxEntries in 101..500;
        ) =
        {linear probe table keeping value stored directly with key}
    . . .
    end HashTable;
scheme HashTable                                                    (h3)
        type keytype
            needs attributes(procedure Hash(keytype) returns 0..maxEntries-1);
        type valuetype;
        maxEntries: integer needs maxEntries in 501..1000
        ) =
        {chained hash table to reduce collisions at the expense of space}
    . . .
    end HashTable;
```

Scheme definition (h1) constrains the *keytype* parameter to be either **string** or **integer** by using **needs** and the equality relation on types (we assume that the scheme provides a hashing function for these types). Definition (h2) uses the "**attributes**" operator in a needs specification to indicate that this *HashTable* scheme requires a user-supplied *Hash* function. Last, (h3) is intended to be used for large tables.

6.7. IMPLEMENTATION NOTES

In this section we shall lay out what appear to be the main issues in implementing schemes and shall sketch ways in which these issues may be handled. One of the necessary properties of the scheme system is that schemes are fully resolved during compilation: They determine what code is produced, but schemes per se appear nowhere in the run-time environment. Thus our discussion is confined to how the compiler deals with schemes. To confine this discussion to the prominent points, we shall make the simplifying assumption that all procedures are compiled together. We shall ignore issues which arise in loading and binding separately compiled modules.

Four language constructs require special treatment because of schemes:

1. Scheme definitions, e.g., **scheme** *Queue*(**type** *ItemType*) = ...
2. Scheme instantiations, e.g., **type** *IntQueue* = *Queue*(**integer**);.
3. Procedure calls in which the procedure name is a scheme attribute name, e.g., *Add* in *Add*(3, *q*).
4. Procedure calls in which an argument is a scheme attribute name, e.g., *Add* in *Foo*(*q*, *x*, *Add*).

We shall consider these constructs in turn.

6.7.1. Scheme Definitions

A scheme definition is processed to build tables which facilitate instantiation and to check so far as possible that the scheme is type-correct; however, no code is generated. Checking type correctness of a scheme is desirable in order to detect errors early—at the point of definition—rather than later in an instantiation where the fault may be confounded with errors of instantiation. The **needs** specification on the scheme formal parameters provides information which allows partial checking of the scheme's body. However, it is not always possible to make a complete type check on the basis of the definition alone.

For example, the scheme for *ListLink* in Section 6.4.3 is written with a **needs** clause which specifies that the argument *PtrType* has attributes *link* and *item* with certain type structures. The specification for *PtrType* is so written that the type correctness of expressions such as *p.item* in *Cons* can be checked from its definition alone; any admissible *PtrType* must result in a *ListLink* instance having a type-correct version of *Cons*. However, similar considerations cannot be applied to the definition of PLUS in the scheme *Complex* (Section 6.4.6). We want PLUS to be defined *whenever used* for all pairs of *Complex* instances. It would be too restrictive to demand in a **needs** clause that there be a PLUS routine for each pair of *Field* types used as arguments. Many of these might never be used in the actual program.

The issue is a conflict between two features, both of which are desirable:

1. Specifying precisely the requirements a scheme imposes on its arguments, and
2. Imposing no more constraints than actually required by the use of a scheme instance.

We intend that the **needs** specification be used to strike the appropriate balance in each scheme definition. The writer of the scheme specifies criteria for admissible parameters. The compiler will type-check the scheme using the information they provide. Any expressions in a scheme which are demonstrably type-incorrect are flagged as errors. Those expressions which can be certified as type-correct are all to the good.

The others will have to be checked for type correctness in each instantiation. In any case, compile-type type checking is complete; the only issue is where it takes place.

6.7.2. Scheme Instantiations

A scheme instantiation results in a type definition which can be treated much like any other type definition. Processing an instantiation can be loosely thought of as first reducing the scheme instantiation to a type and then processing the type. Actually, the processing is complicated by some additional semantic issues and a few space-optimization considerations.

When a scheme instantiation is encountered, actual parameters are substituted for formal parameters in the scheme definition, and constraints on the parameter specifications are checked. If the actual parameters form an admissible binding set, the scheme body is instantiated with these bindings, and the body is checked for type correctness.

As a matter of implementation strategy, it seems desirable not to treat each instance as a completely separate type or to generate code for each scheme procedure in an instance. There are two reasons for this:

1. A scheme may export a large number of procedure attributes, but many of these may never be used in a particular program for a particular instance. We would like to compile code and allocate space only for those procedure instances that are actually needed.
2. It may be possible to use the same piece of code to implement a given procedure in several different scheme instances if these instances have the same physical layout. In this case, the several scheme instances form an *equivalence class* with respect to the implementation of the given procedure. We want all members of the equivalence class to share one code block.

We suggest that a scheme instance be processed only to check the admissibility of the instantiating arguments and to build tables, e.g., those describing physical storage layout, attribute names and their types, etc. The entire program is processed to determine which procedure instances are actually needed and which instances fall into the same equivalence class. On a subsequent pass, code can be generated as actually needed and shared where possible.

6.7.3. Procedure Calls in Which the Operator Is a Scheme Attribute Name

Whenever a procedure call occurs, the generic selection mechanism uses type structure to choose a single meaning for the procedure name from the possible set of procedures, some of which may be scheme attributes. Scheme procedures may be divided into two groups, depending on their parameter specifications: those which are fully instantiated in a scheme instance and those containing unbound formal types (Section 6.4.6) in their parameter specifications.

Fully instantiated scheme procedures are the simpler case. For example, the procedure *Negate* in the scheme *Complex* has the type specification

procedure *Negate*(*Complex*) **returns** *Complex*

An instantiation of *Complex*, e.g.,

RC: *Complex*(**integer**)

behaves *as if* an instance of *Negate* were created such that *Complex* in the specification is bound to the type *Complex*(**integer**). Choosing this instance upon encountering a procedure call, e.g.,

Negate(*c*)

where *c* has type *RC*, entails normal application of the generic selection mechanism. Recall that code generation is deferred, so a table describing instance types is maintained separately from any code.

Scheme procedures that contain unbound formal types require more involved processing. For example, the procedure PLUS in the scheme *Complex* has the type specification

procedure PLUS(*Complex*(*t1*), *Complex*(*t2*)) **returns** *Complex*(PLUS(*t1*, *t2*))

where *t1* and *t2* are unbound scheme formals. Suppose *c1* and *c2* have type *RC* as defined above. We consider the processing of

PLUS(*c1*, *c2*).

The relevant symbol table information may be summarized as

c1 :: type is *RC*;
c2 :: type is *RC*;
RC :: type is **type**; value is ⟨*some type table entry*⟩; is an instance of *Complex* with *FieldType* bound to **integer**
PLUS :: generic procedure name; possible interpretations are:
. . .*Complex*.PLUS. . .

The generic selection mechanism examines the list of possible interpretations for PLUS, looking for those having a type structure compatible with the argument type structure—here (*RC*, *RC*), which is equal to (*Complex*(*integer*), *Complex*(*integer*)). Since *RC* is an instance of *Complex* with *FieldType* bound to **integer** and since the formal parameter list for *Complex*.PLUS has the type structure (*Complex*(*t1*), *Complex*(*t2*)), this is a match with *t1* and *t2* each bound to **integer.** If there is a single admissible interpretation for PLUS, then it is used. If there were no admissible interpretations, then the program would be incomplete. If there were more than one, the program would be ambiguous.

When a scheme procedure is selected, two activities are performed:

1. The compiler checks to see if a suitable code body has already been generated (either because the procedure has been generated for this scheme instance or

because a shared code body has been generated). If not, code is generated and becomes available to all procedures in the implementation equivalence class.

2. The **returns** specification for the selected procedure determines the type of the result. In the case of scheme procedures with unbound formals, this may require binding any formals which occur in the **returns** specification and invoking the generic selection machinery. For example, to process the specification **returns** *Complex*(PLUS(*t1*, *t2*)), the bindings for *t1* and *t2* are obtained; call these *t1** and *t2**. The generic selection mechanism is invoked to find meanings for PLUS with argument structure (*t1**, *t2**). Suppose a unique meaning is found and that it specifies **returns** *t3**. Then, **returns** *Complex*(PLUS(*t1*, *t2*)) reduces to **returns** *Complex*(*t3**).

6.7.4. Procedure Calls Where an Argument Is a Scheme Procedure Name

The situation is more involved when the meaning of an argument can be determined only by considering the calling procedure. This occurs when a generic procedure is used as a procedure-valued argument in a procedure call, for example,

```
Foo(13, PLUS)
```

Suppose *Foo* has the type specification

```
procedure Foo(integer;
        procedure(Complex(real), Complex(real)) returns Complex(real));
```

The type of *Foo*'s second formal parameter dictates that *Complex*(**real**).PLUS be chosen as the meaning of the second argument to *Foo*.

The issue is further complicated if the calling procedure name is itself generic. In the above example, suppose that *Foo* has two interpretations—the one shown and another with the type structure

```
procedure Foo(integer;
        procedure(string) returns string);
```

We adopt the following rule: All possible meanings for caller and argument are considered, and their type specifications checked for type consistency. If exactly one interpretation is type-consistent, then that one is chosen. Otherwise, the expression is considered to be in error.

Observe that these program phenomena and our need for selection rules result from generic procedure names being used as arguments to procedures. Whether the procedures are scheme attributes or not does not affect the selection rule; it does increase the number of cases to be considered in its implementation.

6.8. SUMMARY

We have developed a notation and semantics for parameterized implementation mechanisms called *schemes*. Schemes are built upon five basic notions:

- Extensible data types,
- The ability to refer to the attributes of an object in a uniform way,
- The ability to override the system-defined meanings of attributes,
- The ability to encapsulate a set of definitions, and
- The ability to control external access to the attributes of an encapsulated set.

Schemes extend the state of the art for generalizing implementation techniques to serve a wide variety of applications. Once a scheme such as *ListLink* is correctly programmed, that concept need not be coded again. This may help to make safe and palatable implementation techniques which involve low-level but powerful programming concepts such as pointers. The user of a scheme may be assured of its correctness, and encapsulation may be used to ensure that it cannot be misused.

Viewed from outside, a scheme can be regarded as providing one possible implementation of some abstract specification. A set of schemes may be used to provide alternative realizations of a single abstraction having different performance characteristics. It proves convenient to give all the schemes in the set a common name and to use constraint specifications to choose among them based on the properties of a particular use.

Type errors can occur in schemes, their instantiations, and the uses of these instances. Since it is desirable to detect and report errors as early as possible, the **needs** specification was introduced as a means for doing limited type checking within schemes and for checking the parameters to a scheme instance. It was shown that complete error checking within the scheme imposes an overly strong constraint on the programmer; hence, some of the error checking occurs when scheme instances are used. All type checking is, however, carried out during compilation.

Finally, we have discussed compilation techniques for schemes. We outlined delayed code generation and considerations of code sharing among separate scheme instances.

CHAPTER 7

PROGRAM GENESIS AND THE DESIGN OF PROGRAMMING LANGUAGES

J. T. SCHWARTZ
Computer Science Department
New York University
New York, New York

7.1. THE CIRCUMSTANCES OF PROGRAMMING

A useful programming language is a tool intended to facilitate programming and to alleviate either problems typical for present-day programming practice or problems which can be expected to arise as programming is extended to new areas. Language design must therefoıe be based on some overall view of programming as an activity. Three main subareas of programming deserve to be distinguished:

(a) *Clean-slate* programming, i.e., the design and development of systems of programs "from scratch."

(b) Programming of adaptations, extensions, and corrections to large preexisting systems.

(c) *Programming for nonprogrammers*, i.e., the design of software systems which can be used by persons with little technical training and who lack the fundamental programmer skills: procedure manipulation and debugging know-how.

Most language-design effort has provided tools usable only by the trained programmer and useful in "from-scratch" rather than in adaptation programming. But adaptation and maintenance programming, rather than the development of new programs, continues to occupy the overwhelming majority of programmers. Thus the language designer may rightfully be accused of ignoring the requirements of the most numerous group of programmers.

A somewhat more detailed survey of their characteristics will show that the three areas of programming which we have listed above differ substantially.

Clean-Slate Programming by Skilled Programmers

This is the type of programming which has been most discussed in the literature; it is also the area of programming on which we shall concentrate in this chapter. Our view of the characteristic difficulties of this area can be summarized as follows. The development of a complex program, like the construction of any highly structured object, consists of a progression of steps that supply piece after piece of a total. For the total to be correct it is of course necessary that all these separate elements cohere correctly. Each element must therefore satisfy certain constraints. The set of all those constraints that affect the choice of a program element E may be called the *local context* of E. Note that in typical programming situations local context will be defined by a miscellany of restrictions, particularly including the following:

1. Syntactic restrictions determined by the programming language being used and by any definitional extensions to the language that may be operative in a given context.
2. Semantic requirements reflecting particular properties of subprocesses (already defined or to be defined) that are to be invoked in a given context.
3. Semantic requirements related to the structure of the data objects to be manipulated in a given code section.
4. Accumulated odds and ends, as, for example, restrictions implied by the previous uses of particular data items, subroutine names, and so forth.

As noted, a program is built by choosing a sequence of elements, each correct in its local context. The probability that a given element E will be correctly chosen falls off rapidly with increasing complexity of its local context, and, beyond a certain threshold T of complexity, this probability will effectively be zero. The inverse of this probability measures the *difficulty* of choosing a given program element correctly or, what comes to much the same thing, the number of debugging cycles that will be required before the fully corrected form of an element is attained. It is useful to bear in mind the (merely suggestive) shape of the difficulty versus context-complexity curve shown in Figure 7.1.

The line of thought which leads us to draw the curve shown in Figure 7.1 may be extended to a somewhat more comprehensive statement concerning the difficulty of programs. Specifically, suppose that a total program P consists of elements $E_1, \ldots, E_n$ and that the local complexity of context of the element E_j is C_j. Then we suggest that the overall effort required to complete the entire program P will be measured by

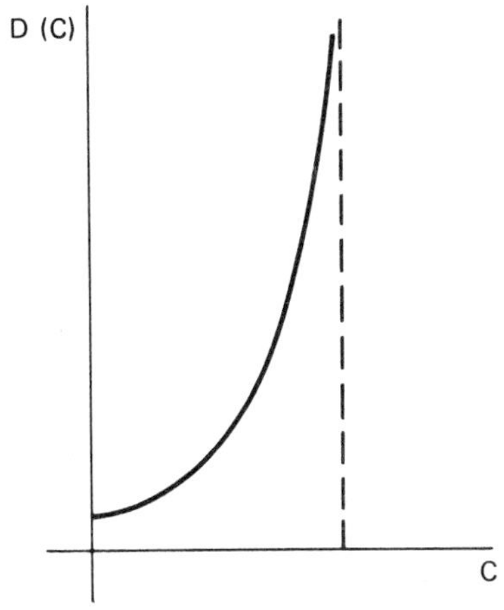

Figure 7.1. Local context complexity C vs. the difficulty $D(C)$ of completing an item in a compound structure.

$$D(P) = D(C_1) + \cdots + D(C_n)$$

where D is a function growing rapidly with C and becoming quite large at some finite complexity threshold T.

Adaptation Programming

A programmer trying to adapt, extend, or correct an existing system needs first to understand and then to expose relevant portions of the system which he is modifying, down to the level at which the change which he wants to install finds its expression. He must also reconstruct enough of the logic of his subject system to convince himself that the change to be installed will have its intended effects and no others. The baneful influence of accumulated complexity is always felt even more keenly in adaptation programming than in clean-slate programming. Current programming techniques make it quite difficult to avoid the accumulation of complexity in developing systems since they encourage the construction of systems devoid of internal boundaries isolating system portions from each other; such boundaries, if present, would allow each change to be regarded as an adaptation of a system subportion rather than as a change in the system as a whole. A much more satisfactory situation would prevail if applications, especially large applications, were systematically developed: first, by defining a *one-shot* language tailored to the application at hand; then by using this language to write the actual application code, which should be transparently and succinctly expressible in the language; and finally, by implementing the language to run efficiently. Such techniques, which will smooth the initial development of programs, should also make their subsequent maintenance and adaptation much easier.

Languages for Nonprogrammers

The procedural constructs of programming arise when a predicate which defines some desired output but whose original form implies some catastrophically inefficient computation is optimized by transformation into procedural form. The nonprogrammer is distinguished from the programmer precisely by the degree of discomfort he feels for procedural constructions; languages for the nonprogrammer must therefore seek to avoid such constructions.

For the rest, any attempt to provide languages for nonprogrammers will raise much the same problems as would arise in an effort to build other advanced, specialized, and comfortable languages for algorithm specification.

7.2. PROTO-PROGRAMS AND THEIR DEVELOPMENT INTO PROGRAMS

The intellectual structures which eventually become (large) programs arise as incompletely expressed *proto-programs* in which only major rules governing process activity and data transformation appear. Manual optimization and algorithm completion/correction based in part upon the use of various "generalized coercions" subsequently transform proto-programs into full, executable programs. The evolution of proto-program into program can usefully be viewed as a progression through various levels of language, from higher (more abstract and incomplete) to lower (more rich in detail and more carefully restricted to individual operations which machines can handle well). The designer of general-purpose programming languages should aim to make as much of this evolution as possible amenable to automatic handling. This requires two things: languages incorporating well-selected and aggressively high-level semantic constructs, and a sustained attack on the optimization problems which must be solved if very high-level languages are to be made to perform efficiently.

Let us trace the evolution of proto-program into program in more detail. In its genesis, a proto-program, like any other structure on which the mind has just finished acting creatively, must arise as a *rubble* of loosely interrelated fragments. The most favorable case for programming is that in which one succeeds in dealing with this rubble directly, i.e., in building up a system which can directly digest *rubble programs*. These are structures in which program elements are very loosely related to each other, can be freely added and removed, and for which each program output can be ascribed to some individual program element rather than to the cooperative action of many interrelated elements. A hypothetical general-purpose concordance generator whose "programs" are simply lists of words and where the presence of a word causes all its occurrences to be tabulated in some appropriately arranged listing exemplifies this notion of rubble program.

Where rubble programs can be used, they will of course be maximally easy to develop, to debug, and to adapt to new uses. Programs of this kind are ideally suited for use by nonprogrammers. In developing such programs, one simply adds elements until all desired effects have been obtained, perhaps subtracting elements whose effects are undesired. A rubble program is correct if its individual elements are correct.

One knows that one has devised the ideal language for treating a given problem when the problem can be solved in the language by a rubble program. Beyond its description by a rubble there will in many cases be no simpler description of the problem; with a rubble, one will have reached a level at which the elemental action of the mind can become directly manifest.

Structured complex programs which solve a problem may be considered to arise from the problem's defining rubble by a process of optimizing transformation (a transformed program can of course be vastly more efficient than the rubble program which underlies it). The ultimate goal of programming language design is to allow the programmer to express himself directly in rubble form, leaving it to an automatic optimization system to transform this rubble into a complex structure which realizes the same effects as the rubble but does so much more efficiently. However, presently available optimizers handle only limited classes of superficial transformations. Currently, therefore, the programmer is himself required to take over much of the work of optimization and to express himself in dictional structures complicated, by manual optimization, to the point at which they generally approach the threshold of humanly sustainable complexity.

An example will illustrate the points just made. A business application system is a programmed model of the enterprise in which it is to be used. Written in an appropriate language, such a system can be a rubble, each of whose elements will describe the rule according to which some kind of exogenous or endogenous event is handled when it comes to the attention of some person or group within the firm being described. These rules are interrelated logically, but only in a loose way, and the misstatement of a few rules will produce a system that malfunctions slightly rather than catastrophically. For describing business applications, an appropriate language might be one which allows definition of systems of intercommunicating "clerks," each with one or more in-baskets, and who follow some simple rule of procedure. We imagine all the clerks to act in parallel, sending messages to each other and all sharing the use of certain centralized files and access to certain central data objects. Certain clerks are sensitive to the time and date and periodically emit messages. A few fragments from such a rubble serve to clarify what is meant:

```
order-receipt: whenever exists order in input
               check name = customer_name(order) and address =
                            customer_address(order) filled-out
                 ifnot finish by
                  send ⟨customer_info_defective, order⟩
                                          to wrongorder_clerk
               check record =
                    customer_record(name = name,address = address)exists
                 ifnot finish by
                  send ⟨unknown_customer, order⟩
                                       to wrongorder_clerk
```

```
/* else */       finish by send <order,record>
                                    to order_classification_clerk
billing-clerk:   whenever exists invoice in input
                 let itemlist = item_list(invoice)
                 let total = sum price(item) over all item in
                          item_list(invoice) such that
                                available(item) is true;
                 let total-tax = sum price(item)*taxrate(category(item))
                    over all item in item_list(invoice) such that
                       available(item) is true, . . . (and so forth)
```

It is worth noting that the rubble underlying programs of business application type lies closer to the surface than is the case for programs of other types, since the transformations which generate such an application from its defining rubble are generally of routine rather than of highly specialized mathematical character. It is this consideration that justifies the decision of several currently active "automatic programming" groups to study systems of business application type rather than programs of some other kind.

Application programs of the type ordinarily seen arise when characteristic optimizations are applied to an underlying rubble like that displayed above. Typical steps of optimization are

(a) Introduction of a *procedural structure*, which groups together all processes dealing with the direct and indirect consequences of certain classes of exogenous events, thus allowing incoming "transactions" to be processed serially to completion. This allows the data files which must be consulted during processing to be kept in special arrangements which make access to needed records efficient and predictable; incoming groups of transactions can be presorted into an order determined by the pattern of file accesses which they will collectively require, etc.

(b) Introduction of auxiliary procedures which produce *special data arrangements, auxiliary mappings, and combinatorial structures*, etc., that expedite the calculations called for under (a). The use of these special arrangements and mappings can increase efficiency by immense factors and can even change the asymptotic rate at which calculation time grows with mass of data to be processed.

(c) Reduction of the number of expressions which must be expensively and repeatedly calculated. This is done by *maintaining current values* of important expressions (or even values produced by lengthy code sequences); these values are updated differentially whenever one of their input parameters is changed. This technique, emphasized by Earley (1974), generalizes John Cocke's method of *operator strength reduction.*

(d) Choice of *data structures* which reduce the amount of machine-level computation required to realize some abstractly specified algorithm and which ensure that needed data are held in suitably condensed form. A key aim here is to ensure that map values can be obtained efficiently by direct indexing and that important machine-level opportunities, e.g., the possibility of performing set-theoretic operations using high-speed Boolean instructions, are exploited when available.

(e) Exploitation of a wide range of other *special opportunities for code elision*, e.g., recognition of cases in which some construct occurs in some special form allowing unusually direct, efficient calculation. Programs can be transformed to create such opportunities even where they do not exist originally. This technique is applicable at both abstract and concrete levels of programming.

7.3. VERY HIGH-LEVEL FEATURES OF FUTURE GENERAL-PURPOSE LANGUAGES

A construction is *ordinary* if its use is justified by assertions of predictable form which can be generated by processing families of statements whose examination is predictably profitable. On the other hand, a construction is *mathematical* if it can only be justified using some fact found, by good fortune, within an area too large or disorganized to be profitably subject to systematic search. Future languages should rely increasingly on automatic optimizers, which should ultimately handle most ordinary constructions. However, mathematical constructions will for a long period remain the province of the manual programmer. Of course, the boundary drawn between these two types of construction will steadily change as our understanding of high-level program structure and optimization becomes more profound.

We expect future very high-level languages to embody and emphasize semantic concepts of broad simplifying power which make it possible to describe large classes of algorithms either by expressing something close to their underlying rubble directly or, where this is not possible, by writing algorithms in the form which they take on after the mathematical transformations (a) and (b) of Section 7.2 have been applied but before application of the more routine transformations (c), (d), and (e). Certain central semantic concepts are already known to possess this broad simplifying power; in the course of time, more such concepts will come to be understood, and these in their turn will have to be included in future languages. Among the language features which are presently known to simplify algorithm statements dramatically, the following deserve emphasis:

1. Availability, within a harmonious object/operator family, of sets, mappings, and all the operations of finite set theory, together with pointers, arrays, and structures. Any language which provides these general and powerful objects and operations, which deserve to be regarded as the common coin of very high-level programming, will be able to deal comfortably with a wide variety of ordinary mathematical constructions. Note that these objects are inherently of dynamically varying size, so that a language incorporating them will manage memory using some type of garbage collector.

2. The conventional control structures, including procedures, recursion, and procedure variables.

3. A logical environment supporting multiple processes, each one activated when some condition for which it monitors comes to hold: As the fragmentary business application example of Section 7.2 illustrates, such a logical environment allows many real-world situations, in which process parallelism is always inherent, to be expressed naturally. A diction, perhaps having the form

```
await C;
```

which causes a process to become suspended until the Boolean condition C is satisfied, will be central to such a logical environment. In addition, one will require an operation which creates and initializes new processes, and perhaps also a *copy process* operation, and rules which define a relationship between the internal data environment of one process and the internal data environment of others, allowing information to be communicated by interprocess reference.

If multiple processes are being used only as a descriptive tool, then it is appropriate to impose the semantic rule that processes only lose control by executing some explicit **await** primitive; this avoids many complex coordination problems that would otherwise have to be faced. (It is the common origin and purpose attaching to multiple processes used in this way that makes it reasonable to allow processes to communicate by writing directly into each other's data environment.) To decide which of several processes, all having their *await* conditions satisfied, is to run next, some simple notion of process priority can be used.

Languages intended for the description of multiple processes acting in true temporal parallelism, competing with each other for resources, and suspicious of each other's intent and correctness face more difficult semantic problems and must make use of more carefully restricted and more complex interprocess communication and coordination facilities. Among the semantic mechanisms appropriate to this situation (which we do not intend to explore in depth) are explicitly programmable scheduling relationships among processes; interprocess communication via shared global data objects which processes are able to manipulate only in restricted, preprogrammed ways under appropriate rules of exclusive access; and some notion of "ownership" and "accounts" which allows demand for storage space to be controlled.

4. Mathematical descriptions of a procedure often use powerful but impractical set-theoretic *selection* operations which must be replaced by *constructions* if these abstract procedure descriptions are to be turned into algorithms, and analysis of this stage of algorithm development suggests certain potentially useful semantic constructs. To illustrate what is meant, consider the abstract notion of sorting in its relationship to algorithms actually used for sorting. To define the notion of sorting in an *algorithm-free* way we can proceed as follows: An n-permutation is a 1-1 map p from the set $\{i, 1 \leq i \leq n\}$ to itself; given two vectors v and $\bar{v}$ of length n, $\bar{v}$ is said to be in the *permutation range* of v [we write $\bar{v} \in \text{permrange}(v)$] if there exists a permutation p such that $\bar{v}(i) \equiv v(p(i))$. To sort v is to find a $\bar{v}$ in its permutation range such that $\bar{v}(i) \leq \bar{v}(i + 1)$ for all $1 \leq i < n$. What we have just given is a problem statement rather than

an algorithm since the collection of n permutations contains $n!$ elements and is thus far too large to be searched explicitly. To obtain an algorithm from this problem statement one transforms it mathematically using a method which may be described abstractly and generally as follows: An object x satisfying a predicate C is to be found within a set S which cannot be searched explicitly, either because S is too large or because C is expressed in terms which make C very difficult to compute. To construct x algorithmically, one typically chooses some initial object x_0 in S and finds a transformation f of S into itself which has the property that $f(x) = x$ implies $C(x)$ (fixed point method). Then one generates the sequence $x_0, f(x_0), f^2(x_0), \ldots$. If f has been chosen appropriately, this sequence will stabilize, and the first element $f^n(x_0)$ satisfying $f^n(x_0) = f(f^n(x_0))$ is the desired x. We may then say that x has been found by *generation* rather than by *selection*.

Many variants of this paradigm will occur. It may, for example, be convenient to embed S in some even larger set T and to use an auxiliary transformation f which maps T into T but where $f(x) = x$ implies $x \in S$. One may make use of an auxiliary predicate C' for which $C'(x_0)$ holds and for which $C'(y)$ implies $C'(f(y))$; then one need only prove that the two propositions $C'(x)$ and $f(x) = x$ together imply $C(x)$. (A predicate C' with these properties is said to be a *continuing assertion* of the iteration x_0, $f(x_0), f^2(x_0), \ldots$.) The target predicate $C(x)$ may be decomposable as a conjunction $C_1(x)$ *and* $C_2(x)$; in this case, one can try to find two transformations f_1, f_2 of S into itself such that $f_1(x) = x$ implies $C_1(x)$, such that $f_2(x) = x$ implies $C_2(x)$, and such that $C_1(y)$ implies $C_1(f_2(y))$. When these are found, one can select x_0 in S, carry the sequence $x_0, f_1(x_0), f_1^2(x_0), \ldots$ to convergence to obtain an element x_0', and then carry the sequence $x_0', f_2(x_0'), f_2^2(x_0'), \ldots$ to convergence to obtain the desired x.

The very fundamental optimization which takes us from a predicate which selects to a loop which generates can well be called *mathematical expansion*, and we can say that the *while* and *until* loops which originate during such optimization arise by mathematical expansion of the set-theoretic expressions which underlie the final algorithms. Within loops arising in this way, subsidiary set-theoretical expressions can occur, and these will themselves expand into *while* loops, nested to some modest depth.

To be solved, a mathematical problem P must first be recognized and must therefore have a set-theoretic statement which is not too complicated. This set-theoretic description of P will be loosely reflected in the loop structure of the program's final form, and the overall structure of P should therefore correspond to the structural facts which flow analysis of the program will reveal.

The way in which we choose to expand a set-theoretic expression E into a loop will depend on the fact-context within which E is to be evaluated. For example, to find the smallest component x of a vector v requires a full search of v in the general case but only a binary search if v is known to be sorted. Thus, it will sometimes be advantageous when transforming a set-theoretic expression E into a loop to begin with a loop L within which set-theoretic expressions E_1 just as complicated as E or even identical to E appear, provided that the context of assertions available inside L makes calculation of E_1 relatively inexpensive. The total cost of evaluating E_1 repeatedly within the loop L will be the cost of a single typical evaluation times the expected number of times that L is executed. To evaluate E efficiently, we choose L, the fact context within L, and E_1 so as to minimize this product. Calculating similar evaluation costs recursively for all the nested subparts of an algorithm under development gives the expected cost of the total algorithm. The essence of algorithm design is to structure an algorithm P in such a way as to guarantee, to each significant expression E appearing in P, a surrounding fact context which allows E to be evaluated in an especially efficient way.

The fact that constructions of fixed-point type will occur frequently in routines which construct special data arrangements and combinatorial objects suggests that dictions embodying the idea "iterate-to-convergence" should be useful in a high-level programming language. A possible syntactic form is

```
(while)
        block
end while;
```

where "while" is a key word and *block* is a block of code to be executed until its continued execution ceases to affect any variable. The important special case

```
x = expn1;
(while)
        x = x op expn2;
end while;
```

is worth abbreviating as

```
x =:: expn1 op expn2.
```

As an example of the power of the diction thus introduced, note that we can calculate the transitive closure t of a set s under a map f simply by writing

$$t =:: s \cup f[t];$$

where [as in SETL; cf. Kennedy and Schwartz (1975)] the notation $f[t]$ has been used to denote the range of the map f on the set t. For more extended and convincing examples of the use of this $x =:: y$ construct, see Schwartz (1975).

Iterate-to-convergence constructions like those shown above are optimized by determining the variables or parts of variables which might be changed by the code appearing in *block* and by setting flags appropriately when changes occur, thereby making it possible to transform converge iterators to loops of ordinary kind.

5. In situations in which a desired structure x cannot be found using the "step to the goal" approach outlined in the preceding paragraphs, one must fall back on some much less efficient search technique. To locate x within s in such cases, one typically starts with some x_0 and with a *family* of mappings $f_1, \ldots, f_n$ having the property that by applying the f_j to x_0 in all possible ways one will eventually generate the whole of s. Then generation begins and continues until x is found. Various well-known methods to improve the efficiency of such searches exist. For example, whenever a new element y is generated, one can

a. Make some calculation which determines whether the desired x is reachable from y, and if not, suppress y.

b. In some way, estimate the number of mapping steps that separate y from the desired x and always work forward from the "most promising" y.

Often in applying this technique to significant cases the transformations f_j will be complex and the objects x, y, etc., to which they apply will be complex structures processing large numbers of attributes. To deal effectively with such situations, one will want to use a powerful language of transformations for definition of the f_j, and this language should also make it convenient to describe structured objects x possessing numerous and disparate parts. It is therefore natural to allow the transformations f_j to be arbitrary procedures written in a general-purpose language and to represent the objects x as process data environments. This can be done by specializing the multiple process framework described in 3. above as follows:

a. Make some address, which we shall call A, available to all processes. The value stored in A will always be a pair ⟨prc,val⟩, where *prc* is a process and *val* is an arbitrary value.

b. Set aside a private address *valuereceived* in each process. Restrict all inter-process control transfers to have the form

```
(1)    A = ⟨otherprocess,⟨thisprocess,valsent⟩⟩;
       await A(1) eq thisprocess;
       valreceived = A(2);
```

The transfer-of-control macro (1) can be abbreviated as

```
(2)    valreceived = cocall(otherprocess,valsent) .
```

Here, *thisprocess* identifies the "current" process, which is temporarily yielding control to *otherprocess*; *valsent* can be any arbitrary value.

The *cocall* primitive (2) can serve to define quite a variety of useful backtracking regimes. One can, for example, use one process P as a master scheduler to which all other processes return control; then P can record the existence and relevant properties of all other processes and select one of them for execution. A simple but useful backtracking scheme results if P is always sent one of the two values true, false by an environment Q which cocalls it and if P simply maintains a stack S of environments, stacking a copy of Q and returning true when the value true is transmitted by Q to P but erasing Q, popping the topmost element Q' of S, and transmitting the value false to Q' when the value false is transmitted by Q to P. In this case it is reasonable to abbreviate cocall(P, true) by the symbol ok, and cocall(P, false) by the symbol fail. The function ok, as seen by its user, then acts as an oracle: When evaluated, it looks ahead over the whole *future* course of the program in which it is embedded and seems to return either the value true or the value false, choosing that one of these two values whose return will guarantee that the fail primitive will not have to be executed later. For all this, see Hewitt (1972) and McDermott and Sussman (1972).

6. A significant language feature is the ability to use very general expressions on the left-hand side of statements. ALGOL 68 provides this by allowing any pointer-

valued expression to appear on the left-hand side of an assignment. Even though this approach is quite general, it is limited by the fact that pointers are data objects rather than procedures, for which reason the range of things that can be pointed at is a fixed, inextensible part of a language's initial definition. It is, for example, impossible in ALGOL 68 to create an object which "points to" a physically noncontiguous subsequence of a one-dimensional array a and after this to modify the elements (and only the elements) belonging to this subsequence by writing $p = aa$. An approach allowing substantially more general left-hand sides, and as a matter of fact one which gives the left-hand side L of an assignment all the generality normally associated with an assignment's right-hand side R, is as follows. Allow arbitrary constructs having the syntax of function calls to appear as L in $L = R$, but if $f(\ldots)$ appears as L, treat this semantically as a call on a special "assignment" entry to f, to which all the explicit parameters of f, plus an extra parameter which is the calculated value of R, are passed. The code belonging to this "assignment entry" and the code belonging to the normal "retrieval" entry to the function f must be related in a way guaranteeing that immediately after the execution of $f(\ldots) =$ val calculation of $f(\ldots)$ will necessarily yield *val* and also guaranteeing that immediately after the execution of $x = f(\ldots.)$ the assignment operation $f(\ldots) = x$ has no effect. If this is the case, then the fundamental hypothesis upon which a programmer relies in using the logical notion "assignment" is valid, so that f's "assignment" entry and its ordinary "retrieval" entry can justifiably be called a storage/retrieval pair.

The functional approach to the assignment notion outlined in the preceding paragraph is used in SIMSCRIPT II and in SETL (which latter language also incorporates nesting rules allowing new storage/retrieval pairs to be defined by compounding).

In addition to the fundamental semantic mechanisms discussed in the preceding pages, there exist a number of important *semisemantic* issues which can have great impact on a language's value to its ultimate user. Among these issues, the selection of useful name scope rules and of useful mechanisms for the disambiguation of references to generic operators is particularly important.

A name-scoping system should allow large systems of routines to be built up without "name crowding" becoming a problem. Neither a language's name-scoping rules nor anything else in its design should make it impossible to compile large programs in multiple independent sections. The name-scoping rules should not make it necessary to arrange a program text in any narrowly defined, possibly uncomfortable order, which probably means that one wants to provide statements which allow name scopes to be managed explicitly.

Certain important syntactic constructions, in particular the technique of indicating a call on a two-operand operation by writing a single infix operator symbol between symbols for its operands, are so generally useful that the language designer will wish to make them available for a wide variety of purposes. Moreover, in part because to do so suggests profitable analogies, it is useful to allow one single operator sign to represent various operations, depending on context. This corresponds to mathematical practice; e.g., the sign $+$ is used in mathematics to designate a wide variety of commutative and associative operations, e.g., integer, real, vector, and array addition; direct sum of groups; addition of residue classes; etc. It can quite advantageous to make similar mechanisms available in a programming language. A system which does this can be developed in many ways, of which the following is fairly typical:

a. Allow indefinitely many new "basic" object type names to be declared. These names, which can be treated in a purely formal way, are intended to represent the conceptual object categories which a programmer finds convenient in thinking through the program which he wishes to construct. Incorporate these names into a calculus of types by allowing compound types to be formed as follows: If $t, t_1, \ldots, t_n$ are type names, then so are $t_1 \mid t_2 \mid \ldots \mid t_n$ (denoting an object which is of any one of the types $t_1, \ldots, t_n$); $\{t\}$ and $[t]$ (respectively designating sets/sequences of elements of type t); $\langle t_1, \ldots, t_n \rangle$ (denoting an n-tuple with components of designated types); $\langle t_1\!:\text{name}_1, \ldots, t_n\!:\text{name}_n \rangle$ (designating an n-tuple with named components of designated types, i.e., a "structure"); $(t_1, \ldots, t_n)$ (denoting a programmed subroutine with parameters of types $t_1, \ldots, t_n$); and $(t_1, \ldots, t_n)t$ (denoting a programmed function with parameters of types $t_1, \ldots, t_n$, returning a value of type t). A type name for objects of "general" type should also be available.

b. Allow the type of variables $x_1, x_2, \ldots$ to be declared, perhaps in the syntactic form

```
dcl x1:t1,x2:t2,...;
```

where $t_1, t_2, \ldots$ are type names.

c. Allow the types of the parameters expected by a programmer-defined procedure, and the type of value returned, to be declared. Possible syntactic forms are

```
define procedure_name(x1:t1,x2:t2,...);     (for subroutines)
define function_name(x1:t1, x2:t2,...)t;    (for functions)
```

The following rules can then be applied: Only expressions of appropriate type can be assigned to a variable whose type has been declared. If types have been declared for the parameters of a procedure, the procedure can only be invoked with arguments (variables or expressions) of appropriate type. However, any number of procedures, functions, and infix operators with the same name can be defined, provided that the declared types of their parameters suffice to determine the procedure which is to be invoked at each formal call.

d. As already stated, the type declarations attached directly to the parameters of a procedure determine the type of argument for which the procedure can be called. Within the body of the procedure, each of its parameters may have a second, different, declaration. For example, we might write

```
definef((m1:sparsematrix),(m2:sparsematrix))matrix;
dcl m1:{<integer,integer,real>},
   m2:{<integer,integer,real>}; ...
```

The second declaration supplied for a procedure parameter exposes the parameter's internal details for manipulation within the procedure.

7.4. COMMENTS ON PROGRAM OPTIMIZATION

Stages (c), (d) and (e) of the evolution of a program, as listed in Section 7.2, belong to the routine portion of its development rather than to its initial creation and expression. We shall now discuss these optimization phases in more detail.

(a) *Maintaining and using current values of important and hard-to-compute expressions* (Earley's method of *iterator inversion*): Suppose that a program P to be optimized contains an expression $E = E(a_1, \ldots, a_n)$ involving n free parameters and that repeated evaluation of E is worth avoiding. Suppose also that E has the following property: If some of the parameters of E, say, for example, $a_1, \ldots, a_j$, are changed "slightly" or *differentially*, then E changes slightly, in the sense that the new value of E can be obtained from its old value by some "easy" calculation $E_{\text{new}} = f(E_{\text{old}})$. In this case, we shall say (suggestively though only heuristically and of course not in the standard technical sense) that E is *continuous* in the parameters $a_1, \ldots, a_j$. Suppose finally that, in some loop or more general program region R of interest, all the operations which change $a_1, \ldots, a_j$ change them only slightly. Then we can

i. Keep E's current value $C(a_{j+1}, \ldots, a_n) = E(a_1, \ldots, a_{j+1}, \ldots, a_n)$ available for appropriately chosen values of the parameters $a_{j+1}, \ldots, a_n$. [This means that some of the values $C(a_{j+1}, \ldots, a_n)$ must be stored; suppose for the moment that we store all previously calculated values $C(a_{j+1}, \ldots, a_n)$, collecting these values together as a mapping C.]

ii. Use $C(a_{j+1}, \ldots, a_n)$ rather than $E(a_1, \ldots, a_n)$ wherever the value of $E(a_1, \ldots, a_n)$ is required.

iii. For all values $a_{j+1}, \ldots, a_n$ in the domain of the mapping C, update $C(a_{j+1}, \ldots, a_n)$ using an appropriate rule $C_{\text{new}} = f(C_{\text{old}})$ whenever one of the $a_1, \ldots, a_j$ is changed (these parameters will only change differentially).

iv. Update or calculate $C(a_{j+1}, \ldots, a_n)$ using the rule

(1)
```
C(aj+1,...,ak-1,b,ak+1,...,an) =
    if C(aj+1,...,ak-1,b,ak+1,...,an) is val ne Ω then val
      else E(a1,...,ak-1,b,ak+1,...,an)
    /* obtained by evaluation of E */
```

whenever $j < k \leq n$ and a_k is changed by an assignment $a_k = b$. [In (1), the is operator merely assigns its left-hand operand to its right-hand operand x and returns x; the symbol Ω is used as an abbreviation for "undefined."]

Note that considerable memory may be needed to store values of C; thus, in some cases, we may prefer to keep only a small section $C'(a_j, \ldots, a_k) = C(a_j, \ldots, a_k, \ldots, a_n)$, $j < k < n$, of $C(a_j, \ldots, a_k)$ available and to perform a full recalculation using the expression E each time one of the parameters $a_{k+1}, \ldots, a_n$ is changed. In an extreme case, we may only keep one single value $C' = C(a_j, \ldots, a_n)$ available and will then recalculate C' whenever any of $a_{j+1}, \ldots, a_n$ is changed.

Let us consider a few examples. The assignments

(2) $$s = s \cup \{x\} \quad \text{and} \quad s = s - \{x\}$$

represent slight changes to the set s, as do

(2′) $$s = s \cup t \quad \text{and} \quad s = s - t$$

when t has only a few elements. If f is a set of pairs used as a mapping, then

(3) $$f(x) = a$$

causes f to change slightly. If f is a set of $(n + 1)$-tuples used as a multiparameter mapping, then

(3′) $$f(x_1, \ldots, x_n) = a$$

is a slight change to f. The expression $r = f[s]$ (which designates the range of f on the set s) is continuous in s; to adjust it after the change $s = s \cup t$ of s, execute $r = r \cup f[t]$. (Note that the ordinary rule "continuous functions of continuous functions are continuous" can be applied to the set-theoretical operations we have been considering.)

As Earley has emphasized, expressions involving set formers provide more interesting examples of the phenomenon of *continuity* which we have been discussing. The expression

(4) $$C' = \{x \in s \mid f(x) \ \underline{\text{eq}}\ a\}$$

is a prototypical example. This expression is continuous in s and f but discontinuous in a. When s is changed by addition of an element y_0, then C' can be updated by executing

(5) $C' = C' \cup (\text{if } f(y_0)\ \underline{\text{eq}}\ a \text{ then } \{y_0\} \text{ else } \underline{nl});$

and a similar rule applies for deletions. (Here as elsewhere, $\underline{nl}$ denotes the null set.) When f is changed by executing $f(y_0) = z$, then C' can be updated by executing

(6) $C' = \text{if } y_0 \in s \text{ then } (C' - (\text{if } f(y_0)\ \underline{\text{eq}}\ a \text{ then } \{y_0\} \text{ else } \underline{nl})$
$\qquad \cup \text{ if } z\ \underline{\text{eq}}\ a \text{ then } \{y_0\} \text{ else } \underline{nl}) \text{ else } C';$

[the update operation should be inserted just before the assignment $f(y_0) = z$]. More insight is gained by writing (6) as

(7) $C' = C' - \{x \in \{u \in s \mid u\ \underline{\text{eq}}\ y_0\} \mid f(x)\ \underline{\text{eq}}\ a\}$
$\qquad \cup \{x \in \{u \in s \mid u\ \underline{\text{eq}}\ y_0\} \mid z\ \underline{\text{eq}}\ a\};$

since (7) begins to suggest a rule for updating more general set-theoretical expressions than (4). For example, just before changing f by $f(y_0) = z$, the set

(8) $$C_1 = \{x \in s \mid g(f(x))\ \underline{\text{eq}}\ a\}$$

can be updated by executing

(9) $C_1 = C_1 - \{x \in \{u \in s \mid u\ \underline{\text{eq}}\ y_0\} \mid g(f(x))\ \underline{\text{eq}}\ a\}$
$\qquad \cup \{x \in \{u \in s \mid u\ \underline{\text{eq}}\ y_0\} \mid g(z)\ \underline{\text{eq}}\ a\};$

and the set

(10) $$C_2 = \{x \in s \mid f(g(x)) \ \underline{\text{eq}}\ a\}$$

can be updated by executing

(11) $$C_2 = C_2 - \{x \in \{u \in s \mid g(u)\ \underline{\text{eq}}\ y_0\} \mid f(g(x))\ \underline{\text{eq}}\ a\} \cup \{x \in \{u \in s \mid g(u)\ \underline{\text{eq}}\ y_0\} \mid z\ \underline{\text{eq}}\ a\};$$

All the updating operations (7), (9), and (11) are to be performed just *prior* to the change $f(y_0) = z$ for which they compensate.

An appropriate term for the class of program transformations which we have just been describing is *formal differentiation.* This type of transformation often acts, at a profound level, to shape programs during their development. As a small example, consider the rudimentary transitive closure program

$$t =:: s \cup f[t];$$

introduced above. This can be written using a conventional "while" loop as

```
t = s;
t_old = nl; /* as before, nl abbreviates nullset */
(while t_old ne t)
    t_old = t;
    t = t ∪ f[t];
end while; /* end of while loop */
```

Using a suitably extended variant of formal differentiation, we transform this into the more efficient code

```
t = s;
t_new = s;
(while t_new ne nl)
    t_new = f[t_new] - t;
    t = t ∪ t_new;
end while;
```

For much deeper illustrations of transformations of this kind, see Earley (1975).

(b) *Data structure choice:* The sets and mappings which appear in the abstract version of an algorithm can be represented by concrete data structures in quite a number of ways. Effective choice of concrete data representations is essential if abstract algorithms are to be turned into efficient codes. To determine the data structure which can most appropriately represent some particular object x in an abstract procedure p, one must know how x is used within p and also how x is related to other objects appearing in p. An important idea in this connection is that of *basing*. An abstract quantity x is said to be represented in *based form*, or to be *based*, if it is not kept in whatever form is standard for abstract objects of its type but instead is kept in a special form which relates it to a set s called the *base* for the representation of x. A very wide collection of useful nonstandard representations could be devised; however, in our present remarks we shall consider a modest but typical (and probably adequate) system of representations.

For each basing to be considered, a symbolic notation will be introduced. The family of notations which thereby arises (or perhaps some equivalent family of notations chosen for greater syntactic convenience) defines a language of data structures which can be used declaratively as a *data structure elaboration language*. An example of such a notation is "$\subseteq s$," which we shall use to describe sets which are subsets of s and which are represented by bits either stored locally with the individual elements of s or grouped together in a bit vector. To indicate that s_1 has this representation we shall write $s_1 :: \subseteq s$, which may be read "s_1 is represented as a subset based on s."

A reasonably adequate list of based representations might be as follows:

$s_1 :: \subseteq s$	The subset s_1 of s is represented by a collection of bits either stored locally with the individual elements of s or grouped together in a bit vector. If a bit vector is used, then a generated serial number referencing a particular bit position must be stored locally with each individual element of s.
$s_1 :: L \subseteq s$	The subset s_1 of s is represented using both a collection of bits and a list of pointers to elements of s. This list serves to expedite iterations over s_1.
$x :: \in s$	The object x is represented by a pointer to an element of s.
$x :: \langle \beta_1, \ldots, \beta_n \rangle$	The object x is represented as an n-tuple, whose components have the basings $\beta_1, \ldots, \beta_n$, respectively; e.g., one might write $x :: \langle \subseteq s, \in s, L \subseteq s' \rangle$.
$x :: \{\beta\}$	The object x is represented by a hash table with locally stored overflow, whose entries point to objects having the basing β; e.g., one might write $x :: \{\subseteq s\}$.
$f :: M(s, \beta)$	The set f is a single-valued map defined on (a subset of) s, with map values (or pointers thereto) either stored locally with the individual elements of s or collected in a vector of map values. The map values themselves are represented using the basing β.
$f :: MM(s, \beta)$	f is a multivalued map defined on (a subset of) s, the values constituting $f\{x\}$ being stored as a list referenced by an initial list element pointer either stored locally with each element x of s or collected in a vector of pointers. The map values are represented using the basing β.
$x :: \mathrm{INT}(k)$	x is an integer of known size k.
$x :: \mathrm{STR}(k)$	x is a string of known maximum size k.
$x :: \mathrm{BIT}(k)$	x is a bit string of known maximum size k.

Other, less critical, variations of the basings listed above might also be considered. For example, an object x for which a basing of the type $\{\beta\}$ is desirable might in some cases be represented still more effectively simply by a list of elements, each with the basing β; for a multivalued map f, representation by a pair of arrays FIRST and LAST of indices to a third array FVALS, where the values of f for a given x are

FVALS(FIRST(x)) through FVALS(LAST(x)), might be preferable to the MM(s, β) type of basing; etc. In certain situations, use of multidimensional arrays and other special mapping schemes may also be advantageous. We shall, however, avoid discussion of these subtler possibilities.

Using the fundamental basings which appear in the preceding list and compounding them in obvious ways, we obtain a large family of possible basings. Given an abstract program and a variable x in it, we can allow any of these basings to be declared for x. Then given a binary operation x_1 $\underline{\text{op}}$ x_2 (in an abstract program) and assuming that basings have been declared for its inputs, both the manner in which the operation is to be performed and the manner in which its result will ordinarily be represented are determined.

As an example of this remark, consider the operation $s_1 + \{x\}$ that adds an element x to the set s_1. Suppose first that s_1 has the basing s_1 $::\subseteq$ s. Then to calculate $s_1 + \{x\}$ we first locate x as a member of s; if this location operation is successful, we set a bit (the "s_1-bit") attached to the member of s that has been located. If this changes the bit, we may also wish to adjust an element count maintained as part of the representation of s_1. On the other hand, if x cannot be located as a member of s, we shall probably wish to consider the basing declared for s_1 to be unusable, since in this case the calculation of $s_1 + \{x\}$ can make necessary some very extensive reconstruction of s_1, which we may not wish to allow.

All of this is shown in detail in the following code, which realizes the operation $s_1 + \{x\}$ in the case s_1 $::\subseteq$ s:

```
(*)     lx = locate(x,s);
        if lx ≠ undefined then
         if s1_bit(lx) = 0 then
          s1_bit(lx) = 1; /* set flag bit */
          count(s1) = count(s1) + 1;
            /* adjust count field of s1 if necessary */
         end if s1_bit;
        else
         error('basing violation in s with x operation,
                              x not present in base');
        end if locate;
```

In this code, *locate*(x, s) is a subprocedure that returns a pointer lx to the item of s which is equal to x if such an item exists, but *undefined* otherwise; *count*(s_l) is a field of s_1 in which the current number of elements of s_1 is maintained (if it is necessary to maintain such a count). The 1-bit field s_1_bit(lx) contains the bit which flags membership/nonmembership of the item lx in the set s_1.

Depending on the way in which x and s are represented and on the global context in which x and s appear, the code (*) will represent a larger or smaller amount of calculation; moreover, in certain cases opportunities to elide parts of this code will arise. The most drastic variations in the time needed to execute (*) will come from variations in the time needed to calculate the function locate(x,s). If x has the basing x $::\in$ s, we are at one extreme, since locate(x,s) simply reduces to x. If x has some quite different basing and s has a basing like $s :: L \subseteq s_2$, then we are at another extreme, since locate(x,s) is calculated using what may be a long list search and a sequence of identity tests (which check x for identity with successive elements of this list). In addition to the execution-time variability involved in calculating *locate*, elision of parts of the code (∗) will speed it up in certain cases. If s_1 is used only for membership testing but is not itself tested for equality with the null set or any other set, then no count need be maintained for it, so that a line of (∗) can be removed and (∗) elided to

```
lx = locate(x,s);
if lx ≠ undefined then
    s1_bit(lx) = 1;
else
    error('basing violation . . . etc.');
end if;
```

Finally, if global inclusion-membership analysis shows that $x \in s$ must hold, then the test appearing in this last code is unnecessary, and (∗) reduces to

```
s1_bit(locate(x,s)) = 1;
```

or, even, if x has the basing $x :: \in s$, to

```
s1_bit(x) = 1   .
```

To choose an effective representation for the objects appearing in an abstract algorithm, and to map the algorithm manually into a specific code utilizing these data representations, is at present a central part of a programmer's work. Very high-level languages will only gain wide acceptance if substantial automation of this process proves possible. Two approaches to such automation now seem possible. A conservative, and only semiautomatic, approach could require that a representation be declared for all (or for all critical) variables occurring in an algorithm to be compiled. Given these declarations, the specific code sequences to be used could be elaborated automatically and in a fairly straightforward way. The necessary declaration language can be built up by compounding from the vocabulary of basic data representations listed above, with extensions as needed.

A more ambitious, fully automatic approach is also possible. The main elements of such an approach would be as follows. Let some algorithm A which we wish to develop into an efficient program be made available as a text in an abstract set-theoretic language whose repertoire of semantic objects includes finite sets, ordered n-tuples, and sets of ordered n-tuples usable as mappings. Then A can be subjected to a compile-time global analysis, whose results determine the data representations possible a priori for the data objects of A. The main stages of such an analysis are as follows. First, one calculates *value flow* relationships for A, i.e., finds all the points q in A at which a data object x (which can be created or modified at other program points) can reappear. Once these relationships have been worked out and expressed as a set of maps, then operation-application functions, which determine the operators that might be applied to an object at any of its appearances in A, can be built up. Additionally, "stack" objects which can be allocated within a pushdown stack rather than a garbage-collected heap can be detected, and "allocate/free" patterns which allow more efficient space management than is provided by garbage collection can be set up automatically. After this, one can go on to detect various relationships of inclusion and membership, such as the fact that one set-valued variable s is always a subset of another s', or that some x is always a member of s', or that the domain or range of a map f is contained in s'. The methods used to deduce these relationships can also be used to establish other similar facts, as, for example, that particular maps are single-valued or particular sets disjoint from each other.

Once having determined what data representations are possible a priori, we can collect frequency information on all the explicit loops and branches of a program P and information on the sizes of the sets and vectors which appear in it. Using this information, an execution frequency can be assigned to each of the primitive operations of P, and the time required to execute each such primitive can be calculated as a function of the data representations which might be used. This in turn allows us to estimate the total time required to execute P, as a function of these data representations.

With this information in hand, representations can be assigned to the objects of P in all possible ways, the resulting execution times calculated, and an efficient scheme of representations chosen. For this purpose, a branch and bound algorithm incorporating appropriate heuristic principles can be used; such an algorithm can drastically reduce the number of different data representations that need to be considered.

(c) *Exploitation of other special opportunities:* At all levels of programming, there exist numerous special situations which can be handled with considerably greater efficiency than is suggested by the treatment required for the general case of which they are specializations. We shall list a number of opportunities of this kind, concentrating on those which belong to the set-theoretic programming level.

(a) The combination

$$\# \{x \in a \mid C(x)\}$$

(where # denotes the "number of elements" operation) can be compiled as the iterative loop

```
n = 0;              /* initialization */
(∀x ∈ a | C(x))     /* iterative loop over the members
                                     of a */
    n = n + 1;
end ∀x;             /* end of loop */
```

(b) The membership test

$$y \in \{e(x), x \in a \mid C(x)\}$$

can be compiled as the loop

```
ismember = false;
(∀x ∈ a | C(x))
    if y = e(x) then
        ismember = true;
        quit; /* i.e., exit from loop */
    end if;
end ∀x;         /* end of loop */
```

(c) The union operation

$$s \cup \{e(x),\ x \in a \mid C(x)\}$$

can be compiled as

```
temp = s;              /* initialization */
(∀x ∈ a | C(x))
   temp = temp with e(x);
   /* the with operator inserts a single element
                                  into a set */
end ∀x;
```

(d) The constructions

```
(∀x ∈ (s ∩ t))   and   (∀x ∈ (s − t))
      ...                     ...
end x;                 end x;
```

can be transformed into

```
(∀x ∈ s | x ∈ t)   and   (∀x ∈ s | x not ∈ t)
      ...                       ...
end ∀x;                  end ∀x;
```

respectively.

(e) Let *block* denote some block of code. Then the iteration

```
(∀x ∈ (s ∪ t))
      block
end ∀x;
```

can be improved to

```
(∀x ∈ s)
      block
end ∀x;
(∀x ∈ t | x not ∈ s)
      block
end ∀x;
```

For various other set-theoretic "peephole" optimizations of this kind, see Schwartz (1974a, 1974b, 1974c).

7.5. PROGRAMMING DISCIPLINE AS A LANGUAGE DESIGN ISSUE; DEBUGGING AND PROGRAM VERIFICATION

(a) Sources of Error and Their Elimination Through Disciplined Programming

In the ordinary process of manual programming in a low-level language, the several stages of program evolution that we have sketched are all fused together. Working from an unwritten proto-program and from some incomplete, purely mental view of some of its salient algorithmic details, the programmer works out the results of optimizations like those described in (c), (d), and (e) of Section 7.2 and may even develop still more irregular, machine-dependent optimizations, all in his head; often the first and even the only thing which he then writes down is the code emerging from these complex transformations. It is not surprising that when so many logical layers are brought together the context complexity which faces the programmer should rise above the critical threshold described in Section 7.1, resulting in program failure. Error can insinuate itself during the application of any of the optimizing transformations (c), (d), or (e). In trying to keep the value of some important expression E available, it is easy to forget to insert some necessary update operation at some point at which one of the parameters of E is modified. In transposing an algorithm to use a data structure chosen for efficiency and rich in pointers and indirection, it is easy to misconceive the manner in which some auxiliary data item is represented or accessed. In noting and exploiting facts on which special opportunities for code elision can be based, it is easy to overlook the existence of some operation or flow path which invalidates an assumed fact. Even if the last type of error is avoided, properly elided code can be written only if one correctly recalls all relevant internal details of the objects which the code is meant to manipulate, and the elisions remain correct only if neither the internal representations of these objects nor the context within which the elision has been supplied is subsequently changed in any significant way. In exploiting algebraic or set-theoretic identities, it is easy to make some small algebraic error, especially when the unsimplified expression whose simplified form one is trying to supply is never written down.

Given the existence of these rich sources of error, it is not surprising that programs written in low-level languages should be error-prone. Moreover, the difficulty of coping with error is compounded by the fact that a low-level language realizes not the semantic environment proper to high-level algorithms being transposed into it but a much more anonymous, permissive environment. This allows an erroneous low-level code to run on long past the point at which it has ceased to bear any relationship to the algorithm which it is supposed to represent, so that the first symptom of an error can be something bizarrely remote from the logical fault which the error represents.

It is important that the structure of a language should be such as to repress the intrusion of error and to prevent errors from disguising themselves when they do intrude. The most effective way of doing this is to use very high-level languages which allow algorithms, or still more ideally their underlying proto-programs, to be expressed without heavy transformation. Even though we still have only limited experience with this approach, this experience seems to show not only that high-level versions of algorithms are much shorter than their low-level equivalents (which is unsurprising) but also that, since high-level programs are more natural in logical structure and distort an underlying thread of ideas less, they tend to contain fewer bugs per line of code.

If efficiency requirements preclude direct use of a code written in a very high-level language, the next best thing is to proceed in two stages, using a very high-level language to specify the code and then to transcribe it manually, but in essentially mechanical spirit, into a lower-level form. The high-level code form from which one then works makes the underlying logic of the final low-level code visible, allowing the reasoning which justifies the elisions and other optimizing transformations embodied in the low-level code to be explicit and to be scrutinized. Experience shows that by approaching a complex programming task in this multilevel way, one can both reduce the density of error in the code ultimately produced and, by raising the level of sophistication of the optimizing transformations which can be perceived and safely applied, can wind up with a product which is at once simpler and more efficient than that which would result from a more haphazard approach.

The level of efficiency which can be reached without falling back on a manually produced low-level version of a high-level program is still debatable, and for this reason language designers have generally been rather more concerned to prevent the intrusion of error in low-level programs than to explore the debugging advantages of high-level techniques. Many of the kinds of programming discipline which designers have suggested relate in a direct way to some of the important sources of error depicted above. By restricting the flow structure of programs, and especially by emphasizing the use of single-entry, single-exit subgraphs, one can limit the complexity and elusiveness of the paths along which influences invalidating programmer assumptions can propagate, thus making one type of error less likely. By disciplining the use of complex, context-specific elisions, e.g., by insisting that no code module can be longer than one printed page, one takes a further step toward the control of much the same type of error; the efficiency losses imposed by such a rule will generally be modest. By requiring the types of all variables, and the types of arguments expected and returned by all functions, to be declared, one can catch most erroneous patterns of data structure access and use.

(b) Program Verification

Although the various program disciplines sketched in the preceding paragraphs can do much to keep a program closely in contact with the underlying algorithm which it is supposed to represent, the full intent and logic of the program only becomes explicit, and its solidity is only guaranteed, when a formal proof of program correctness is given. To develop a correctness proof for a program we shall ordinarily have to

(a) Attach assertions A (*Floyd assertions*) to the formal text T of the algorithm, and verify a number of symbolic relationships which tie these assertions to the statements of T and which have the form "if A_j can be asserted at point P_j of a program PR, then A can be asserted at point P." The verification of propositions of this sort will generally be rather routine, as the symbolic relationships which need to be checked are all recursive. All that will ordinarily be involved is symbolic manipulation of a conventional sort, which must, however, be guided by a semantic knowledge of the programming language employed.

(b) Step (a) will yield a family of propositions C, one such proposition being attached to each (significant) point in PR. These propositions will have the form "if A [which by step (a) is a consequence of assertions attached to other points of PR] holds, then B (a proposition directly attached to some point of PR) is implied." The propositions C will be of standard set-theoretic form, i.e., will be mathematical statements no longer having any explicit tie to the details of PR, or for that matter to the semantics of the language in which PR is expressed. To verify PR one must then prove all the propositions C. The proof which here becomes necessary should itself be checked by an automatic proofchecker (if indeed it is not constructed by an automatic theorem prover), since a merely written proof, even if carefully and repeatedly read, still leaves open the possibility of error; e.g., a crucial (if perhaps marginal) execution case can easily be glossed over erroneously.

Of the steps just outlined, it is the last one, construction of a family of proofs in a form acceptable to an automatic proof checker, that is apt to be most onerous. Two reasons buttress this expectation. In the first place, proof-checker technology is still only weakly developed; proof checkers can take only very small steps themselves and must therefore be guided in great detail. Moreover, step (a) above will often transform the assertions A originally attached to a program in such a way as to obscure whatever intuitive flavor these assertions may originally have possessed.

For this reason, it will be quite important in developing proofs of program correctness to ensure that the Floyd assertions with which such a proof begins are in fact correct. However, as originally set up, these assertions, which will often be roughly equivalent in bulk to the programs to which they attach, are just as likely to attract numerous small errors as programs are. Of course, this objection falls away for any set of assertions for which we are ultimately able to give a mechanically verified proof. However, in most cases we shall not even want to try generating a formal proof until the set of assertions to be proved has been subjected to a preliminary check for plausibility, probably by verifying that these assertions do remain true as the program PR is run against various admissible data inputs. Thus we expect informal techniques like those presently used in debugging to remain useful in the early stages of development of fully detailed correctness proofs.

Note also that by attaching carefully constructed sets of Floyd assertions to a program we make its intended logical structure explicit. This is information that anyone modifying or correcting the program will need to know anyhow, so that a program annotated in this way must count as a distinctly more valuable item than a program not annotated with assertions.

The initial aim of very high-level language design is to simplify the process of programming and make it more productive. But these same language-design efforts are bound to play an essential role in the development of program verification techniques convenient enough for their use to become a part of standard practice. By writing an algorithm in a very high-level language, we shorten and simplify its text, thereby reducing the number of Floyd assertions which must be supplied as part of a correctness proof, and also the cost of proving these assertions, proportionately. Moreover, an algorithm's high-level statement will generally be substantially less obscure than its optimized restatement in a lower-level language; accordingly, the Floyd assertions constructed in verifying a high-level algorithm version will generally have a clearer intuitive meaning and be less difficult to deal with than the assertions needed to verify a lower-level version of the same algorithm. The optimizing transformations which carry an algorithm's initial high-level form into some more efficient low-level form will belong to some limited, carefully stereotyped transformation family, and a relatively small number of general lemmas can establish once and for all that these transformations are correctness preserving. Thus use of very high-level languages is seen to give at least a partial answer to the important question of how to find general lemmas on which substantial portions of many program correctness proofs may be based. Note also that the facts needed to justify application of particular optimizing transformations will often be superficial enough to be discussed and proved, without programmer intervention, by a global program analysis routine; these are often facts which would be more deeply hidden in an algorithm's lower-level versions. Thus use of very high-level languages also helps answer another important question of program verification technology: how to automate as much as possible of the work of constructing Floyd assertions from program text.

7.6. A FEW COMMENTS ON SPECIAL-PURPOSE LANGUAGES

Special-purpose programming languages are one of the sources from which important new semantic ideas, eventually to be incorporated in general-purpose languages, arise. Ideally, the semantic structure of a special-purpose language defines a logical framework in which the objects and processes typical for the language's intended application area can be described rapidly and conveniently, while the language's syntax allows the customary dictions of this application area to be used without much distortion. The range of "typical" programs for which a special-purpose language must guarantee adequate performance can vary quite widely, depending on the language's intended application. Thus implementation of special-purpose languages will pose a wide variety of challenges to the language optimizer. In the present relatively undeveloped state of optimization technique, one may not be able to assure adequate performance if a maximally broad range of semantic facilities are all incorporated into one language. When this is the case, the language designer may be forced to split what he would prefer to regard as one integrated set of facilities along several lines of cleavage, producing not one but several languages, each adapted to allow efficient compilation for some particular spectrum of applications. On the other hand, when they first arise, application-oriented languages may make use of unduly specialized or restricted facilities simply because it is not perceived that these facilities are special cases of something more general and broadly useful or because the possibility of an efficient implementation which integrates these with other important semantic facilities is not seen. However, as special-purpose languages are improved, regularized, and extended, the semantic inventions which they embody will come increasingly to be seen as specializations of ideas of broad simplifying power. We may, for example, observe that one of the first places in which formal multiprocess notions made their appearance was in specialized simulation languages such as GPSS and SIMULA and that the SNOBOL pattern-matching mechanisms, as well as the more general but still specialized semantic mechanisms such as PLANNER and CONNIVER, were important sources for the idea of backtracking.

7.7. THE POSSIBILITY OF STILL MORE ADVANCED PROGRAMMING LANGUAGES: AUTOMATIC PROGRAMMING AS THE AUTOMATIC DISAMBIGUATION OF INCOMPLETELY EXPRESSED ALGORITHMS

To push programming technique beyond the level to which it can be brought by full utilization of the powerful semantic mechanisms described in Section 7.3 and of other similar mechanisms still to be discovered, one will probably need to make use of techniques, resembling those which play an important role in natural language, for the automatic disambiguation of incompletely expressed algorithms. By suitably generalizing the way in which we use systems of declarations like those described in the final three paragraphs of Section 7.3, we begin to define the outlines of a scheme allowing this. Nouns appearing in English-language discourse are typically very highly "typed," i.e., are known to refer to objects of particular "types" and thus to appear only in certain argument positions in the family of semantic relationships around which a given discourse is structured; conversely, each of the arguments of a relationship (or function) appearing in a typical English discourse is known to have some specific type and the type of the output of each function which appears is known. In a programming environment, information of this sort can be used systematically to elide patterns of reference and make them flexible. The "coercion" mechanisms used in many languages illustrate this general principle. For example, if $+$ can designate either an operator with two integer parameters or with two real parameters, if a mapping "float" sending an integer into a real is available, and if i is an integer while r is a real, then the combination $i + r$, illegal in itself, can be regarded as an abbreviation for the related, but legal, combination $\text{float}(i) + r$. As natural language shows, much more general elisions are possible in a semantic environment in which the type of every object and the types of objects which can enter into every relationship are known. Specifically,

(i) In a context in which a vector with components of a given type t is required, and if x is known to be of type t, then x can stand for $\langle x \rangle$; similarly, in a context in which a set of elements of type t is required, x can stand for the singleton set $\{x\}$.

(ii) If the arguments of a function or relation have known types, all of which are distinct, then when the function is invoked its arguments can be written in arbitrary order (since the correct order can be deduced from the known argument types).

(iii) Generalizing rule (ii), suppose that we extend a device inherent in the "expression" construct and agree that in each local context C of any program P the last referenced object of each of the types declared within P is implicitly available in C. Then a function argument can be omitted if its type is known and if the argument value desired is the implicit value of this type, in the sense just explained. This rule can be applied to set-theoretic iterators in two ways: If xt denotes an object of type t and if some set st of objects of type t is available, then $\forall xt$ can stand for $\forall xt \in st$. Also, if st denotes a set of objects of type t, then $\forall st$ can stand for $\forall x \in st$; note that within the scope of this last iteration an implicit object x of type t is available.

(iv) One or more of the arguments of a function producing a result of known type t can stand for a call to the function in a context in which an object of type t is known to be required. We can even allow several functions to be involved if the type relationships are sufficient to disambiguate the sequence of mappings which must be applied. Syntactically, we can allow a single argument to stand for itself and use the notation $\cdot(a_1, a_2, \ldots, a_n)$ when we have reason to list a few of the arguments, to one or more nested functions, explicitly. For example, imagine a context in which an object of type t_1 is required and where functions f and g, with arguments, respectively, of distinct types t_2, t_3 and t_4, t_5, and returning values of respective types t_1 and t_3, are available. Let x and y be variables of types t_2 and t_4, respectively. Then the notation $\cdot(x, y)$ [or, if one must be more specific, $t_1(x, y)$] can serve as an abbreviation for $f(x, g(y, z))$, where z is an "implicit" value of type t_5, assumed to be available. We can also allow an object of "record" type containing several declared "fields" or "attributes" to stand for some one of its attributes, provided that the particular attribute required is determined by the attribute's type and the requirements of context.

(v) Rule (iv) can be extended by *pluralizing* it, e.g., by agreeing that if a sequence x of elements of a given type t is available, if x appears in a context in which a sequence of elements of type t' is required, and if a map f coercing elements of type t into elements of type t' is available, then x may be coerced to $\langle f(x(1)), f(x(2)), \ldots \rangle$. A similar remark applies to sets.

(vi) If a function returns as value an object having as attributes several objects of various types, we can use an explicit or implicit call to the function solely for the value of some one of the attributes of the object it returns. In this case the other attributes of the object become implicitly available values of their several types. This remark applies in particular to iterators over objects of sequence type. Suppose, for example, that *t*seq denotes an object of sequence type (whose components are objects of type *t*). Then within the scope of the iteration $\forall xt \in t$seq the integer portion *k* of the component *xt* of *t*seq is implicitly available.

In natural language, the semantic nature of an object or object type is often made apparent in the internal structure of the noun or adjective which describes it; e.g., a "mailman" is a person who deals with mail. It is worth introducing similar mechanisms into programming languages; e.g., after a type name "typ*n*" is introduced, then "typ*ns*" can designate the "plural" form of typ*n*, which we would otherwise write as {typ*n*}; similarly, "typ*n*seq" can be used as a sequence object whose components are objects of type typ*n*. Moreover, we can agree that variable names of the form "typ*nx*," "typ*ny*," "typ*nxy*," "*x*typ*n*," etc., will denote quantities of type "typ*n*." In addition, we can also use "typ*n*," with no letters appended, to denote the currently implicit value of type "typ*n*." If we allow all of this to be done *en passant* without formal definitions being required, then we begin to attain some of the dictional flexibility of natural language.

The conventions which have just been outlined may allow numerous small steps of program completion and correction to be supplied automatically. A nonnegligible part of the ordinary process of programming consists of the manual application of very similar steps to an implicit, unwritten proto-program. By making the mechanisms that have been outlined available within a programming language, one may make it possible to write programs in a form closer to their underlying proto-program or rubble than could otherwise be used.

7.8. APPENDIX: A BRIEF CRITIQUE OF SOME CURRENT SUGGESTIONS CONCERNING CLUSTERS

An idea that has recently become popular is that of supplying linguistic tools which allow the definition of a new data type to be associated closely with the definition of each of the operations which is allowed to access internal data of objects of type *t*. Such object-type/operation groups or *clusters* seem to have originated in the SIMULA language [see Dahl et al. (1970)], where they were called *classes*; for more recent cluster-like proposals, see Liskov (1974), Liskov and Zilles (1974), and Wulf (1974). Recent work has emphasized that access to the internal representation of an object *o* of type *t* should be allowed *only* via the operations belonging to *o*'s cluster (which we shall call the cluster's *entries*).

The following arguments, all quite significant, support this approach:

(i) The proposed mechanism allows data objects to be treated "abstractly"; i.e., once a cluster t is defined, the programmer using objects of type t only needs to know the logical effects of all the various operations applicable to such objects but need not be concerned with the detailed way in which objects of type t are represented internally. This allows one to change the internal data representation of a cluster, perhaps in order to attain efficiency.

(ii) The cluster mechanism allows objects to be defined by their properties rather than their details and thus stands in analogy to the axiomatic method which is so useful in mathematics. If facilitates the development of reliable programs and also of proofs that programs are correct, since it allows one to prove, first, that the operations of a cluster are correctly realized and, then, using operation correctness as a lemma, that more extensive programs are correct.

(iii) In parallel programming, the cluster notion is doubly valuable since it can be used to ensure exclusive data access during the execution of "critical sections" of code: Once one of the entries of a cluster is invoked, and before return from the entry, all other cluster-entry invocation can be blocked. Moreover, the cluster mechanism can also provide protection: The right to use a given entry can be treated as a protected "capability." [For a development of these ideas, see Hoare (1974) and Shaw (1976).]

The weight of those arguments will vary with the type of programming to which they are applied. Let us first consider them in relation to an unfavorable case: the programming of procedures which have a mathematical flavor and which make use of relatively complex objects (e.g., procedures for symbol manipulation or combinatorial analysis). Here the following observations, which seriously undercut at least the first two of the arguments offered above, can be made:

(a) Regardless of what other object and operation types one wants to build up in clusters, one will always want to be able to form sets of these objects and use mappings defined on them, and hence one will always find it desirable to make the standard operations of set theory available. Even in an "axiomatic" approach, set theory is likely to be required; after all, mathematicians rarely investigate any system of axioms without assuming that the axioms of set theory are available along with the more particular axioms on which attention is concentrated. But if set theory is to be available anyhow, it is tempting to use set-theoretic representations for all the objects with which one intends to deal. Since set theory is quite powerful, these representations will generally not be terribly complex. Thus if set-theoretic data representations are used, the amount of internal detail which a cluster mechanism could serve to conceal will be greatly diminished from the detail to be expected when more primitive base-level representations are used, and this vitiates the utility of the cluster concept.

(b) It can be desirable, for clarity and programming discipline, to insist that all operations affecting objects of a given type be centralized in some single place; and the cluster approach seems to do this. However,

(bi) The protection afforded by clusters can easily be evaded: All that is necessary is for the programmer of a cluster to write entries which make internal details of its data manipulable. This may be bad form, but it is legal and can tempt a programmer who rejects sound practice. Evasion of the cluster mechanism's intent is impossible only in a system in which a cluster's author can isolate himself from its users; this implies an environment in which other protection mechanisms also exist. Since evasion is possible in a more ordinary environment, the cluster mechanism can be regarded simply as a device which (by making lack of structure highly visible) encourages, but does not enforce, use of standardized data objects and operations.

(bii) Interesting operations will often have multiple parameters, and often several of these parameters will be logically compound objects. The cluster mechanism cannot treat these parameters symmetrically, but perforce regards one of them, call it x, as a principal parameter to which the operation belongs, while the others are auxiliary. Invocation of an entry belonging to the cluster of x exposes the internal data structure of x but leaves all other parameters still "packaged" and accessible only through entries of their own clusters. In effect, this assumes either that all the composite logical structures used in a program will have parts which are elementary (as, e.g., in an array of pointers) or that these parts are composite objects of some lower type, and it is also assumed that objects x will typically interact with other objects x' which resemble the parts of x. This approach is not well suited to the description of operations which use multiple logically compound parameters in relatively symmetric ways (or even in fully symmetric ways, as, e.g., in determining isomorphism of two graphs or of two groups). When one writes an operation involving several equally important logically complex parameters there is no unique, parameter-type-determined, place in which to put the code representing the operation. Thus one important support of the cluster approach breaks down.

(c) A potential advantage of the cluster mechanism is that by concealing the inner details of abstract objects it can allow these details to be varied, and efficient representations to be built up, perhaps from machine-related and hence highly efficient primitive elements. However, this hope meets significant obstacles:

(ci) If the objects realized by a cluster have set-like semantics or are potentially members of sets, they need to be integrated into a system supporting set-theoretic operations efficiently. But simply to provide these operations is already an intricate task, and once they have been built up it is tempting to use them in realizing other operations.

(cii) A scheme which is intended to make efficient realization of abstract operations possible must, when multiple logically compound operation arguments exist, allow a single procedure call to expose the inner details of multiple arguments. As noted in (b) above, the cluster mechanism does not do this.

In view of the objections just enumerated, we do not expect cluster notions like those presently proposed to have broad importance in all fields of programming. However, it is possible to discern certain special areas to which this approach is particularly suited:

(i) Parallel process and operating system programming, where, as already noted, clusters can also support mutual exclusion and protection, and

(ii) Data base programming. Here one does normally deal with composites (records) whose parts are elementary; composites interact only with objects resembling their parts; record format designers are generally distinct from the programmers who access the records; and finally data and programs lead independent lives and must be carefully isolated from one another.

For use in other situations, a variant of the cluster scheme providing some of the discipline inherent in the cluster approach, but one which does not insist on associating each operator with just one object type, might be desirable. Such a scheme might use a system of declarations something like that sketched at the end of Section 7.3; the rule that a procedure can only be called with arguments of the types which it expects and that only values having the type declared for a variable can be assigned to the variable will then impose substantial discipline upon the programmer. Of course, the protective barriers defined by this scheme can easily be evaded, since one can always "convert" between types simply by writing

```
define convert(s:t1)t2;
return s;
end convert;
```

In spite of this, the scheme does make nonstandard use of data objects stand out, and this is enough to provide a useful measure of programming discipline.

ACKNOWLEDGMENT

This work was sponsored by the National Science Foundation, Office of Computer Activities, Grant NSF-GJ-1202X3.

CHAPTER 8

FORMAL MODELS FOR STRING PATTERNS

A. C. FLECK
Computer Science Dept. and
University Computer Center
The University of Iowa
Iowa City, Iowa

8.1. INTRODUCTION

Our purpose in this chapter is to deal in some detail, and in a fairly formal manner, with the topic of string patterns and their use in structuring collections of strings. We shall treat two mathematical models. The first of these models is based on a formal languages approach and the second on an algebraic approach. Thus the prerequisites for the best understanding of this chapter include some familiarity with a pattern-oriented programming language, some knowledge of formal languages, and a bit of background in abstract algebra. However, appropriate background material will be included to make the treatment reasonably self-contained, though in too condensed a form to be useful without prior exposure.

Originally the SNOBOL family of languages integrated the idea of a "pattern" type of structure for strings with a powerful pattern matching system. This has proven to be a useful facility in many areas of application. Recognition of this fact has led to numerous implementations of SNOBOL4 [see Griswold et al. (1971)] and to the addition of such facilities to other languages such as PL/I [Furtado and Pfeffer (1973)], LISP [Smith and Enea (1973) and Tesler et al. (1973)], and others. For a discussion of the role of these facilities in AI languages, the reader can consult Bobrow and Raphael (1974).

As Stewart (1975) points out, "One of the most pressing problems in the design of better string manipulation languages arises in the specification of patterns. SNOBOL4 patterns, although extremely flexible and powerful, are notoriously difficult to explain and use." Our concern will be with the underlying concepts common to such systems, and we shall avoid idiosyncratic aspects. In this way we attempt to foster a deeper understanding of patterns and the pattern matching process. Thus while our development is strongly influenced by existing systems, notably SNOBOL4, we shall prefer to make assumptions that lead to conceptual simplicity rather than remaining completely faithful to a particular language or implementation.

Our approach in this chapter will be to develop a static analysis of the pattern facility. That is, patterns will be considered in isolation and apart from other programming features. We shall not be concerned with questions relating to what can be programmed using patterns but with more primitive or basic issues relating to just what structures can be imposed by various classes of patterns and how this may affect the speed and complexity of the pattern matching process and other algorithms of interest for such classes. We shall also emphasize the closely related issues of how patterns can be carefully defined and the relations among several pattern combination operations.

8.2. BACKGROUND MATERIAL

It is presumed that the reader will most likely peruse this section and possibly refer back to it in case questions of technical detail later arise. This section has been included for completeness. As compactness is one of our major goals in this section, examples, proofs, and exposition are avoided; only necessary definitions and results are included. For each of the topics included, references to expository treatments are given.

Formal Languages

For a more detailed discussion of the material in this section, the reader can consult one of the standard references in the area such as Hopcroft and Ullman (1969) or Salomaa (1969).

In this section Σ will denote a finite, nonempty set of abstract symbols. We shall denote by Σ^* the set of all finite sequences of elements from Σ; we specifically include in Σ^* the null sequence (i.e., the sequence of length 0), which is denoted by λ. The usual notation for the empty set, $\varnothing$, is used throughout. For $w \in \Sigma^*$ we sometimes use the notation w^n to denote the concatenation of n copies of w, where w^0 is interpreted as λ. The concatenation operation will also be applied to sets; for $A, B \subseteq \Sigma^*$, $AB = \{ab \mid a \in A \text{ and } b \in B\}$.

Definition 1. A *regular expression* over the alphabet Σ is defined recursively by the following:

(1) α, Φ, Λ, and σ for each $\sigma \in \Sigma$ are regular expressions [we assume α, Φ, Λ, (,), $+$, and $*$ are abstract elements distinct from Σ];

(2) If x and y are regular expressions, then so are
   (a) $(x)(y)$,
   (b) $(x) + (y)$, and
   (c) $(x)^*$;

(3) An object is a regular expression only if it is followed by repeated applications of (1) and (2).

Definition 2. Each regular expression x denotes a subset of Σ^*, written $|x|$, and such sets are called *regular*. The regular sets are defined inductively following Definition 1:

(1) $|\alpha| = \Sigma^*, |\Phi| = \varnothing, |\Lambda| = \{\lambda\}$, and $|\sigma| = \{\sigma\}$ for each $\sigma \in \Sigma$;

(2) If there are regular expressions y and z so that
 (a) $x = (y)(z)$, then $|x| = |y||z|$;
 (b) $x = (y) + (z)$, then $|x| = |y| \cup |z|$; or
 (c) $x = (y)^*$, then $|x| = \{\lambda\} \cup |y| \cup (|y|)^2 \cup \ldots$

$$= \bigcup_{i=0}^{\infty} (|y|)^i = |y|^*.$$

Theorem 1

Each regular set is accepted by some finite state acceptor (and conversely).

Theorem 2

There are algorithms, given regular expressions x and y, for deciding if

(a) $|x| = \varnothing$,

(b) $|x| = \Sigma^*$, and

(c) $|x| = |y|$.

Definition 3. A *context-free grammar* G is a 4-tuple $G = (V, \Sigma, v_0, P)$, where V is a nonempty set and $V \cap \Sigma = \varnothing, v_0 \in V$, and $P \subseteq V \times (V \cup \Sigma)^*$ is a finite set. The elements $(v, x) \in P$ are called productions and are written $v \longrightarrow x$.

Definition 4. Let $G = (V, \Sigma, v_0, P)$ be a context-free grammar. For $w_1, w_2 \in (V \cup \Sigma)^*$ we say w_1 *directly derives* w_2, written $w_1 \Longrightarrow w_2$, provided that $w_1 = w_1'vw_1''$, $w_2 = w_1'xw_1''$, and $v \longrightarrow x \in P$. We say w_1 *derives* w_2, $w_1 \overset{*}{\Longrightarrow} w_2$, if there exist $z_0, z_1, \ldots, z_n \in (V \cup \Sigma)^*$, for some $n \geq 0$, so that $w_1 = z_0$, $w_2 = z_n$, and $z_i \Longrightarrow z_{i+1}, 0 \leq i < n$.

Definition 5. Let $G = (V, \Sigma, \alpha, P)$ be a context-free grammar. The *language of* G, $L(G)$, is $L(G) = \{x \mid \alpha \overset{*}{\Longrightarrow} x \text{ and } x \in \Sigma^*\}$. A subset $K \subseteq \Sigma^*$ is called a *context-free language* if there exists a context-free grammar G so that $K = L(G)$. An arbitrary subset $K \subseteq \Sigma^*$ is sometimes referred to as a *language*.

Theorem 3

Each regular subset $K \subseteq \Sigma^*$ is a context-free language. However, there are context-free languages which are not regular, for instance, $\{a^nb^n \mid n \geq 1\} \subseteq \{a, b\}^*$.

Theorem 4

There is an algorithm which, given a context-free grammar G, will decide whether or not $L(G) = \varnothing$.

Theorem 5 [Valiant (1975)]

For each context-free grammar G there is an algorithm which for any $x \in \Sigma^*$ correctly decides if $x \in L(G)$ and which executes in time proportional to n^t where $t < 3$ and $n = \text{length}(x)$.

Theorem 6

There is no algorithm which, given a context-free grammar G, will always correctly decide whether or not $L(G) = \Sigma^*$.

Corollary 6.1

There is no algorithm which, given context-free grammars G_1 and G_2, will always correctly decide whether or not $L(G_1) = L(G_2)$.

For both the class of regular languages and the class of context-free languages, languages in a class may be combined by the operations of union, concatenation, and iteration (*), and the result is in the same class. The complement and intersection of regular sets are also regular, but there are context-free languages whose complement and intersection are not context-free. One frequently cited example of a non-context-free language which arises in this way is $\{a^nb^nc^n \mid n \geq 0\} = \{a^nb^nc^m \mid n, m \geq 0\} \cap \{a^nb^sc^s \mid n, s \geq 0\}$.

Algebraic Concepts

We shall introduce one nonstandard concept here. For the most part, the reader can consult any of the standard references on abstract algebra for more details, for instance, Jacobson (1951).

We use the notation N for the set of nonnegative integers, $N = \{0, 1, 2, \ldots\}$, and I for the set of all integers, $I = \{\ldots, -2, -1, 0, 1, 2, \ldots\}$.

> **Definition 6.** A *counted set* (of nonnegative integers) is a function $f: N \longrightarrow I$. The counted set is said to be *finite* provided that $N - f^{-1}(0)$ is finite [i.e., for all but finitely many n, $f(n) = 0$].

Usually we use the ordinary set notation, augmenting it with an element prefix to denote the value $f(n)$. That is, we write $\{f(0) * 0, f(1) * 1, f(2) * 2 \ldots\}$ but omit the entire entry for i if $f(i) = 0$ and omit the element prefix $f(i)*$ if $f(i) = 1$. Thus for

$$f(n) = \begin{cases} -1, & \text{if } n = 1, 2, 7 \\ 1, & \text{if } n = 3, 10 \\ 0, & \text{otherwise} \end{cases}$$

we use the notation $\{-1 * 1, -1 * 2, 3, -1 * 7, 10\}$.

Definition 7. For counted sets f and g we defined the counted sets $i * f$, where $i \in I$ by $(i * f)(n) = i \cdot f(n)$ and the *union* of f and g, $f \cup g$, by $(f \cup g)n = f(n) + g(n)$.

We shall also have occasion to refer to the *empty counted set*, written $\varnothing$, which designates the function $f(n) = 0$ for all $n \in N$. For a counted set f we use the notation $m \in f$ to mean that $f(m) \neq 0$; the notation $i * m \in f$ means that $f(m) = i$ $(i \in I)$.

Definition 8. A *ring* is a system consisting of a set R and two binary operations $+$ and $\cdot$ on R which satisfy the following for all $a, b, c \in R$:

(A1) $(a + b) + c = a + (b + c)$,

(A2) $a + b = b + a$,

(A3) There is an element $0 \in R$ so that $a + 0 = 0 + a = 0$,

(A4) There is $-a \in R$ so that $a + (-a) = (-a) + a = 0$,

(M1) $(a \cdot b) \cdot c = a \cdot (b \cdot c)$,

(D1) $a \cdot (b + c) = a \cdot b + a \cdot c$, and

(D2) $(b + c) \cdot a = b \cdot a + c \cdot a$.

Definition 9. If $\langle R, +, \cdot \rangle$ is a ring, then an element $1 \in R$ is called a *multiplicative identity* (or *unit*) if $1 \cdot a = a \cdot 1 = a$ for all $a \in R$. An element b is called a (*right*) *multiplicative inverse* of a provided that $ab = 1$.

Definition 10. An *integral domain* is a ring $\langle R, +, \cdot \rangle$ such that the following holds:

(I1) For all $a, b \in R$, if $a \neq 0$ and $b \neq 0$, then $a \cdot b \neq 0$.

Theorem 7

A ring $\langle R, -, \cdot \rangle$ is an integral domain if and only if the following hold for all $a, b, c \in R$:

(C1) $a \cdot b = a \cdot c$ and $a \neq 0$ imply $b = c$, and

(C2) $b \cdot a = c \cdot a$ and $a \neq 0$ imply $b = c$.

Given a set S with an operation $\cdot$ (which may be binary or unary; we assume binary here) a subset $T \subseteq S$ is said to be *closed* with respect to $\cdot$ provided that for all $t_1, t_2 \in T$, $t_1 \cdot t_2 \in T$. The *closure* of a subset T is the smallest closed T' so that $T \subseteq T' \subseteq S$.

String Patterns

For more extended exposition on the topics discussed here, the reader is probably best advised to consult one of the available texts on SNOBOL4, such as Griswold et al. (1971) or Maurer (1976).

Patterns are constructed from various primitive elements by means of certain rules of combination. Each pattern both describes a collection of strings and a structure foı the collection. In what is to follow we shall consider the effect of restricting attention to certain subsets, both of element types and operations. Our intent here is to descirbe each of these items without significant consideration of interactions.

We shall generally be concerned with strings of symbols from some finite nonempty set of characters C. By a *string constant* over C we generally mean a nonnull sequence from C. We use the symbol λ to denote the *null string*. For a string $s = c_1c_2 \ldots c_n$, where $c_i \in C$, we use several notations: (1) len $(s) = n$ [of course, len $(\lambda) = 0$]; (2) $s(i, j) = c_ic_{i+1} \ldots c_j$ for $1 \leq i \leq j \leq n$; and (3) $s(i) = c_i$ for $1 \leq i \leq n$.

> **Definition 11.** Let C be a finite, nonempty character set, and let $V = \{v_1, \ldots, v_m\}$ be a set of identifiers. The following are *primitive pattern elements*:
>
> (1) α (this is ARB in SNOBOL4),
>
> (2) Φ (this is FAIL in SNOBOL4),
>
> (3) Λ (this is NULL in SNOBOL4),
>
> (4) Any string constant over C, written $c_1c_2 \ldots c_n$,
>
> (5) Any identifier (simple variable) from V.

There are several other primitive pattern elements which could be introduced, and attention is called to some of these later. However, the detailed treatment in the following is concerned with those mentioned above. We shall discuss the effect of these elements shortly.

> **Definition 12.** The following are pattern combination operators (given pattern expressions P and Q):
>
> (1) *Alternation*, a binary operator written $P \mid Q$,
>
> (2) *Concatenation*, a binary operator written PQ,
>
> (3) *Iteration*, a unary operator written P^* (in SNOBOL4 this is the ARBNO function),
>
> (4) *Assignment*, a binary operator written identifier $= P$.

To avoid undue parentheses nesting we establish a precedence for these operators as follows (from highest to lowest): iteration, concatenation, alternation, and assignment.

We shall associate in pattern expression P two collections of strings: (1) the collection of strings *represented by P*, $L(P)$, and (2) the collection of strings *matched by P*, $M(P)$. $M(P)$ will denote all those strings which have some substring represented by P; thus $M(P) = C^*L(P)C^*$.

We shall now present one definition which describes both how valid patterns are formed by the combination of other valid patterns and what collection of strings is represented by the result.

Definition 13. Let C be a character set, and let $V = \{v_1, v_2, \ldots, v_m\}$ be a collection of identifiers. The *pattern expressions* over C and V and the set of strings represented are defined recursively by

(1) The primitive pattern elements are pattern expressions, and
  (a) $L(\alpha) = C^*$,
  (b) $L(\Phi) = \varnothing$,
  (c) $L(\Lambda) = \{\lambda\}$, and
  (d) $L(c_1c_2 \ldots c_n) = \{c_1c_2 \ldots c_n\}$;

(2) If P and Q are pattern expressions, so are each of the following:
  (a) $P|Q$, and $L(P|Q) = L(P) \cup L(Q)$,
  (b) PQ, and $L(PQ) = L(P)L(Q)$,
  (c) P^*, and $L(P^*) = (L(P))^*$;

(3) Nothing is a pattern expression unless it follows by repeated application of (1) and (2).

This defines the pattern expressions and for any pattern expression P which contains no identifier, $L(P)$ as well. If P contains variables, we define $L(P)$ only in the following setting:

Definition 14. Let C be a character set, and let $V = \{v_1, v_2, \ldots, v_m\}$ be a collection of identifiers. A *pattern expression system* over C and V consists of a distinguished identifier (taken to be v_1 if not explicitly stated otherwise) called the *start variable* and a collection of assignments

$$\begin{aligned} v_1 &= P_1 \\ v_2 &= P_2 \\ &\vdots \\ v_m &= P_m, \end{aligned}$$

where each P_i, $1 \leq i \leq m$, is a pattern expression over C and V. For each i we define $L(v_i) = L(P_i)$; we understand $L(v_1), \ldots, L(v_m)$ to be the collection of smallest sets which satisfy this system of equations (hence the identifiers may be thought of as set variables). The *language of the system* is taken as the language of the start variable.

This approach results in a recursive system of definitions which we leave on a very informal basis here. For instance, for

$$A = aA \mid B$$
$$B = bB \mid \Lambda$$

one should understand that $L(B) = b^*$ and $L(A) = a^*b^*$. That is, $L(B)$ is the smallest set which satisfies the equation $B = \{\lambda\} \cup \{b\} \cdot B$ and $L(A)$ is the smallest set which satisfies the equation $A = L(B) \cup \{a\} \cdot A$. Note that our use of a variable v_i in a pattern expression here corresponds to the unevaluated expression $*v_i$ in SNOBOL4. This is because of our static view—we do not assume that assignment (=) is executable but only that it prescribes a relation. For similar reasons, the order in which the assignments of a system are written will not be considered significant. More examples are given in the following sections, and we shall later hint at how this recursive definition can be made precise.

In the following sections, when presenting examples, we shall adopt the convention that variables are written as capitals: A, B, C, etc., and character symbols are written in lowercase: a, b, c, etc. Also for patterns or pattern systems X and Y we sometimes use the notation $X \equiv Y$ to denote that $L(X) = L(Y)$.

8.3. FORMAL LANGUAGES MODEL

In this section the formal languages model of string patterns is adopted. The theme of the section is to show analogs of various classes of mechanisms among the string patterns. This allows conclusions to be made about the impossibility of certain pattern algorithms of interest and about potential optimality of various algorithms of interest. It should perhaps be emphasized that this model takes a *global* view of a pattern and is not suited to questions relating to the combination of patterns to produce new patterns. The model treated in the next section is more useful for such questions but too *local* to be manageable for the investigations in this section.

Literature relating to the material presented in this section includes Fleck (1971, 1975), Furtado (1972), and Thompson (1968). Also, for another model which was developed for a different purpose but which has many similarities to that discussed here, the reader may see Conway (1963), Lomet (1973), Winograd (1976), and Woods (1970).

Regular Expression Patterns

To establish some perspective for the results of later sections, we shall treat here a relatively simple subclass of patterns. This subclass has a limited but nontrivial potential for application.

Definition 15. A *regular expression pattern* over the character set C [which we assume does not contain the symbols (,), |, $*$, α, Φ, or Λ] is defined recursively by the following:

(1) α, Φ, Λ and any string constant over C are regular expression patterns;

(2) If x and y are regular expression patterns, then so are
(a) $(x)(y)$,
(b) $(x)|(y)$, and
(c) $(x)^*$;

(3) An object is a regular expression pattern only if it may be constructed by repeated applications of (1) and (2).

Note that since $(L(\Phi))^* = L(\Lambda)$ and $L(\alpha) = L((c_1|c_2|\ldots c_n)^*)$ (where $C = \{c_1, c_2, \ldots, c_n\}$), Λ and α need not have been included as axiomatic regular expression patterns, but it is convenient to do so. Also we shall not in general use all the parentheses dictated by a strict interpretation of Definition 15; instead we shall use the precedence ordering mentioned earlier. For example, we write $a|b^*c$ in place of $(a)|(((b)^*)(c))$ as technically required by Definition 15.

To the reader with the anticipated background, the properties of this subclass of patterns are clear. Nonetheless, for completeness and comparison with later results, we shall include here a statement of properties of interest and a few examples. These examples are presented without justification, which in some cases is not easy to provide. The reader should be skeptical, and the insight gained in personal justification of a few of the examples will be helpful for later understanding.

Example 1

ALGOL indentifiers:

$$(a|b|\ldots|z)(a|b|\ldots|z|0|1|\ldots|9)^*$$

Example 2

All finite sequences of $\{a, b\}$ with an even number of b's:

$$a^*(ba^*ba^*)^*$$

Example 3

All finite sequences of $\{a, b\}$ which include at least one a and one b:

$$(aa^*b|bb^*a)(a^*b^*)^*$$

Example 4

Decimal constants:

$$((1|2|\ldots|9)(0|1|\ldots|9)^*|\Lambda)\cdot(0|1|\ldots|9)^*$$

Example 5

All finite sequences of $\{a, b\}$ without three consecutive a's:

$$(b|ab|aab)^*(\Lambda|a|aa)$$

Example 6

All finite sequences of $\{a, b\}$ with an odd number of a's and odd number of b's:

$$(aa \mid bb)^*(ab \mid ba)(aa \mid bb)^*((ab \mid ba)(aa \mid bb)^*(ab \mid ba))^*(aa \mid bb)^*$$

Theorem 8

For each regular expression pattern R there is a (isomorphic) regular expression ρ so that $L(R) = |\rho|$ and similarly if the regular expression is given.

Proof: No proof of this result is required; the same notation was purposefully used in both definitions to emphasize the interpretation of regular expressions as patterns.

We can also observe that for a regular expression pattern R the set of strings matched, $M(R)$, is $M(R) = C^*L(R)C^*$. Hence $M(R) = L(R')$, where R' is some other regular expression pattern and we lose no generality by restricting our attention to the sets $L(R)$.

Corollary 8.1

For each regular expression pattern there is a bounded space, linear time recognition algorithm which given any string will determine whether or not that string is represented by the pattern. Conversely, any set of strings for which such an algorithm exists occurs as the set represented by some regular expression pattern.

Proof: This result is just a restatement of the fact that the class of regular sets is exactly the class accepted by finite state acceptors.

In automata theory, consideration is generally given to the existence of a number of different algorithms. We shall mention just two here which seem to have particular significance for pattern-oriented string manipulation systems. One relates to the resolution of the question, Is $R \equiv \Phi$? If this is the case, then clearly execution time is improved if at compile time the more complicated pattern R is replaced by Φ (which fails *immediately*). But of more importance than the efficiency issue is the assistance in debugging. While one probably does not want to prohibit patterns R (other than Φ itself) where $R \equiv \Phi$, it is surely, in the preponderance of cases, an inadvertent error when one writes a more complicated pattern which always fails. Similar arguments can be put forth with respect to the question, Is $R \equiv \alpha$?

Corollary 8.2

There is an algorithm which for any regular expression pattern R will determine whether or not $R \equiv \Phi$. Similarly, there is an algorithm which will determine whether or not $R \equiv \alpha$.

Proof: Again this result is a direct corollary to the existence of algorithms for the corresponding questions for finite automata.

An algorithm to decide $R \equiv \alpha$ which performs within polynomial bounded storage requirements is known, but one is not known which will perform within polynomial bounded time requirements [see Aho et al. (1974)]. Thus while algorithms for these questions do exist for this subclass of patterns, the practical utility of the algorithms which are actually known is questionable.

The second algorithm we mention here relates to the question, Given patterns R_1 and R_2, is $R_1 \equiv R_2$? The positive resolution of such equivalence questions is sometimes given exaggerated significance. It is many times claimed that such an equivalence algorithm leads to optimization procedures. Given a pattern R, one could simply generate each of the finitely many patterns "smaller" than R and test each for equivalence with R and thus find the "smallest" pattern equivalent to R. This is of course in principle correct; however, in practice it is so inefficient as to be useless. What is needed is a direct technique for optimization, and an equivalence algorithm does not help in this regard. Furthermore, it is conceivable that an optimization algorithm exists even when an equivalence algorithm does not. Thus establishing that an equivalence algorithm does not exist is not conclusive, although it can be taken as a fairly discouraging sign. Hence the importance of the existence of an equivalence algorithm must stand on its own. This it can do, as the test for equivalence has proved to be of considerable value for many varieties of entities in many languages. For example, it could be conveniently used in the definition of pattern-valued functions of patterns, e.g., $\mathcal{P}(Q) := \underline{\text{if}}\ (Q\,|\,a)^* \equiv \alpha\ \underline{\text{then}}\ Q\ \underline{\text{else}}\ \mathcal{P}(Q\,|\,b)$. Unfortunately, as we shall see, the situation is not too favorable for this operation on patterns.

Corollary 8.3

There is an algorithm which for any two regular expression patterns R_1 and R_2 will determine whether or not $R_1 \equiv R_2$.

Proof: This result, too, is a direct consequence of the corresponding result for finite state acceptors.

Clearly, there can be no more efficient algorithm for the question $R_1 \equiv R_2$ than for $R \equiv \alpha$. Hence the comments made above, questioning the practicality of those algorithms, also apply here. For a quantitative treatment of the equivalence problem, the interested reader can consult Stockmeyer and Meyer (1973).

The results and observations made here concerning regular expression patterns have set the stage for the observations which are to follow on more powerful mechanisms. Also these patterns serve as a prototype of a useful subclass, exhibiting the following desirable properties:

1. They may be detected on the basis of form alone (i.e., there is easy compile-time detection),
2. Optimal (or near optimal) recognition (pattern matching) techniques are known.

3. Other algorithms of interest (such as testing for impossibility of success or failure) are known to exist for the class, and
4. There is a sound conceptual understanding of the type of collection of strings for which patterns in the class can (or cannot) be applied to provide a definition.

Context-Free Pattern Systems

In this section we shall examine a more general model which essentially corresponds to the collection of all SNOBOL4 patterns which include no "special" features (e.g., functions, immediate value assignment, etc.).

Definition 16. A *context-free pattern system* over character set C and identifier set V is any pattern system (see Section 9.2) which can be constructed from only

(1) Alternation, concatenation, and assignment operators;

(2) The primitive pattern Λ and string constants; and

(3) Simple variables.

Example 7

All finite sequences of $\{a, b\}$ with an even number of b's:

$$A = aA \mid bB \mid \Lambda$$
$$B = aB \mid bA$$

Example 8

ALGOL identifiers:

$$I = L \mid IL \mid ID$$
$$L = a \mid b \mid \ldots \mid z$$
$$D = 0 \mid 1 \mid \ldots \mid 9$$

Example 9

All sequences of n a's followed by n b's, $n = 1, 2, \ldots$:

$$A = ab \mid aAb$$

Example 10

All well-formed parentheses nestings:

$$P = (\;\;) \mid (P) \mid PP$$

Example 11

All finite sequences of $\{a, b, c\}$ where the (number of a's) + (number of b's) = number of c's:

$$S = \Lambda \mid cSR \mid RcS$$
$$R = aS \mid bS$$

Lemma

For each context-free pattern P there is a context-free pattern Q which is an alternation of concatenations and so that $L(P) = L(Q)$.

Proof: This is a type of normal form result familiar from logic and switching theory. The conclusion follows from the observation that $L(R(S \mid T)) = L(RS \mid RT)$ and $L((S \mid T)R) = L(SR \mid TR)$ for any context-free patterns R, S, and T.

Theorem 9

For each context-free grammar G there is a context-free pattern system P (which is *isomorphic* to G) so that $L(G) = L(P)$, and similarly if the pattern system P is given.

Proof (*outline*): We shall include only a description of the correspondence; the remainder of the detail is tedious but not difficult to verify. The variables of the grammar and the variables of the pattern system are in one-to-one correspondence. From the lemma we may assume the equation for each pattern variable is in alternation of concatenation form; then there is a one-to-one correspondence between the productions for a variable in the grammar and the alternatives for a variable in the pattern system, each alternative being the right-hand side of the corresponding production.

Example 12

The pattern system of Example 11 corresponds to the productions

$$S \longrightarrow \lambda, \quad S \longrightarrow cSR, \quad S \longrightarrow RcS, \quad R \longrightarrow aS, \quad R \longrightarrow bS.$$

Example 13

The pattern system of Example 10 corresponds to the productions

$$P \longrightarrow (\ \ ), \quad P \longrightarrow (P), \quad P \longrightarrow PP.$$

Corollary 9.1

Each collection of strings represented by a regular expression pattern is also represented by a context-free pattern.

Proof: Follows from the corresponding result for grammars.

For example, a context-free equivalent of regular expression Examples 1 and 2 is given in Examples 8 and 7, respectively. Of course, the context-free extension is a proper one; that is, there are collections which cannot be represented by the regular expression patterns but can be represented by context-free patterns. Examples 9, 10, and 11 are in this category.

Corollary 9.2

For each context-free pattern system there is a recognition algorithm that operates in less than cubic time and determines whether or not a given string is represented by the pattern.

Proof: We need only appeal to the corresponding result for grammars.

Corollary 9.3

There is an algorithm which for any context-free pattern P will determine whether or not $P \equiv \Phi$.

The standard grammar algorithm for this problem operates in time proportional to $p \cdot v$, where p is the number of productions and v the number of variables, and hence is eminently practical. On the other hand, contrast the following result with the results for regular expression patterns:

Corollary 9.4

There are no algorithms which will determine for arbitrary context-free pattern systems P_1 and P_2 whether or not $P_1 \equiv \alpha$ or whether or not $P_1 \equiv P_2$.

The preceding corollary of the results in Section 9.2 provides a strong contrast and gives a quantitative indication of the increased complexity of the context-free case over the regular expression case. Note, however, that to a considerable extent the context-free case retains the desirable attributes referred to at the end of the last section—this despite a substantial increase in the expressive power.

We shall introduce here one other representation technique for context-free pattern systems, the *diagram*. This is the type of graphical presentation frequently used, for example, in LISP [McCarthy et al. (1962)] and strongly advocated by Winograd (1976). We shall not provide a careful definition here [see Fleck (1971)], as it is fairly involved to do and is counter to our purpose, which is to suggest an aid to intuition, not precision.

Example 14

The diagram representation of the system of Example 9 is

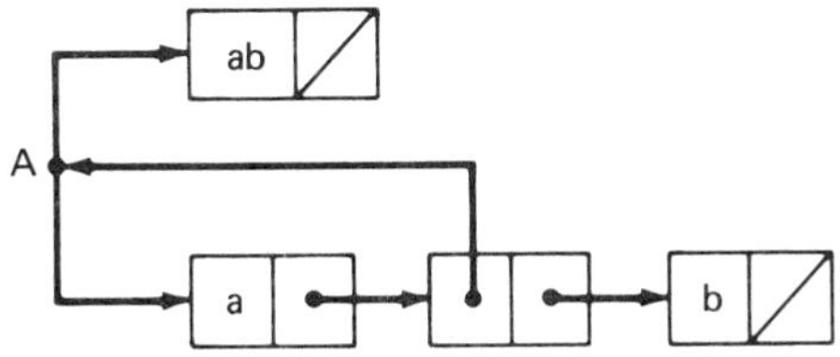

One has a *head cell* (which contains no data) for each identifier and a linearly linked collection of cells for the right side of each production [each cell holds a string constant or (pointer to an) identifier].

Example 15

The diagram representation of the system of Example 7 is

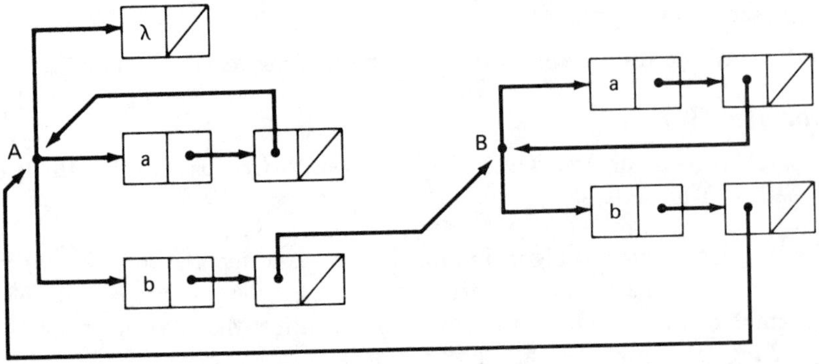

A number of properties of interest may be readily determined by inspection of the diagram representation. For instance, the system involves recursive definition if (and only if) the diagram has a cycle, and only in this case can the set of strings represented be infinite. Also the set represented will be empty if each terminating path from the head cell has a segment in common with a cycle.

Extensions to Context-Free Patterns

One of the most natural extensions to consider is the augmentation by the set operations, complement, and intersection. That is, for patterns P_1 and P_2 over C we allow the definition of new patterns $\neg P_1$ and $P_1 \wedge P_2$, where $L(\neg P_1) = C^* - L(P_1)$ and $L(P_1 \wedge P_2) = L(P_1) \cap L(P_2)$. For the regular expression patterns these operations do not increase the expressive power, as regular sets still result. However, even here there is a definite improvement in conciseness. That is, often sets which can be described have simpler and more natural expressions when these operations are allowed; for instance, the expression of Example 3 can be replaced by $\neg(a^*) \wedge \neg(b^*)$. The situation for the context-free patterns is more dramatic. In this case a substantial increase in expressive power is achieved by adding these two pattern operations (of course by De Morgan's laws, one need only add complementation). As pointed out in Section 9.2, the context-free languages are not closed under complement and intersection.

Example 16

$$A = Ac \mid B$$

$$B = aBb \mid \Lambda$$

$$C = aC \mid D \qquad L(E) = \{a^n b^n c^n \mid n \geq 0\}$$
$$D = bDc \mid \Lambda$$
$$E = A \wedge C$$

An indication of this increase in expressive power has been given by Liu and Weiner (1973), who show that an infinite hierarchy arises depending on the number of times the intersection operation is used. Note that even so, the context-free pattern matching technique (refer to Corollary 9.2) can be applied here practically intact; when the complement operation is involved, the success or failure response is simply reversed, and the intersection response is determined by the results of the responses for each of the constituents. Hence for such patterns it is still possible to perform pattern matching efficiently. It also would be natural to augment the context-free patterns by the iteration operator $*$. This would not increase their expressive capacity, as context-free languages still result. However, it does improve the conciseness of the mechanism and allows more readable definitions. For instance, Example 8 can be written

Example 17

ALGOL idetifiers:

$$I = L(L \mid D)^*$$
$$L = a \mid b \mid \ldots \mid z$$
$$D = 0 \mid 1 \mid \ldots \mid 9$$

Another possibility is to augment the context-free patterns with function elements in the spirit of the manner in which SNOBOL allows programmer-defined or system functions as pattern primitives. A careful study of such an extension would require that we specify the mathematical properties of the functions to be admitted. We shall not enter into any of these details here, but even with very restrictive assumptions concerning the properties of the function elements and the way they can occur in patterns, it turns out that expressive power is increased so greatly that efficient algorithms for most problems of interest are impossible [see Fleck (1971, 1975)].

A third interesting extension to the context-free patterns is augmentation by the immediate value assignment of SNOBOL4. A careful definition of the semantics of this operation is difficult, and we shall not attempt it here. Informally, one understands a left-to-right, top-down matching algorithm; at any point in this process the occurrence of an element of the form "element \$ var" causes the substring matched by the element to be assigned to the variable. This value may, of course, be referenced later by mention of the variable.

Example 18

Immediate value assignment pattern for $\{a^{2^n} \mid n \geq 0\}$:

$$A = a \mid (A \,\$\, X)X$$

As is seen by this example, the augmentation by immediate value assignment allows definition of sets which are not context-free. Hence it serves as a mechanism for properly extending the capacity of the context-free patterns. The interested reader can see Fleck (1975) for more analysis.

The last extension we shall mention is suggested by a facility of MLISP2 [Smith and Enea (1973)], although our proposal takes a substantially different form. The suggestion is to allow conditional pattern elements. These would be of the form "if cond then P_1 else P_2," where P_1 and P_2 are other (possibly conditional) elements. Again we appeal to an intuitive understanding of the semantics; if the "cond" is true, then the element represents whatever P_1 represents and otherwise whatever P_2 represents. In a programming system the conditions could involve testing of flags set elsewhere, etc. For our static view there are far fewer options. However, we can imagine conditions based on immediate value assignment.

Example 19

A pattern using immediate value assignment and conditional elements:

$$A = a \mid aA$$

$$B = b \mid bB \qquad L(D) = \{a^n b^n c^n \mid n \geq 1\}$$

$$C = c \mid cC$$

$$D = (A \,\$\, X)(B \,\$\, Y)(C \,\$\, Z)(\underline{\text{if}}\ \text{len}\,(X) = \text{len}\,(Y)\ \&\ \text{len}\,(Y) = \text{len}\,(Z)\ \underline{\text{then}}\ \Lambda\ \underline{\text{else}}\ \Phi)$$

8.4. AN ALGEBRAIC MODEL

In this section we shall discuss a model which is more closely related to implementation details. The model allows better approximation to the element relations in a composition. Thus the interrelationships of the pattern operations can be carefully treated. In fact suitable abstraction leads naturally to suggestions for extensions and generalizations with considerable appeal. Hence our interest naturally turns from a consideration of the existence and potential efficiency of algorithms to a consideration of the semantics of patterns and pattern matching.

The development in this section is based on work by Gimpel (1973) and Stewart (1974, 1975). These papers develop similar but somewhat different models, Gimpel (1973) being more implementation-oriented and Stewart (1974, 1975) more conceptually natural. As suggested by the philosophical comments in the introduction, we shall follow the latter line here.

Basic Definitions

In this section we shall adhere more carefully to the terminology introduced in Section 9.2. In particular we shall be interested in discriminating between a *pattern expression* and a *pattern function*.

Definition 17. A *pattern function* $\hat{P}$ on the character set C is a partial function, $\hat{P}: C^* \times N \longrightarrow$ {finite counted sets}; $\hat{P}(s, n)$ is defined just in the event $0 \leq n \leq \text{len}(s)$, and we shall assume that if $m \in \hat{P}(s, n)$, then $0 \leq m \leq \text{len}(s)$. In the event, for each $s \in C^*$ and $n \in N$, $i * m \in \hat{P}(s, n)$ implies $i \geq 0$, $\hat{P}$ is said to be *nonnegative*; if $i * m \in \hat{P}(s, n)$ implies that $m > n$, $\hat{P}$ is said to be *monotone*. Sometimes n is referred to as the *precursor position*, and the members of the resulting counted set as the *postcursor positions*.

Of course, this definition is far too general; it includes nonconstructive elements in which we shall never have any interest. We shall shortly focus on constructive classes of pattern functions of particular interest.

The semantic interpretation of a pattern function is as a recording of the set of *actions* of a pattern matching algorithm on a pattern expression. As suggested by the terminology introduced in the definition, the motivation is essentially an implementation-oriented modeling of the pattern matching process. For a given string s, at any moment a certain portion of the string will have been processed by the matching algorithm. The present character position of interest is the precursor position, and the possible positions (together with their multiplicities) to which processing can have continued after the pattern element P has been matched are given by $\hat{P}(s, c)$. Examples will be given shortly.

Definition 18. Let $\hat{P}$ be a pattern function on C. We extend $\hat{P}$ to $\bar{P}: C^* \times$ {finite counted sets} as follows: $\bar{P}(s, \{n1 * c1, n2 * c2, \ldots, np * cp\}) = (n1 * \hat{P}(s, c1)) \cup (n2 * \hat{P}(s, c2)) \cup \ldots \cup (np * \hat{P}(s, cp))$ while $\bar{P}(s, \varnothing) = \varnothing$. Usually no confusion will arise and we simply write $\hat{P}$ in place of $\bar{P}$.

We shall be interested in the operations on pattern functions given in the following:

Definition 19. Let $\hat{P}$ and $\hat{Q}$ be pattern functions on character set C. Then for each $s \in C^*$ and $n \in N$,

(a) $-\hat{P}$ is defined by $(-\hat{P})(s, n) = (-1) * \hat{P}(s, n)$ and is called the *negation* of $\hat{P}$;

(b) The *alternation* of $\hat{P}$ and $\hat{Q}$, written $\hat{P} | \hat{Q}$, is defined by $(\hat{P} | \hat{Q})(s, n) = \hat{P}(s, n) \cup \hat{Q}(s, n)$;

(c) The *concatenation* (or composition) of $\hat{P}$ and $\hat{Q}$, denoted $\hat{P}\hat{Q}$, is defined by $(\hat{P}\hat{Q})(s, n) = \hat{Q}(s, \hat{P}(s, n))$;

(d) If $\hat{P}$ is nonnegative and monotone, the *iteration* of $\hat{P}$, written $\hat{P}^*$, and the Λ-*free iteration* of $\hat{P}$, written $\hat{P}^+$, are defined by $\hat{P}^*(s, n) = \cup_{i=0}^{\infty} \hat{P}^i(s, n)$ and $\hat{P}^+(s, n) = \cup_{i=1}^{\infty} \hat{P}^i(s, n)$, where $\hat{P}^{i+1} = \hat{P}\hat{P}^i$ for $i \geq 0$ and $\hat{P}^0(s, n) = \{n\}$ for all $0 \leq n \leq \text{len}(s)$; we are to understand that these "infinite" unions only contain the designated elements for which $\hat{P}^i(s, n)$ is actually defined.

Lemma

If $\hat{P}$ is nonnegative and monotone, then the operations $\hat{P}^*$ and $\hat{P}^+$ result in well-defined pattern functions.

Proof: It is easy to verify, under these assumptions, that as soon as $i + n$ exceeds len (s), $\hat{P}^i(s, n)$ is no longer defined (or is empty).

Definition 20. Consider the context-free pattern systems introduced in Section 9.3. We shall now indicate how to associate a pattern function (actually a system of pattern functions) with such a system:

(1) If x is a string constant, the associated pattern function $\hat{x}$ is defined by the following: For a string $s \in C^*$ and for all $0 \leq m \leq \text{len}(s)$,

$$\hat{x}(s, m) = \begin{cases} \{m + \text{len}(x)\}, & \text{if } s(m + 1, m + \text{len}(x)) = x \\ \varnothing, & \text{otherwise;} \end{cases}$$

(2) For the primitive pattern Λ, the associated pattern function $\hat{\Lambda}$ is defined by the following: For all $s \in C^*$ and all $0 \leq m \leq \text{len}(s)$, $\hat{\Lambda}(s, m) = \{m\}$;

(3) If pattern expressions P and Q are associated with pattern functions $\hat{P}$ and $\hat{Q}$, respectively, then
(a) $P \mid Q$ is associated with $\hat{P} \mid \hat{Q}$, and
(b) PQ is associated with $\hat{P}\hat{Q}$;

(4) Finally, the (recursive) system of pattern function definitions is arrived at as follows: Each simple identifier in the system has associated with it a definition determined by the pattern expression assigned to it according to the rules (1)–(3) above.

Example 20

$P_1 = ab, s = abab$:

c	$\hat{P}_1(s, c)$
0	{2}
1	$\varnothing$
2	{4}
3	$\varnothing$
4	$\varnothing$

Example 21

$P_2 = ab \mid abc, s = abcd$:

k	$\hat{P}_2(s, k)$
0	{2, 3}
1	$\varnothing$
2	$\varnothing$
3	$\varnothing$
4	$\varnothing$

Example 22

$P_3 = (ab \mid abc)(c \mid \Lambda)$, $s = abcc$:

k	$\hat{P}_3(s, k)$
0	$\{2, 2 * 3, 4\}$
1	$\varnothing$
2	$\varnothing$
3	$\varnothing$
4	$\varnothing$

Note that $\hat{P}_3(s, 0) = (\hat{c} \mid \hat{\Lambda})\hat{P}_2(s, 0) = (\hat{c} \mid \hat{\Lambda})(s, \{2, 3\}) = \hat{c}(s, \{2, 3\}) \cup \hat{\Lambda}(s, \{2, 3\}) = \hat{c}(s, 2) \cup \hat{c}(s, 3) \cup \hat{\Lambda}(s, 2) \cup \hat{\Lambda}(s, 3) = \{3\} \cup \{4\} \cup \{2\} \cup \{3\} = \{2, 2 * 3, 4\}$.

Example 23

Let $\hat{P} = \hat{a}\hat{b} \mid \hat{b}\hat{a}$ and $s = aabbabab$. Then $\hat{P}^*(s, n)$ is as follows:

n	$\hat{P}^*(s, n)$
0	$\{0\}$
1	$\{1, 3, 5, 7\}$
2	$\{2\}$
3	$\{3, 5, 7\}$
4	$\{4, 6, 8\}$
5	$\{5, 7\}$
6	$\{6, 8\}$
7	$\{7\}$
8	$\{8\}$

where, for instance, the details of one of these evaluations can be expressed by

$$\begin{aligned}\hat{P}^*(s, 3) &= \hat{P}^0(s, 3) \cup \hat{P}(s, 3) \cup \hat{P}(s, \hat{P}(s, 3)) \cup \ldots \\ &= \{3\} \cup \{5\} \cup \{7\} \cup \ldots.\end{aligned}$$

But notice that $\hat{P}^3(s, 3) = \hat{P}(s, \hat{P}^2(s, 3))$ and $\hat{P}(s, 7) = \varnothing$. Hence $\hat{P}^i(s, 3) = \varnothing$ for all $i \geq 3$ and so we may conclude that $\hat{P}^*(s, 3) = \{3, 5, 7\}$.

Example 24

Context-free pattern system:

$$\begin{aligned}A &= aA \mid bB \mid \Lambda \\ B &= aB \mid bA\end{aligned}$$

gives rise to the system of pattern function definitions

$$\begin{aligned}\hat{A}(s, c) &= \hat{A}(s, \hat{a}(s, c)) \mid \hat{B}(s, \hat{b}(s, c)) \mid \hat{\Lambda}(s, c) \\ \hat{B}(s, c) &= \hat{B}(s, \hat{a}(s, c)) \mid \hat{A}(s, \hat{b}(s, c)).\end{aligned}$$

Hence, for example, $\hat{A}(ababb, 0) = \{0, 1, 4\}$ as

$$\begin{aligned}\hat{A}(ababb, 0) &= \hat{A}(ababb, 1) \cup \varnothing \cup \{0\}\\ &= (\varnothing \cup \hat{B}(ababb, 2) \cup \{1\}) \cup \{0\}\\ &= (\hat{B}(ababb, 3) \cup \varnothing) \cup \{0, 1\}\\ &= (\hat{A}(ababb, 4) \cup \varnothing) \cup \{0, 1\}\\ &= (\varnothing \cup \hat{B}(ababb, 5) \cup \{4\}) \cup \{0, 1\}\\ &= (\varnothing \cup \varnothing) \cup \{0, 1, 4\} = \{0, 1, 4\}.\end{aligned}$$

We shall leave the meaning of the recursive definition of pattern functions on an informal basis here. One of the valuable assets of this approach is that the means to make this aspect precise is close at hand (via the fixed point approach). However, we shall not pursue this here, as it would detract from our main goals; the interested reader can consult Stewart (1974, 1975).

In terms of the concepts introduced earlier, we can think of a pattern function as an equivalence class of pattern expressions which define this function. In terms of the strings recognized and matched we can write $L(P) = \{s \mid n * \text{len}(s) \in \hat{P}(s, 0) \text{ and } n > 0\}$ and $M(P) = \{s \mid \exists\, 0 \leq c_1, c_2 \leq \text{len}(s) \text{ with } n * c_2 \in \hat{P}(s, c_1) \text{ and } n > 0\}$.

There are a large number of identities involving the various operations on pattern functions. An exhaustive listing of these is beyond our reach. Before turning to suggestions from algebraic systems, we shall consider another source for suggestions (which does not work out nearly so well). This is the so-called *regular expression* identities [see Salomaa (1969)]. Several problems arise here, however. First, $\hat{P}^*$ is never monotone, so expressions of the form $(\hat{P}^*)^*$ are invalid. Second, the counted set approach carries multiplicities along, so many of the usual identities are lost. For example, the reader can verify that $\hat{a}^*(a, 0) = \{0, 1\}$, while $\hat{a}^*\hat{a}^*(a, 0) = \hat{a}^*(a, \hat{a}^*(a, 0)) = \hat{a}^*(a, \{0, 1\}) = \hat{a}^*(a, 0) \cup \hat{a}^*(a, 1) = \{0, 1\} \cup \{1\} = \{0, 2 * 1\}$.

The following result indicates some of the identities which do carry over. This result is presented without proof. The proofs are straightforward (though tedious) to obtain.

Theorem 10

Let $\hat{P}$ and $\hat{Q}$ be nonnegative, monotone pattern functions. Then

(a) $\hat{\Phi}^* = \hat{\Lambda}$,

(b) $\hat{P}^* = \hat{\Lambda} \mid \hat{P}^+$,

(c) $\hat{P}^*\hat{P} = \hat{P}\hat{P}^* = \hat{P}^+$, and

(d) $(\hat{P}\hat{Q})^*\hat{P} = \hat{P}(\hat{Q}\hat{P})^*$.

Patterns with Negation

Consider now the unary operation of negation on pattern functions introduced in Definition 19. We extend this to a binary operator in the natural way, namely,

$\hat{P} - \hat{Q} = \hat{P} | -\hat{Q}$. This negation operation is suggested by the underlying algebraic structure. We may also extend the negation operation from pattern functions to pattern expressions. We of course assume that the semantics for such pattern expressions are defined by the associated pattern function. The existence of some particularly important identities is asserted by

Theorem 11

The context-free pattern functions augmented by negation (i.e., the closure of the context-free pattern functions under negation, alternation, and concatenation) form an integral domain with unit element.

Proof: The pattern function $\hat{\Phi}$ which is defined by $\hat{\Phi}(s, c) = \varnothing$ for all s and c serves as the additive identity (and is context-free) and $\hat{\Lambda}$ as the multiplicative identity. For any such pattern functions $\hat{P}$, $\hat{Q}$, and $\hat{R}$ the integral domain axioms can be verified (using, of course, alternation as the ring addition and concatenation as the ring multiplication). We shall not do this here, but we suggest that it can be a helpful exercise in understanding the formalism so far developed. We shall suggest here the verification of the distributive property for those who would otherwise avoid all details. $[\hat{P}(\hat{Q} | \hat{R})](s, c) = (\hat{Q} | \hat{R})(s, \hat{P}(s, c)) = \hat{Q}(s, \hat{P}(s, c)) \cup \hat{R}(s, \hat{P}(s, c)) = \hat{P}\hat{Q}(s, c) \cup \hat{P}\hat{R}(s, c) = (\hat{P}\hat{Q} | \hat{P}\hat{R})(s, c)$.

In particular it might be pointed out that with this approach we maintain the commutativity property of alternation. Also we remark that the above result also holds for all pattern functions, but as indicated earlier, we shall be interested in constructive classes. This theorem gives a particularly strong interpretation of the algebraic axioms for the case of patterns; the equality is achieved in a much stronger sense than just set equality for the represented strings; that is, equality of pattern functions not only requires the set of strings matched to be equivalent in the formal languages sense but furthermore requires the cursor movements to be identical, including multiplicities.

The negation operation is rather unique. From the algebraic point of view it is quite trivial. On the other hand, understanding its properties in terms of string matching is another matter. Stewart (1974) points out that it has some of the properties of the primitive pattern ABORT in SNOBOL4, as in

Example 25

A SNOBOL4 pattern to match any character except an asterisk is

'*' ABORT | LEN(1).

Using the negation, we would have

—'*' | LEN(1).

(Note that because of such special functions, the commutativity of alternation is lost in SNOBOL4 but not with this formalism.)

Also negation has some of the properties of complementation, as is seen by

Example 26

$$A = aAa \mid bAb \mid \Lambda$$
$$B = aB \mid bB \mid \Lambda$$
$$C = B - A$$

Then $\hat{A}(s, 0) = \{2k \mid 2k \leq \text{len}(s) \text{ and } s(1, 2k) = \sigma_1\sigma_2 \ldots \sigma_k\sigma_k \ldots \sigma_2\sigma_1, \sigma_i \in \{a, b\}\}$ and $L(A) = \{\sigma_1\sigma_2 \ldots \sigma_k\sigma_k \ldots \sigma_2\sigma_1 \mid k \geq 0, \sigma_i \in \{a, b\}, 1 \leq i \leq k\}$. Also $\hat{B}(s, 0) = \{0, 1, 2, \ldots, \text{len}(s)\}$ and $L(B) = \{\text{all finite sequences of } \{a, b\}\}$. Hence $\hat{C}(s, 0) = \{j \mid j \leq \text{len}(s) \text{ and either } j \neq 2k \text{ or } j = 2k \text{ and } s(1, j) \neq \sigma_1\sigma_2 \ldots \sigma_k\sigma_k \ldots \sigma_2\sigma_1, \sigma_i \in \{a, b\}\}$. Thus $L(C) =$ complement of $L(A)$.

Note, however, that to use negation to realize complementation in this fashion considerable caution must be exercised. It is crucial that the multiplicities of elements in the two sets be identical, as they were in the example here; otherwise, negation does not result in element deletion. Hence the negation operation cannot be identified with complementation. For instance, $-a$ does not represent all strings except for a; in fact, $L(-a) = L(\Phi)$. But while $-a$ represents the same collection of strings as Φ, it behaves entirely differently when composed with other patterns. This is reflected in the difference in the pattern functions for $-a$ and Φ, and this is the sense in which the pattern function model is finer or more detailed than the string representation model.

We see that the negation operation provides a definite increase over the expressive power of context-free patterns. As stated in Section 9.2 and pointed out again in Section 9.3, the context-free languages are not closed under complementation. So we can describe collections of strings using negation which cannot be described without negation.

Notice that in our approach here we have been careful to adjoin the negation operation to context-free pattern functions. This is, we have not admitted negation to occur in the recursive systems of equations defining these functions. Stewart (1975) points out that the fixed point theory cannot be used to formalize recursive definition involving negation, as negation lacks a necessary property (continuity). The failure of this formalism in this case does not concern us here, but it does serve as a warning that natural intuitive interpretations may not work out. For example, the reader may want to consider the recursive "definition" $P = \Lambda \mid (-\Lambda)P$ of a pattern expression which gives the pattern function "definition" $\hat{P}(s, m) = \hat{\Lambda}(s, m) \cup \hat{P}(s, -\hat{\Lambda}(s, m))$. We choose to avoid rather than overcome these difficulties in this presentation.

Modeling Other Features

Each of the models presented here has aspects to which it seems best suited. For instance, the negation operation is naturally suggested by the algebraic model. Another feature which can be easily treated with the algebraic model is *built-in* pattern function definitions. For instance, $\hat{\alpha}(s, c) = \{c, c + 1, \ldots, \text{len}(s)\}$ for all $0 \leq c \leq \text{len}(s)$. More important are the examples which seem to have no natural interpretation in the formal languages model, for instance, the SNOBOL4 functions

$$\text{TAB}\ (n)(s, c) = \begin{cases} \{n\}, & \text{if } 0 \leq n \leq \text{len}\ (s) \\ \varnothing, & \text{otherwise} \end{cases}$$

and for string t

$\text{SPAN}\ (t)(s, c) = \{c + m\}$

where m is the largest value so that $s(c + 1), \ldots, s(c + m) \in t$.

Of course this approach could also be used to advantage to provide a careful definition of the semantics of programmer-defined functions as well as built-in functions. Again this would require the development of a constructive mechanism within which the definitions could be phrased. While we shall not pursue such a development here, the potential of the model for such an extension is a desirable attribute.

Stewart (1974, 1975) considers the possibilities of pattern functions which will serve as multiplicative inverses. $\hat{P}^{-1}$ would be a (right) inverse of $\hat{P}$ if $\hat{P}\hat{P}^{-1} = \hat{\Lambda}$. But this will never be possible for patterns of interest since if there is $s \in C^*$ and $n \in N$ so that $\hat{P}(s, n) = \varnothing$ (i.e., P fails somewhere), then $\hat{P}\hat{P}^{-1}(s, n) = \hat{P}^{-1}(s, \hat{P}(s, n)) = \hat{P}^{-1}(s, \varnothing) = \varnothing \neq \hat{\Lambda}(s, n)$. Following Stewart (1974, 1975), we say that $\hat{P}^{-1}$ is a (right) *semiinverse* pattern function for $\hat{P}$ provided that for all $s \in C^*$ and $n \leq \text{len}\ (s)$, $\hat{P}\hat{P}^{-1}(s, n) = \{n\} = \hat{\Lambda}(s, n)$ if $\hat{P}(s, n) \neq \varnothing$. For a number of patterns a (right) semiinverse exists but is not unique. For instance, $\hat{a}^{-1}$ must have the property that $\hat{a}^{-1}(s, n) = \{n - 1\}$ if $s(n) = a$ and otherwise may have any value. By this technique, *context-sensitive* (in a very informal sense) definitions can be given. For instance, $\hat{a}\hat{a}^{-1}$ does not behave as $\hat{\Lambda}$ does in element compositions. For instance $\hat{a}\hat{a}^{-1}\hat{a} = \hat{a} = \hat{\Lambda}\hat{a}$, but $\hat{a}\hat{a}^{-1}\hat{b} = \hat{\Phi}$, while, of course, $\hat{\Lambda}\hat{b} = \hat{b}$. As a somewhat different approach we suggest a definition of *quotient* of pattern functions $\hat{P}_1$ and $\hat{P}_2$,

$$(\hat{P}_1/\hat{P}_2)(s, n) = \{k * p \mid \text{there exist } i * m \in \hat{P}_1(s, n) \text{ and } j * m \in \hat{P}_2(s, p) \text{ and } kj = i\}.$$

Then, of course, $\hat{\Lambda}/\hat{P}_1$ serves as the multiplicative inverse. Schematically this quotient can be viewed as

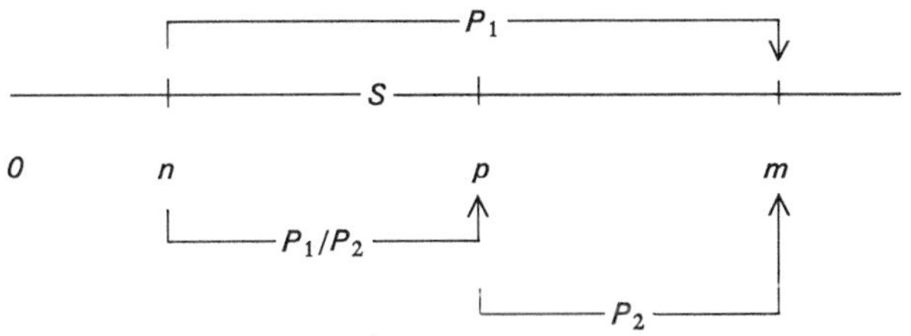

and also as

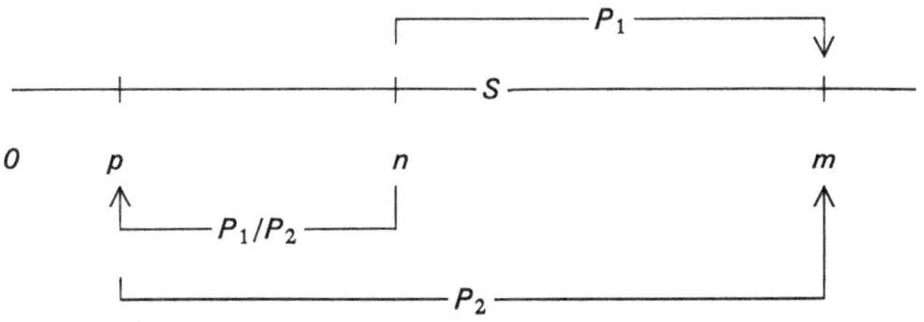

Doyle (1973) has proposed programmer control of *scanner direction* to achieve a similar effect. Using his approach, one could write $\hat{a}$ LEN (-1) in place of $\hat{a}\hat{a}^{-1}$. The algebraic interpretation suggested here may be conceptual improvement, but more investigation and experience are needed with both concepts. The *scanner direction control* seems more natural from the implementation point of view and is in the spirit of automata with two-way input tapes. The algebraic approach seems conceptually clearer, especially when one tries to understand the effect of combining such pattern elements with others.

ACKNOWLEDGMENT

A portion of the author's work reported here was supported by the National Science Foundation, Grant No. DCR75-05296.

CHAPTER 9

NOTES ON RELATIONAL DATA STRUCTURES

SUNG-YANG BANG
Data Systems Department
Michigan Bell Telephone Co.
Southfield, Michigan

RAYMOND T. YEH
Dept. of Computer Science
University of Texas
Austin, Texas

9.1. INTRODUCTION

Models of data structures have been developed based on sets, graphs, binary relations, lists, and labeled graphs [Bang (1975), Childs (1968), Codd (1970), Gray (1967)]. In this study, a model of data structure based on relations is described. It is well known that the concept and the use of relations are very important in pattern descriptions [Fu (1974), Raphael (1968)], the internal representation of sentences in natural languages [Raphael (1968), Simmons and Slocom (1970)], and data management systems [Codd (1970), McGee (1969)]. The advantage of the proposed model is that one can approach various data in a unified way via relations. For example, a table of data can be handled as a relation [Codd (1970)]. This unified approach seems especially attractive when data to be handled are diverse and heterogeneous. We do not, however, intend to become very much involved with many of the more theoretical developments of relational algebra here. Readers are referred to Bang (1974) and Yeh (1968)–(1973).

The structure of this chapter is as follows. In Section 9.2, some preliminary definitions are given. In Section 9.3, we derive some results which describe how a relation can be naturally decomposed into relations of lower rank. In Section 9.4, a method will be given for constructing a relation from a set of relations of lower rank. In Section 9.5, we propose a model for relational data structures based on results of Sections 9.2 and 9.3. The problem of consistency of representational power is discussed in the Appendix.

9.2. PRELIMINARY

In this section, we shall provide some preliminary definitions which are necessary for understanding the subsequent sections.

Definition 1. An *n-ary relation* α on a sequence of sets $S_1, \ldots, S_n$ is simply a subset of the Cartesian product $X_{i=1}^n S_i$. If each S_i is identical to S, then we simply say α is an n-ary relation on S. The number n is referred to as the *rank* of S.

Usually, we shall use lowercase Greek letters to denote relations. It is well known that binary relations can be represented by directed graphs. It is also possible to provide a graph-like representation of higher rank relations. More specifically, let α be an n-ary relation; then each element $(a_1^i, a_2^i, \ldots, a_n^i)$ of α can be represented graphically by drawing an arc from a_j^i to a_{j+1}^i for $1 \leq j < n$. However, distinct elements of α must be represented by distinct types of arcs, as illustrated in the following example.

Example 1

Let $S_1 = \{1, 2, 3\}$, $S_2 = \{a, b\}$, and $S_3 = \{1, 2\}$, and let $\alpha = \{(1, a, 2), (1, a, 1), (2, b, 1), (3, a, 1)\}$; then the graph-like representation of α is given in Figure 9.1.

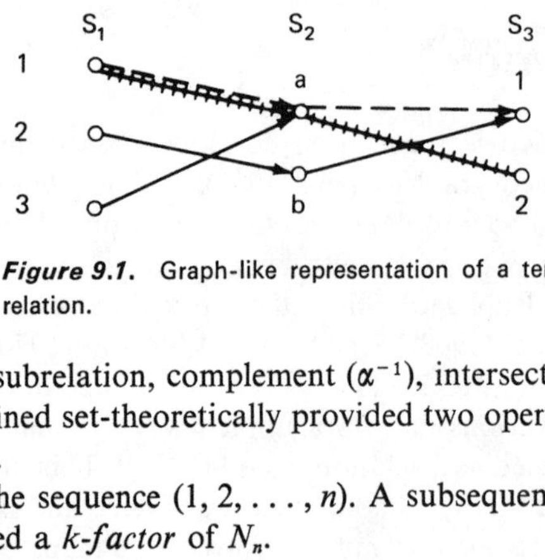

Figure 9.1. Graph-like representation of a tenary relation.

The concept of subrelation, complement (α^{-1}), intersection ($\cap$), and union ($\cup$) of relations α are defined set-theoretically provided two operand relations are defined on the same domain.

Let N_n denote the sequence $(1, 2, \ldots, n)$. A subsequence of N_n consisting of k elements will be called a *k-factor* of N_n.

Definition 2. Let α be an n-ary relation on $(S_1, \ldots, S_n)$, and let $L = (i_1, \ldots, i_k)$ be a k-factor of N_n. Then the *partial relation of α induced by L*, denoted of α_L, is the relation obtained by restricting α to the domain $(S_{i_1}, \ldots, s_{i_k})$. α_L is also referred to as a k-factor of α.

The *L-projection* of α, denoted by $P_L(\alpha)$, is the relation

$$\{(a_{i_1}, \ldots, a_{i_k}) \mid (\exists a_1, \ldots, a_{i_1-1}, a_{i_1+1}, \ldots, a_{i_k+1}, \ldots, a_n) \cdot (a_1, \ldots, a_n) \in \alpha]\}.$$

It is easily seen that given L, we have $\alpha_L = P_L(\alpha)$.

Example 2

Let $\alpha \subset S^4$ and $\alpha = \{(1, 4, 2, 3), (2, 3, 4, 3), (4, 2, 1, 3), (4, 3, 2, 1)\}$, where $S = \{1, 2, 3, 4\}$; then its 2-factors are

$$\alpha_{12} = \begin{Bmatrix} (1, 4) \\ (2, 3) \\ (4, 2) \\ (4, 3) \end{Bmatrix}, \quad \alpha_{13} = \begin{Bmatrix} (1, 2) \\ (2, 4) \\ (4, 1) \\ (4, 2) \end{Bmatrix}, \quad \alpha_{14} = \begin{Bmatrix} (1, 3) \\ (2, 3) \\ (4, 1) \\ (4, 3) \end{Bmatrix},$$

$$\alpha_{23} = \begin{Bmatrix} (2, 1) \\ (3, 2) \\ (4, 2) \\ (3, 4) \end{Bmatrix}, \quad \alpha_{24} = \begin{Bmatrix} (2, 3) \\ (3, 1) \\ (3, 3) \\ (4, 3) \end{Bmatrix}, \quad \alpha_{34} = \begin{Bmatrix} (1, 3) \\ (2, 3) \\ (2, 1) \\ (4, 3) \end{Bmatrix}.$$

Its 3-factors are

$$\alpha_{123} = \begin{Bmatrix} (1, 4, 2) \\ (2, 3, 4) \\ (4, 2, 1) \\ (4, 3, 2) \end{Bmatrix}, \quad \alpha_{124} = \begin{Bmatrix} (1, 4, 3) \\ (2, 3, 3) \\ (4, 2, 3) \\ (4, 3, 1) \end{Bmatrix},$$

$$\alpha_{134} = \begin{Bmatrix} (1, 2, 3) \\ (2, 4, 3) \\ (4, 1, 3) \\ (4, 2, 1) \end{Bmatrix}, \quad \alpha_{234} = \begin{Bmatrix} (2, 1, 3) \\ (3, 2, 1) \\ (3, 4, 3) \\ (4, 2, 3) \end{Bmatrix}.$$

Definition 3. The *natural join* of two partial relations α_{L_1} and α_{L_2}, denoted by $\alpha_{L_1} * \alpha_{L_2}$, of an n-ary relation α on S is an n-ary relation such that

$$\alpha_{L_1} * \alpha_{L_2} = \{A \in S^n \mid P_{L_1}(A) \in \alpha_{L_1} \text{ and } P_{L_2}(A) \in \alpha_{L_2}\}.$$

Example 3

Consider a file α defined by the following table, where A, B, C, D, and E are attributes of the records:

$$\alpha = \begin{Bmatrix} & A & B & C & D & E & \\ (& 1, & 1, & 1, & 1, & 1 &) \\ (& 1, & 2, & 2, & 1, & 2 &) \\ (& 1, & 2, & 2, & 2, & 2 &) \\ (& 2, & 1, & 2, & 1, & 1 &) \end{Bmatrix}.$$

Let $L_1 = (A, B, C)$ and $L_2 = (B, C, D, E)$. Then

$$\alpha_{L_1} = \{(1, 1, 1), (1, 2, 2), (2, 1, 2)\}$$

and

$$\alpha_{L_2} = \{(1, 1, 1, 1), (2, 2, 1, 2), (2, 2, 2, 2), (1, 2, 1, 1)\}.$$

Then $\alpha_{L_1} * \alpha_{L_2} = \alpha$.

Note that in the above example it is natural to say that the file α is "decomposable" into α_{L_1} and α_{L_2}. This notion is used by Codd (1970).

A generalization of the notion of natural join will now be given.

Definition 4. The *k-ary closure* of a relation $\alpha \subseteq S^n$, denoted by α_k^*, is a n-ary relation consisting of elements A in S^n such that for each k-factor L of N_n, $P_L(A) \in \alpha_L$.

Note that α_k^* as defined above is unique.

Example 4

Let α be the relation given in Example 2. Then

$$\alpha_2^* = \{(1, 4, 2, 3), (2, 3, 4, 3), (4, 2, 1, 3), (4, 3, 2, 1), (4, 3, 2, 3), (4, 2, 1, 1), (4, 3, 1, 1), (4, 3, 2, 3)\}$$

$$\alpha_3^* = \{(1, 4, 2, 3), (2, 3, 4, 3), (4, 2, 1, 3), (4, 3, 2, 1)\} = \alpha.$$

Theorem 1

If α is an n-ary relation on S, then

$$\alpha \subseteq \alpha_{n-1}^* \subseteq \alpha_{n-2}^* \subseteq \cdots \subseteq \alpha_1^* \subseteq S^n.$$

9.3. DECOMPOSITION OF RELATIONS

A method for decomposing a relation into nondecomposable lower rank relations will be given in this section.

Definition 5. An n-ary relation α is said to be *k-decomposable* (for $k < n$) if $\alpha < \alpha_k^*$.

We observe that the relation α in Example 4 is 3-decomposable but not 2-decomposable.

We shall give here two results which are corollaries of Theorem 1 in the previous section.

Corollary 1

If α is not k-decomposable, then it is not j-decomposable for $j < k$.

Corollary 2

A relation α is k-decomposable if $\alpha_k^* \subseteq \alpha$.

We shall now develop a few side lemmas which will be utilized for developing a method to decompose a relation into n-ary relations which are not k-decomposable for any $k < n$.

Definition 6. Let α be an n-ary relation on S, A an element of α, and L an m-factor of N_n. Then the partial relation $\{A\}_L$ is said to be *k-covered* by a set of elements $\{A_i\}_{i \in I}$, $A_i \in S^n$, for $k \leq m \leq n$, if for each k-factor L' of L there exists an A_i such that $P_{L'}(A) \in P_{L'}(A_i)$.

When $k = m$, we shall simply say $\{A\}_L$ is *covered.*

Example 5

Let $A = (1, 2, 1, 2)$ be an element of a relation α. Let

$$\beta = \{(1, 1, 1, 1), (1, 1, 2, 1), (2, 2, 1, 1), (2, 2, 1, 2), (2, 2, 2, 2)\}$$
$$\gamma = \{(1, 1, 1, 2), (1, 2, 1, 1)\}$$

and

$$\delta = \{(1, 2, 1, 1), (1, 1, 2, 2), (2, 1, 1, 2)\}.$$

Then $P_{134}(A) = (1, 1, 2)$ is 2-covered by r as well as by δ. However, $P_{134}(A)$ is not 2-covered by β.

Lemma 1

If $A \in (\alpha_k^* - \alpha)$ and A is k-covered by $\{A_i\} \subseteq \alpha$, then $|\{A_i\}| \geq k + 1$.

Proof: Since $A \in (\alpha_k^* - \alpha)$, $A \neq A_i$ for $A_i \in \alpha$. Obviously $A \neq A_i$ if there exists a j such that $a_j \neq a_j^i$, where $A = (a_1, a_2, \ldots, a_n)$ and $A_i = (a_1^i, a_2^i, \ldots, a_n^i)$. Therefore, there must exist at least one $a_{j(i)}$ which does not appear in A_i for each A_i. Let us consider the best case, that is, each A_i is different from A just at one domain $j(i)$. Suppose, without loss of generality, that A and A_1 differ only at domain 1; i.e., $a_1 \neq a_1^1$ and $a_j = a_j^1$ for $j \neq 1$. Then the number of k-ary components of A which are not covered by A_i is $\binom{n-1}{k-1}$. Therefore, these $\binom{n-1}{k-1}$ k-ary components whose first element is a_1 have to be convered by other A_i's. Let A_2 be a member with $a_1^2 = a_1$. Such A_2 always exists since at least (a_1, a_2) has to be convered by some A_i. Since $A_2 \neq A$, let $a_2^2 \neq a_2$ and $a_j^2 = a_j$ for $j \neq 2$, again without loss of generality. The number of k-ary components of A which have not been covered by A_2 among $\binom{n-1}{k-1}$ k-ary components above is $\binom{n-2}{k-2}$. Repeating this process, we eventually come to the point where the number of k-ary components which are not covered by A_k either is $\binom{n-k}{0}$. Therefore, we need one more member A_{k+1} to completely cover A. Since $A_1, A_2, \ldots, A_{k+1}$ obtained above is a best possible case, $|\{A_i\}| \geq k + 1$ in general.

Note that the best case described above can be chosen as follows: Let $A \in (\alpha_k^* - \alpha)$ and $A = (a_1, a_2, \ldots, a_n)$; then

$$\{A_i\} = \{(a_1, a_2, \ldots, a_{i-1}, b_i, a_{i+1}, \ldots, a_n), i = 1, 2, \ldots, k + 1\}.$$

Here b_i can be any member of S such that $b_i \neq a_i$.

We shall now illustrate the above process by the following example:

Example 6

Let $\alpha \subset S^6$ and $A = (1, 1, 1, 1, 1, 1) \in (\alpha_2^* - \alpha)$; then A is 2-covered by $\{A_i\} = \{A_1 = (2, 1, 1, 1, 1, 1), A_2 = (1, 2, 1, 1, 1, 1), A_3 = (1, 1, 2, 1, 1)\}$.

The following is an immediate consequence of Lemma 1 on the minimum number of members necessary for a relation to be not k-ary decomposable.

Corollary 3

If $\alpha \subsetneq \alpha_k^*$, then $|\alpha| > k$.

Definition 7. Let α be an n-ary relation on S and α_L a partial relation of α. We say there is a *functional dependence* from α_L to α, denoted by $\alpha_L \longrightarrow \alpha$, if for A, A' in α, $A \neq A'$ implies that $P_L(A) \neq P_L(A')$. If there is no such functional dependence, then we shall denote it by $\alpha_L \not\rightarrow \alpha$.

Theorem 2

Let α be an n-ary relation on S. If $\alpha_{n-1}^* - \alpha \neq \varnothing$, then for each $(n-1)$-factor L of N_n, $\alpha_{L'} \not\rightarrow \alpha_L$ for any $(n-2)$-factor L' of L.

Proof: Let $A \in \alpha_{n-1}^* - \alpha$. Then by Lemma 1, A is covered by n relations $\{\alpha_1, \ldots, \alpha_n\}$. Without loss of generality, we may assume that there exists $A_i \in \alpha_i$ such that A_i differs from A only in the ith component. Hence $\alpha_{(1,2,\ldots,n-2)} \not\rightarrow \alpha_{(1,2,\ldots,n-1)}$. Similarly, it can be shown that $\alpha_{L'} \not\rightarrow \alpha_{(1,2,\ldots,n-1)}$ for any $(n-2)$-factor L' of $(1, 2, \ldots, n-1)$. By the same arguments, it is easily shown that $\alpha_{L'} \not\rightarrow \alpha_L$ for any $(n-1)$-factor L.

Corollary 4

Let α be an n-ary relation on S. If there exists an $(n-1)$-factor α_L of α and an $(n-2)$-factor $\alpha_{L'}$ of α such that $\alpha_{L'} \longrightarrow \alpha_L$, then α is $(n-1)$-ary decomposable.

Proof: Let L and L' be the $(n-1)$-factor and $(n-2)$-factor of N_n, respectively. Pick an $(n-1)$-factor M of N_n such that $L \cap M = L'$. Then since $\alpha_{L'} \longrightarrow \alpha_L$ by assumption, we have $\alpha_L * \alpha_M = \alpha$. Furthermore, $\alpha_L * \alpha_M \supseteq \alpha_{n-1}^*$. Hence, we must conclude that $\alpha = \alpha_{n-1}^*$ by Theorem 3.

We shall now apply Corollary 4 to determine whether a specific relation is decomposable.

Definition 8. A triangle relation α is a tenary relation satisfying the following properties:

(i) $(a, b, c) \in \alpha \longrightarrow a, b$, and c are all distinct.

(ii) $(a, b, c) \in \alpha \longrightarrow$ all its permutations are in α.

(iii) $(a, b, x), (a, y, c), (z, b, c) \in \alpha \longrightarrow (a, b, c) \in \alpha$.

Theorem 3

A triangle relation is 2-decomposable.

Proof: Suppose that there exists $A = (a, b, c) \in \alpha_2^* - \alpha$. Then there exist A_1, A_2, A_3 in α such that

$$A_1 = (a, b, x) \quad \text{and} \quad x \neq c$$
$$A_2 = (a, y, c) \quad \text{and} \quad y \neq b$$
$$A_3 = (z, b, c) \quad \text{and} \quad z \neq a.$$

Since α is a triangle relation, by property (iii), $(a, b, c) \in \alpha$.
Hence, $A \in \alpha$, a contradiction. Therefore, we must conclude that $\alpha = \alpha_2^*$.

In the following, we shall illustrate a method for systematically decomposing a given relation into primitive nondecomposable lower rank relations.

Definition 9. A partial relation α_L of rank m of a relation is called an *elementary relation* of α if α_L is not k-ary decomposable for any $k < m$. The set of all elementary relations of α, denoted by α^*, is called the *maximal decomposition* of α.

Example 7

Let $\alpha \subset S^4$ be defined by

$$\alpha = \begin{Bmatrix} (1, 1, 1, 1) \\ (1, 2, 2, 2) \\ (2, 2, 1, 3) \\ (3, 1, 3, 3) \end{Bmatrix},$$

Then the maximal decomposition of α is $\{\alpha_{123}, \alpha_{12}, \alpha_{24}, \alpha_{14}, \alpha_{13}, \alpha_{34}, \alpha_{234}\}$, as illustrated in Figure 9.2, where each terminal node represents an elementary relation of α.

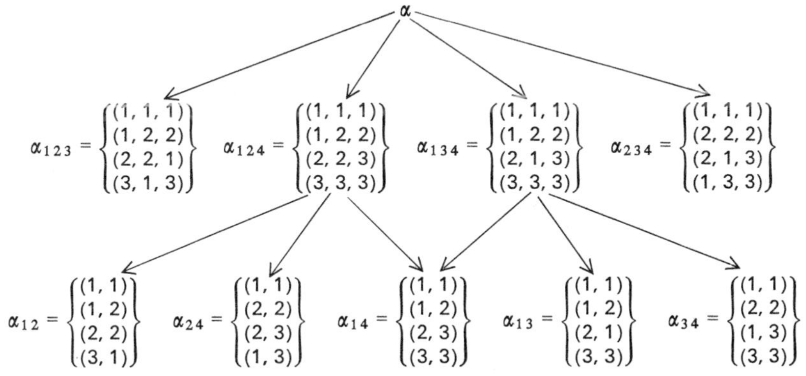

Figure 9.2. Maximal decomposition of α.

Note that if we performed the maximal decompositions to a set of relations, instead of one, on S, then it is quite possible that some of the elementary relations are identical. In other words, it will be necessary to keep only the irredundant set of elementary relations to reproduce the entire set of relations. This idea is equivalent to what underlines the irredundancy of a relational data base system by Codd (1970).

Algorithm (for maximal decomposition)

We can obtain the maximal decomposition α^* of a given relation $\alpha \subseteq S^n$ by a recursive procedure as follows:

(1) Set $R = \alpha$ and $K = n$.

(2) If $K = 1$, stop. Otherwise, if $R^*_{K-1} = R$, obtain $P_L(R)$ for all $(K - 1)$-factor L; otherwise, stop.

(3) Apply (2) to each partial relation obtained above after setting $R = P_L(R)$ and $K = K - 1$.

The previous algorithm is now applied to a specific relation in the following example:

Example 8

Let α be the relation given below:

$$\alpha = \begin{Bmatrix} (1\ 1\ 1\ 2) \\ (1\ 2\ 1\ 2) \\ (1\ 2\ 2\ 2) \\ (2\ 1\ 1\ 1) \\ (2\ 1\ 2\ 2) \\ (2\ 2\ 1\ 1) \end{Bmatrix}.$$

Since $\alpha_3^* = \alpha$, we obtain the following four partial relations:

$$\alpha_{123} = \begin{Bmatrix} (1\ 1\ 1) \\ (1\ 2\ 1) \\ (1\ 2\ 2) \\ (2\ 1\ 1) \\ (2\ 1\ 2) \\ (2\ 2\ 1) \end{Bmatrix}, \quad \alpha_{124} = \begin{Bmatrix} (1\ 1\ 2) \\ (1\ 2\ 2) \\ (2\ 1\ 1) \\ (2\ 1\ 2) \\ (2\ 2\ 1) \end{Bmatrix}, \quad \alpha_{134} = \begin{Bmatrix} (1\ 1\ 2) \\ (1\ 2\ 2) \\ (2\ 1\ 1) \\ (2\ 2\ 2) \end{Bmatrix}, \quad \alpha_{234} = \begin{Bmatrix} (1\ 1\ 1) \\ (1\ 1\ 2) \\ (1\ 2\ 2) \\ (2\ 1\ 1) \\ (2\ 1\ 2) \\ (2\ 2\ 2) \end{Bmatrix}.$$

Although $\alpha_{123} \neq (\alpha_{123})_2^*$, $\alpha_{124} \neq (\alpha_{124})_2^*$, and $\alpha_{134} \neq (\alpha_{134})_2^*$, $\alpha_{234} = (\alpha_{234})_2^*$. Therefore, we have the following three binary partial relations by decomposing α_{234}:

$$(\alpha_{234})_{12} = \begin{Bmatrix} (11) \\ (12) \\ (21) \\ (22) \end{Bmatrix} = (\alpha_{234})_{13} \quad \text{and} \quad (\alpha_{234})_{23} = \begin{Bmatrix} (11) \\ (12) \\ (22) \end{Bmatrix}.$$

Obviously α_{23} and α_{24} are decomposable, and hence we have the following unary relations:

$$((\alpha_{234})_{12})_1 = ((\alpha_{234})_{12})_2 = ((\alpha_{234})_{13})_1 = ((\alpha_{234})_{13})_2 = \begin{Bmatrix}(1)\\(2)\end{Bmatrix}.$$

Hence, α is decomposed into the set of elementary relations

$$\{\alpha_{123}, \alpha_{124}, \alpha_{134}, ((\alpha_{234})_{12})_1, (\alpha_{234})_{23}\}.$$

9.4. SYNTHESIS OF RELATIONS

In this section we shall discuss briefly a method of constructing relations from a set of relations of lower ranks. The method can be considered to be the converse of the concept of decomposition discussed in the last section.

Definition 10. Let $\alpha = \{(a_i, \ldots, a_n)\}$ be an n-ary relation and π be a permutation of N_n. Then the relation

$$\pi(\alpha) = \{(a_{\pi(1)}, \ldots, a_{\pi(n)}) \mid (a_1, \ldots, a_n) \in \pi\}$$

is called a *permutation of* α (induced by π).

If $\beta = \pi(\alpha)$ for some permutation π, then we say α and β are *permutation-equivalent*, denoted by $\alpha \simeq \beta$.

We say a relation β is *derivable* from a relation α if β is permutation-equivalent to some partial relation of α.

Example 9

Consider three relations:

$$\alpha = \begin{Bmatrix}(1, 1, 3)\\(1, 3, 1)\\(2, 1, 1)\\(2, 1, 2)\\(2, 1, 3)\end{Bmatrix}, \quad \rho = \begin{Bmatrix}(1, 1, 2)\\(1, 2, 2)\\(1, 3, 1)\\(1, 3, 2)\\(3, 1, 1)\end{Bmatrix}, \quad \gamma = \begin{Bmatrix}(1, 1)\\(1, 2)\\(3, 1)\end{Bmatrix}.$$

We see that $\beta = \pi_1(\alpha)$ for $\pi_1 = (2, 3, 1)$. Hence $\alpha \simeq \beta$. On the other hand, $\gamma = \pi_2(\alpha_{12})$ for $\pi_2 = (2, 1)$. Therefore γ is derivable from α.

Definition 11. Let Ω be a set of relations (not necessarily of the same rank) on S, and let Σ be the set of all k-factors of N_n, $1 \leq k \leq n$. Let m be an integer such that $m \geq \max_{\alpha \in \Omega}$ rank (α). We define

$$\hat{\Omega}_m = \{\pi(\alpha) \mid \alpha \in \Omega \text{ and } \pi \text{ is a permutation on } N_{\text{rank}(\alpha)}\} \cup \{S, S^2, \ldots, S^m\}.$$

If ϕ is a mapping from Σ to $\hat{\Omega}_m$ such that for each k-factor $L \in \Sigma$, $\phi(L)$ is a relation of rank k in $\hat{\Omega}$, then the *m-synthesis of* Ω *by* ϕ, denoted by $\phi(\Omega)$, is an m-ary relation on S such that

$$\phi(\Omega) = \{A \in S^m \mid (\forall L \in \Sigma) [P_L(A) \in \phi(L)]\}.$$

Example 10

Let $\Omega = \{\alpha, \beta\}$, where $\alpha = \{(1)\}$ and $\beta = \{(1, 1), (1, 2)\}$ on $S = \{1, 2\}$; then $\hat{\Omega}_3 = \{\alpha, \beta, \beta^{-1}\} \cup \{S, S^2, S^3\}$ and $\Sigma = \{(1), (2), (3), (1, 2), (1, 3), (2, 3), (1, 2, 3)\}$. Let the mapping ϕ be defined by

$$\begin{aligned}\phi\colon\quad (1, 2, 3) &\longrightarrow S^3\\ (1, 2) &\longrightarrow \beta\\ (1, 3) &\longrightarrow S^2\\ (2, 3) &\longrightarrow \beta^{-1}\\ (1) &\longrightarrow \alpha\\ (2) &\longrightarrow S\\ (3) &\longrightarrow S.\end{aligned}$$

Then the 3-synthesis of Ω by ϕ is

$$\begin{aligned}\phi(\Omega) &= \{(a, b, c) \mid (a, b, c) \in S^3 \text{ and } (a, b) \in \beta \text{ and } (a, c) \in S^2\\ &\qquad \text{and } (b, c) \in \beta^{-1} \text{ and } a \in \alpha \text{ and } b \in S \text{ and } c \in S\}\\ &= \{(a, b, c) \mid (a, b) \in \beta \text{ and } (b, c) \in \beta^{-1} \text{ and } a \in \alpha\}\\ &= \{(1, 1, 1), (1, 2, 1)\}.\end{aligned}$$

Definition 12. In a synthesis $\phi(\Omega)$, a factor $L \in \Sigma$ is called *essential* if there exists $\alpha \in \Omega$ such that $\phi(L) \simeq \alpha$. Similarly, a relation $\beta \in \Omega$ is called *essential* if there exists $L' \in \Sigma$ such that $\beta \simeq \phi(L')$.

It follows from the definition that essential factors or relations are those which make a definite contribution to the specification of the relation being synthesized. Thus, factors (1, 2), (2, 3), and (1) are essential in Example 10. Since a decomposition is the representation of a relation by a set of lower rank relations, there always exists a synthesis which yields the original relation from the set of relations. Is the converse also true? In other words, suppose that $\alpha = \phi(\Omega)$; then does the decomposition of α give exactly the same set of relations as Ω? The answer is clearly negative since if a relation of Ω is not essential in ϕ, then it cannot be expected to be derivable from α.

Definition 13. A synthesis $\phi(\Omega)$ is said to be *full* if each relation of Ω is essential.

Therefore a full synthesis $\phi(\Omega)$ is one in which every relation of the given set of relations participates in constructing the relation $\phi(\Omega)$. Note that the synthesis in Example 10 is full.

Since in an arbitrary set of relations some relation may be permutation-equivalent to another and some may be derivable from another, the following definition of a normal form will be useful. Let E be the set of all elementary relations of relations in a given set of relations, Ω; then we can partition E by the equivalence relation induced by the relation $\simeq$. Let us denote the set of the equivalence classes by $[E]$ and each class of $[E]$ by $[\beta]$, where β is a representative of the class $[\beta]$.

Definition 14. The *skeleton* of a set of relations Ω, denoted by Ω^*, is the collection of class representatives of the relation $\simeq$; i.e., $\Omega^* = \{\beta | [\beta] \in [E]\}$. If $\Omega = \Omega^*$, we say that Ω is in a *skeleton form.*

Now let us assume further that $\alpha = \phi(\Omega)$ is full and in a skeleton form. But still in general not all relations in Ω can be obtained by decomposing α. Therefore we need to distinguish the following special syntheses from others:

Definition 15. A synthesis $\phi(\Omega)$ is *loss-free* (*lossless*) if $P_L(\phi(\Omega)) \simeq \phi(L)$ for each essential factor L.

Example 11

Let $\Omega = \{\alpha, \beta, \gamma\}$, where α, β, γ are specified as

$$\alpha = \begin{Bmatrix}(1, 1, 2)\\(2, 1, 2)\\(2, 2, 1)\end{Bmatrix}, \qquad \beta = \begin{Bmatrix}(2, 1)\\(2, 2)\end{Bmatrix}, \qquad \gamma = \{(2, 2)\}.$$

Let a 4-synthesis be defined by ϕ as follows:

$$\begin{aligned}\phi\colon\quad (1, 2, 3) &\longrightarrow \alpha\\ (3, 4) &\longrightarrow \beta\\ (1, 4) &\longrightarrow \gamma.\end{aligned}$$

All other factors are nonessential. Then $\phi(\Omega) = \{2, 1, 2, 2)\}$. Therefore $\phi(\Omega)$ is not lossless since α and β are not derivable from $\phi(\Omega)$ and only $\gamma = \phi(\Omega)_{1,4}$.

Next, let a 5-synthesis be defined by ϕ' as follows:

$$\begin{aligned}\phi'\colon\quad (1, 2) &\longrightarrow \gamma\\ (2, 3) &\longrightarrow \beta\\ (3, 4, 5) &\longrightarrow \alpha.\end{aligned}$$

All other factors are nonessential. Then

$$\phi'(\Omega) = \begin{Bmatrix}(2, 2, 1, 1, 2)\\(2, 2, 2, 1, 2)\\(2, 2, 2, 2, 1)\end{Bmatrix}.$$

Since $\alpha = \phi'(\Omega)_{3,4,5}$, $\beta = \phi'(\Omega)_{2,3}$, and $\gamma = \phi'(\Omega)_{1,2}$, $\phi'(\Omega)$ is lossless.

The following result is a straightforward consequence of the previous definitions:

Theorem 4

Let α be an n-ary relation, and let Ω be the maximal decomposition of α. If ϕ is a mapping of factors of N_n to Ω such that $\phi(L) = P_L(\alpha)$ for each elementary relation $P_L(\alpha)$ of α, then $\phi(\Omega)$ is a full and lossless n-synthesis. Furthermore, $\phi(\Omega) = \alpha$.

The last sentence says that the original relation can be obtained through a synthesis. This is true because the condition that Ω is the maximal decomposition guarantees that no additional elements will be generated by the synthesis. And none of the nonessential factors affect the reconstruction of the original relation.

Before we consider the converse problem, let us see what we have done. We started with a relation and obtained the maximal decomposition. Then we obtained the original relation through a synthesis with the set of relations derived by the maximal decomposition, i.e., $\alpha = \phi(\alpha^*)$. The characterization of such synthesis was the main concern of Theorem 4. In the converse, we start with an arbitrary set of elementary relations and we want to regain the original set of relations by the maximal decomposition of a synthesis over the given set of relations, i.e., $\Omega = \phi(\Omega)^*$. Again, the characterization of such syntheses is our concern. Obviously fullness and losslessness are necessary. But are they enough to guarantee that the synthesis is decomposable and that, if so, $\phi(\Omega)^* = \Omega$? Let us look at an example.

Let $\Omega = \{\beta, \gamma\}$, and let a lossless and full synthesis $\phi(\Omega) = \alpha$ be defined by the essentials $\phi(1, 2, 3) = \beta$ and $\phi(3, 4) = \gamma$. That is, $\alpha = \beta * \gamma$. This is equivalent to saying that $\alpha = \alpha_{123} * \alpha_{34}$ because ϕ is lossless. On the other hand,

$$\begin{aligned}\alpha \subseteq \alpha_3^* &= \alpha_{123} * \alpha_{124} * \alpha_{134} * \alpha_{234} \\ &\subseteq \alpha_{123} * \alpha_{124} * (\alpha_{13} * \alpha_{14} * \alpha_{34}) * \alpha_{234} \\ &= \alpha_{123} * \alpha_{34} * (\alpha_{124} * \alpha_{13} * \alpha_{14} * \alpha_{234}) \\ &\subseteq \alpha_{123} * \alpha_{34}.\end{aligned}$$

Therefore $\alpha = \alpha_3^*$. Also we know that at least one of α_{134} and α_{234} is 2-decomposable so that α_{34} is obtained.

Lemma 2

Let Ω be a set of elementary relations and $\phi(\Omega)$ be a full and lossless synthesis; then $\phi(\Omega)^* \supseteq \Omega$.

Example 12

Applying the following real relations to the above example, we shall verify the above lemma. Let $\Omega = \{\beta, \gamma\}$, where

$$\beta = \begin{Bmatrix}(112)\\(211)\\(212)\end{Bmatrix} \quad \text{and} \quad \gamma = \begin{Bmatrix}(11)\\(12)\\(21)\end{Bmatrix}.$$

Note that β and γ are both elementary. The synthesis is specified by the following two essentials:

$$\phi(1, 2, 3) = \beta$$
$$\phi(3, 4) = \gamma,$$

and we have

$$\alpha = \phi(\Omega) = \begin{Bmatrix} (1121) \\ (2111) \\ (2112) \\ (2121) \end{Bmatrix}.$$

Note that since $\alpha_{123} = \beta$ and $\alpha_{34} = \gamma$, ϕ is full and lossless.

Now we shall obtain the maximal decomposition of α. First, α is 3-decomposable since $\alpha = \alpha_3^*$, and

$$\alpha_{123} = \begin{Bmatrix} (112) \\ (211) \\ (212) \end{Bmatrix}, \quad \alpha_{124} = \begin{Bmatrix} (111) \\ (211) \\ (212) \end{Bmatrix}, \quad \alpha_{134} = \begin{Bmatrix} (121) \\ (211) \\ (212) \\ (221) \end{Bmatrix}, \quad \alpha_{234} = \begin{Bmatrix} (111) \\ (112) \\ (121) \end{Bmatrix}.$$

Among these, all except α_{123} are 2-decomposable, and we have the following partial relations:

$$\alpha_{12} = \begin{Bmatrix} (11) \\ (21) \end{Bmatrix}, \quad \alpha_{13} = \begin{Bmatrix} (12) \\ (21) \\ (22) \end{Bmatrix}, \quad \alpha_{14} = \begin{Bmatrix} (11) \\ (21) \\ (22) \end{Bmatrix},$$

$$\alpha_{23} = \begin{Bmatrix} (11) \\ (12) \end{Bmatrix}, \quad \alpha_{24} = \begin{Bmatrix} (11) \\ (12) \end{Bmatrix}, \quad \alpha_{34} = \begin{Bmatrix} (11) \\ (12) \\ (21) \end{Bmatrix}.$$

Immediately we see that α_{12}, α_{23}, and α_{24} are 1-decomposable and that

$$\alpha_1 = \alpha_3 = \alpha_4 = \begin{Bmatrix} (1) \\ (2) \end{Bmatrix}$$

$$\alpha_2 = \{(1)\}.$$

Consequently, we have the maximal decomposition of α as follows:

$$\begin{aligned} \alpha &= \alpha_{123} * \alpha_{124} * \alpha_{134} * \alpha_{234} \\ &= \alpha_{123} * (\alpha_{12} * \alpha_{14} * \alpha_{24}) * (\alpha_{13} * \alpha_{14} * \alpha_{34}) * (\alpha_{23} * \alpha_{24} * \alpha_{34}) \\ &= \alpha_{123} * ((\alpha_1 * \alpha_2) * \alpha_{14} * (\alpha_2 * \alpha_4)) * (\alpha_{13} * \alpha_{14} * \alpha_{34}) \\ &\qquad * ((\alpha_2 * \alpha_3) * (\alpha_2 * \alpha_4) * \alpha_{34}). \end{aligned}$$

Therefore $\alpha^* = \{\alpha_{123}, \alpha_1, \alpha_2, \alpha_{13}, \alpha_{14}, \alpha_{34}\}$. This shows that $\phi(\Omega)^* \supset \Omega$.

Now we know from the above example that a certain set of factors should all be essential in the synthesis. Otherwise we may have relations which were not in the original set, as seen in the above example. In other words, we need to specify a special type of syntheses.

Definition 16. A k-factor is said to be *hypoessential* if when $k = 1$ the factor is essential, and when $k > 1$ only one of the following conditions is satisfied:

1. The factor is essential, and none of its subfactors are essential.
2. The factor is nonessential, and its $k(k-1)$-factors are all hypoessential.

Definition 17. An n-synthesis is called *regular* either if there are no essentials or if the n-factor is hypoessential and the essential factors in the synthesis are only those accrued from the hypoessentialness of the n-factor.

Example 13

Let $\Omega = \{\beta, \gamma, \delta, \epsilon\}$, where $\beta, \delta \subset S^3$ and $\gamma, \epsilon \subset S^2$. Let a 4-synthesis be defined by the essentials

$$\phi(1, 2, 3) = \beta$$
$$\phi(1, 3, 4) = \beta^{-1}$$
$$\phi(2, 3, 4) = \delta.$$

Then ϕ is not regular. For, since there is at least one essential, (1, 2, 3, 4) has to be hypoessential. And since (1, 2, 3, 4) itself is not essential, its 3-factors have to all be hypoessential. But the factor (1, 2, 4) is not hypoessential. Therefore ϕ is not regular.

However, if we add the essentials $\phi(1, 2) = \gamma$, $\phi(1, 4) = \phi(2, 4) = \epsilon$ to the above list, ϕ becomes regular since now the factor (1, 2, 4) is hypoessential. For, although (1, 2, 4) itself is not essential, (1, 2) (1, 4), and (2, 4) are essential, i.e., hypoessential, since none of their subfactors are essential, and hence (1, 2, 4) is hypoessential. And, moreover, all essential factors are derived from the fact that (1, 2, 3, 4) is hypoessential.

Finally we shall state the converse of Theorem 4 below:

Theorem 5

Let Ω be a set of elementary relations; then $\Omega = \phi(\Omega)^*$ if ϕ is full, lossless, and regular.

The relationship between decomposition and synthesis is summarized in the following table:

Decomposition	*Synthesis*
1. Relations derivable from α	A relation constructed from a set of relations Ω
2. Method—projection: $P_L(\alpha)$	Method—synthesis: $\phi(\Omega)$
3. Decomposition of α: $\alpha = *_{L_i} P_{L_i}(\alpha)$	Lossless synthesis of Ω: $\phi(L) = P_L(\alpha)$
4. Maximal decomposition: α^*	Lossless, full, and regular synthesis of Ω

9.5. DESCRIPTION OF A RELATIONAL DATA STRUCTURE

It is pointed out in the introduction that there is a need for data structure definitions which are independent of the embedding languages. The relational data structure described in this section utilizes the theoretical development of the previous sections and hence is independent of embedding languages. Furthermore, it may be regarded as an extension of the several existing relational models of data structures, namely Codd's relational model (1970), Childs' set-theoretical model (1968), and LEAP's model based on the use of association.

> **Definition 18.** A *relational data structure* D is a triple (E, R, O), where E is a set of data elements, R is a set of relations on E, and O is a set of operations on R.

We note that every relational data structure D has an underlying relational system (E, R). Since operations on relations such as decomposition and synthesis do generate new relations, the question arises as to whether the resulting system is consistent with the original one in terms of power of representation. This question is partially answered in the Appendix. In the following, we shall describe some operations on relation and use two examples to illustrate the power of the relational data structure proposed.

Since relations are sets, all set operations are intrinsically applicable here if the relations are of the same rank. Other relation operations are also given. For each operation below the abbreviation of the name may be attached.

1. UNION$(R_1, R_2, \ldots, R_k)$; U$(R_1, R_2, \ldots R_k)$:

$$\bigcup_{i=1}^{k} R_i = \{A \mid (\exists\, R_i)[A \in R_i]\}$$

2. INDEXED UNION(I); IU(I):

$$\text{U(RELATION}(I))$$

3. INTERSECTION$(R_1, R_2, \ldots, R_k)$; I$(R_1, R_2, \ldots, R_k)$:

$$\bigcap_{i=1}^{k} R_i = \{A \mid A \in R_i, 1 \leq i \leq k\}$$

4. INDEXED INTERSECTION(I); II(I)

$$\text{I(RELATION}(I))$$

5. SYMMETRIC DIFFERENCE(R_1, R_2); SD(R_1, R_2):

$$R_1 \oplus R_2 = \{A \mid (A \in R_1 \vee A \in R_2) \wedge A \notin (R_1 \cap R_2)\}$$

6. RELATIVE COMPLEMENT(R_1, R_2); RC(R_1, R_2):

$$R_1 - R_2 = \{A \mid A \in R_1 \wedge A \notin R_2)\}$$

7. COMPLEMENT(R); C(R):

$$\bar{R} = \{A \mid A \in S^m \wedge A \notin R\}$$

8. CARTESIAN PRODUCT($S_1, S_2, \ldots, S_k$); CP($S_1, S_2, \ldots, S_k$):

$$S_1 \times S_2 \times \cdots \times S_k = \{(a_1, a_2, \ldots, a_k) \mid a_1 \in S_1 \wedge a_2 \in S_2 \wedge \cdots \wedge a_k \in S_k\}$$

9. INVERSE(R); INV(R):

$$R^{-1} = \{(a_n, a_{n-1}, \ldots, a_1) \mid (a_1, a_2, \ldots, a_n) \in R\}$$

10. CARDINALITY(S); CARD(S):

$|S|$: the number of members in S

11. RANGE(R); RAN(R):

$$P_1(R) \times P_2(R) \times \cdots \times P_n(R)$$

12. PROJECTION(L, R); PRO(L, R):

$P_L(R)$: projection of R by L

13. PERMUTATION(π, R); PERM(π, R):

$\pi(R)$: permutation of R by π

14. RESTRICTION(L, S, R); REST(L, S, R):

$$\{A \mid A \in R \wedge P_L(R) \in S\}$$

15. RANK(R):

$r(R)$: rank of R

16. SYNTHESIS($m, L_1\colon R_1, L_2\colon R_2, \ldots, L_k\colon R_k$); SYN($m, L_1\colon R_1, L_2\colon R_2, \ldots, L_k\colon R_k$):

m-synthesis by ϕ: $\phi(L_i) = R_i, \quad i = 1, 2, \ldots, k$

17. RELATION($E_1, E_2, \ldots, E_k$); $R(E_1, E_2, \ldots, E_k)$:

$\{R_i \mid$ the name of R_i is the same as that of $E_i\}$

18. ELEMENT($R_1, R_2, \ldots, R_k$); $E(R_1, R_2, \ldots, R_k)$:

$\{E_i \mid$ the name of E_i is the same as that of $R_i\}$

Also the following predicates are defined.

19. SUBSET(A, B); SUB(A, B):

T if $A \subset B$, F otherwise

20. EQUAL(A, B); $E(A, B)$:

T if $A = B$, F otherwise

21. EQUIVALENT(A, B); EQUIV(A, B):

T if $|A| = |B|$, F otherwise

22. DISJOINT(A, B); DIS(A, B):

T if $A \cap B = \varnothing$, F otherwise

23. DECOMPOSABLE(L_1, L_2, R); DEC(L_1, L_2, R):

$$T \text{ is } R = P_{L_1}(R) * P_{L_2}(R), \qquad F \text{ otherwise}$$

24. REGULAR DECOMPOSABLE(k, R); RDEC(k, R):

$$T \text{ if } R = (R_k)^*, \qquad F \text{ otherwise}$$

The relational data structure described above is general enough to handle the structures of sets, relations, and tables. Therefore, one of the most significant features of the data structure is that all these structures can be used simultaneously and in a uniform manner. Some potential fields for the application include data management systems, pattern recognition, semantic information processing, graph theory, and network analysis.

It should be noted that the design of an efficient data base is the responsibility of the user. All relations have to be defined in advance if they are referred to without specification. The point is that a user should have choices as to which relations should contain real data and which ones should be described only by other relations in order to optimize the speed and the space.

It should be noted that the above set of operations and predicates can be used to develop query languages based on either an algebra or a calculus [Codd (1971), Date (1975)]. However, in the following we shall use a relational algebra.

Example 14

Let us consider family lineage. Given a population of people, unary relations specify special classes in the population, for example, the sets of males, females, children, boys, girls, those who are older than 40, etc. Then we have various binary relations, e.g., father, mother, brother, sister, son, daughter, aunt, and senior by more than 10 years. Also we have higher rank relations. For example, parent, grandfather-father-son, and three brothers are ternary relations.

In the case of family lineage, most high rank relations are binary decomposable. As a matter of fact, only three binary relations, "husband-wife," "brothers or sisters," and "parent-child" relations, along with appropriate unary relations may be enough to generate any other relations of family lineage. Therefore, to make the example more interesting, we add the following two tables.

Let the data of the following relations actually be given:

Unary relations:

S: a population of people

M: the set of males

F: the set of females

X: any subset of S.

Binary relations:

$$\alpha = \{(x, y) \mid x \text{ is the husband of } y\}$$

$$\beta = \{(x, y) \mid x \text{ is a brother or a sister of } y\}$$

$$\gamma = \{(x, y) \mid x \text{ is a parent of } y\}.$$

Ternary relation:

$$\delta = \{(a, b, c) \mid a \text{ is the household head of } b \text{ and } c \text{ is the age of } b \ \forall\ b \in S\}.$$

4-ary relation:

$$\lambda = \{(a, b, c, d) \mid b \text{ is the blood type, } c \text{ is the hair color, and } d \text{ is the eye color of } a \text{ for all } a \in S\}.$$

Then the following are some examples which show how one may obtain specific relations including sets by using the operations of the relational data structure defined earlier:

1. The set of ages A:

   A = PRO (3, δ)

2. The set of blood types B:

   B = PRO(2, λ)

3. The set of hair colors HC:

   HC = PRO(3, λ)

4. The set of eye colors EC:

   EC = PRO(4, λ)

5. The relation ω "is the wife of":

   ω = INV(α)

6. The relation μ "is the mother of":

   μ = REST(1, F, γ)

7. The relation $\gamma\mu$ "is the grandmother of":

   $\gamma\mu$ = PRO((1, 3), SYN(3, (1, 2) : μ, (2, 3) : γ))

8. The set of fathers FA of the people in X:

   FA = I(M, PRO(1, REST(2, X, γ)))

9. The number p of mother-child pairs whose blood types are the same:

   p = CARD(SYN(3, (1, 20 : μ, (1, 3) : PRO((1, 2), λ), (2, 3) : PRO((1, 2), λ))))

10. The relation κ "is a cousin of":

    κ = PRO((1, 4), SYN(4, (1, 2) : INV(γ), (2, 3) : β, (3, 4) : γ))

11. The set of people with no brother or sister N:

    N = C(PRO(1, β))

12. The number q of households whose head is not related to any other member by blood or marriage:

$$q = \text{CARD}(\text{PRO}(1, \text{REST}((1, 2), \text{U}(\beta, \gamma, \text{INV}(\gamma), \alpha, \text{INV}(\alpha), \text{PRO}((1, 3), \text{SYN}(3, (1, 2) : \gamma, (2, 3) : \gamma))), \delta)))$$

13. The number r of households whose head is of an age in a subset of A' of A:

$$r = \text{CARD}(\text{PRO}(1, \text{REST}(3, A' \delta)))$$

14. The set of people T whose blood type is $b \in B$, whose hair color is $h \in \text{HC}$, and whose eye color is $e \in \text{EC}$:

$$T = \text{PRO}(1, \text{REST}(2, b, \text{REST}(3, h, \text{REST}(4, e, \lambda))))$$

Example 15

Let $G = (S, \Gamma)$ be a graph; then the sets of various subgraphs can be expressed as high rank relations. And they are binary decomposable. Therefore one needs only the binary *connection* relation Γ.

Unary relation:

S: the set of nodes.

Binary relation:

$$\alpha = \{(a, b) \mid (a, b) \in \Gamma\}.$$

1. The set of complete subgraphs K_4 of order 4:

$$K_4 = \text{SYN}(4, (1, 2) : \alpha, (1, 3) : \alpha, (1, 4) : \alpha, (2, 3) : \alpha, (2, 4) : \alpha, (3, 4) : \alpha)$$

2. The set of simple cycles C_4 of order 4:

$$C_4 = \text{SYN}(4, (1,2) : \alpha, (2, 3) : \alpha, (3, 4) : \alpha, (1, 4) : \alpha, (1, 3) : C(\alpha), (2, 4) : C(\alpha))$$

3. The set of nodes which can/are directly connected from X, R:

$$R = \text{PRO}(2, (\text{REST}(1, X, \alpha)))$$

4. The set of all paths of length 3 from a node x to a node y, P_{xy}:

$$P_{xy} = \text{SYN}(4, (1, 2) : \text{REST}(1, \{x\}, \alpha), (2, 3) : \alpha, (3, 4) : \text{REST}(2, \{y\}, \alpha))$$

9.6. CONCLUDING REMARKS

In previous sections we have investigated high rank relations by means of decomposition and synthesis. Based on the theoretical studies, a relational data structure is proposed, since a relational data structure is one in which everything is represented by relations. This kind of data structure is suitable when the information can be expressed by a set of relations of finite ranks, which is not uncommon when we notice that sets are unary relations and graphs are binary relations and that even tables can be also regarded as higher rank relations. It is emphasized that this data structure is advantageous not for data of one type but for a unified treatment of various types of data. The efficiency problem of the data structure is left to be worked out on the implementation level.

APPENDIX

Every relational data structure $D = (E, R, O)$ as defined in Section 9.5 has an underlying relational system (E, R). Since operations on relations such as decomposition or loss-free synthesis do generate new relations, the question arises as to whether the resulting systems are consistent with the original one insofar as the power of representation is concerned. This question is partially answered here in that we can show that any relational space constructible from a set of relations Γ can also be constructed from the skeleton Γ^* of Γ.

> **Definition 19.** A relation α is *constructible* from a set of relations Ω if there exists a synthesis $\phi(\Omega)$ such that $\alpha = \phi(\Omega)$.

Therefore we easily have the following:

Lemma 3

If α is constructible from Ω and β is constructible from $\{\alpha\} \cup \Omega'$, then β is constructible from $\Omega \cup \Omega'$.

> **Definition 20.** The *m-constructible space*, denoted by $\Gamma^m(\Omega)$, is the set of all m-ary relations which are constructible from Ω by m-syntheses, i.e., $\Gamma^m(\Omega) = \{\alpha \mid \alpha = \phi(\Omega) \text{ is an } m\text{-synthesis}\}$.

Other simple facts about m-constructible spaces are the following: In general $\Omega \not\subset \Gamma^m(\Omega)$ and $\Gamma^m(\Gamma^m(\Omega)) = \Gamma^m(\Omega)$ by using Lemma 2.

On the other hand, it was earlier defined that a relation α is derivable from a relation β if α is an equivalent of some projection of β. It will be convenient to have the following operator:

> **Definition 21.** The *derivable space* of a set of relations Ω, denoted by $\Delta(\Omega)$, is the set of all relations which are derivable from Ω. We may write $\Delta(\Omega)$ instead of $\Delta(\{\alpha\})$ if $\Omega = \{\alpha\}$.

The following result is straightforward:

Lemma 4

If α is derivable from β and β is derivable from γ, then α is derivable from γ.

It is easily seen that in general $\Omega \subset \Delta(\Gamma^m(\Omega))$ if Ω contains only relations of ranks m or less than m. Also it is self-evident that $\Omega \subset \Delta(\Gamma^m(\Omega))$ if Ω is a subset of elementary relations of some m-ary relation. In the converse case, again $\Delta(\Delta(\alpha)) = \Delta(\alpha)$, but $\alpha \in \Gamma^m(\Delta(\alpha))$ since all elementary relations of α are in $\Delta(\alpha)$, provided that the rank of α is m. We summarize the above arguments below.

Theorem 6

Let α be an m-ary relation and Ω consist of relations of rank m or less; then the following are true:

(1) $\Omega \not\subset \Gamma^m(\Omega)$,

(2) $\Gamma^m(\Gamma^m(\Omega)) = \Gamma^m(\Omega)$,

(3) $\Omega \subset \Delta(\Gamma^m(\Omega))$,

(4) $\alpha \in \Delta(\alpha)$,

(5) $\Delta(\Delta(\alpha)) = \Delta(\alpha)$,

(6) $\alpha \in \Gamma^m(\Delta(\alpha))$.

Now suppose that a set of relations is given. Then the set of relations which are constructible is infinite because the ranks of the syntheses which are used for constructions are not specified, which leads to the following concept:

Definition 22. The set of all relations that are constructible from a set of relations Ω is termed the *constructible space* of Ω, denoted by $\Gamma(\Omega)$. That is, $\Gamma(\Omega) = \bigcup_{i=0}^{\infty} \Gamma^i(\Omega)$.

Lemma 5

For any set of relations Ω, if a relation is constructible from Ω, then it is also constructible from the skeleton of Ω, Ω^*, i.e., $\Gamma(\Omega) \subseteq \Gamma(\Omega^*)$.

Proof: Let a relation β be constructible from Ω; i.e., $\beta = \phi(\Omega)$, where $\phi: \Sigma \longrightarrow \hat{\Omega}$. We shall show that $\beta = \phi'(\Omega^*)$ by some ϕ' which is obtained by modifying ϕ as follows. Let $\phi(x) = \alpha^i$, $\alpha^i \in \Omega$, and α^i be decomposable; then $(\alpha^i)^* \subset \Omega^*$. For each such x define $\phi'(x) = S^k$, where $|x| = k$ and $\phi'(y) = (\alpha^i)_y$ for each $(k-1)$-factor y of x, where $(\alpha^i)_y$ denotes the $(k-1)$-ary partial relation corresponding to y except for those y's such that $\phi(y) \subset (\alpha^i)_y$, in which case we define $\phi'(y) = \phi(y)$. Then for those y's such that $\phi(y) = (\alpha^i)_y$ is decomposable, we apply the above process. And we repeat this procedure until all lower relations are not decomposable, which corresponds to the maximal decomposition of α^i. Then we claim that the synthesis of Ω^* thus constructed, $\phi'(\Omega^*)$, yields β, for α^i is equivalent to, as a constraint for all $B \in \beta$, $\bigwedge_y \{B_y \in \phi(y)\} \wedge \{B_x \in \alpha^i\} = \bigwedge_{\{y|\phi(y) \subset (\alpha^i)y\}} \{B_y \in \phi(y)\} \wedge \{B_x \in \alpha^i\}$, which is, in turn, the same as $\bigwedge_{\{y|\phi(y)\subset(\alpha^i)y\}} \{B_y \in \phi(y)\} \bigwedge_{\{y|\phi(y)\supset(\alpha^i)y\}} \{B_y \in (\alpha^i)_y\} \wedge \{B_x \in \alpha^i\}$. The same argument is applicable to the factors of ranks lower than k.

So far we have considered relational spaces for each operator separately. Next we shall define relational spaces which are obtained by using both projection and synthesis.

Definition 23. Let Ω be a set of relations; then the *relation space* of Ω, denoted by $\Sigma(\Omega)$, is the set of all relations which can be obtained from Ω by using any number of projections and syntheses.

The following lemma is a straightforward consequence of the definitions:

Lemma 6

If $\Omega \subseteq \Omega'$, then

(1) $\Gamma^m(\Omega) \subseteq \Gamma^m(\Omega')$,

(2) $\Gamma(\Omega) \subseteq \Gamma(\Omega')$,

(3) $\Delta(\Omega) \subseteq \Delta(\Omega')$,

(4) $\Sigma(\Omega) \subseteq \Sigma(\Omega')$.

Let Ω be a set of relations; then any relation of Ω can be constructed from its skeleton Ω^* by the definition. Therefore $\Omega \subset \Gamma(\Omega^*)$. Then, since $\Sigma(\Omega) \subseteq \Sigma(\Gamma(\Omega^*)) = \Sigma(\Omega^*)$, we have the following:

Theorem 7

For any set of relations Ω,

$$\Sigma(\Omega) \subseteq \Sigma(\Omega^*).$$

In practice we may use other operations, especially set operations such as union, intersection, and complement, in relational systems. However, the above results hold even if set operations are added to the operation set for relational spaces.

CHAPTER 10

STORAGE MAPPINGS FOR EXTENDIBLE ARRAYS

ARNOLD L. ROSENBERG
Mathematical Sciences Department
IBM Thomas J. Watson Research Center
Yorktown Heights, New York

Abstract

This chapter is a survey of papers devoted to and related to the problem of allocating storage for multidimensional arrays that can expand dynamically.

10.0. INTRODUCTION

Theoretical studies of computation have led to fresh insights into the nature of the computational process, to bounds on the efficiency of classes of techniques for performing certain computations, and to novel approaches to a number of computational problems. A variety of mathematical constructs have proven, by their recurrence in these investigations, to be basic to the study of computing. Among these basic constructs are the integer lattices in finite-dimensional Euclidean spaces.

Rather diverse computational problems can be formulated as problems concerning sets of integer lattice points. We mention only a small sample: Amoroso and Epstein (1974) were motivated by problems concerning iterative arrays of automata and logical circuits to study neighborhood-preserving dimension-reducing maps of the Euclidean lattices; Karp et al. (1975) studied ways of laying out records on a two-dimensional storage medium in terms of distance-minimizing configurations of lattice points; Mylopoulos and Pavlidis (1971) were led by consideration of picture processing and pattern recognition to study certain topological properties of discrete spaces; and Wong and Maddocks (1975) studied discrete d-dimensional spheres in order to gain insight into some problems of multimodule computer memory organization. It is our purpose here to survey a set of papers that study imbeddings of higher-dimensional Euclidean lattices in the one-dimensional lattice (specifically, in the set N of positive integers) with an eye to using these imbeddings to store rectangular arrays that can grow dynamically.

Rectangular arrays are among the most useful and structurally uniform of data structures. The usefulness of arrays is attested to by the fact that virtually every high-level programming language includes at least rudimentary array-handling facilities; some languages, notably APL, are designed with arrays as the basic data type. (Indeed, if one contemplates the task of designing a compiler for a language like APL, one appreciates the desirability of efficient techniques for storing dynamic rectangular arrays.) The structural uniformity of arrays is somewhat harder to pin down. One facet of this structural simplicity is captured by the notion of *regularity* considered by Turski (1971). Closely related to the regularity of arrays is their susceptibility to the *direct-access* storage techniques of Ehrich (1974). Also explaining arrays' structural niceness is their enjoyment of the properties of *addressability* and *free-rootedness* studied by Rosenberg (1971). Indeed, one sees in Rosenberg (1973) that the property of addressability guarantees susceptibility to direct-access storage mappings. In a fundamental sense, all of these facets of arrays' uniformity ensue from the fact that arrays can be accessed by means of systems of coordinates that are essentially "rectangular" sets of integer lattice points. These sets of coordinates give rise to the regular naming systems of Turski, to Rosenberg's addressing schemes for arrays, and to the ease with which Ehrich's scheme generates array-storing functions *op. cit.*

Historically, arrays have been stored using the *sequential allocation* techniques described by Knuth (1968, Section 2.2.6). For simplicity, we shall discuss only the two-dimensional case in this introduction, and we shall refer to these restricted storage mappings suggestively as *store-by-row* methods. As a running example, consider the four-column store-by-row storage mapping

$$\text{(0.1)} \qquad \mathbf{ADDRESS}(i, j) = j + 4(i - 1).$$

[We shall consider array storage mappings (which are defined precisely later) as operating on the positive integer tuple that comprises an array position's coordinates and as yielding the positive integer address of the location assigned to the position. We shall abjure the precise but cumbersome "$\mathbf{f}(\langle i, j\rangle)$" in favor of the more graceful "$\mathbf{f}(i, j)$." Finally, we shall accompany almost every definition of an array storage mapping by a figure depicting schematically the layout of storage under that mapping. These figures will depict an array, with position $\langle i, j\rangle$ containing the "address" $\mathbf{f}(i, j)$.]

Now, store-by-row storage mappings are strikingly efficient in several respects. The function that yields the address of array position $\langle i, j\rangle$ is very simple to compute, being merely a linear combination of i and j. Further, these storage mappings lay arrays out in storage so that both the rows and the columns of the arrays are stored in arithmetic progressions, thereby facilitating traversal of the array. Finally, store-by-row methods utilize storage perfectly in that they relegate an $m \times n$ array to a contiguous block of mn locations. The most noteworthy deficiency in this genre of array storage mapping is the inflexibility of such mappings relative to expansions of stored arrays, which inflexibility results from the dependence of the storage function on the dimensions of the stored array. Consider, for example, the 3×4 array A depicted in

Figure 10.1 stored by the store-by-row mapping **ADDRESS** of (0.1). If one were to

1	2	3	4
5	6	7	8
9	10	11	12

Figure 10.1. A 3 × 4 array stored "by rows."

append a row to A, changing its dimensions to 4×4, one would still be able to use **ADDRESS** to store the augmented array: The new row would merely be assigned to locations 13, . . ., 16, and no already-stored position would have to be moved. (We assume here and henceforth that the storage abutting any stored array is vacant so that demands for storage are never denied because of alternative utilization.) Contrasting with the ease of appending a row to A is the dilemma one faces when trying to adjoin a column to A, changing its dimensions to 3×5. (One faces this dilemma since **ADDRESS** is not one-to-one on the 3×5 array; it stores positions $\langle 1, 5 \rangle$ and $\langle 2, 1 \rangle$ in the same location.) One can effect this expansion either by storing the three new array positions in some arbitrarily chosen available locations or by reallocating storage for the entire augmented A via the five-column store-by-row mapping **ADDRESS**$'(i, j) = j + 5(i - 1)$. However, one sees immediately that the former alternative loses for one the computational simplicity (of accessing and traversal) inherent in the store-by-row regimen; no less unfortunately, the latter alternative entails moving every position of A, save those in the old first row, to a new storage location, a truly expensive option should the current expansion be followed by others.

At an informal level, we shall encapsulate the asymmetry in expandability just observed by saying that store-by-row storage mappings are *extendible* along columns but not along rows; that is, they admit adjunction of rows gracefully but not adjunction of columns. Such asymmetry in extendibility is not inevitable: Array storage mappings that are insensitive to the dimensions of the array being stored, hence fully extendible, can be devised, as the following example testifies:

(0.2) $$\textbf{SPARSE}(i, j) = 2^{i-1}3^{j-1}.$$

See Figure 10.2. This storage mapping contrasts dramatically with **ADDRESS**. Accessing a position of an array stored by **SPARSE** is computationally expensive,

1	3	9	27
2	6	18	54
4	12	36	108

Figure 10.2. A sparse allocation of a 3 × 4 array.

requiring roughly $\log n$ multiplications to access an arbitrary position of an n-position array. Although traversal of rows and columns does not require onerous computation, the necessary multiplications are certainly more costly than the additions called for by

ADDRESS. Finally, **SPARSE**'s utilization of storage is very poor: In the worst case, **SPARSE** spreads an n-position array over 3^{n-1} storage locations, thus leaving huge and growing gaps in the storage set aside for arrays. However, **SPARSE** *is* fully extendible: Any combination of row adjunctions and column adjunctions can be accommodated by **SPARSE** without any change in its computational form and without any moving of already-stored positions.

We now have a fully extendible array storage mapping. Are its inefficiencies inevitable concomitants of extendibility? Certainly not in degree! Let us consider the following alternative to **SPARSE**:

(0.3) $$\mathbf{DIAG}(i,j) = (i+j-1)(i+j-2)/2 + i.$$

See Figure 10.3. The storage mapping **DIAG**, so named since it stores arrays by diagonals, is attributed to Georg Cantor (1878), who used the fact that **DIAG** maps

1	2	4	7
3	5	8	12
6	9	13	18

Figure 10.3. A 3 × 4 array stored by **DIAG**.

$N \times N$ one-to-one onto N to prove that the source and target sets were equal in cardinality. We use the same property of **DIAG** to establish the storage mapping's extendibility. With regard to the three measures of computational efficiency that we have been considering, **DIAG** fares much better than **SPARSE** but nowhere nearly so well as **ADDRESS**. Being a polynomial, **DIAG** is not hard to compute—it requires a fixed number of arithmetic operations in contrast to **SPARSE**—but it is not just a linear combination of i and j. While **DIAG** does not store rows and/or columns in arithmetic progressions, it does afford relatively easy traversal since its first partial differences [the functions

$$\Delta_1\mathbf{DIAG}(i,j) = \mathbf{DIAG}(i+1,j) - \mathbf{DIAG}(i,j) \quad \text{and} \quad \Delta_2\mathbf{DIAG}(i,j) = \mathbf{DIAG}(i,j+1) - \mathbf{DIAG}(i,j)]$$

along rows and columns do form arithmetic progressions, specifically, tails of 1, 2, 3, 4, ... Finally, **DIAG**'s utilization of storage is far from the perfect storage of **ADDRESS**, but it is just as far from **SPARSE**'s exponentially sparse use of storage; in fact, an n-position array is never "spread" by **DIAG** over more than $n\cdot(n+1)/2$ storage locations.

Although **DIAG** affords us extendibility without the abysmal inefficiency of **SPARSE**, it still does not approach the efficiency of a store-by-row mapping. Can we maintain extendibility and do better than **DIAG** with regard to the measures of efficiency mentioned? This question, in a depersonalized form, underlies most of the work surveyed here: What inefficiencies inevitably accompany extendibility in array storage mappings? How can one quantify these inefficiencies? Our three criteria for measuring quality (or lack thereof) are the following (the reader may well wish to consider others also):

(0.4) (a) *Complexity of Computation:* How hard is the storage function to compute?

(b) *Complexity of Traversal:* How hard is it to traverse rows, columns, and their multidimensional analogs?

(c) *Efficiency of Storage Utilization:* We distinguish two aspects of storage use. To what extent are positions that are close together in the array stored close together? To what extent are arrays stored compactly, with regard to the existence and size of "gaps?"

Of course, deciding what to study and what to measure is only half the battle: One must determine how to study and how to quantify these notions of quality. This determination in turn demands precise definitions of the objects and notions to be studied, and these definitions, in Section 10.1, will be our first order of business.

Organization

The chapter comprises seven technical sections. Sections 10.1–10.5 are concerned in the main with *computed-access* array storage mappings, namely those that, in common with the three examples in this introduction, assign an address to a given array position as a displacement from the address assigned to position $\langle 1, 1, \ldots, 1\rangle$, the displacement being computed from the position's coordinates. In Section 10.1 we begin with definitions of the basic objects studied, arrays and array storage mappings. Then we describe a technique for constructing extendible computed-access array storage mappings. Finally, we present two variants on the obvious view of such mappings. In Section 10.2 we study storage mappings that are polynomials (as is **DIAG**), culminating in a result that points out the rarity of such mappings. Section 10.3 is devoted to one facet of the study of efficient storage utilization, specifically, the extent to which closeness of array positions can be retained by extendible storage mappings. Depending on how stringent are one's demands, such proximity can be preserved in some senses and not in others; in the former cases, the "radius of preservation" can be bounded. In Section 10.4 we study extendible storage mappings that afford one easy traversal in the sense that arrays are stored in arithmetic progressions along some direction. As in the previous section, we find here that such *additive* traversal is attainable only if one's demands are modest. Assuming these favorable demands, we present algorithms for constructing such easily traversed storage mappings, and we present bounds on their behaviors. In Section 10.5 we consider the presence and size of gaps in storage allocated by extendible storage mappings. Attainable lower bounds on the size of such gaps are presented for the general case and for two special classes of extendible mappings. It is then shown how to circumvent these bounds in special cases when one can predict the "pattern of expansions" of his arrays. In Sections 10.6 and 10.7 we consider alternatives to computed-access storage of arrays. In Section 10.6, we present three alternative linked allocation schemes for extendible arrays, and we evaluate their quality relative to the criteria of (0.4), with "cost of access/insertion" replacing the criterion "complexity of computation," which is inappropriate for these storage methods. Finally, in Section 10.7, one of the linking techniques of Section 10.6 is combined with the idea of computed access to yield external hashing schemes for extendible arrays. An efficient family of such hashing schemes is presented; a number of bounds on the efficiency of such schemes are discussed to lend perspective to the presentation. We close the paper in Section 10.8 with a brief discussion of open questions in this area.

Throughout this chapter, proofs of cited results are omitted, although hints at the direction of the proofs are presented whenever the proof admits such encapsulation. In an effort to enhance readability, citations are not given in the text but are rather relegated to a paragraph entitled "Attributions" at the end of each section.

Related Work

In writing any survey, one faces the problem of distinguishing between related and relevant work. With resignation at the realization of the imperfection of the partition here, we cite some sources of related work. We have already noted the studies by Turski (1971) and Rosenberg (1971), both of which are concerned with uniformities in data structures, with special reference to arrays. Hellerman (1962) surveys computed-access techniques for storing nonextendible arrays. Rosenberg (1973) and Ehrich (1974) attempt to put the development of computed-access storage mappings for more general classes of data structures on a theoretical footing. deVilliers and Wilson (1973, 1974) study empirically the feasibility of hashing schemes for storing sparse matrices. Amble and Knuth (1974) demonstrate the benefits that accrue when one exploits the order of keys when hashing. Rosenberg and Stockmeyer (1977b) consider a computed-access compromise between the nonextendibility of store-by-row mappings and the limitless extendibility of the extendible storage mappings we shall study in this survey: They consider mappings that allow arrays to expand in all directions but not beyond a prespecified size (= number of positions). Finally, Rosenberg (1974a, 1976/77) investigates the applicability of the ideas that follow (especially in Sections 10.5 and 10.7) to the problems of storing nonrectangular arrays. The books by Knuth (1968, 1973) will provide the reader valuable background and indications of yet other related sources.

10.1. BASIC NOTIONS AND RESULTS

This section is intended as a technical introduction to the chapter and to Sections 10.2–10.5 in particular. In Section 10.1.A, we shall present the notational and terminological conventions for the chapter. In succeeding subsections, we shall introduce the reader to computed-access array storage mappings, and we shall describe techniques for devising extendible such mappings, in preparation for the study of such mappings in Sections 10.2–10.5.

A. Notation and Terminology

Let N denote the positive integers $N = \{1, 2, \ldots\}$. For $d \in N$, N^d denotes the set of d-tuples of positive integers. For arbitrary $d \in N$, ϵ will be the *origin* element $\langle 1, \ldots, 1 \rangle$ of N^d; we rely on context to specify the dimensionality of any given instance of ϵ. For $\pi \in N^d$ and $i \in \{1, \ldots, d\}$, π_i is the ith coordinate of π; *e.g.*, $\epsilon_i = 1$ for all i.

The following functions from $N^d \longrightarrow N$ will be used repeatedly in what follows. For $\pi \in N^d$, we have $\Sigma(\pi) = \sum_{i=1}^{d} \pi_i$, $\Pi(\pi) = \prod_{i=1}^{d} \pi_i$, and $M(\pi) = \max_i \{\pi_i\}$.

We shall employ the following notation for familiar notions. For nonnegative real x, $\lfloor x \rfloor$ will be the integer part of x, $\lceil x \rceil$ will be the smallest integer $\geq x$, and $\log x$ ($x > 0$) will be the base 2 logarithm of x. Letting $n! = \prod_{i=1}^{n} i$ for $n \in N$ and $0! = 1$, we use the notation $C(m, n) = m!/n!(m-n)!$ for the binomial coefficient, where $m,n \leq m \in N$. For any finite set S, $\#S$ denotes the cardinality of S. Finally, let $\mathbf{f}$ and $\mathbf{g}$ be functions from N to the nonnegative reals. We say $\mathbf{f}(p) = O(\mathbf{g}(p))$ or, equivalently, $\mathbf{g}(p) = \Omega(\mathbf{f}(p))$ if there is a constant $c > 0$ such that $\mathbf{f}(p) \leq c \cdot \mathbf{g}(p)$ for all but finitely many p.

Finally we come to our formal notion of array. Throughout this chapter, we shall be concerned only with storage methods that determine the storage location of an array position on the basis of the position's coordinates, without regard to the data residing at the position. Accordingly, we can study these array storage mappings in terms of the following simple mathematical construct:

(1.1) The *d-dimensional array scheme of shape* $\langle n_1, \ldots, n_d \rangle$, each $n_i \in N$, is the set $A = \{1, \ldots, n_1\} \times \ldots \times \{1, \ldots, n_d\}$. Each element π of A is called a *position*. The cardinality $\#A = \prod_i n_i$ of A is termed A's *size*. If $\#A \leq p$, then we call A a $\langle p \rangle$-array scheme.

To facilitate exposition, we shall usually elide the word *scheme* when talking about array schemes.

B. Computed-Access Storage Mappings

The storage mappings we shall be studying in Sections 10.2–10.5 offer *computed access* to array positions in the following sense. Each storage mapping assigns an address to array position π as a displacement from the address assigned to array position ϵ, the displacement being computed from π's coordinates. We shall not, therefore, consider any storage mappings that are associative—that is, content-dependent—or adaptive—that is, context-dependent.

To simplify our exposition, we shall always place position ϵ in location 1, and we shall have our computed-access storage mappings deliver the actual address of π's residence rather than the displacement to this address (which is address -1). The former convention, in particular, yields material simplification later on.

The following formal notion yields a simple and useful embodiment of the intuitive notion of a computed-access array storage mapping:

(1.2) Let A be a d-dimensional array scheme. A (*computed-access*) *storage mapping for* A is a total function $\mathbf{A}: N^d \longrightarrow N$ satisfying (a) $\mathbf{A}(\epsilon) = 1$ and (b) $\mathbf{A}$ is one-to-one on A.

Computed-access storage mappings are the most satisfactory general-purpose way of storing arrays since they combine easy probing (characteristic of hashing schemes; cf. Section 10.7) with easy traversal (characteristic of chaining schemes; cf. Section 10.6.C). In fact, individual probes into an array so stored require but a single function evaluation, and traversing a (d-dimensional) "row" requires only computing first partial differences of the function $\mathbf{A}$.

As noted in the introduction, our concern here is not with array storage mappings in general but rather only with *fully extendible* storage mappings. As we note further there, an array storage mapping will be deemed worthy of this designation only if it accommodates *any* extension to an already-stored array without moving any stored positions and without requiring any alteration of its functional form. Definition (1.2) was designed intentionally to afford us a graceful formal notion of extendible array storage mapping.

(1.3) Let $\mathbf{A}: N^d \longrightarrow N$ be a storage mapping for the array scheme A. We say that $\mathbf{A}$ is *extendible* (or that $\mathbf{A}$ is an *extendible array storage mapping*, *esm*, for short) if $\mathbf{A}$ is a storage mapping for any super-array $A' \supset A$.

It is no accident that the term esm avoids mention of the "base array" A; in fact, A is immaterial in the following sense:

Proposition 1

The function $\mathbf{A}: N^d \longrightarrow N$ is an extendible array storage mapping iff $\mathbf{A}$ is one-to-one on all of N^d.

The functions we shall be studying are, thus, *d-tupling functions*, in the sense of computability theory.

The theory exposed in the sequel degenerates when $d = 1$. Accordingly, from this point on, we shall always understand that *our arrays are of dimensionality* $d > 1$.

C. A Technique for Constructing esm's

When faced with the task of constructing an esm, one might do well to view the construction as an incremental process. One first assigns addresses to some small set of positions in N^d (ϵ always being assigned address 1), then to some finite subset of the yet-to-be-addressed positions, and so on. If the sets in this never-ending iteration are chosen judiciously, the efficiency of the resulting esm relative to the quality criteria mentioned in (0.4) may be enhanced. We now present a vehicle for rendering systematic the choice of the successively stored sets:

(1.4) A function $\mathbf{s}: N^d \longrightarrow N$ is a *shell index* if (a) $\mathbf{s}(\epsilon) = 1$ and (b) for all $n \in N$, the set $\mathbf{s}^{-1}(n) = \{\pi \in N^d \mid \mathbf{s}(\pi) = n\}$ is finite.

The sets in the informally described iteration are, respectively, the *shells* $\mathbf{s}^{-1}(1)$, $\mathbf{s}^{-1}(2), \ldots$. Put another way, we design our esm to linearize the partial order on N^d induced by the function $\mathbf{s}$, *viz.*, $\pi < \pi'$ iff $\mathbf{s}(\pi) < \mathbf{s}(\pi')$.

The esm **DIAG** of (0.3) is an example of a *shell-linearizing* storage mapping. It is not hard to verify that **DIAG** linearizes the partial order induced by the shell index $\mathbf{s}(i, j) = i + j - 1$.

One other shell-induced esm merits mention at this point, since it was the stimulus for most of the research reported in this survey (and, indeed, it plays a central role in Section 10.5). Say that one plans to solve systems of linear equations of undetermined size and that one wishes to devise an esm tailor-made for the accompanying square coefficient matrices. One notes that the shell index $\mathbf{s}(\pi) = M(\pi)$ partitions $N \times N$ into just the right shells since, for all $n \in N$, $\cup_{i=1}^{n} \mathbf{s}^{-1}(i)$ is precisely the array scheme of shape $\langle n, n \rangle$. Even if one generalizes the problem of linearizing these shells to a d-dimensional problem in the obvious way, one finds that the shell technique leads one to a readily computed family of esm's:

(1.5) The *cubic shell esm's* $\mathbf{CUBE}_d: N^d \longrightarrow N$ are defined as follows:

(a) $\mathbf{CUBE}_2(\pi) = (m-1)^2 + m + \pi_2 - \pi_1$, where $m = M(\pi)$.

(b) $\mathbf{CUBE}_{d+1}(\pi) = \mathbf{CUBE}_d(\pi_2, \pi_3, \ldots, \pi_{d+1}) + (\pi_1 - 1)(m-1)^d + m^d \cdot (m - \pi_1)$, where $m = M(\pi)$.

Since we shall be concerned especially with the case $d = 2$, we shall simplify terminology by renaming $\mathbf{CUBE}_2$ as **SQ**.

See Figure 10.4.

1	4	9	16	25	36	49	64	81	100
2	3	8	15	24	35	48	63	80	99
5	6	7	14	23	34	47	62	79	98
10	11	12	13	22	33	46	61	78	97
17	18	19	20	21	32	45	60	77	96
26	27	28	29	30	31	44	59	76	95
37	38	39	40	41	42	43	58	75	94
50	51	52	53	54	55	56	57	74	93
65	66	67	68	69	70	71	72	73	92
82	83	84	85	86	87	88	89	90	91

Figure 10.4. The array scheme of shape $\langle 10, 10 \rangle$ stored by the esm **SQ**.

Several other applications of this shell technique will appear in later sections.

D. Esm's in a Paging Environment

Although we discuss esm's as though our entire array will always reside in high-speed memory, the construction of esm's can be modified easily to accommodate arrays that are to be segmented for use in a paging scheme with a random access back-up store. Specifically, we segment (= partition) N^d into identically shaped blocks, and we assign each array position π an address of the form $\mathbf{H}(\pi) + \mathbf{B}(\pi)$, where $\mathbf{H}$ is an esm modified to assign addresses only to the *headers* of the blocks of the partition and $\mathbf{B}$ is a finite-range function that indicates π's position within its block. The vagueness of this description will dissipate as we formalize our notion of block and exemplify the proposed technique.

(1.6) For each dimensionality $d \in N$, let $u^{(1)}, u^{(2)}, \ldots, u^{(d)} \in N^d$ denote the unit vectors defined by

$$u_j^{(i)} = \begin{cases} 1 & \text{if } i = j \\ 0 & \text{otherwise.} \end{cases}$$

A d-dimensional *stencil* is a finite subset $\Sigma \subset (N \cup \{0\})^d$ such that (a) $\omega = \langle 0, 0, \ldots, 0 \rangle \in \Sigma$ and (b) Σ is *connected* in the sense that, for all $\sigma \in \Sigma$, there exists a sequence $\omega = \sigma^{(0)}, \sigma^{(1)}, \ldots, \sigma^{(n)} = \sigma$ of elements of Σ for which each $\sigma^{(k)} = \sigma^{(k-1)} +$ (some $u^{(i)}$). (As usual, addition is coordinate-wise.)

(1.7) A d-dimensional stencil Σ is a *block basis* if there is a subset $H \subset N^d$ (of *block headers*) satisfying the following two conditions. Let $\eta + \Sigma = \{\eta + \sigma \mid \sigma \in \Sigma\}$ for $\eta \in H$. Then, (a) $\cup_{\eta \in H}(\eta + \Sigma) = N^d$, and (b) for $\eta, \eta' \neq \eta$ in H, $(\eta + \Sigma) \cap (\eta' + \Sigma) = \varnothing$. The finite set $\eta + \Sigma$ is called the *block headed* by η, and the pair (H, Σ) is called a *block scheme*.

A paging-oriented esm will be constructed using a block scheme (H, Σ), as the sum of a $(\#\Sigma)$-to-one function $\mathbf{H}: N^d \longrightarrow \{(\#\Sigma) \cdot n \mid n \in N \cup \{0\}\}$ and an infinite-to-one function $\mathbf{B}: N^d \longrightarrow \{1, \ldots, \#\Sigma\}$. Specifically, $\mathbf{H}$ maps all positions π of a given block $\eta + \Sigma$ to the same *block address*, while $\mathbf{B}$ associates with each π the unique $\sigma \in \Sigma$ such that $\pi = \eta + \sigma$. An example may be helpful at this point:

(1.8) Let $\Sigma = \{\langle 0, 0 \rangle, \langle 0, 1 \rangle, \langle 1, 0 \rangle, \langle 1, 1 \rangle, \langle 2, 0 \rangle, \langle 2, 1 \rangle\}$. Let $H = \{\langle m, n \rangle \mid m \equiv 1 \text{ (mod. 3)}, n \equiv 1 \text{ (mod. 2)}\}$. It is not hard to verify that Σ is a two-dimensional stencil which is a block basis. Moreover, (H, Σ) is a block scheme. Each block of N^2 has the form

$\langle 3k + 1, 2l + 1 \rangle$	$\langle 3k + 1, 2l + 2 \rangle$
$\langle 3k + 2, 2l + 1 \rangle$	$\langle 3k + 2, 2l + 2 \rangle$
$\langle 3k + 3, 2l + 1 \rangle$	$\langle 3k + 3, 2l + 2 \rangle$

Let us choose **SQ** as the esm to adapt to a paging environment. Since our chosen stencil has six elements, we alter the form of **SQ** from (1.5a) to

$$\mathbf{H}(i,j) = 6\cdot(M\cdot(M-1) + \lceil j/2 \rceil - \lceil i/3 \rceil),$$
$$\text{where } M = \max(\lceil i/3 \rceil, \lceil j/2 \rceil).$$

Since our blocks are, in fact, copies of the array scheme of shape $\langle 3, 2\rangle$, we can choose for the function **B** the following adaptation of a two-column store-by-row array storage mapping:

$$\mathbf{B}(i,j) = [j, 2] + 2([i, 3] - 1), \qquad \text{where } [a, b] = a - b\cdot(\lceil a/b \rceil - 1).$$

The final esm that stores N^2 in 3×2 blocks is simply $\mathbf{BLOCK}(i,j) = \mathbf{H}(i,j) + \mathbf{B}(i,j)$.

See Figure 10.5.

1	2	19	20	49	50
3	4	21	22	51	52
5	6	23	24	53	54
7	8	13	14	43	44
9	10	15	16	45	46
11	12	17	18	47	48
25	26	31	32	37	38
27	28	33	34	39	40
29	30	35	36	41	42

Figure 10.5. The array scheme of shape $\langle 9, 6\rangle$ stored in 3×2 blocks by the esm **BLOCK**.

The task of constructing the function **B**, and hence the esm **BLOCK** in (1.8), was simplified materially by the fact that the stencil Σ there was "rectangular" in the sense that the blocks were array schemes. The shape of Σ was not just a fortuitous choice.

(1.9) A stencil Σ is *rectangular* if the set $\epsilon + \Sigma$ is an array scheme, that is, if Σ has the form $\Sigma = \{0, \ldots, m_1\} \times \ldots \times \{0, \ldots, m_d\}$ for $m_1, \ldots, m_d \in N \cup \{0\}$.

Theorem 2

A stencil Σ is a block basis, if and only if, it is rectangular.

The proof of Theorem 2 is most easily visualized in two dimensions. Since some block must nestle neatly at the origin, all blocks (since all are shaped identically) must have left and bottom sides that are free of "bulges". By the assumption of connectedness of stencils (1.6b), these two sides must be free of "dents" also, since there would be no way for a connected, bulge-free left or bottom to fill in a space left by a dent from another block. Hence, the left and bottom sides of blocks must be flat. Since blocks must fit flush with one another, right and top sides must be flat also, leaving us with the asserted rectangles. It is obvious that any rectangular shape will work. (Note that, in formalizing this sketch, the "musts" need to be verified as well as their purported implications.)

The construction of a page-oriented esm is thus simplified even further: It is the sum of an appropriately modified esm (that yields *block addresses*) and an appropriately modified (not necessarily extendible) array storage mapping (that yields *block displacements*).

E. On Storing Many Extendible Arrays

Our final remark in this introductory section is to note that although we have thus far discussed using esm's to store individual arrays, these mappings can be adapted easily to the task of storing arbitrarily many extendible arrays of arbitrary dimensionalities. The reason for the ease of adaptation is that the problem of storing even infinitely many extendible arrays reduces easily to the problem of storing a single two-dimensional array scheme extendibly. Specifically, let us be given the indexed family $A_1, A_2, \ldots$ of (possibly extendible) arrays, and with each, let us be given a compatible esm $\mathbf{A}_i$. We can use any two-dimensional esm $\mathbf{A}$ to store all of these arrays as follows. We merely assign to position π of A_n the address $\mathbf{A}(n, \mathbf{A}_n(\pi))$. Note that we need the index n as well as the address $\mathbf{A}_n(\pi)$ as an argument to $\mathbf{A}$ just in case several of the A_i are of equal dimensionality and so share positions. The results in the following sections all view esm's as being used to store a single extendible array. The reader can easily reinterpret these results in the context of esm's storing many arrays, and this alternative vantage point may suggest a number of interesting new questions.

Attributions

The material in this section is adapted almost entirely from Rosenberg (1974b); terminology and notation have been altered when deemed appropriate. For instance, we have adopted the streamlined notion of array scheme found in Rosenberg (1975b) in preference to the more cumbersome notion in Rosenberg (1974b). Further, in (1.2), we have replaced the term *realization*, which traces back to Rosenberg (1971), by the more transparent *storage mapping*. The cubic shell esm's in (1.5) originate in Rosenberg and Strong (1972), and the stencils of (1.6), with the attendant block bases (1.7), were discussed first in Rosenberg (1973). Finally, the remark in Section 10.1.E, that esm's can be used to store many arrays, formed the basis of Rosenberg (1975a).

10.2. POLYNOMIAL STORAGE MAPPINGS

Perhaps the most elusive measure of the quality of an extendible array storage mapping is the ease of computing the mapping function. What is an appropriate repertoire of basic operations against which to gauge the complexity of these functions? In certain computing situations one would deem arithmetic operations preferable to bit-string operations, while under other circumstances, one might opt in the converse direction. One class of functions that would likely appear high on anyone's easy-to-compute list is the class of polynomials, especially given the considerable attention paid to these functions in recent years by computation theorists. We shall now review some results germane to the use of polynomials as array storage mappings. Of course, polynomials that map N^d one-to-one into N have been studied for many years since their computational simplicity renders them attractive as *tupling* functions, which functions play an important role in set theory and in logic.

Polynomial esm's are not difficult to devise: In two dimensions, for instance, the polynomials $(x + y)^n + x - 2^n$ yield such mappings for every integer $n > 1$. Polynomial esm's begin to exhibit interesting structure, however, only when one investigates polynomials that map N^d one-to-one *onto* N. It is such polynomial *packing functions*, in the terminology of Lew and Rosenberg (1975), that will occupy our attention here.

Although polynomial packing functions are not as easy to invent as are their nonsurjective relatives, such functions do exist for any dimensionality:

(2.1) For $\pi \in N^d$,

$$\mathbf{POLY}(\pi; d) = \sum_{k=1}^{d} C(\mathbf{t}(\pi; k), k) + 1, \qquad \text{where } \mathbf{t}(\pi; k) = \sum_{l=1}^{k} \pi_l - 1.$$

The $d = 2$ member of this family is simply the diagonal *pairing function* **DIAG** of (0.3).

Theorem 3

For each $d \in N$, $\mathbf{POLY}(\cdot\,; d)$ is a d-dimensional polynomial packing function.

The proof of the theorem is facilitated by noting that each function $\mathbf{POLY}(\cdot\,; d)$ stores N^d by the shells specified by the shell index $\mathbf{s}(\pi) = \Sigma(\pi) - d + 1$.

One verifies easily that the composition of any collection of polynomial packing functions is again a polynomial packing function. The polynomials in (2.1) can, therefore, be combined in manifold ways to create polynomial packing functions of a given dimensionality. For instance, one can construct the three mappings $\mathbf{POLY}(\cdot\,; 3)$, $\mathbf{POLY}(\pi_1, \mathbf{POLY}(\pi_2, \pi_3; 2); 2)$, and $\mathbf{POLY}(\mathbf{POLY}(\pi_1, \pi_2; 2), \pi_3; 2)$ from the building blocks of (2.1) to store three-dimensional arrays. It is easily verified that one can view each composition of the polynomials in (2.1) as specifying a finite rooted tree; this viewpoint affords one a way of enumerating the distinct polynomial packing functions of a given dimensionality obtainable from the basic building blocks of (2.1). Let $\mathcal{P}_d$ denote the set of d-dimensional polynomials so obtained.

Theorem 4

(a) For each dimensionality $d > 1$, there are 2^{d-2} polynomials in $\mathcal{P}_d$ of (total) degree 2^{d-1}. No polynomial in $\mathcal{P}_d$ has higher degree. (b) No polynomial in $\mathcal{P}_d$ has degree less than d. The number of degree d polynomials in $\mathcal{P}_d$ satisfies the recurrence

$$\nu(d) = \sum_{\substack{n \mid d \\ n>1}} \nu(d/n)^n.$$

The case $d = 2$ is an especially intriguing one. First, most applications of tupling functions are studied in terms of iterated compositions of pairing functions; *cf.* Minsky (1967). Second, and more germane to our purpose here, dimensionality 2 is the only case where the recipe "the polynomials in (2.1) combined by iterated composition" yields but a single result, namely **DIAG**. Are there, in fact, any other two-dimensional polynomial packing functions? We think not!

> **Conjecture.** **DIAG** and its sibling, $\mathbf{DIAG}'(i, j) = j + (i + j - 1)(i + j - 2)/2$, are the only two-dimensional polynomial packing functions.

This conjecture, in its full generality, remains open; however, it has been verified for a number of situations.

Theorem 5

(a) **DIAG** and **DIAG**$'$ are the only quadratic two-dimensional polynomial packing functions. (b) There is no two-dimensional polynomial packing function of degree 1, 3, or 4. (c) There is no two-dimensional polynomial packing function of degree greater than 2 that is eventually monotonic in both variables.

The remainder of the conjecture (that is, degrees greater than 4) remains an intriguing research problem.

We remark in closing this section that **DIAG**'s utilization of storage is not drastically different from **SQ**'s, being about a factor of 2 bigger, and this similarity persists in the higher-dimensional analogs of these esm's. In addition, it is not computationally difficult to traverse the rows or the columns of an array stored by **DIAG**, since **DIAG** stores both rows and columns in a simple quadratic progression. (The second differences of adjacent addresses are constantly 1.) These properties, in conjunction with **DIAG**'s being easy to compute, may render **DIAG** attractive as an array storage mapping in certain situations, despite its failure to be "optimal" under any of the criteria we shall look at.

Attributions

Chowla (1961) presents the family (2.1) of polynomials and states Theorem 3 without proof. As noted earlier, **DIAG** dates back at least to 1878, when Cantor (1878) used it in his study of cardinal numbers. The elegant view of the compositions of the polynomials in (2.1) and the associated enumeration of $\mathcal{P}_d$ in Theorem 4 are due to Lew (1977). Finally, the stated conjecture and its partial verification in Theorem 5 comprise the most easily summarized portion of the contents of Lew and Rosenberg (1975), which paper is devoted to studying the cited conjecture and closely related topics. Minsky (1967) discusses pairing functions at some length.

10.3. PROXIMITY-PRESERVING STORAGE MAPPINGS

Algorithms that process arrays tend to access their input arrays by groups of neighboring positions; that is, the position accessed after position π is likely to reside in a small "neighborhood" of π. Matrix-multiplication algorithms illustrate this tendency: The conventional algorithm accesses matrices along rows and columns; and the more recent algorithm of Strassen (1969) accesses matrices, at the bottom of the recursions, in blocks of four positions. The efficiency of such algorithms will likely be enhanced if bookkeeping can be minimized by storing array positions in a proximity-preserving manner, so that positions that are close to one another in the array do not get separated inordinately in storage. Preservation of proximity is all the more desirable in a paging environment, where the expense of page swaps makes it crucial that significant processing be done while a page resides in main memory. Therefore, when implementing any algorithm that processes arrays that are extendible, hence apt to grow beyond the limits of page size, one must take pains to store one's arrays so as to minimize these expensive page swaps. Unfortunately, there is no way to store extendible arrays so that distances are dilated by a bounded amount, that is, so that positions that are distance n apart in the array (via some path of up-down-left-right's) are placed in storage locations whose addresses differ by at most δn, where $\delta \in N$ is the "dilation factor". Moreover, this intransigence of arrays persists even if we allow our storage space to be organized as a tree of any bounded degree. Proximity remains unpreservable in a linear address space even if we permit certain types of dynamic reorganization of the array storage mapping, at least for some kinds of computational problems; there remain other computational problems where we still do not know if dynamic reorganization will suffice to store arrays with bounded dilation. In contrast with these negative facts are a number of senses in which proximity can be preserved by extendible array storage maps. Specifically, if we measure all distances relative to a single position in N^d, one can devise proximity-preserving array storage mappings, and, at the cost of greater dilation, one can extend this preservation to proximities measured relative to any fixed finite set of positions in N^d. This section is devoted to surveying a number of results that assert either the possibility or the impossibility of preserving proximity when storing arrays.

A. Bounds on Dilation by Storage Mappings

We need a formal notion of the distance between two points in N^d. For convenience, we shall study the *rectilinear* (or L_1) metric, although we could just as well employ the *Euclidean* (or L_2) or the *maximum* (or L_∞) metric except in the few instances noted.

(3.1) For $\pi, \pi' \in N^d$, the *distance* between π and π' is given by

$$\text{dist}(\pi, \pi') = \sum_i |\pi_i - \pi'_i|.$$

(3.2) For $\pi \in N^d$ and $r \in N \cup \{0\}$, the *radius r neighborhood* of π is the set

$$\mathfrak{N}(\pi; r) = \{\pi' \in N^d \mid \text{dist}(\pi, \pi') \leq r\}.$$

Lemma 6

For all $\pi \in N^d$ and all $r \in N \cup \{0\}$,

$$C(r + d, d) \leq \#\mathfrak{N}(\pi; r) \leq \sum_{k=0}^{d} C(d, k) \cdot C(r, k) \cdot 2^k.$$

Hence, $\#\mathfrak{N}(\pi; r)$ is bounded both above and below by constant multiples of r^d, the constants depending only on d.

It is already obvious from this lemma that no one-to-one map $\mathbf{F}$ of N^d into N^e, $e < d$, can preserve neighborhoods in the sense that, for all π, r,

(3.3) $$\mathbf{F}(\mathfrak{N}(\pi; r)) \subset \mathfrak{N}(\mathbf{F}(\pi); \delta r)$$

for some $\delta \in N$. However, a more detailed and interesting proof of this nonpreservability for the case $e = 1$ can be derived as follows [indeed, yet other proofs of this fact for the case $e = 1$ are derived in Rosenberg (1975c)]:

(3.4) For any esm $\mathbf{A}: N^d \longrightarrow N$, define the functions $\mathbf{d_A}: N^d \times N \longrightarrow N$ and $\mathbf{d_A^*}: N^d \times N \longrightarrow N$ as follows:

(a) For each $\pi \in N^d$ and $r \in N$,

$$\mathbf{d_A}(\pi, r) = \max(\mathbf{A}(\mathfrak{N}(\pi; r))) - \min(\mathbf{A}(\mathfrak{N}(\pi; r))) + 1.$$

$\mathbf{d_A}$ is $\mathbf{A}$'s *local diameter of proximity preservation:* $\mathbf{d_A}(\pi, r)$ is the size of the smallest interval that contains the image under $\mathbf{A}$ of $\mathfrak{N}(\pi; r)$.

(b) For each $\pi \in N^d$ and $r \in N$,

$$\mathbf{d_A^*}(\pi, r) = \max\{\mathbf{d_A}(\pi', r) \mid M(\pi') \leq M(\pi)\}.$$

$\mathbf{d_A^*}$ is $\mathbf{A}$'s *cumulative* local diameter of proximity preservation.

The advantage of measuring preservation of proximity by $\mathbf{A}$ in terms of $\mathbf{d_A^*}$ rather than $\mathbf{d_A}$ is that the cumulative measure smooths out the possibly erratic behavior of the latter measure caused by $\mathbf{A}$'s nonmonotonicities. This smoothing permits us to bound from below the rate of growth of cumulative local diameters of proximity preservation.

Theorem 7

For each dimensionality $d > 1$, there is a constant $c_d > 0$ such that, for all d-dimensional esm's $\mathbf{A}$ and for all $\pi \in N^d$ and $r \in N$,

$$\mathbf{d_A^*}(\pi, r) > c_d \cdot r \cdot (\max\{r, M(\pi)\})^{d-1}.$$

Theorem 7, which depends ultimately on Lemma 6, yields the following infinitely-often lower bound on $\mathbf{d_A}$:

Corollary 8

For each dimensionality $d > 1$, there is a constant $c_d > 0$ such that, for all d-dimensional esm's **A** and all $r \in N$, $\mathbf{d}_{\mathbf{A}}(\pi, r) > c_d \cdot r \cdot M(\pi)^{d-1}$ for infinitely many points $\pi \in N^d$.

The nonpreservability of proximity by extendible array storage mappings, in the sense of (3.3), follows directly.

The lower bounds of Theorem 7 and Corollary 8 are reasonably tight, at least in order of growth.

Theorem 9

For every dimensionality d, there are d-dimensional esm's **A** with $\mathbf{d}_{\mathbf{A}}(\pi, r) \leq c \cdot (M(\pi) + r)^d$ for some constant c.

Example of such esm's are the d-dimensional versions of **DIAG** [(0.3) and (2.1)] for which $\mathbf{d}_{\mathbf{POLY}(\cdot;\, d)}(\pi, r) \leq C(\Sigma(\pi) + r, d)$ as well as the d-dimensional versions of **SQ** (1.5) for which $\mathbf{d}_{\mathbf{CUBE}_d}(\pi, r) \leq (2M(\pi) + r)^d$.

B. List-Structured Memory

Up to this point, we have considered only linearly structured memory, addressed by the integers. We now make a brief digression to a more general memory structure.

(3.5) A d-dimensional *array* $\longrightarrow$ *tree mapping* (*atm*, for short) is a one-to-one function $\mathbf{T}\colon N^d \longrightarrow \Sigma^*$. Here (a) Σ is a finite set of symbols, and (b) Σ^* denotes the set of all finite strings of symbols from Σ, including the empty string e.

The set Σ^* can be viewed as the set of addresses of an infinite rooted tree of degree $\#\Sigma$. The root of the tree is addressed by e, and, generally, the successor of node x reached by following the σth branch out of x is given address $x\sigma$. (Note that we are assuming tacitly that all branches are labeled by symbols from Σ.)

(3.6) For $x \in \Sigma^*$ and $r \in N \cup \{0\}$, the *radius r tree neighborhood* of x is defined as follows:

(a) $\mathfrak{J}(x; 0) = \{x\}$;

(b) $\mathfrak{J}(x; r + 1) = \{z \in \Sigma^* \mid \text{for some } \sigma \in \Sigma \text{ and } y \in \mathfrak{J}(x; r) \text{ either } z = y\sigma \text{ or } y = z\sigma\}$.

As in (3.2), the radius r neighborhood of a position x is the set of positions accessible from x in r or fewer "steps".

It is transparent that, providing only that $\#\Sigma > 1$, $\#\mathfrak{J}(x; r)$ is exponential in r. Hence $\mathfrak{J}(x; r)$ is certainly sufficient in capacity to accommodate the image under an atm of any dimensionality of an array neighborhood $\mathfrak{N}(\pi; r)$. It is, therefore, surprising that atm's cannot preserve neighborhoods even as esm's cannot.

Theorem 10

Let $\mathbf{T}: N^d \longrightarrow \Sigma^*$ be an atm. There is no constant c such that $\mathbf{T}(\mathfrak{N}(\pi; r)) \subset \mathfrak{Z}(\mathbf{T}(\pi); cr)$ for almost all $\pi \in N^d$ and $r \in N$.

As we remarked, volumetric arguments are of no avail with this result. The key observation needed to prove the theorem is that trees have "bottlenecks", while arrays do not. Consider, for contrast, an arbitrary $n \times n$ array A and a finite tree Tr(A) containing A's image under some atm **T**. Now, subsets of any array are *exposed* in the sense that no matter what subset S of A we choose, with $\#S$ roughly $n^2/2$, there will be approximately n positions in S that are adjacent (i.e., distance 1) to positions in $A - S$. In sharp contrast, if we select any subtree of Tr(A), in its entirety, only *one* position of the subtree (namely, its root) will be adjacent to a position in Tr(A) — (the subtree). Therefore, if we select S to be some portion of A of the right size that is relegated to its own subtree of Tr(A), the roughly n exposed positions of S are easily seen to get buried in this subtree. Precisely, the images of some two positions that are adjacent in A (one position from S and one from $A - S$) will be at a distance not less than about $\log_{\#\Sigma} n$ in Tr(A). (This discussion suggests what an atm version of Theorem 7 might look like.)

The significance of Theorem 10 lies in a number of orthogonal directions. First, the theorem supersedes the proof in Section 10.3.A of the nonpreservability of proximity by esm's (although without supplying the structural information of, say, Theorem 7). Second, it points the way to a potentially fruitful study of memories with other than linear structure. Finally, it points up a weakness in the arguments of those who propose using VDL data objects [basically labeled trees; see Lee (1972)] to generate the computer representations of data objects as in "A multidimensional array is merely a list of lists of . . . of lists." Traversal-oriented algorithms are bound to come to grief if such representations are used.

C. Simple Algorithms on Extendible Arrays

Another digression from our main topic is in order here. Although we have depicted our study as being concerned with random access devices, there is a sense in which many of the cited results are really talking about linear representations of multidimensional storage media, irrespective of the mode of access. Two results in the literature of time-restricted Turing machines (TM's) seem particularly appropriate to the topic of preservation of proximity by dimension-reducing maps $N^d \longrightarrow N^e$, $e < d$.

We have a Turing machine operating on a d-dimensional tape. The instructions it responds to are (1) move one step forward in the direction of axis i; (2) move one step backward along axis i; (3) print symbol 1 on the tape square currently scanned; (4) flash YES if there is a 1 printed on the current tape square, NO otherwise. [In two dimensions, UP and RIGHT would comprise the moves of type (1) and DOWN and LEFT the moves of type (2).]

We shall consider the following simple programming language L_d. The atomic operations of L_d are (1) F_i, $i \in \{1, \ldots, d\}$, symbolic for MOVE FORWARD ALONG

AXIS i; (2) B_i, $i \in \{1, \ldots, d\}$, symbolic for MOVE BACKWARD ALONG AXIS i; (3) W, symbolic for WRITE; and (4) P, symbolic for PROBE FOR 1. Programs in the language L_d are finite strings of operation symbols, whose meanings should be obvious given that TM's always start on a blank tape: The response to an L_d-program should be the response given by a d-dimensional TM following the directions specified by the operation symbols.

Now, we assume that the reader is familiar with the fact that TM's of any dimensionality are universal in the sense that they can compute any "effectively computable" function. All we need of this far-reaching result is the fact that, for any pair d, e of dimensionalities, there are TM's on d-dimensional tapes that can execute any L_e-program. However, the speed of such execution depends heavily on the relative sizes of d and e. Let T be a TM capable of executing L_e-programs (e is fixed). We say that T *operates in time* $\mathbf{t}: N \longrightarrow N$ if T never requires more than $\mathbf{t}(n)$ steps to execute a length-n L_e-program.

Theorem 11

Let T be any d-dimensional TM that executes L_e-programs, $d \leq e$. Then T operates in time $\mathbf{t}(n) = \Omega(n^{2-d/e})$.

The theorem is proved by an adversary technique. Given T, one demonstrates that, no matter how T organizes (and reorganizes) its storage, the nonpreservability of proximity by maps from $N^{e>d}$ into N^d renders T vulnerable to certain sequences of walks-*cum*-probes; and one designs a set of programs of increasing lengths that exploit this vulnerability. The programs operate in two stages: Initially, T is directed (in the language L_e) to proceed in a "spiral" to visit some k^e tape squares, marking some (with 1's) as it goes, and then to return as directly as possible to the home square (where it started); the second stage comprises a sequence of searches, each search being a sequence of F_i's and B_i's, followed by a single P, followed by a direct return to the home square. As one can see intuitively, these programs exploit adjacencies in N^e in a quintessential way.

The lower bound of Theorem 11 is, at least for the case $d = 1$, best possible. A sophisticated simulation technique can be used to prove the following:

Theorem 12

Given any d-dimensional TM that operates in time $\mathbf{t}(n)$, one can find a (behaviorally) equivalent one-dimensional TM that operates in time $(\mathbf{t}(n))^{2-1/d}$.

The adversary programs just mentioned lead T back to its home square and thence on another search. Does T "know" on its own when the home square has been reached? This is a crude paraphrase of the *origin-crossing* problem.

Let $\mathcal{O}_d$ be that set of L_d-programs that have equal numbers of occurrences of F_i and B_i for each $i \in \{1, \ldots, d\}$.

Theorem 13

For every $d \in N$, there is a single-tape one-dimensional TM operating in time $\mathbf{t}(n) = n$ that flashes YES on an L_d-program precisely when the program is in the set $\mathcal{O}_d$.

A TM cannot only recognize its home square; it can do so expeditiously, regardless of the dimensionality of the program being executed. Given the ease of solving this origin-crossing problem, one might assume similar facility with the closely related *axis-crossing* problem, but this assumption has yet to find basis in fact. Let $\mathcal{A}_d$ be that set of L_d-programs that have equal numbers of occurrences of F_i and B_i for *some* $i \in \{1, \ldots, d\}$. The switch from $\mathcal{O}_d$'s universal quantifier to $\mathcal{A}_d$'s existential quantifier transforms the completely settled Theorem 13 to the thorny (even for $d = 2$)

Question

Does there exist a single-tape one-dimensional Turing machine operating in time $\mathbf{t}(n) = n$ that flashes YES on an L_d-program precisely when the program is in the set $\mathcal{A}_d$?

D. Centered Storage Mappings

There are senses in which esm's can preserve proximity, but they obviously require weakening the demands of (3.3). One feasible weakening is to measure proximities relative to a single reference point.

(3.7) The point $\pi \in N^d$ is the *center* of the esm $\mathbf{A}: N^d \longrightarrow N$ if $\mathbf{d}_{\mathbf{A}}(\pi, r) = \#\mathfrak{N}(\pi, r)$ for all $r \in N$.

The main facts about centers of esm's are summarized in the following:

Theorem 14

(a) There are onto esm's with no center. (b) For every $\pi \in N^d$ there are esm's $\mathbf{A}: N^d \longrightarrow N$ centered at π. (c) No esm has two centers.

Part (a) is immediate using examples like $\mathbf{A}(\pi_1, \pi_2) = 2^{\pi_1 - 1}(2\pi_2 - 1)$ in two dimensions. Part (b) can be established by assigning addresses in a "spiral" about π. Part (c), which holds for any L_p metric (p finite) but not for the L_∞ metric, depends on the way neighborhoods overlap. Specifically, distances relative to distinct points in N^d must conflict in the sense that there exist radii a, b such that the radius a neighborhood about π and the radius b neighborhood about π' each contain points not contained by the other.

An exemplary centered esm is **DIAG** (0.3), which is centered at ϵ. Being centered about any point other than ϵ has an unexpected effect on the structure of an esm.

Theorem 15

Let the esm **A** have center π. If **A** is monotonic in every variable, then $\pi = \epsilon$.

Theorem 15 exploits the "shape" of neighborhoods and is not valid for the L_∞ metric, though it is true for the L_2 metric.

If one is willing to lower his sights by weakening the stringent demands of (3.7), then one can devise esm's with any finite number of *quasi-centers*.

Theorem 16

Given any k points $\pi^{(1)}, \ldots, \pi^{(k)} \in N^d$, there is an esm $\mathbf{A}: N^d \longrightarrow N$ that is quasi-centered at these points in the following sense. For all $\pi, \pi' \in N^d$, if $\pi, \pi' \in \cap_{i=1}^{k} \mathfrak{N}(\pi^{(i)}; r_i)$, then $|\mathbf{A}(\pi) - \mathbf{A}(\pi')| < k \cdot \min \#\mathfrak{N}(\pi^{(i)}; r_i)$.

The proof of Theorem 16 involves a spiraling process more complicated than that needed for Theorem 14(b).

E. Adjacency-Preserving Maps

We have just discussed a way in which esm's can preserve proximity providing that one localizes the notion of proximity to neighborhoods of some finite set of points. An alternative way to weaken the demands of (3.3) is to weaken the notion of neighborhood. This ploy does permit a type of proximity preservation by dimension-reducing maps, but not, unfortunately, by esm's. For simplicity of exposition, we shall consider here one-to-one maps from Z^d into Z^e, Z being the set of all integers.

(3.8) For $d \in N$, a d-dimensional *template* is a finite set $T \subset Z^d$.

Intuitively, a template specifies an adjacency structure, that is, those points that are to be considered unit distance from a given point. For instance, the adjacencies of the L_1 metric are given by the template $T = \{\langle \pm 1, 0, \ldots, 0\rangle, \langle 0, \pm 1, 0, \ldots, 0\rangle, \ldots, \langle 0, \ldots, 0, \pm 1\rangle\}$ since $\text{dist}(\pi, \pi + \tau) = 1$ for all $\pi \in Z^d$ and $\tau \in T$.

(3.9) Let T be a d-dimensional template. The one-to-one function $\mathbf{F}: Z^d \longrightarrow Z^e$ is *T-adjacency-preserving* if $\mathbf{F}(\pi + \tau) = \mathbf{F}(\pi) + \mathbf{F}(\tau)$ for all $\pi \in Z^d$ and $\tau \in T$.

Theorem 17

Let $T \subset Z^d$ be a template. There is a T-adjacency-preserving map $\mathbf{F}: Z^d \longrightarrow Z^{d-1}$ if, and only if, T generates a space of dimensionality less than $d - 1$.

Necessity is established by a crowding argument and sufficiency by a sieve-like construction.

Attributions

Sections 10.3.A and D are adapted from Rosenberg (1975c) with the exception of the upper bound of Lemma 6, which is derived by Wong and Maddocks (1975), and Theorem 16, which is due to Bollman (1974, 1976). Section 10.3.B excerpts only the most easily quoted result from Lipton et al. (1975), who actually establish an analog of Theorem 7 for a memory structured as an "ancestor" tree (from which result Theorem 10 follows). Theorem 11 is adapted from Hennie (1966), and Theorem 12 is taken from Pippenger and Fischer (1977), both of which papers deal generally with retrieval problems that are easily computed with one type of tape structure but only arduously with another structure. Theorem 13 is taken from Fischer and Rosenberg (1968). Finally, Section 10.3.E is adapted from Amoroso and Epstein (1974). Aside from the open problems stated directly in the text, there remains the inviting challenge of finding an analog of Theorem 7 for maps from N^d into N^e.

10.4. ADDITIVE TRAVERSAL OF EXTENDIBLE ARRAYS

One of the most common regimens for accessing arrays is by traversing rows/columns or their multidimensional analogs. This method of access is encountered in such disparate applications as matrix multiplication and table searching. The familiar store-by-row type of nonextendible array storage mappings are superbly suited for traversal-oriented algorithms in that they store rows/columns and their analogs in arithmetic progressions so that traversing, say, a row reduces to a simple indexing operation. It is our purpose in this section to investigate the extent to which extendible array storage mappings can be designed to accommodate traversal-oriented array-processing algorithms in a like manner.

(4.1) Let $u^{(1)}, \ldots, u^{(d)}$ be the d unit vectors as in (1.6). The function $\mathbf{F}: N^d \longrightarrow N$ is *additive in direction i* if, for every $\pi \in N^d$, the sequence of integers $\mathbf{F}(\pi)$, $\mathbf{F}(\pi + u^{(i)})$, $\mathbf{F}(\pi + 2u^{(i)}), \ldots$ forms an arithmetic progression; that is, each is obtained from its predecessor by adding the constant $\delta_\pi \in N$. Additionally, $\mathbf{F}$ is *uniformly additive in direction i* if all the δ_π coincide, that is, if there is a constant $\delta \in N$ such that $\mathbf{F}(\pi + u^{(i)}) = \mathbf{F}(\pi) + \delta$ for all $\pi \in N^d$. The constants δ and δ_π are called *displacements*.

The store-by-row type of mappings we have been alluding to are easily seen to be uniformly additive in every direction. No such "total" additivity is achievable with esm's. In fact, when discussing esm's, we must distinguish between uniform and non-uniform additivity, and we need to specify the direction of additivity, as the following result demonstrates.

Theorem 18

(a) Either of the following two properties guarantees that the function $\mathbf{F}: N^d \longrightarrow N$ is not one-to-one, and hence not an esm: (i) **F** is uniformly additive in some direction; (ii) **F** is additive in directions i and $j \neq i$ ($i, j \in \{1, \ldots, d\}$). (b) For each $i \in \{1, \ldots, d\}$, there are esm's that are additive in direction i.

The impossibility of a uniformly additive esm can be seen as follows. Say that the function $\mathbf{F}: N^2 \longrightarrow N$ is additive along the rows of N^2, i.e., in direction 2. Each row of N^2 will consume, as images of F, all but a finite segment of some residue class modulo the (uniform) displacement δ. But there are infinitely many rows and only finitely many residue classes. We conclude that **F** cannot be one-to-one. Not dissimilar pigeonholing verifies the impossibility of a "doubly" additive esm. Say that $\mathbf{F}: N^2 \longrightarrow N$ is additive along direction i with displacement $\delta_\epsilon^{(i)}$, $i = 1, 2$. Then $\mathbf{F}(1, \delta_\epsilon^{(1)} + 1) = \mathbf{F}(\epsilon) + \delta_\epsilon^{(1)} \cdot \delta_\epsilon^{(2)} = \mathbf{F}(\delta_\epsilon^{(2)} + 1, 1)$, and **F** is not one-to-one. Clearly, these two-dimensional arguments generalize directly to arbitrary finite dimensionality. Finally, the existence of additive esm's can be established by construction. Note that it suffices to establish the existence of two-dimensional additive esm's, since a d-dimensional such esm can be constructed by composing a two-dimensional additive esm with an arbitrary $(d-1)$-dimensional esm as in $\mathbf{A}(\pi_1, \ldots, \pi_d) = \mathbf{B}(\pi_1, \mathbf{C}(\pi_2, \ldots, \pi_d))$. The remainder of this section will be devoted to developing techniques for constructing additive two-dimensional esm's. For further simplification, we shall look only at esm's that are additive in direction 2, that is, along rows.

(4.2) Let **b** and **d** be total functions from $N \longrightarrow N$. The $\langle \mathbf{b}, \mathbf{d} \rangle$*-function* is the function $\mathbf{F}: N^2 \longrightarrow N$ defined by

$$\mathbf{F}(i, j) = \mathbf{b}(i) + (j - 1) \cdot \mathbf{d}(i).$$

b and **d** are, respectively, **F**'s *base* and *displacement* functions.

Clearly, if a $\langle \mathbf{b}, \mathbf{d} \rangle$-function is one-to-one, then it is an additive esm (in direction 2), and we call it a $\langle \mathbf{b}, \mathbf{d} \rangle$*-esm*.

Theorem 19

The $\langle \mathbf{b}, \mathbf{d} \rangle$-function is one-to-one if, and only if, for all $i, i' \neq i \in N$, there is an $n \in N$ such that (a) n divides $\gcd(\mathbf{d}(i), \mathbf{d}(i'))$ and (b) $\mathbf{b}(i) \not\equiv \mathbf{b}(i') \pmod{n}$.

The theorem follows by direct calculation. We are now assured of a certain level of structural complexity in $\langle \mathbf{b}, \mathbf{d} \rangle$-esm's. For instance, we have immediately

Corollary 20

Any one of the following conditions guarantees that the $\langle \mathbf{b}, \mathbf{d} \rangle$-function is not one-to-one: (a) $\mathbf{b}(i) = \mathbf{d}(i)$ for at least two distinct $i \in N$. (b) $\mathbf{b}(i) = \mathbf{b}(i')$ for distinct $i, i' \in N$. (c) $\mathbf{d}(i) = c$ for some $c \in N$ and more than c values of i.

Let **A** be a $\langle \mathbf{b}, \mathbf{d} \rangle$-esm. Speaking very roughly, approximately $1/\mathbf{d}(i)$ of the available integer addresses are used in storing row i of N^2. This intuition can be rendered rigorous in order to prove the following limitation on **d**:

Theorem 21

For any $\langle \mathbf{b}, \mathbf{d} \rangle$-esm **A**, $\sum_{i=1}^{\infty} \mathbf{d}(i)^{-1} \leq 1$. If, moreover, **A** is onto, then $\sum_{i=1}^{\infty} \mathbf{d}(i)^{-1} = 1$.

A general method for constructing $\langle \mathbf{b}, \mathbf{d} \rangle$-esm's can be described easily in terms of a class of infinite rooted edge-labeled leaf-labeled trees.

(4.3) Let $r > 1$ (for *radix*) be a positive integer. A *degree r BD-tree* is an infinite rooted tree with infinitely many leaves. Each nonleaf of the tree has r sons; the branches to these sons are labeled uniquely by the integers $0, 1, 2, \ldots, r - 1$. The leaf nodes are labeled bijectively by the positive integers so that each $n \in N$ resides at precisely one leaf.

The name of *BD*-trees was motivated by the following.

(4.4) Let T be a degree-r *BD*-tree. We construct from T the pair of functions **b**, **d**, each from N to N. For each $i \in N$, let $\langle l_0, l_1, \ldots, l_{k-1} \rangle$ be the sequence of edge labels on the (unique, length-k) path in T from the root to the leaf labeled i. Then define

$$\mathbf{b}(i) = \sum_{j=0}^{k-1} l_j r^j - 1 \quad \text{and} \quad \mathbf{d}(i) = r^k.$$

The importance of *BD*-trees and their associated $\langle \mathbf{b}, \mathbf{d} \rangle$-functions [which arise by combining (4.4) with (4.2)] resides in the following result:

Theorem 22

Let the pair of functions $\langle \mathbf{b}, \mathbf{d} \rangle$ be constructed from a *BD*-tree as in (4.4). Then the $\langle \mathbf{b}, \mathbf{d} \rangle$-function is an esm that maps N^2 one-to-one onto N.

The proof of Theorem 22 builds on the same intuition as that of Theorem 21: One can view each r-way branching in the *BD*-tree as splitting one residue class modulo r^k (k is the depth of the node being split) into r residue classes modulo r^{k+1}.

We can finally use (4.3) and (4.4) to construct additive esm's. We let two families of examples suffice.

(4.5) For $r \in N - \{1\}$, the degree r *BD*-tree T_r is defined as follows. The leaf labeled 1 is attained by following edge 0 from the root, and, for $n > 1$, the leaf labeled n is reached by following the path labeled $\langle l_1, l_2, \ldots, l_k, 0 \rangle$ from the root, where $l_k l_{k-1} \cdots l_2 l_1$ is the $(r-1)$-adic representation of $n - 1$; that is, $n - 1 = \sum_{j=1}^{k} l_j (r-1)^{j-1}$.

See Figure 10.6.

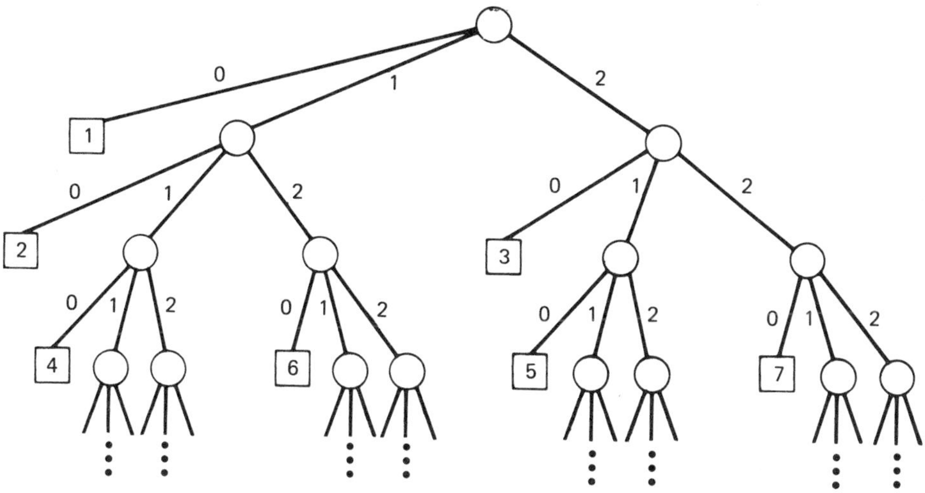

Figure 10.6. A portion of the BD-tree T_3 of (4.5).

The BD-trees just defined give rise to the following additive esm's.

(4.6) For $\langle i, j \rangle \in N \times N$ and $r \in N - \{1\}$,

$$\mathbf{ADD}_1(i, j; r) = \mathbf{b}(i) + (j - 1)\mathbf{d}(i),$$

where

$$\mathbf{b}(i) = \begin{cases} 1 & \text{if } i = 1 \\ \sum_{j=1}^{k} l_j r^{j-1} + 1 & \text{if } i > 1 \end{cases}$$

and $\mathbf{d}(i) = r^{k+1}$, the l_j and k being determined from T_r as in (4.5).

See Figure 10.7.

1	4	7	10	13	16	19	22	25	28
2	11	20	29	38	47	56	65	74	83
3	12	21	30	39	48	57	66	75	84
5	32	59	86	113	140	167	194	221	248
6	33	60	87	114	141	168	195	222	249
8	35	62	89	116	143	170	197	224	251
9	36	63	90	117	144	171	198	225	252
14	95	176	257	338	419	500	581	662	743
15	96	177	258	339	420	501	582	663	744
17	98	179	260	341	422	503	584	665	746

Figure 10.7. The array scheme of shape $\langle 10, 10 \rangle$ stored by the esm $\mathbf{ADD}_1(\cdot, \cdot; 3)$.

An alternative scheme can be described as follows.

(4.7) For $r \in N - \{1\}$, the degree-r BD-tree T_r^* is defined as follows. Consider any nonleaf node v of T_r^*. The nodes reached by following edges $0, \ldots, r-2$ from v are all leaves. The integers they contain are, in order, the $r-1$ smallest integers not assigned to shallower leaves. The son of v along edge $r-1$ is not a leaf.

See Figure 10.8.

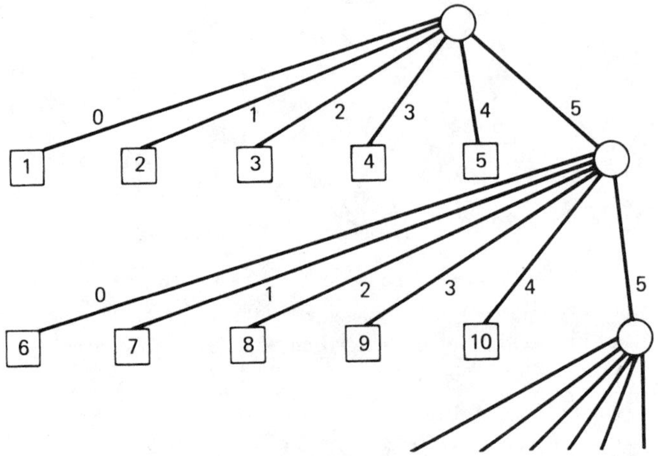

Figure 10.8. A portion of the BD-tree T_6^* of (4.7).

The BD-trees T_r^* can be shown to yield the following additive esm's:

(4.8) For $\langle i, j\rangle \in N \times N$ and $r \in N - \{1\}$,

$$\mathbf{ADD}_2(i, j; r) = \mathbf{b}(i) + (j-1)\mathbf{d}(i),$$

where $\mathbf{b}(i) = r^{k-1}\cdot(i + (k-1)(1-r))$ and $\mathbf{d}(i) = r^k$, with $k = \lceil i/(r-1)\rceil$.

See Figure 10.9.

1	7	13	19	25	31	37	43	49	55
2	8	14	20	26	32	38	44	50	56
3	9	15	21	27	33	39	45	51	57
4	10	16	22	28	34	40	46	52	58
5	11	17	23	29	35	41	47	53	59
6	42	78	114	150	186	222	258	294	330
12	48	84	120	156	192	228	264	300	336
18	54	90	126	162	198	234	270	306	342
24	60	96	132	168	204	240	276	312	348
30	66	102	138	174	210	246	282	318	354

Figure 10.9. The array scheme of shape $\langle 10, 10\rangle$ stored by the esm $\mathbf{ADD}_2(\cdot, \cdot; 6)$.

Attributions

Theorem 18 is obtained from the more general study of additive traversal by Rosenberg (1974b). (In that paper the general problem of linearizing partial orders that are unions of disjoint chains is considered.) Corollary 20 and the esm $\mathbf{ADD}_2$ appear in Rosenberg (1975a). The remainder of the section is taken from the in-depth study of additive esm's by Stockmeyer (1973). The reader interested in easily traversed extendible arrays should look also at Section 10.6 of this chapter.

10.5. EFFICIENCY OF STORAGE UTILIZATION

An extendible array storage mapping is allocating storage not only for the array currently being stored but also for all possible extensions of that array. It is, therefore, not surprising that esm's cannot utilize storage as well as can their nonextendible counterparts: An esm has no way of knowing whether the current array will be expanded by a series of adjunctions of rows (we speak about two-dimensional arrays for simplicity), by a series of adjunctions of columns, or by a series of adjunctions of "bands", each band comprising, say, two rows and three columns. Optimal utilization of storage would demand different storage layouts for the three depicted possibilities, but, as we noted, an extendible array storage mapping can lay out storage but once. The deficiencies in storage use by esm's are well illustrated by **SQ** (1.5). While **SQ** stores square arrays perfectly, allocating each $n \times n$ array to locations $1, \ldots, n^2$, it leaves sizable (and growing) gaps in storage when storing nonsquare arrays. In the worst case, **SQ** stores the p-position array $\{1\} \times \{1, \ldots, p\}$ in locations $1, 4, 9, \ldots, p^2$, thus "spreading" a p-position array over p^2 storage locations. Although **SQ** is typical of esm's in its leaving large gaps when storing arrays, how representative is it in the size of these gaps? How, indeed, would one measure the utilization of storage by extendible array storage mappings?

A. General Storage Utilization

The measure we shall study evaluates an esm's utilization of storage by its behavior on arrays of ever-increasing sizes.

(5.1) For any d-dimensional esm $\mathbf{A}$ and all $p \in N$,

$$\begin{aligned} \mathcal{S}(p; \mathbf{A}) &= \max\{\mathbf{A}(\pi) \mid \pi \in N^d \text{ resides in a } \langle p \rangle\text{-array}\} \\ &= \max\{\mathbf{A}(\pi) \mid \pi \in N^d \text{ and } \Pi(\pi) \leq p\}. \end{aligned}$$

Because of our convention that $\mathbf{A}(\epsilon) = 1$ for any esm $\mathbf{A}$, the *spread* function $\mathcal{S}$ measures the extent to which $\mathbf{A}$ spreads $\langle p \rangle$-arrays out in storage. It is not hard to verify that $\mathcal{S}(p; \mathbf{SQ}) = p^2$ for all p.

More interesting than the spread function are the *utilization* functions defined as follows:

(5.2) For $d, p \in N$,

$$\mathcal{U}_d(p) = \min\{\mathcal{S}(p; \mathbf{A}) \mid \mathbf{A} \text{ is a } d\text{-dimensional esm}\}.$$

The utilization function $\mathcal{U}_d$ sets an absolute limit on the efficiency of storage utilization by d-dimensional esm's. In fact we can evaluate this limit exactly. Moreover, for each dimensionality d, we can devise an esm $\mathbf{A}_d: N^d \longrightarrow N$ that achieves this limit in the sense that $\mathcal{S}(p; \mathbf{A}_d) = \mathcal{U}_d(p)$ for all p. These esm's are thus minimax optimal among esm's in their utilization of storage.

Theorem 23

(a) For each dimensionality $d \in N$,

$$\mathcal{U}_d(p) = \sum_{\substack{\langle k_1, \ldots, k_{d-1}\rangle \in N^{d-1} \\ \text{with } \Pi k_i \le p}} \lfloor p/\Pi k_i \rfloor = \Omega(p \cdot (\log p)^{d-1}).$$

(b) For each dimensionality $d \in N$, there is an esm $\mathbf{A}_d: N^d \longrightarrow N$ such that

$$\mathcal{S}(p: \mathbf{A}_d) = \mathcal{U}_d(p) = O(p \cdot (\log p)^{d-1}).$$

Part (a) of Theorem 23 is proved via the d-dimensional analog of the following two-dimensional argument. For each $k \in N$, the kth *column* $N \times \{k\}$ of $N \times N$ can contribute no more than $\lfloor p/k \rfloor$ positions to a $\langle p \rangle$-array, since each column $N \times \{i\}$ with $i < k$ must match the kth column's contribution (because our arrays are rectangular); moreover, a contribution of $\lfloor p/k \rfloor$ positions is feasible, as witnessed by the $\langle p \rangle$-array of shape $\langle k, \lfloor p/k \rfloor \rangle$. It follows that the number of positions in $N \times N$ that can take part in constructing $\langle p \rangle$-arrays is precisely $\sum_{k \le p} \lfloor p/k \rfloor$. Since every esm is one-to-one, $\mathcal{U}_2(p)$ can be no smaller than this quantity, which can easily be shown to grow like $p \cdot \log p$. The fact that $\mathcal{U}_2(p)$ does not exceed this lower bound is verified via part (b) of the theorem. Moving on to part (b), we claim that any esm that maps N^d one-to-one *onto* N and that linearizes the partial order, $\pi < \pi'$ iff $\Pi(\pi) < \Pi(\pi')$, utilizes storage optimally among esm's. To wit, any d-dimensional such esm $\mathbf{A}$ has storage spread

(5.3) $$\mathcal{S}(p; \mathbf{A}) = \#\{\pi \in N^d \mid \Pi(\pi) \le p\},$$

which quantity can be shown to be

$$\sum_{\substack{\langle k_1, \ldots, k_{d-1}\rangle \in N^{d-1} \\ \text{with } \Pi k_i \le p}} \lfloor p/\Pi k_i \rfloor$$

which in turn can be shown to grow like $p \cdot (\log p)^{d-1}$. One specific minimax optimal esm is given by the following:

(5.4) Letting $\delta_d(p) =$ (the number of $\langle n_1, \ldots, n_d \rangle \in N^d$ with $\Pi n_i = p$), we define

$$\mathbf{HYP}_d(\pi) = \sum_{k=1}^{\Pi(\pi)-1} \delta_d(k) + \left[\begin{array}{l}\text{the position of } \pi \text{ among factorizations of } \Pi(\pi) \\ \text{into } d \text{ parts, in reverse lexicographic order}\end{array}\right].$$

See Figure 10.10.

$\mathbf{HYP}_d$ stores N^d by linearizing the *hyperbolic* shell index $\mathbf{s}(\pi) = \Pi(\pi)$. The first term in the expression for $\mathbf{HYP}_d$ in (5.4) is the number of positions in shells lower than

1	3	5	8	10	14	16	20	23	27
2	7	13	19	26	34	40	49	57	65
4	12	22	33	44	56	69	82	94	109
6	18	32	48	64	81	99	117	137	156
9	25	43	63	86	108	130	155	180	205
11	31	55	80	107	136	165	194	224	256
15	39	68	98	129	164	200	236	271	309
17	47	79	116	154	193	235	277	321	364
21	54	93	135	179	223	270	320	371	420
24	62	106	153	204	255	308	363	419	478

Figure 10.10. The array scheme of shape $\langle 10, 10\rangle$ stored by the esm $\mathbf{HYP}_2$.

π's; the second term specifies π's position within its shell. A computationally superior expression for $\mathbf{HYP}_2$ issues from the following identity:

$$\sum_{k=1}^{p} \delta_2(k) = \sum_{k=1}^{p} \lfloor p/k \rfloor = 2\cdot \sum_{k=1}^{\lfloor\sqrt{p}\rfloor} \lfloor p/k \rfloor - \lfloor \sqrt{p}\, \rfloor^2. \tag{5.5}$$

Even though (5.5) cuts down dramatically the range of the summation needed to compute $\mathbf{HYP}_2$, it still leaves one with a lengthy computation to perform. If one is willing to forgo the optimal compactness of $\mathbf{HYP}_2$, then, at the cost of no more than a factor of 3 in spread, one can use the following esm in place of $\mathbf{HYP}_2$:

(5.6) For $\langle i, j\rangle \in N \times N$,

$$\mathbf{CONCAT}(i, j) = 2^{m(i,j)}(j + (i-1)2^{l(j)}) + l(j),$$

where $m(i, j) = \lceil \log (l(i) + l(j) + 1)\rceil$ and $l(x) = \lfloor \log x \rfloor$, $x = i, j$.

See Figure 10.11. The name "**CONCAT**" derives from our ability to regard the computation of **CONCAT** as the concatenation (in this order) of the minimal-length binary representation of i, the corresponding representation of j, and a short ($l(j)$-)bit string telling where i ends and j begins.

1	5	7	18	22	26	30	35	39	43
4	17	21	34	38	42	46	131	139	147
6	25	29	50	54	58	62	195	203	211
16	33	37	130	138	146	154	259	267	275
20	41	45	162	170	178	186	323	331	339
24	49	53	194	202	210	218	387	395	403
28	57	61	226	234	242	250	451	459	467
32	129	137	258	266	274	282	515	523	531
36	145	153	290	298	306	314	579	587	595
40	161	169	322	330	338	346	643	651	659

Figure 10.11. The array scheme of shape $\langle 10, 10\rangle$ stored by the esm **CONCAT**.

Theorem 24

CONCAT is an esm, and

$$\mathcal{S}(p; \mathbf{CONCAT}) \leq (2p + 1)\cdot \log p \leq 3 \sum_{k=1}^{p} \lfloor p/k \rfloor.$$

The fact that esm's like **SQ** and **DIAG** [(1.5) and (0.3)] and their higher-dimensional analogs have spreads that grow polynomially in p can be explained definitively:

Theorem 25

Say that the esm $\mathbf{A}: N^d \longrightarrow N$ linearizes the partial order, $\pi < \pi'$ iff $\mathbf{n}(\pi) < \mathbf{n}(\pi')$, where $\mathbf{n}$ is a norm on Euclidean d-space. Then, for all $p \in N$, $\mathcal{S}(p; \mathbf{A}) > \lfloor (p-1)/d \rfloor^d$.

Thus, **SQ** and **DIAG** have close to optimal spreads considering their origins, i.e., among norm-preserving esm's.

Norm-preserving esm's are not the only readily specified class of esm's that cannot attain optimal storage utilization. Additive esm's suffer similarly, but not with such severity. Call a $\langle \mathbf{b}, \mathbf{d} \rangle$-esm *standard* if $\mathbf{b}(i) \leq \mathbf{d}(i)$ for all i [see (4.2)].

Theorem 26

(a) For any standard $\langle \mathbf{b}, \mathbf{d} \rangle$-esm $\mathbf{A}: N \times N \longrightarrow N$,

$$\liminf_{p \to \infty} \frac{\mathcal{S}(p; \mathbf{A})}{p \cdot \log p} = \infty.$$

(b) For every $e > 0$, there is a constant $c_e > 0$ and a standard $\langle \mathbf{b}, \mathbf{d} \rangle$-esm $\mathbf{A}_e: N \times N \longrightarrow N$ such that

$$\mathcal{S}(p; \mathbf{A}_e) \leq c_e \cdot p \cdot (\log p)^{1+e}.$$

B. Arrays of Favored Shapes

In spite of the sizable difference between the spreads of $\mathbf{HYP}_2$ and **CONCAT** on the one hand and **SQ** on the other, it is not unusual to encounter circumstances wherein the last esm would be far preferable to either of the former ones. Although **SQ** stores certain arrays very inefficiently, it stores square arrays perfectly and nearly square arrays quite well. $\mathbf{HYP}_2$ and **CONCAT**, in contrast, lay out all arrays with almost equal mediocrity. Should one know that the arrays his algorithms will process are likely to be (nearly) square, he would most assuredly opt for **SQ**'s perfect storage of square arrays over the other esms' uniform mediocrity. But what of another hypothetical user who, no less than the fellow with growing square arrays, can predict how his arrays are likely to grow but whose arrays will be decidedly nonsquare (e.g., $n^2 \times n$)? This user will be glad to know that one can construct analogs of **SQ** for *any* well-defined pattern of array expansions. Moreover, with only minor degradation of performance on well-stored arrays, esm's can "favor" any finite set of expansion patterns. Even more, with only negligible additional degradation in performance, this pattern-favoring esm can come within a constant multiple of $\mathbf{HYP}_d$'s behavior on all arrays that do not conform to any of the specified patterns. The apparatus needed to construct these efficient esm's will be developed now.

(5.7) A d-dimensional array *shape* S is a d-tuple of functions $S = \langle \mathbf{h}_1, \ldots, \mathbf{h}_d \rangle$, where each $\mathbf{h}_i: N \longrightarrow N$ is total, nondecreasing, and unbounded and where there is no $n \in N$ for which all $\mathbf{h}_i(n) = \mathbf{h}_i(n + 1)$.

Although this notion of array shape differs from the notion of the *shape* of an array scheme in (1.1), there is an intimate connection between the two that justifies our abuse of language:

(5.8) The array scheme of shape $\langle n_1, \ldots, n_d \rangle$—in the sense of (1.1)—*belongs* to the array shape $\langle \mathbf{h}_1, \ldots, \mathbf{h}_d \rangle$—in the sense of (5.7)—if there is an integer $k \in N$ for which $\mathbf{h}_i(k) = n_i$ for each $i \in \{1, \ldots, d\}$.

An array shape thus specifies a family $\{A_k\}_{k \in N}$ of arrays, each A_k having shape $\langle \mathbf{h}_1(k), \ldots, \mathbf{h}_d(k) \rangle$; $\mathbf{h}_i(k)$ is the *height* of the kth array in the ith dimension. This family is guaranteed to be infinite since the $\mathbf{h}_i$ are unbounded (hence have infinite range); all the A_k are distinct since some $\mathbf{h}_i(n) \neq \mathbf{h}_i(n + 1)$ for each n; the A_k are nested, i.e., $A_k \subset A_{k+1}$, since the $\mathbf{h}_i$ are nondecreasing; and the "limit" of this nested family is all of N^d since all the $\mathbf{h}_i$ are unbounded. As an aid to the reader, we include Table 10.1, which describes some two-dimensional array shapes; for simplicity we denote a two-dimensional array shape by $\langle \mathbf{h}, \mathbf{w} \rangle$ for $\langle$*height*, *width*$\rangle$.

Table 10.1. Some Array *Shapes* and Their Formal Analogs

Informal Specification	*Formal Specification*
Square arrays	$\mathbf{h}(n) = n,\ \ \mathbf{w}(n) = n$
Even-sided square arrays	$\mathbf{h}(n) = 2n,\ \mathbf{w}(n) = 2n$
$n \times n^2$ arrays	$\mathbf{h}(n) = n,\ \ \mathbf{w}(n) = n^2$
$2^n \times \lceil \log(n + 1) \rceil$ arrays	$\mathbf{h}(n) = 2^n,\ \mathbf{w}(n) = \lceil \log(n + 1) \rceil$

We now have a generalization of the *square* arrays that **SQ** stores perfectly. What, however, does "perfectly" mean?

(5.9) Let $\mathbf{A}: N^d \longrightarrow N$ be an esm.

(a) $\mathbf{A}$ stores the array $A \subset N^d$ with *bound* $b \in N$ if $\max \mathbf{A}(A) \leq b \cdot (\# A)$.

(b) $\mathbf{A}$ is *b-linear* ($b \in N$) on the d-dimensional array shape S if $\mathbf{A}$ stores every array belonging to shape S with bound b.

(c) $\mathbf{A}$ is *compact* on the d-dimensional array shape S if $\mathbf{A}$ is b-linear on S for some $b \in N$.

Our informal assertion about **SQ** can now be formalized: **SQ** is 1-linear on array shape $\langle \mathbf{h}, \mathbf{w} \rangle$, where $\mathbf{h}(n) = \mathbf{w}(n) = n$. Our claim that analogs of **SQ** can be found for any array shape can similarly be formalized:

Theorem 27

For any array shape S, there is an esm $\mathbf{A}_S$ that is 1-linear on S.

In fact, the array shape S gives rise naturally to a shell index $\mathbf{s}_S$; any esm that linearizes the induced partial order, $\pi < \pi'$ iff $\mathbf{s}_S(\pi) < \mathbf{s}_S(\pi')$, will satisfy the theorem. Let $S = \langle \mathbf{h}_1, \ldots, \mathbf{h}_d \rangle$. Then, for $\pi \in N^d$,

$$(5.10) \quad \mathbf{s}_S(\pi) = \max\{\text{least } k \text{ with } \mathbf{h}_1(k) \geq \pi_1; \; \text{least } k \text{ with } \mathbf{h}_2(k) \geq \pi_2; \ldots; \; \text{least } k \text{ with } \mathbf{h}_d(k) \geq \pi_d\}$$
$$= \text{least } k \text{ such that } \pi \in \text{the array of shape } \langle \mathbf{h}_1(k), \ldots, \mathbf{h}_d(k) \rangle.$$

In fact, the esm's that linearize these shells needn't be that forbidding computationally if the $\mathbf{h}_i$ and $\mathbf{s}_S$ aren't. In two dimensions, for instance, let $S = \langle \mathbf{h}, \mathbf{w} \rangle$. The following esm is 1-linear on shape S:

$$(5.11) \quad \mathbf{A}_S(i, j) = \mathbf{h}(s)\cdot(j-1) + \mathbf{h}(s-1)\cdot(\mathbf{w}(s-1) - \min\{j, \mathbf{w}(s-1)\}) + i, \quad \text{where } s = \mathbf{s}_S(i, j).$$

Some concrete instances of (5.11) may be of interest; compare the following esm **SQU** with **SQ** (1.5):

(5.12) Let $\mathbf{h}(n) = \mathbf{w}(n) = n$. The devised esm is given by

$$\mathbf{SQU}(i, j) = (m-1)^2 - (m-1)\cdot\min(j, m-1) + m\cdot(j-1) + i,$$

where $m = \max(i, j)$.

See Figure 10.12.

1	3	7	13	21	31	43	57	73	91
2	4	8	14	22	32	44	58	74	92
5	6	9	15	23	33	45	59	75	93
10	11	12	16	24	34	46	60	76	94
17	18	19	20	25	35	47	61	77	95
26	27	28	29	30	36	48	62	78	96
37	38	39	40	41	42	49	63	79	97
50	51	52	53	54	55	56	64	80	98
65	66	67	68	69	70	71	72	81	99
82	83	84	85	86	87	88	89	90	100

Figure 10.12. The array scheme of shape $\langle 10, 10 \rangle$ stored by the esm **SQU**.

(5.13) Let $\mathbf{h}(n) = n$ and $\mathbf{w}(n) = n^2$. The derived esm is given by

$$\mathbf{NBYNSQ}(i, j) = (r-1)^3 - (r-1)\cdot\min(j, (r-1)^2) + r\cdot(j-1) + i,$$

where $r = \max(i, \lceil\sqrt{j}\,\rceil)$.

See Figure 10.13.

1	3	5	7	13	16	19	22	25	37
2	4	6	8	14	17	20	23	26	38
9	10	11	12	15	18	21	24	27	39
28	29	30	31	32	33	34	35	36	40
65	66	67	68	69	70	71	72	73	74
126	127	128	129	130	131	132	133	134	135
217	218	219	220	221	222	223	224	225	226
344	345	346	347	348	349	350	351	352	353
513	514	515	516	517	518	519	520	521	522
730	731	732	733	734	735	736	737	738	739

Figure 10.13. The array scheme of shape $\langle 10, 10\rangle$ stored by the esm **NBYNSQ**.

By combining Theorem 27 with the following lemma, we can devise esm's that are compact on any finite collection of array shapes:

Lemma 28

Let $\mathbf{A}_1, \ldots, \mathbf{A}_k$ be d-dimensional esm's. Define the esm $\mathbf{A}: N^d \longrightarrow N$ by

(5.14) $$\mathbf{A}(\pi) = \min_l k\cdot\mathbf{A}_l(\pi) + l - k.$$

For all $\pi \in N^d$, $\mathbf{A}(\pi) \leq k\cdot\min_l \mathbf{A}_l(\pi)$.

Basically, **A** makes each $\mathbf{A}_l$ use only addresses in the residue class $l \bmod k$; the address that **A** assigns to π is then the smallest address assigned by the modified $\mathbf{A}_l$'s. It is obvious, since **A** operates on esm's rather than directly on shapes, that one can add **HYP** to the collection of esm's to be *dovetailed* via (5.14) and thereby construct an esm that is at once compact on all the desired array shapes and close to minimax optimal on arrays of unfavored shapes.

Regarding constants of linearity, one has in fact more leeway than (5.14) might suggest at first blush. A direct application of (5.14) to the three esm's **SQU**, **NBYNSQ**, and **HYP**, for example, would result in an esm that stores square arrays 3-linearly, $n \times n^2$ arrays 3-linearly, and all other arrays with a spread of roughly $3\cdot\mathfrak{U}_2(p)$. See Figure 10.14. If one expects most arrays of interest to be square, the dilation factor of 3 might be deemed unacceptable. Such a situation needn't cause despair. One could first combine **NBYNSQ** with **HYP** using (5.14) and then combine **SQU** with the resulting esm. The esm obtained by this two-level process would store square arrays 2-linearly, $n \times n^2$ arrays 4-linearly, and all other arrays with a spread of roughly $4\cdot\mathfrak{U}_2(p)$. Compare Figure 10.15 with Figure 10.14. In fact, one can describe quite

1	7	14	20	30	42	48	60	69	81
4	10	17	23	41	50	59	68	77	113
12	16	25	35	44	53	62	71	80	116
18	31	34	46	70	98	101	104	107	119
27	52	55	58	73	103	139	181	218	221
33	79	82	85	88	106	142	184	232	286
45	112	115	118	121	124	145	187	235	289
51	141	154	157	160	163	166	190	238	292
63	162	199	202	205	208	211	214	241	295
72	186	250	253	256	259	262	265	268	298

Figure 10.14. The array scheme of shape $\langle 10, 10\rangle$ stored by an equally weighted dovetailing of the esm's **SQU**, **NBYNSQ**, and **HYP**.

1	5	13	25	40	56	64	80	92	108
3	7	15	27	43	63	78	90	102	150
9	11	17	29	45	65	82	94	106	154
19	21	23	31	47	67	91	119	142	158
33	35	37	39	49	69	93	121	153	189
44	53	55	57	59	71	95	123	155	191
60	75	77	79	81	83	97	125	157	193
68	101	103	105	107	109	111	127	159	195
84	131	133	135	137	139	141	143	161	197
96	165	167	169	171	173	175	177	179	199

Figure 10.15. The array scheme of shape $\langle 10, 10\rangle$ stored by an esm that dovetails **SQU**, **NBYNSQ**, and **HYP** according to the prescription $\langle$**SQU**, $\langle$**NBYNSQ**, **HYP**$\rangle\rangle$, thus favoring **SQU**.

precisely how to adapt (5.14) to "favor" differentially the set of esm's to be dovetailed. One constructs a rooted tree with one esm at each leaf in such a way that (a) every nonleaf node has at least two sons, and (b) the more an esm is to be favored, the closer is its leaf to the root. The esm's are then combined via (5.14) according to the usual rules for "evaluating" such a tree: the leaves "are" esm's *ab initio;* a node "becomes" an esm when all of its sons "are" esm's; the esm it "becomes" is the one obtained by combining all of its sons using (5.14). The second technique for combining **SQU**, **NBYNSQ**, and **HYP** (Figure 10.15) issues from the following tree:

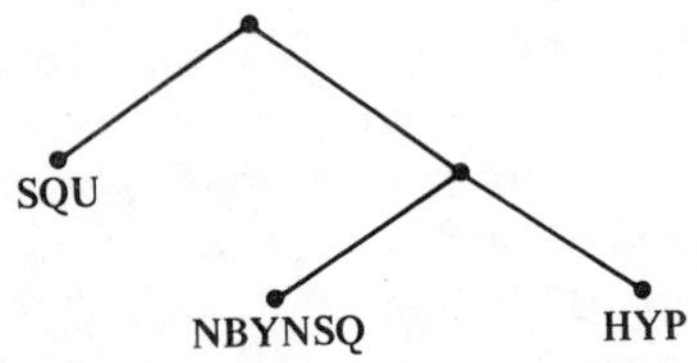

There is, thus, a way to decrease **A**'s constant of linearity on some shapes at the expense of others. We do not know whether this "conservation of dilation" is necessary: there may be techniques for super-favoring one shape without penalizing others. We know only (by detailed study of arrays whose sizes are powers of 2) that one cannot super-favor all k shapes at once. The following result summarizes the preceding discussion:

Theorem 29

(a) For any k d-dimensional array shapes $S_1, \ldots, S_k$, there is an esm **A** that is $(k+u)$-linear on each shape S_i, where $u = 1$ or 0 according as **A**, respectively, does or does not achieve the $O(p \cdot (\log p)^{d-1})$ bound on unfavored arrays. (b) For every k, there exist array shapes $S_1, \ldots, S_k$ such that any esm which is compact on all the S_i must be c-linear on one of them for some $c > (k-1)/2$.

It goes without saying that the residue-class technique of (5.14) cannot be used to combine infinite sets of array shapes. Will any technique permit combining an infinite set of shapes? We now formalize this question:

(5.15) Two array shapes S_1 and S_2 are *distinguishable* if there is an esm which is compact on one of S_1, S_2 but not on the other.

For example, the array shapes $S_1 = \langle \mathbf{h}_1(n) = n, \mathbf{w}_1(n) = n \rangle$ and $S_2 = \langle \mathbf{h}_2(n) = n, \mathbf{w}_2(n) = n^2 \rangle$ are distinguishable, while S_1 and $S_3 = \langle \mathbf{h}_3(n) = n + a, \mathbf{w}_3(n) = n \rangle$ are not, irrespective of the value of the constant a.

Problem

Does there exist an esm **A** and an infinite collection $\mathcal{S}$ of pairwise distinguishable array shapes such that **A** is compact on every shape in $\mathcal{S}$?

We can give only a minor indication of how one might settle this question in the negative:

Lemma 30

Let $\mathbf{A}: N^2 \longrightarrow N$ be an esm. For every $k \in N$, there is an array $A \subset N^2$ of size 2^k such that $\max \mathbf{A}(A) > k \cdot 2^{k-1}$.

Theorem 31

No esm is compact on every array shape.

Proof: It clearly suffices to consider two-dimensional arrays and esm's, for such arrays can trivially be padded out to arbitrary dimensionality by replacing A by $A \times \{1\}^d$. Consider, therefore, an arbitrary two-dimensional esm **A**. Let $A_1, A_2, \ldots$ be the sequence of power-of-two-position arrays guaranteed by Lemma 30: Each A_k has 2^k positions, and $\max \mathbf{A}(A_k) > k \cdot 2^{k-1}$; say that each A_i has shape $\langle 2^{a_i}, 2^{b_i} \rangle$. Now, with no loss of generality, we may assume that $a_i \leq a_{i+1}$ and $b_i \leq b_{i+1}$ for all i, for if this is not the case, we can filter out an infinite subsequence of the A_i that are nested in this sense. We must now consider two cases.

Say first that there are infinitely many distinct a_i and infinitely many distinct b_i in the sequence of A_i-shapes. Then the pair of functions $\langle \mathbf{h}(n) = 2^{a_n}, \mathbf{w}(n) = 2^{b_n} \rangle$ is an array shape; moreover, **A** is not compact on this array shape since, by construction, max $\mathbf{A}(A_k) > k \cdot 2^{k-1} = (1/2) \cdot \text{size}(A_k) \cdot \log \text{size}(A_k)$ for each A_k belonging to the shape.

Alternatively, one of the sequences—say the b_i—is infinite, while the other is finite. (One must be infinite since the A_i are all distinct.) Filter the sequence $\langle a_i, b_i \rangle$ so that in the resulting infinite subsequence $b_{i+1} > 2^{b_i}$, so that $b_n > 2^{2^n}$. Consider now the infinite sequence of arrays $A'_1, A'_2, \ldots,$ each A'_i of shape $\langle 2^{a_n+n}, 2^{b_n} \rangle$ (using the new $\langle a_n, b_n \rangle$ sequence). Now, one verifies easily that the pair of functions $\langle \mathbf{h}(n) = 2^{a_n+n}, \mathbf{w}(n) = 2^{b_n} \rangle$ is an array shape. Moreover **A** is not compact on this shape: to wit, on the one hand, A'_n has size$(A'_n) = 2^n \cdot 2^{a_n+b_n}$ positions. On the other hand, since each A'_n contains the array of shape $\langle 2^{a_n}, 2^{b_n} \rangle$, we know by choice of the original arrays A_i that max $\mathbf{A}(A'_n) > (1/2) \cdot (a_n + b_n) 2^{a_n+b_n} > 2^{2^n-1} \cdot (2^{a_n+b_n})$, which grows with n faster than any constant multiple of size(A'_n).

In either event, there is an array shape specifying only power-of-two-position arrays that **A** does not store compactly.

Attributions

Most of the material in this section is taken from Rosenberg (1975b) and in fact summarizes that paper. The esm **CONCAT** in (5.6) and its behavioral assessment in Theorem 24 are due to Stockmeyer (1973), as is the material on storage utilization by additive esm's encapsulated in Theorem 26. The notion of distinguishability in (5.15) was suggested by J. S. Lew in a conversation concerning how one could formalize the notion of *distinct* array shapes. Finally, Theorem 31 is original, which fact accounts for the inclusion of a complete proof of the theorem.

10.6. LINKED ALLOCATION SCHEMES

In the absence of special information about the patterns of expansions of input arrays, extendible array storage mappings inevitably manage storage poorly. It is worthwhile, therefore, to investigate allocation schemes that do not employ computed access, in the hope that such schemes may have more modest storage demands, together with acceptable time of access. (The time of access for an esm will be viewed as unity, since accessing an array position involves only a single function evaluation.) In the final two sections we shall be concerned with such alternative schemes. In the current section, we shall consider three *pure linking* strategies for storing extendible arrays that exploit successively more information about the structure of arrays. In Section 10.7 we shall combine elements of computed access and linked allocation to arrive at so-called external hashing schemes for extendible arrays.

Although linked allocation schemes tie up dramatically fewer storage locations when storing extendible arrays than do esm's (they need reserve only one location per array position), the "locations" used by linking schemes are larger than those used by esm's. To facilitate comparison of the relative storage demands of the storage schemes we have considered and shall be considering, we shall crystallize our view of the storage in which our arrays will reside. We view the host memory as being composed of addressable units called *words*, each sufficient in size to hold an address (and, thereby, serve as a pointer) or to hold some encoding of the coordinates of an array position (to be used as a key when searching for a position). We shall always assume that the data items stored at the positions of our arrays each occupies a block of δ words. Thus, *any* allocation of a p-position array consumes δp words. The storage demand of an esm in words is obtained directly by replacing each occurrence of p by δp in the expression for its storage demand in locations.

A. Linear Lists

The most straightforward method of linking array positions ignores the fact that the positions come from an array. As array positions are encountered, they are chained together in a linear list. The technique proceeds as follows. Here and in the sequel, the term *key* refers to the image of an array position π under some one-to-one mapping. Keys are used to identify positions during searches. The box "$\square$" indicates completion of the operation.

Algorithm 1 Access/Insertion in a Linear List

Input. Array position π, its key $\mathbf{k}(\pi)$, and (for insertion) its associated data item.

Location Structure. Each location is a contiguous block of $\delta + 2$ words. δ words hold the data, 1 word holds the current key, and 1 word points to this location's successor in the list. See Figure 10.16.

Procedure.
(1) Access the first location of the list.
(2) If the sought location does not yet exist, obtain a new location from the storage allocator, chain it to the just-visited location [or, if we come from step (1), make it the list head], and store π and its associated data here. $\square$
(3) If the sought location exists, compare its key with $\mathbf{k}(\pi)$. If the keys are not identical, access (using the current link) the current location's successor. Go to step (2).
(4) If the keys are equal, access the current data item or, in the case of an insertion, replace the data item. $\square$

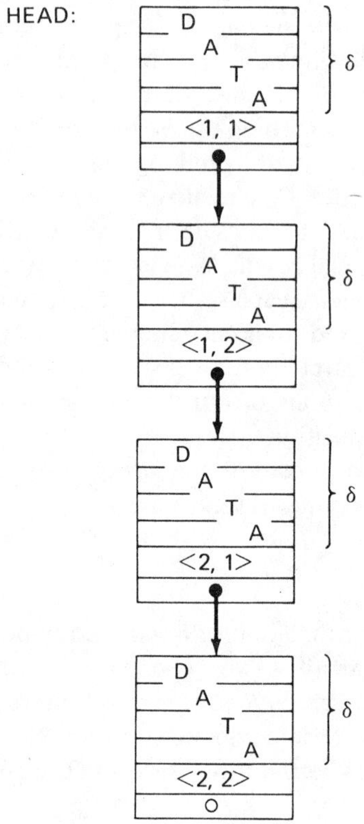

Figure 10.16. The array scheme of shape ⟨2, 2⟩ stored in a linear list.

The extendibility of linear-list allocation schemes is obvious and so also is the evaluation of such schemes' consumption of time and storage. We measure the consumption of the latter quantity in terms of the number of words that must be set aside to store arrays having p or fewer positions. The consumption of time is measured in terms of both the worst-case and expected number of locations that must be accessed in the course of accessing/inserting into an array of p or fewer positions stored according to Algorithm 1. Storage consumption is trivially p locations. Time is also easy to estimate.

Theorem 32

When a p-position array is stored according to Algorithm 1, the worst-case and expected times to access/insert an array position into the resulting p-location linear list are, respectively, p probes and $(p + 1)/2$ probes.

The dramatic savings in storage over esm's comes at a heavy cost in access time.

B. Balanced Search Trees

A first cut at retaining the storage savings of linear lists while improving the poor timing behavior of such lists is to exploit any of a large number of possible total orders on N^d to reorganize our linear lists into balanced search trees. To illustrate one available order (although any will suffice in what follows), say that $\mathbf{k}(\pi) = \pi$ and that $\pi < \pi'$ when there is an integer $l \in \{1, \ldots, d\}$ such that $\pi_i = \pi'_i$ for $i < l$ and $\pi_l < \pi'_l$. (This is lexicographic order.) At the cost of slightly expanded location size, we shall now enjoy much improved time of access.

Algorithm 2 Access/Insertion in a Binary Search Tree

Input. Array position π, its key $\mathbf{k}(\pi)$, and (for insertion) its associated data item.

Location Structure. Each location is a contiguous block of $\delta + 3$ words. δ words hold data; 1 word holds the current key; and 2 words point to this location's successors in the tree. See Figure 10.17.

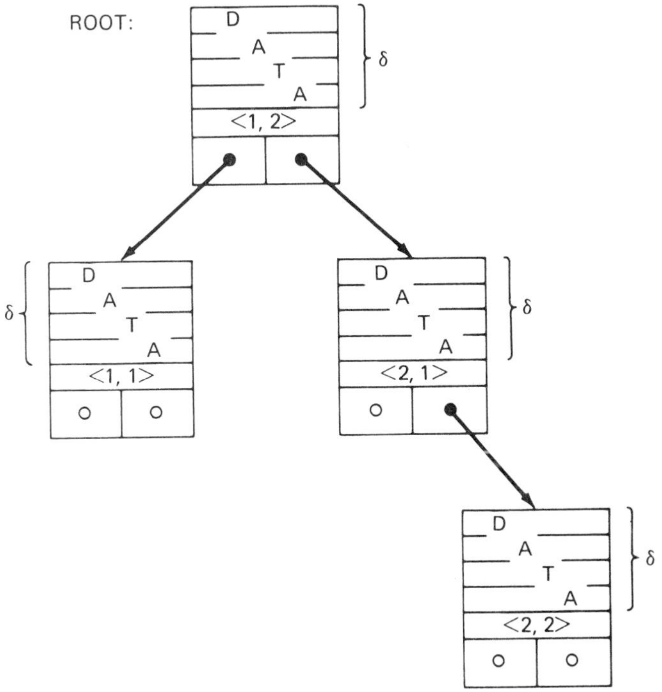

Figure 10.17. The array scheme of shape $\langle 2, 2 \rangle$ stored in a balanced search tree.

Procedure. (1) Access the root location of the tree.

(2) If the sought location does not yet exist, obtain a new location from the storage allocator; chain it to the just-visited location via the just-followed link [or, if we come from step (1), make it the root]; store π and its associated data here; and *Rebalance* the tree. □

(3) If the sought location exists, compare its key with $\mathbf{k}(\pi)$. If $\mathbf{k}(\pi)$ is less than (resp., greater than) the current key, access the left-link (resp., right-link) successor of the current location. Go to step (2).

(4) If the keys are equal, access the current data item (or, in the case of an insertion, replace the data item). □

Rebalance. Since rebalancing such trees requires a reasonable amount of detailed bookkeeping, we shall merely refer the reader to Section 6.2.3 of Knuth (1973) for a description of access/insert with rebalancing.

Theorem 33

When a p-position array is stored according to Algorithm 2, the worst-case and expected times to access/insert an array position into the resulting p-position tree are both constant multiples of $\log(p + 1)$.

The specific multiples in the theorem depend on whether we access or insert and on whether we seek the worst-case or expected time.

At the cost of a more complicated data structure, slightly larger locations, and more costly processing per step, we thus retain the good storage utilization of linear lists and increase timing efficiency exponentially (from roughly p to roughly $\log p$).

C. Orthogonal Lists

If one expects to process arrays by repeated traversal, the two list-oriented allocation schemes just described are quite unsatisfactory, since they ignore completely the adjacency structure in arrays. The following list structure exploits the structure of arrays in much the same way as esm's do: the "logical" destination of an array position depends only on the "logical" residence of position ϵ. Accordingly, these orthogonal lists can be implemented without reference to keys.

Algorithm 3 *Access/Insert in an Orthogonal List*

Input. Array position $\pi \in N^d$ and (for insertion) its associated data.

Location Structure. Each location is a contiguous block of $\delta + d$ words. δ words hold the data; each of the remaining d words points to one of this location's d successors in the list (one successor for each direction). See Figure 10.18.

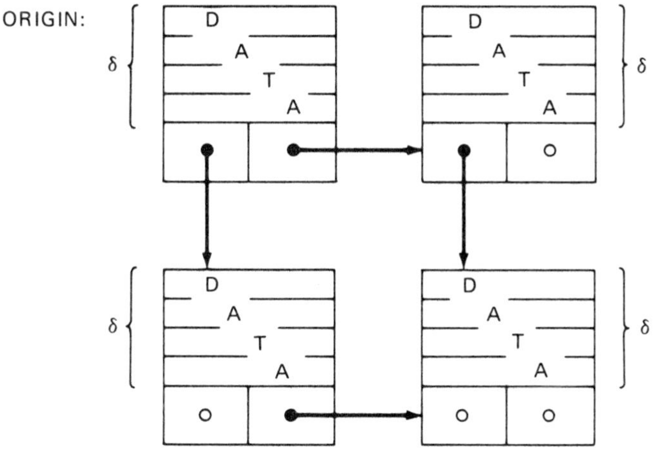

Figure 10.18. The array scheme of shape $\langle 2, 2 \rangle$ stored in an orthogonal list.

Procedure. (1) Access the "origin" location of the list.

(2) Follow, in some arbitrary order, $\pi_1 - 1$ direction-1 successors, $\pi_2 - 1$ direction-2 successors, . . . , $\pi_d - 1$ direction-d successors. If at any point in this "walk" a sought successor is missing, obtain a new location from the storage allocator and chain it to all its (d, at most) predecessors. When the prescribed "walk" is completed, access the data at the attained location or, in the case of an insertion, insert π's data there. □

Orthogonal lists are designed, as we have noted, with traversal in mind, and they are obviously quite efficient for traversal-oriented applications. However, they are almost as bad as linear lists when used for long sequences of independent accesses.

Theorem 34

Let the p-position array $A \subset N^d$ of shape π be stored as an orthogonal list. The worst-case and expected times to access an element of A in the p-location list are, respectively, $\Sigma(\pi) - d + 1$ and $(\Sigma(\pi) - d + 2)/2$. Thus, in the worst case (a "linear" array), these quantities are p and $(p + 1)/2$, respectively, and in the best case (a "hypercubic" array), these quantities are $dp^{1/d} - d + 1$ and $(dp^{1/d} - d + 2)/2$, respectively.

Attributions

The three data structures discussed in this section are described by Knuth (1968). The use of linear lists and balanced trees in searching algorithms is discussed in Knuth (1973), and the costs of these data structures, as exposed in Theorems 32 and 33, are derived. Theorem 34 is original; its proof has been left to the reader since it yields readily to standard techniques.

10.7. ALLOCATION SCHEMES USING HASHING

The storage techniques presented thus far leave in an uncomfortable position the user whose array processing takes the form of many independent probes. At the one extreme, he can opt for the timing efficiency of esm's, but only at the cost of their poor utilization of storage; at the other extreme, he can opt for the compact storage of linked allocation schemes, but only at the cost of expected access time that grows as his array does (at least as the log of the array's size); and we have presented no method for compromising between these extremes. Fortunately, satisfactory compromises can be found if one combines the philosophies underlying computed-access and linked allocation schemes. We shall now discuss a genre of compromise schemes that hash array positions into buckets which are organized as linked lists. We shall exhibit a family of such *external* hashing schemes that are conservative of storage, all the while affording one *constant* expected access time. And we shall discuss several results which indicate that such hashing schemes can degenerate into pessimal (timing or storage use) performance unless designed with care.

Informally, our hashing schemes will operate as follows. There will be a hash function $\mathbf{H}: N^d \longrightarrow N$ which differs from an esm only in that it need not be one-to-one. For the sake of definiteness, we shall organize our buckets as balanced search trees (which, recall, had the best access time of the three linked structures described in Section 10.6). We envisage storage as partitioned into a set W of individual words, indexed by N, and a set B of contiguous blocks of $\delta + 3$ words each (δ words for data, 1 word for a key, and 2 words for links as in Algorithm 2). To access (insert) array position π, we evaluate $\mathbf{H}(\pi)$ to determine the bucket (= tree) in which π is (to be) resident: $\mathbf{H}(\pi)$ is the address of that word in W that contains a pointer to the root of π's tree. (See Figure 10.17.) We then use Algorithm 2 to find π within its bucket. The expected and worst-case times to access/insert position π are composed of the time to evaluate $\mathbf{H}(\pi)$ plus the time to find/insert π in the balanced search tree. The storage consumed by the hashing scheme when storing p-position arrays is $(\delta + 3)p$ words for trees plus however many words $\mathbf{H}$ uses when storing such arrays. To present our results, we shall now formalize the preceding discussion.

Since specifying the hash function $\mathbf{H}$ serves to describe completely the hashing scheme being considered, we shall identify our hashing schemes with their hash functions.

(7.1) A d-dimensional ($d \in N$) *extendible* (*array*) *hashing scheme*, *ehs*, for short, is a total function $\mathbf{H}: N^d \longrightarrow N$ with $\mathbf{H}(\epsilon) = 1$.

As usual we shall be concerned only with dimensionalities $d > 1$.

Our measure of the utilization of storage by ehs's will be the number of bucket-addresses affected by **H** when storing arrays of various sizes.

(7.2) For any d-dimensional ehs **H** and all $p \in N$,

$$\beta(p; \mathbf{H}) = \max\{\mathbf{H}(\pi) \mid \pi \in N^d \text{ resides in a } \langle p\rangle\text{-array}\}$$
$$= \max\{\mathbf{H}(\pi) \mid \pi \in N^d \text{ and } \Pi(\pi) \leq p\}.$$

β is the hash-function analog of the spread measure $\mathcal{S}$ for esm's (5.1). We shall focus on the measure β rather than on any measure of total storage consumption because of the fixed difference of $(\delta + 3)p$ between the two quantities.

To measure the access behavior of **H**, we recall that the worst-case and expected times to access/insert a node in a n-node balanced search tree is a modest multiple of $\log(n + 1)$ (Theorem 33). Since all of our results in this section, save one, will be concerned only with the rate of growth of our complexity measures, we can ignore these multiples and assess the cost of accessing array position π when the ehs **H** stores the array A ($\pi \in A$) as follows (we equate, henceforth, the costs of accessing and inserting):

(7.3) $$\mathbf{Access}(\pi; A; \mathbf{H}) = \log(1 + \#(A \cap \mathbf{H}^{-1}(\mathbf{H}(\pi)))).$$

The right-hand quantity is just the log of 1 plus the population of π's bucket when **H** stores A. This measure of the cost of accessing a single position affords us a device for measuring **H**'s access efficiency.

(7.4) (a) Worst-case time of access:

$$\alpha(p; \mathbf{H}) = \text{worst access time when } \mathbf{H} \text{ stores } \langle p\rangle\text{-arrays}$$
$$= \max\{\mathbf{Access}(\pi; A; \mathbf{H}) \mid \pi \text{ resides in the } \langle p\rangle\text{-array } A\}.$$

(b) Maximum expected time of access:

$$\bar{\alpha}(p; \mathbf{H}) = \text{the expected time to access a position of that } \langle p\rangle\text{-array whose expected access time under } \mathbf{H} \text{ is maximal}$$
$$= \max\{(1/\#A) \sum_{\pi \in A} \mathbf{Access}(\pi; A; \mathbf{H}) \mid A \text{ is a } \langle p\rangle\text{-array}\}.$$

Note that although $\bar{\alpha}$ averages access times over positions of each array, it does *not* average over arrays.

To place the coming results, especially the lower bounds, in context, we remark that there exist d-dimensional esm's **H** with $\beta(p; \mathbf{H}) = O(p \cdot (\log p)^{d-1})$ and that *every* ehs **H** has $\bar{\alpha}(p; \mathbf{H}) = O(\log p)$ (Theorems 23b and 33, respectively).

We shall begin our survey of ehs's by exhibiting a family of ehs's that affords one the sought compromise between good-access/bad-storage esm's and compact-storage/slow-access linked allocation schemes.

A. A Family of Efficient Hashing Schemes

Our compromise storage schemes are defined as follows:

(7.5) (a) $d = 2$: For $\pi \in N^2$,

$$\mathbf{HASH}_2(\pi) = \pi_2 + (\pi_1 - 1)2^{\lfloor \log \pi_2 \rfloor}.$$

(b) $d > 2$: For $\pi \in N^d$,

$$\mathbf{HASH}_d(\pi) = \mathbf{HASH}_2(\pi_1, \mathbf{HASH}_{d-1}(\pi_2, \ldots, \pi_d)).$$

One can fruitfully view the computation of $\mathbf{HASH}_d$ as a computation on bit strings. Let $\xi_i = 1\omega_i$ ($\omega_i \in \{0, 1\}^*$) be the minimum-length binary representation of π_i, $i = 1, \ldots, d$. Then the minimum-length binary representation of $\mathbf{HASH}_d(\pi_1, \ldots, \pi_d)$ is $1\omega_1\omega_2 \ldots \omega_d$. Note the dropped initial 1's from $\xi_2, \ldots, \xi_d$.

See Figure 10.19.

1	2	3	4	5	6	7	8	9	10
2	4	5	8	9	10	11	16	17	18
3	6	7	12	13	14	15	24	25	26
4	8	9	16	17	18	19	32	33	34
5	10	11	20	21	22	23	40	41	42
6	12	13	24	25	26	27	48	49	50
7	14	15	28	29	30	31	56	57	58
8	16	17	32	33	34	35	64	65	66
9	18	19	36	37	38	39	72	73	74
10	20	21	40	41	42	43	80	81	82

Figure 10.19. The array scheme of shape $\langle 10, 10 \rangle$ stored by the ehs $\mathbf{HASH}_2$.

Theorem 35

For each dimensionality $d \geq 2$, the ehs $\mathbf{HASH}_d$ has the following properties:

(a) $\beta(p; \mathbf{HASH}_d) = p$;

(b) $\alpha(p; \mathbf{HASH}_d) \leq (d - 1) \cdot \log \log p + O(1)$;

(c) $\bar{\alpha}(p; \mathbf{HASH}_d) = O(1)$; in particular, $\bar{\alpha}(p; \mathbf{HASH}_2) < 3.36$.

Part (a) of the theorem is easily established: On the one hand, $\mathbf{HASH}_d(p, 1, \ldots, 1) = p$, and $\langle p, 1, \ldots, 1 \rangle$ resides in a $\langle p \rangle$-array, so $\beta(p; \mathbf{HASH}_d) \geq p$. On the other hand, a straightforward argument shows that $\beta(p; \mathbf{HASH}_d) \leq p$; the argument relies on the facts that $\mathbf{HASH}_d(\pi) \leq \Pi(\pi)$ and that π resides in a $\langle p \rangle$-array only if $\Pi(\pi) \leq p$. Part (b) builds on part (a). If π resides in some $\langle p \rangle$-array, then $\mathbf{HASH}_d(\pi) \leq p$, so the bit string representing $\mathbf{HASH}_d(\pi)$ has length not exceeding $\lceil \log (p + 1) \rceil$. This string, therefore, admits only $(\lceil \log(p + 1) \rceil + 1)^{d-1}$ "parses" into d bit strings, and this quantity bounds from above the number of synonyms of π under $\mathbf{HASH}_d$. A reference to definition (7.4a) completes the proof. The bound of part (c) is more delicate. Consider an arbitrary p-position array A to be stored by $\mathbf{HASH}_d$; we try to maximize A's expected access time. Let $u = \lfloor \log p \rfloor$. Now, when $\mathbf{HASH}_d$ stores A, no bucket with a hash address longer than u is used (longer in length of binary representation). Moreover, those buckets whose addresses have length u never contain more than one array position. (If, say, A were $m \times n$, any synonym of $\langle m, n \rangle$ would have first coordinate $\geq 2^i m$ for some i or second coordinate $\geq 2^j n$ for some j and, hence, not be in A.) More generally, one shows that for each $k = 1, 2, \ldots, u + 1$ there are 2^{k-1} bucket addresses of length k, and each of these buckets contains no more than roughly $(u - k + d)^{d-1}$ array positions. Direct evaluation of the expected time to access an element of A yields a constant upper bound to $\bar{\alpha}(p; \mathbf{HASH}_d)$, and a slightly more detailed version of this argument yields the cited bound on $\bar{\alpha}(p; \mathbf{HASH}_2)$.

The possibility of finding ehs's with expected access time superior to $\mathbf{HASH}_d$'s is intriguing. However, it is conceivable that $\mathbf{HASH}_d$'s expected access time cannot be improved without increasing its consumption of storage. This question of optimality remains open, but we do know that $\mathbf{HASH}_d$'s worst-case access time is asymptotically optimal among ehs's with β's that are linear in p.

Theorem 36

For any d-dimensional ehs $\mathbf{H}$, if $\beta(p; \mathbf{H}) = O(p)$, then

$$\alpha(p; \mathbf{H}) \geq (d - 1) \cdot \log \log p + O(1).$$

Say that $\beta(q; \mathbf{H}) = c \cdot q$. Then, when $\mathbf{H}$ stores the q^d-position array A of shape $\langle q, q, \ldots, q \rangle$, some bucket gets filled with at least $k \cdot (\log q)^{d-1}$ array positions for some $k > 0$. This is so since A contains all positions $\pi \in N^d$ with $\Pi(\pi) \leq q$; $\mathbf{H}(\pi) \leq c \cdot q$ for each of these positions; and these positions are roughly $q \cdot (\log q)^{d-1}$ in number. By definition (7.4a), then, the theorem is established for $p = q^d$. The full theorem follows by calculation since α is monotonic in p.

We remark in passing that by replacing an ehs $\mathbf{H}$ by the ehs $\mathbf{H}^{(k)}(\pi) = \lceil \mathbf{H}(\pi)/k \rceil$, $k \in N$, one obtains an ehs which is more conservative of bucket addresses by a factor of k and which is slower by only the term $\log k$.

Proposition 37

For all $k \in N$, $\beta(p; \mathbf{H}^{(k)}) = \lceil \beta(p; \mathbf{H})/k \rceil$, and $\bar{\alpha}(p; \mathbf{H}^{(k)}) \leq \bar{\alpha}(p; \mathbf{H}) + \log k$. In particular, if $\bar{\alpha}(p; \mathbf{H}) = O(1)$, then the same is true for $\bar{\alpha}(p; \mathbf{H}^{(k)})$.

The proposition affords one an avenue for trading a multiplicative savings in bucket storage for an incremental increase in time of access.

We shall now turn to some lower bounds on ehs performance in order to put the preceding results in perspective.

B. Overly Conservative Hashing Schemes

Any attempt to have an ehs approximate the optimal access behavior of esm's must condemn the ehs to consume storage at roughly the same rate as an esm. Even more striking, any attempt to have an ehs enlist buckets at a rate that grows slower than linearly inevitably destroys all hope of constant expected access time: If the consumption of buckets proceeds much slower than linearly, the ehs will have access behavior close to that of linked allocation schemes.

Theorem 38

Let **H** be a d-dimensional ehs.

(a) If $\alpha(p; \mathbf{H}) = O(1)$, then $\beta(p; \mathbf{H}) = \Omega(p \cdot (\log p)^{d-1})$.

(b) Let $\mathbf{f}: N \longrightarrow N$ bem onotonic increasing. If $\beta(p; \mathbf{H}) = O(p/\mathbf{f}(p))$, then $\bar{\alpha}(p; \mathbf{H}) = \Omega(\log \mathbf{f}(p))$. In particular, if $\beta(p; \mathbf{H}) = O(p^{1-e})$ for some $e > 0$, then $\bar{\alpha}(p; \mathbf{H}) = \Omega(\log p)$.

Part (a) follows from the observation that bounded worst-case access time implies bounded bucket sizes. We can, thus, mimic the proof of Theorem 23a with "oversize" locations. Part (b) follows from the following lemma in conjunction with the observation that $\beta(p; \mathbf{H}) \geq \#\mathbf{H}(A)$ for any $\langle p \rangle$-array A.

Lemma 39

For any ehs **H**, for all $p \in N$,

$$\bar{\alpha}(p; \mathbf{H}) \geq \max\{\log(\#A/\#\mathbf{H}(A)) \mid A \text{ is a } \langle p \rangle\text{-array}\}.$$

This lemma in turn follows from the definitions of **Access** and $\bar{\alpha}$, and from the convexity of the function $x \cdot \log(x + 1)$ in the region $x \geq 1$.

C. Unexpected Efficiency Inhibitors

The adverse effects on efficiency of the constraints just mentioned are not surprising. Even at an intuitive level, for instance, the insistence that an ehs have constant worst-case access time seems counter to the philosophy of hashing, namely, to sacrifice excellent worst-case behavior relative to one quality measure in order to obtain good expected behavior relative to a number of measures. It is also to be expected, when hashing growing data structures, that restricting the rate of use of bucket addresses will force those buckets that are employed to grow rapidly. In this subsection, we shall discuss two constraints on ehs's that would appear intuitively to enhance efficiency relative to consumption of either time or storage without adversely affecting the unenhanced resource and yet which demonstrably cause close to pessimal behavior relative to one of the quality measures.

The first efficiency-inhibiting restriction we note is that the ehs be *gap-free* in the sense that it uses bucket b whenever it uses bucket $b + 1$ so that for every array A,

$\mathbf{H}(A) = \{1, \ldots, k\}$ for some k. At first blush, gap-free ehs's seem to be commendably conservative of storage, and there seems to be no reason for this conservativeness to affect the ehs's access behavior adversely. Yet, gap-free ehs's exhibit close to pessimal access time.

Theorem 40

If the d-dimensional ehs $\mathbf{H}$ is gap-free, then

$$\bar{\alpha}(p; \mathbf{H}) \geq (1 - 1/d) \cdot \log p + O(1).$$

Gap-freeness forces an ehs to use bucket addresses at a very slow rate. Specifically, if the d-dimensional ehs $\mathbf{H}$ is gap-free, then $\mathbf{H}(\pi) \leq \Sigma(\pi) - d + 1$ for all $\pi \in N^d$. $\mathbf{H}$ must, therefore, have very bad average access on arrays that are close in shape to hypercubes.

The second efficiency inhibitor is to demand that an ehs always keep its buckets level. This is very counterintuitive! If we are given p items to store in k buckets, we minimize the expected time to retrieve an item by distributing the items as evenly as possible among the buckets, that is, by keeping the buckets level. [This assertion relies on the same principle as does Lemma 39, namely, the convexity of $x \cdot \log(x + 1)$ in the region $x \geq 1$.] It is only natural to assume that those ehs's would be most efficient which adhered to this tenet religiously. However, the situation in fact is quite the opposite. Any ehs that stores every array so that its positions are spread evenly over some set of buckets (of course, we don't count buckets that the ehs ignores when storing this array) must suffer close to pessimal growth of either β or $\bar{\alpha}$. Even stronger, this same penalty falls upon any ehs for which the sizes of the largest and smallest buckets are functionally related. The formal statement of the theorem in question is simplified by the following shorthand for the size of π's bucket when $\mathbf{H}$ stores the array A, $\pi \in A$:

$$\mathbf{Size}(\pi; A; \mathbf{H}) = \#(A \cap \mathbf{H}^{-1}(\mathbf{H}(\pi))). \tag{7.6}$$

Theorem 41

Let $\mathbf{H}$ be a d-dimensional ehs. Suppose that there is a function $\mathbf{b}: N \longrightarrow N$ such that, for all arrays $A \subset N^d$,

$$\max_{\pi \in A} \mathbf{Size}(\pi; A; \mathbf{H}) \leq \mathbf{b}(\min_{\pi \in A} \mathbf{Size}(\pi; A; \mathbf{H})).$$

Then either $\beta(p; \mathbf{H}) = \Omega(p \cdot (\log p)^{d-1})$ or $\bar{\alpha}(p; \mathbf{H}) = \Omega(\log p)$.

The intuition behind the theorem is that $\mathbf{H}$ has only two avenues for avoiding grossly disparate growth rates in bucket sizes. On the one hand, $\mathbf{H}$ can make sure that buckets never get too full, so new buckets can be started when needed; but this course of action can be shown to cause β to grow as though $\mathbf{H}$ were an esm. On the other hand, $\mathbf{H}$ can let buckets grow as the situation demands but stop enlisting new buckets when the old ones get too big. A somewhat involved argument shows that any ehs that operates in this manner must have close to pessimal expected access time on hypercubic arrays.

It is interesting to note that the disjunctive conclusion of the theorem is essential: esm's have (trivially) balanced buckets together with unit expected access time; and linked allocation schemes [which can be viewed as ehs's with $\mathbf{H}(\pi) \equiv 1$] have (again trivially) balanced buckets together with linearly growing bucket usage.

D. An Open Problem

Perhaps the major research topic concerning ehs's is to determine whether or not there is a way to design *internal* extendible hashing schemes, that is, hashing schemes with internal collision resolution mechanisms such as *open addressing* [see Section 6.4 of Knuth (1973)]. Such internal ehs's may be able to outperform the $\mathbf{HASH}_d$ schemes of (7.5) and Theorem 35 and, perhaps, attain practical levels of efficiency.

Attributions

The material in this section is excerpted from the in-depth study of extendible array hashing schemes by Rosenberg and Stockmeyer (1977a). deVilliers and Wilson (1973, 1974) report on empirical studies of (nonextendible) hashing schemes for (sparse) matrices. Amble and Knuth (1974) study ways to exploit orderings of the keys when hashing arbitrary sets. These last references are not quite germane to the current survey, but they may be of interest to the reader in that they consider closely related topics.

10.8. CONCLUSION

The topics and results covered in Sections 10.1–10.7 constitute, in the opinion of and to the knowledge of the author, the major developments in the study of storage mappings for extendible arrays as of the end of 1975. The several major problems noted in the text and the even larger number of open questions in the sources reviewed are ample evidence that much challenging and interesting research remains to be done. The major open areas (that is, questions that seem to have the potential of developing into major pursuits) would seem to be the following:

1. What is the inevitable complexity of esm's? Section 10.2 can be viewed as the initial stage of the study of one approach to this problem, namely, characterizing the esm's constructible from a given instruction repertoire.
2. What type of memory structure would form a natural "home" for extendible arrays? The development in Section 10.3 would suggest that neither linear nor list-structured memories are the answer.
3. How large a catalog of efficient special-purpose esm's can be compiled? The additive schemes of Section 10.4 [constructed systematically from *BD*-trees as in (4.4) and (4.5)] and the shape-favoring schemes of Section 10.5 [constructed by dovetailing (5.14) the single-shape esm's of (5.11)] would be appropriate entries in this catalog.

4. Can one devise efficient internal hashing schemes for storing extendible arrays? This question is discussed more fully in Section 10.7.D and in even greater detail in Rosenberg and Stockmeyer (1977a).

5. Finally, can one devise extendible storage mappings that accommodate gracefully operations on stored arrays? A glance at the repertoire of operations in the APL language will give one ample food for thought. The author has recently completed a study of the operation of concatenation of arrays, which culminated in the paper "On storing concatenable arrays," *J. CSS*, 14 (1977), 157–74.

BIBLIOGRAPHY

1. AHO, A. V., J. HOPCROFT, and J. D. ULLMAN [1974], *The Design and Analysis of Computer Algorithms*, Addison-Wesley, Reading, Mass.
2. ALLEN, F. E., and J. COCKE [1971], "A Catalogue of Optimizing Transformations, in Design and Optimization of Compilers," *Courant Computer Symposium 5*, Prentice-Hall, Englewood Cliffs, N.J.
3. AMBLE, O., and D. E. KNUTH [1974], "Ordered Hash Tables," *Computer Journal, 17*, 135–142.
4. AMOROSO, S., and I. J. EPSTEIN [1974], "Maps Preserving the Uniformity of Neighborhood Interconnection Patterns in Tesselation Structures," *Information and Control, 25*, 1–9.
5. BALZER, R. M. [1967], "Dataless Programming," *FJCC*, 525–534.
6. BANG, S. Y. [1974], "Analysis, Decomposition, Synthesis, and Applications of Higher Rank Relations," Ph.D. Dissertation, Department of Computer Sciences, University of Texas at Austin.
7. BERZINS, V. [undated], "Behavioral Specifications as a Design Aid," MIT Position Paper, Version I.
8. BIRKHOFF, G. [1938], "Structure of Abstract Algebras," *Proc. Cambridge Philosophical Society, 31*, 433–454.
9. BIRKHOFF, G. [1967], *Lattice Theory*, Amer. Mathematical Soc. Colloquium Pub. 25, New York (1948). Revised Edition.
10. BIRKHOFF, G., and D. LIPSON [1970], "Heterogeneous Algebras," *Journal of Combinatorial Theory, 8*, 115–133.
11. BIRKHOFF, G., and S. MACLANE [1961], *A Survey of Modern Algebra*, Macmillan, New York.
12. BOBROW, D. G. [1972], "Requirements for Advanced Programming Systems for List Processing," *CACM, 15*, no. 7, 618–627.
13. BOBROW, D. G., and B. RAPHAEL [1974], "New Programming Languages for Artificial Intelligence Research," *Computing Surveys, 6*, 155–174.
14. BOLLMAN, D. [1974], "Some Tailor-Made Extendible Array Realizations," IBM Research Report RC 5121.
15. BOLLMAN, D. [1976], "On Preserving Proximity in Arrays," *SIAM J. Computing, 5*, 318–323.
16. BURSTALL, R. M. [1969], "Proving Properties of Programs by Structural Induction," *Computer Journal, 12*, no. 1, 41–48.
17. BURSTALL, R. M. [1972], "Some Techniques for Proving Correctness of Programs Which Alter Data Structures," *Machine Intelligence 1*, 23–50 (ed. B. Meltzer and D. Michie), Edinburgh University Press.
18. CANTOR, G. [1878], Ein Beitrag zur Mannigfaltigkeitslehre, *Crelle J. Math., 84*, 242–258.
19. CHEATHAM, T. E., JR. and B. WEGBREIT [1972], "A Laboratory for the Study of Automating Programming," *SJCC*, 11–21.

20. Childs, D. L. [1968a], "Description of a Set-Theoretical Data Structure," *EJCC*, 557–561.

21. Childs, D. L. [1968b], "Feasibility of a Set-Theoretic Data Structure," *Proc. IFIP Congress*, 420–430, North Holland, Amsterdam.

22. Chowla, P. [1961], "On Some Polynomials Which Represent Every Natural Number Exactly Once," *Det Kongelige Norske Videnskabers Selskabs Forhandliger*, *34*, 512–513.

23. Church, A., and J. B. Rosser [1936], "Some Properties of Conversion," *Transactions of the American Mathematical Society*, *39*, 472–482.

24. Codd E. F. [1970], "A Relational Model of Data for Large Shared Data Bases," *CACM*, *13*, no. 6, 377–387.

25. Codd E. F. [1971], "Relational Completeness of Data Base Sublanguages," *Courant Computer Science Symposia 6*, *Data Base Systems*, Prentice-Hall, Englewood Cliffs, N.J.

26. Cohen, E., and D. Jefferson [1975], "Protection in the Hydra Operating System," *Proc. of the Fifth Symposium on Operating System Principles*, *ACM SIGOPS Operating System Review*, *9*, no. 5, 141–160.

27. Cohn, P. M. [1965], *Universal Algebra*, Harper and Row, New York.

28. Conway, M. E. [1963], "Design of a Separable Transition-Diagram Compiler," *CACM*, *6*, no. 7, 396–408.

29. Dahl, O-J., E. W. Dijkstra, and C. A. R. Hoare [1972], *Structured Programming*, Academic Press, London.

30. Dahl, O-J., and C. A. R. Hoare [1972], "Hierarchical Program Structures," *Structured Programming* (ed. O.-J. Dahl, E. W. Dijkstra, and C. A. R. Hoare), Academic Press, London.

31. Dahl, O-J., B. Myhrhaug, and K. Nygaard [1968], "The SIMULA 67 Common Base Language," Publication S-22, Norwegian Computing Center, Oslo.

32. Dahl, O-J., B. Myhrhaug, and K. Nygaard [1970], *Common Base Language*, Norsk Regnesentral, Oslo.

33. Darlington, J., and R. M. Burstall [1976], "A System Which Automatically Improves Programs," *Acta Informatica*, *6*, no. 1, 41–60.

34. Date, C. J. [1975], *An Introduction to Data Base Systems*, Addison-Wesley, Reading, Mass.

35. de Villiers, E.v.d.S., and L. B. Wilson [1973], "Hash Coding Methods for Sparse Matrices," Technical Report 45, Computing Lab, University of Newcastle Upon Tyne.

36. de Villiers, E.v.d.S., and L. B. Wilson [1974], "Hashing the Subscripts of a Sparse Matrix," *BIT*, *14*, 347–358.

37. Dijkstra, E. W. [1968], "The Structure of the "THE"-Multiprogramming System," *CACM*, *11*, no. 5, 341–346.

38. Dijkstra, E. W. [1972], "Notes on Structured Programming," *Structured Programming* (ed. O-J. Dahl, E. W. Dijkstra, and C. A. R. Hoare), Academic Press, London.

39. Dijkstra, E. W. [1976], *A Discipline of Programming*, Prentice-Hall, Englewood Cliffs, N.J.

40. Doyle, J. N. [1973], "A New Approach to the Analysis and Synthesis of Strings," Department of Computer Science, University of Arizona.

41. Earley, J. [1971], "Towards an Understanding of Data Structures," *CACM*, *14*, no. 10, 617–627.

42. Earley, J. [1972], "On the Semantics of Data Structures: Data Base Systems," *Courant Computer Science Symposium 6*, Prentice-Hall, Englewood Cliffs, N.J.

43. Earley, J. [1973], "Relational Level Data Structures in Programming Languages," Computer Science Department, University of California at Berkeley.

44. Earley, J. [1974a], "High Level Iterators and a Method for Automatically Designing Data Structure Representations," Electronics Research Laboratory Memo ERL-M425, University of California at Berkeley.

45. Earley, J. [1974b], "High Level Operations in Automatic Programming," *Proc. of a Symposium on Very High Level Languages, SIGPLAN Notices.*

46. Ehrich, H-D. [1974], "Theory of Direct-Access Storage Functions," *Proc. IEIP Congress*, 647–651, North Holland, Amsterdam.

47. Fischer, M. J., and A. L. Rosenberg [1968], "Real-Time Solutions of the Origin-Crossing Problem," *Mathematical Systems Theory*, *2*, 257–263.

48. Fisher, D. [1970], "Control Structures for Programming Languages," Ph.D. Thesis, Carnegie-Mellon University.

49. Fleck, A. C. [1971], "Towards a Theory of Data Structures," *Journal of Computing and Systems Science*, *5*, no. 5, 475–488.

50. Fleck, A. C. [1975], "Theoretical Results on the Use of Patterns to Structure Collections of Strings," submitted for publication.

51. Floyd, R. [1967a], "Nondeterministic Algorithms," *JACM*, *14*, 636–644.

52. Floyd, R. [1967b], "Assigning Meaning to Programs," *Proc. Symposium on Applied Mathematics*, *19*, 19–32, American Mathematical Society, Providence, R.I.

53. Fu, K. S. [1974], "Linguistic Approach to Pattern Recognition," in *Applied Computation Theory* (ed. R. T. Yeh), Prentice-Hall, Englewood Cliffs, N.J.

54. Furtado, A. L. [1972], "Algebraic Concepts in Data Structures," Report No. 7172, Computer Science Department, Pontificia Universidad Catolica do Rio de Janeiro, Brazil.

55. Furtado, A. L., and A. S. Pfeffer [1973], "Pattern Matching for Structured Programming," *Proc. Seventh Asilomar Conf. on Circuits, Systems and Computers*, Pacific Grove, Calif.

56. Geschke, C. M., and J. G. Mitchell [1975], "On the Problem of Uniform References to Data Structures," *IEEE Transactions on Software Engineering*, *SE-1*, no. 2, 207–219.

57. Giarratana, V., F. Gimona, and U. Montanari [1976], "Observability Concepts in Abstract Data Type Specification," *Lecture Notes in Computer Science 45*, Springer-Verlag, 576–587.

58. Gimpel, J. F. [1973], "A Theory of Discrete Patterns and Their Implementation in SNOBOL4," *CACM*, *16*, no. 2, 91–100.

59. Goguen, J. A. [1976], "Correctness and Equivalence of Data Types," *Proc. Conference on Algebraic Systems Theory*, Udine, Italy. Also in *Mathematical Systems Theory*, 352–358 (ed. G. Marchesihi and S. K. Mitter), Springer-Verlag.

60. Goguen, J. A. [1977], "Abstract Errors for Abstract Data Types," UCLA Semantics and Theory of Computation Report 6. Also in *Proc. IEIP Working Conference on Formal Description of Programming Concepts*, 21.1–21.32, St. Andrews, New Brunswick.

61. Goguen, J. A., J. W. Thatcher, E. G. Wagner, and J. B. Wright [1973], "A Junction Between Computer Science and Category Theory: I, Basic Definitions and Examples," Part I, IBM Research Report RC 4526.

62. Goguen, J. A., J. W. Thatcher, E. G. Wagner, and J. B. Wright [1975a], "Initial Algebra Semantics and Continuous Algebras," IBM Research Report RC 5701. Also in *JACM*, *24*, 68–95.

63. Goguen, J. A., J. W. Thatcher, E. G. Wagner, and J. B. Wright [1975b], "Abstract Data Types as Initial Algebras and Correctness of Data Representations," *Proc. Conference on Computer Graphics, Pattern Recognition and Data Structure*, 89–93.

64. Goguen, J. A., J. W. Thatcher, E. G. Wagner, and J. B. Wright [1976a], "A Junction Between Computer Science and Category Theory: I, Basic Definitions and Examples," Part II, IBM Research Report RC 5908.

65. Goguen, J. A., J. W. Thatcher, E. G. Wagner, and J. B. Wright [1976b], "Some Fundamentals of Order-Algebraic Semantics," *Lecture Notes in Computer Science 45*, Springer-Verlag, 153–168. Also in IBM Research Report RC 6020.

66. Graetzer, G. [1968], *Universal Algebra*, Van Nostrand, Princeton.

67. Gray, J. C. [1967], "Compound Data Structures for Computer Aided Design: A Survey," *Proc. ACM National Conference*, 355–365.

68. Gries, D., and N. Gehani [1977], "Some Ideas on Data Types in High Level Languages," *CACM, 20*.

69. Griesmer, J. H., and R. D. Jenks [1971], "SCRATCHPAD/1—An Interactive Facility for Symbolic Mathematics," *Proc. of the Second Symposium on Symbolic and Algebraic Manipulation, ACM*, 42–58.

70. Griswold, R. E., J. F. Poage, and I. P. Polonsky, [1971], *The SNOBOL4 Programming Language*, Prentice-Hall, Englewood Cliffs, N.J.

71. Guttag, J. V. [1975], "The Specification and Application to Programming of Abstract Data Types," Ph.D. Thesis, University of Toronto, Department of Computer Science, available as Computer Systems Research Group Report CSRG-59.

72. Guttag, J. V. [1976], "Abstract Data Types and the Development of Data Structures," *Proc. of Conference on Data: Abstraction, Definition, and Structure, SIGPLAN Notices, 8*, no. 2.

73. Guttag, J. V., E. Horowitz, and D. R. Musser [1976a], "Abstract Data Types and Software Validation," Information Sciences Institute, Report RR-76-48, Marina del Rey, Calif.

74. Guttag, J. V., E. Horowitz, and D. R. Musser, [1976b], "The Design of Data Type Specifications," Information Sciences Institute, Report RR-76-49, Marina del Rey, Calif.

75. Habermann, A. N., [1973], "Critical Comments on the Programming Language Pascal," *Acta Informatica, 3*, 47–57.

76. Hammer, M. M., W. G. Howe, and I. Wladawsky [1974], "An Interactive Business Definition System," *Proc. of a Symposium on Very High Level Languages, SIGPLAN Notices, 9*, no. 4, 25–33.

77. Hearn, A. C. [1971], "Reduce 2: A System and Language for Algebraic Manipulation," *Proc. of the Second Symposium on Symbolic and Algebraic Manipulation, ACM*, 128–133.

78. Hellerman, H. [1962], "Addressing Multidimensional Arrays," *CACM, 5*, 204–207.

79. Hennie, F. C. [1966], "On-Line Turing Machine Computations," *IEEE Transactions on Electronic Computers, EC-15*, 35–44.

80. Hewitt, C. [1972], "Description and Theoretical Analysis (Using Schemata) of PLANNER: A Language for Proving Theorems and Manipulating Models in a Robot," Ph.D. Thesis, Department of Mathematics, Mass. Institute of Technology, Cambridge, Mass.

81. Higgins, P. J. [1963], "Algebras With a Scheme of Operators," *Mathematische Nachrichten, 27*, 115–132.

82. Hoare, C. A. R. [1968], "Record Handling," in *Programming Languages*, 291–347 (ed. F. Genuys), Academic Press, New York.

83. HOARE, C. A. R. [1969], "An Axiomatic Basis for Computer Programming," *CACM*, *12*, no. 10, 576–583.

84. HOARE, C. A. R. [1972], "Proof of Correctness of Data Representations," *Acta Informatica*, *1*, 271–281.

85. HOARE, C. A. R. [1974], "Monitors: An Operating System Structuring Concept," *CACM*, *17*, no. 10, 549–577.

86. HOARE, C. A. R. [1975], "Recursive Data Structures," *Int. Journal of Computer and Information Sciences*, *4*, no. 2, 105–132.

87. HOARE, C. A. R., and N. WIRTH [1973], "An Axiomatic Definition of the Programming Language PASCAL," *Acta Informatica*, 335–355.

88. HOLT, A. W. [1965], "–Theory, A Mathematical Model for the Description and Analysis of Discrete Finite Information Systems," Applied Data Research, Inc.

89. HOPCROFT, J., and J. ULLMAN [1969], *Formal Languages and Their Relation to Automata*, Addison-Wesley, Reading, Mass.

90. HOROWITZ, E., and S. SAHNI [1976], *Fundamentals of Data Structures*, Computer Science Press, Woodland Hills, Calif.

91. IBM System 360 Operating System, [1966], "P1/I Language Specifications," Form C28-6571-4, New York.

92. JACOBSON, N. [1951], *Lectures in Abstract Algebra*, *I*, Van Nostrand Co., Princeton, N.J.

93. JONES, A. [1973], "Protection in Programmed Systems," Ph.D. Thesis, Carnegie-Mellon University.

94. KARP, R. M., A. C. MCKELLAR, and C. K. WONG [1975], "Near-Optimal Solutions to a Two-Dimensional Placement Problem," *SIAM J. Comput.*, *4*, 271–286.

95. KENNEDY, K., and J. T. SCHWARTZ [1975], "Introduction to the Set-Theoretic Language SETL," *Computers and Mathematics with Applications*, *1*, 97–119.

96. KILLDALL, G. A. [1973], "A Unified Approach to Global Program Optimization," *First Symposium on Principles of Programming Languages*, *ACM*, New York.

97. KIVIAT, P. J., R. VILLANUEVA, and H. M. MARKOWITZ [1972], "The SIMSCRIPT II.5 Programming Language," *CACI*, Los Angeles, Calif.

98. KNUTH, D. E. [1968], *The Art of Computer Programming I: Fundamental Algorithms*, Addison-Wesley, Reading, Mass.

99. KNUTH, D. E. [1973], *The Art of Computer Programming III: Sorting and Searching*, Addison-Wesley, Reading, Mass.

100. KNUTH, D. E. [1974], "Structured Programming with GOTO Statements," *Computing Surveys*, *6*, no. 4, 261–301.

101. LAMPSON, B. W., J. J. HORNING, R. L. LONDON, J. G. MITCHELL, and G. J. POPEK [1977], "Report on the Programming Language Euclid," *SIGPLAN Notices*.

102. LANDIN, P. J. [1970], "A Program Machine Symmetric Automata Theory," *Machine Intelligence 5*, 99–120 (ed. B. Meltzer and D. Michie), Edinburgh University Press.

103. LEAVENWORTH, B. M., and J. SAMMET [1974], "An Overview of Nonprocedural Languages," *Proc. of a Symposium of Very High Level Languages*, *SIGPLAN Notices*, *9*, no. 4, 1–12.

104. LEE, J. A. N. [1972], *Computer Semantics*, Van Nostrand Reinhold, New York.

105. LEW, J. S. [1977], "Polynomial Enumeration of Multidimensional Lattices," IBM Research Report RC 6737.

106. LEW, J. S., and A. L. ROSENBERG [1975], "Polynomial Mappings from $N \times N$ into N," IBM Research Report RC 5761; to appear in *Journal of Number Theory*, as "Polynomial Indexing of Integer Lattices, I, II."

107. LINDSEY, C. H., and S. G. VAN DER MEULEN [1971], *Informal Introduction to ALGOL 68*, North Holland, Amsterdam.

108. LIPTON, R. J., S. C. EISENSTAT, and R. A. DEMILLO [1976], "Space and Time Hierarchies for Classes of Control Structures and Data Structures," *JACM*, *23*, 720–732.

109. LISKOV, B. H. [1972], "A Design Methodology for Reliable Software Systems," *FJCC*, 191–199.

110. LISKOV, B. H. [1974], "A Note on CLU," Computation Structures Group, Project MAC, MIT, Memo 112.

111. LISKOV, B. H., and S. N. ZILLES [1974], "Programming with Abstract Data Types," *Proc. of ACM Symposium on Very High Level Languages, SIGPLAN Notices*, *9*, no. 4, 50–59.

112. LISKOV, B. H., and S. N. ZILLES [1975], "Specification Techniques for Data Abstractions," *IEEE Transactions on Software Engineering*, *SE-1*, no. 1, 7–18.

113. LIU, L. Y., and P. WEINER [1973], "An Infinite Hierarchy of Intersections of Context-Free Languages," *Mathematical Systems Theory*, *7*, no. 2, 185–192.

114. LOMET, D. B. [1973], "A Formalization of Transition Diagram Systems," *JACM*, *20*, no. 2, 235–257.

115. LONDON, R. L. [1972], "The Current State of Proving Programs Correct," *Proc. ACM National Conference*.

116. LOW, J. R. [1974], "Automatic Coding: Choice of Data Structures," Ph.D. Thesis, Stanford University.

117. LOWENTHAL, E. I. [1971], "A Functional Approach to the Design of Storage Structures for Generalized Data Management Systems," Ph.D. Dissertation, Department of Computer Sciences, University of Texas at Austin.

118. LUCAS, P., P. LAUER, and H. STIGLEITNER [1968], "Method and Notation for the Formal Definition of Programming Languages," TR25.087, IBM Research Laboratory, Vienna.

119. MACLANE, S., and G. BIRKHOFF [1967], *Algebra*, Macmillan, New York.

120. MACLENNAN, B. J. [1973], "Fen-An Axiomatic Basis for Program Semantics," *CACM*, *16*, no. 8, 468–474.

121. MARTIN, W. A., and R. J. FATEMAN [1971], "The MACSYMA System," *Proc. of the Second Symposium on Symbolic and Algebraic Manipulation, ACM*, 59–75.

122. MAURER, W. D. [1976], *The Programmer's Introduction to SNOBOL*, American Elsevier Pub., New York, N.Y.

123. MCCARTHY, J. [1960], "Recursive Functions of Symbolic Expressions and Their Computation by Machine," *CACM*, *3*, no. 4, 184–195.

124. MCCARTHY, J. [1962], "Towards a Mathematical Science of Computation," *Proc. IEIP Congress*, North Holland, Amsterdam.

125. MCCARTHY, J. [1963], "A Basis for a Mathematical Theory of Computation," *Computer Programming and Formal Systems*, 33–70 (ed. P. Braffort and D. Hirschberg), North Holland, Amsterdam.

126. MCCARTHY, J., P. W. ABRAHAMS, D. J. EDWARDS, T. P. HART, and M. I. LEVIN [1962], *LISP 1.5 Programmer's Manual*, M.I.T. Press, Cambridge, Mass.

127. McDermott, D., and G. J. Sussman [1972], *The Conniver Reference Manual*, MIT Artificial Intelligence Lab. Memorandum 259, Cambridge, Mass.

128. McGee, W. C. [1969], "File Structures for Generalized Data Management," *Proc. IEIP Congress*, North Holland, Amsterdam.

129. Mealy, G. H. [1967], "Another Look at Data," *EJCC*, 525–534.

130. Mealy, G. H. [1974], "Data Structures: Theory and Representation," *Proc. IEIP Congress*, 322–325, North Holland, Amsterdam.

131. Meltzer, B., and D. Michie [1970], "Bibliography on Proving the Correctness of Computer Programs," *Machine Intelligence 5*, New York.

132. Mendelson, E. [1964], *Introduction to Mathematical Logic*, Van Nostrand, Princeton, N.J.

133. Minsky, M. L. [1967], *Computation: Finite and Infinite Machines*, Prentice-Hall, Inc., Englewood Cliffs, N.J.

134. Morris, J. H., Jr. [1973], "Types are Not Sets," *Proc. First ACM Symposium on Principles of Programming Languages*, *ACM*, New York, 120–124.

135. Mylopoulos, J., and T. Pavlidis [1971], "On the Topological Properties of Quantized Spaces, I, II," *JACM*, *18*, 239–246, 247–254.

136. Newman, W. M., and R. F. Sproull [1973], *Principles of Interactive Computer Graphics*, McGraw-Hill, New York.

137. Palme, J. [1973], "Protected Program Modules in Simula 67," Research Institute of National Defense, Stockholm, Sweden.

138. Parnas, D. L. [1971], "Information Distribution Aspects of Design Methodology," *Proc. IFIP Congress*, 339–344, North Holland, Amsterdam.

139. Parnas, D. L. [1972], "A Technique for the Specification of Software Modules with Examples," *CACM*, *15*, 330–336.

140. Pippenger, N. J., and M. J. Fischer [1977], "Relations Among Complexity Measures," IBM Research Report RC 6569.

141. Post, E. [1947], "Recursive Unsolvability of a Problem of True," *Journal of Symbolic Logic*, 1–11.

142. Prenner, C. J. [1972], "Multi-Path Control Structures for Programming Languages," Ph.D. Thesis, Harvard University, Document Number ESD-TR-72-308.

143. Preparata, F. P., and R. T. Yeh [1973], *Introduction to Discrete Structures*, Addison-Wesley, Reading, Mass.

144. Raphael, B. [1968], "SIR: A Computer Program for Semantic Information Retrieval," in *Semantic Information Processing* (ed. M. Minsky), MIT Press, Cambridge, Mass.

145. Reynolds, J. C. [1969], "A Set Theoretic Approach to the Concept of Type," Argonne National Laboratories.

146. Reynolds, J. C. [1970], "GEDANKEN—A Simple Typeless Language Based on the Principle of Completeness and the Reference Concept," *CACM*, *13*, no. 5, 305–319.

147. Richards, M. [1969], "BCPL: A Tool for Compiler and System Writing," *SJCC*, 557–566.

148. Rosenberg, A. L. [1971], "Data Graphs and Addressing Schemes," *Journal of Computing and Systems Science*, 193–238.

149. Rosenberg, A. L. [1973], "Exploiting Addressability in Data Graphs," in *Computational Complexity; Courant Comp. Sci. Symposium 1*, 161–183 (ed. R. Rustin), Algorithmics Press, New York.

150. Rosenberg, A. L. [1974a], "Allocating Storage for Extendible Arrays," *JACM*, *21*, 652–670.

151. Rosenberg, A. L. [1974b], "Computed Access in Ragged Arrays," in *Proc. IEIP Congress*, 642–646, North Holland, Amsterdam.

152. Rosenberg, A. L. [1975a], "Managing Storage for Extendible Arrays," *SIAM J. Comput.*, *4*, 287–306.

153. Rosenberg, A. L. [1975b], "Preserving Proximity in Arrays," *SIAM J. Comput.*, *4*, 443–460.

154. Rosenberg, A. L. [1975c], "On Storing Arbitrarily Many Extendible Arrays of Arbitrary Dimensions," *Int'l J. Computer and Information Sci.*, *4*, 189–196.

155. Rosenberg, A. L. [1976], "Universal Data Objects are Trees," IBM Research Report RC 5872.

156. Rosenberg, A. L. [1977], "On Storing Ragged Arrays by Hashing," *Mathematical Systems Theory*, *10*, 193–210.

157. Rosenberg, A. L., and L. J. Stockmeyer [1977a], "Hashing Schemes for Extendible Arrays," *JACM*, *24*, 199–221.

158. Rosenberg, A. L., and L. J. Stockmeyer [1977b], "Storage Schemes for Boundedly Extendible Arrays," *Acta Informatica*, *7*, 289–303.

159. Rosenberg, A. L., and H. R. Strong [1972], "Addressing Arrays by Shells," *IBM Technical Disclosure Bulletin*, *14*, 3026–3028.

160. Rosenberg, A. L., and J. W. Thatcher [1975], "What is a Multilevel Array?" *IBM Journal of Research and Development*, *19*, no. 2, 163–169.

161. Rosenbloom, P. [1950], *Elements of Mathematical Logic*, Dover Publications.

162. Rosenfeld, A. [1969], *Picture Processing by Computer*, Academic Press, New York.

163. Rulifson, J. F., J. A. Derksen, and R. J. Waldinger [1972], "QA4: A Procedural Language for Intuitive Reasoning," Technical Note 73, Stanford Research Institute, Artificial Intelligence Center, Menlo Park, Calif.

164. Rutledge, J. D. [1973], "Program Schemata As Automata. I," *Journal of Computing and Systems Science*, *1*, 543–578.

165. Salomaa, A. [1969], *Theory of Automata*, Pergamon Press, New York, N.Y.

166. Sammet, J. [1969], *Programming Languages: History and Fundamentals*, Prentice-Hall, Englewood Cliffs, N.J.

167. Sammet, J. [1974], "Roster of Programming Languages for 1973," *Computing Reviews*, *15*, 147–160.

168. Schaefer, M. [1973], *A Mathematical Theory of Global Program Optimization*, Prentice-Hall, Englewood Cliffs, N.J.

169. Schwartz, J. T. [1971a], "More Detailed Suggestions Concerning 'Data Strategy' Elaborations for SETL," *SETL Newsletter 39*, Computer Science Department, New York University.

170. Schwartz, J. T. [1971b], "Optimization of Very High Level Languages. I. Value Transmission and Its Corollaries," *Computer Languages*, *1*, 161–194.

171. Schwartz, J. T. [1973], "On Programming, An Interim Report on the SETL Project. Part I: Generalities; Part II: The SETL Language and Examples of Its Use," Computer Science Department, Courant Inst. Math. Sci., New York University.

172. Schwartz, J. T. [1974a], "Automatic and Semiautomatic Optimization of SETL," *Proc. of a Symposium on Very High Level Languages, SIGPLAN Notices.*

173. Schwartz, J. T. [1974b], "Automatic Data Structure Choice in a Language of Very High Level," *ACM Second Annual Conference on Principles of Programming Languages*, Palo Alto, Calif.

174. Schwartz, J. T. [1974c], "Central Technical Issues in Programming Language Design," Novosibirsk International Symposium on Theoretical Programming, *Lecture Notes on Computer Science 5*, Springer-Verlag, New York.

175. Schwartz, J. T. [1974d], "More Local and Semi-Local SETL Optimizations," *SETL Newsletter 122*, Computer Science Department, New York University.

176. Schwartz, J. T. [1974e], "A Few Peephole Optimizations Applicable to Iterators," *SETL Newsletter 122A*, Computer Science Department, New York University.

177. Schwartz, J. T. [1974f], "Still More Miscellaneous Optimizations," *SETL Newsletter 122B*, Computer Science Department, New York University.

178. Schwartz, J. T. [1975], "General Comments on High Level Dictions, and Specific Suggestions Concerning 'Converge' Iterators'" *SETL Newsletter 133B*, Computer Science Department, New York University.

179. Scott, D. [1972a], "Data Types as Lattices," unpublished notes, Amsterdam (1972), Oxford (1974).

180. Scott, D. [1972b], "Lattice Theory, Data Types and Semantics," in *Formal Semantics of Programming Languages*, 65–106 (ed. R. Rustin), Prentice-Hall, Englewood Cliffs, N.J.

181. Shaw, P. [1976], "GYVE: A Language for the Coordination and Control of Concurrent Processes," Ph.D. Thesis, Computer Science Department, New York University.

182. Simmons, R. F., and J. Slocum [1970], "Generating English Discourse From Semantic Networks," Natural Language Research for Computer Assisted Instruction, Technical Report NL-3, University of Texas at Austin.

183. Smith, D. C., and H. J. Enea [1973], "MLISP2," AIM-195, Stanford AI Lab., Stanford University.

184. Spitzen, J., and B. Wegbreit [1975], "The Verification and Synthesis of Data Structures," *Acta Informatica*, *4*, 127–144.

185. (Staff of the) Center for Research in Computing Technology [1974], "ECL Programmer's Manual," Report 74-23, Harvard University.

186. Standish, T. A. [1973], "Data Structures: An Axiomatic Approach," BBN Report 2639, Bolt Beranek and Newmann, Cambridge, Mass.

187. Stewart, G. F. [1974], "An Algebraic Model for String Patterns," University of Toronto, Computer Systems Research Group, Technical Report No. CSRG-39.

188. Stewart, G. F. [1975], "An Algebraic Model for String Patterns," *Proc. Second ACM Symposium on Principles of Programming Languages*, 167–184, Palo Alto, Calif.

189. Stockmeyer, L. J. [1973], "Extendible Array Realizations with Additive Traversal," IBM Research Report RC 4578.

190. Stockmeyer, L. J., and A. R. Meyer [1973], "Word Problems Requiring Exponential Time," *Proc. Fifth Annual ACM Symposium on Theory of Computing*, 1–9.

191. Strassen, V. [1969], "Gaussian Elimination Is Not Optimal," *Numerische Mathematik*, *13*, 354–356.

192. Suzuki, N., and K. Ishihata [1977], "Implementation of Array Bound Checker," *SIGPLAN Symposium on Principles of Programming Languages*, 132–143.

193. TENENBAUM, A. [1973], "Revised and Extended Algorithms for Deducing the Types of Objects Appearing in SETL Programs," *SETL Newsletter 118*, Computer Science Department, New York University.

194. TESLER, L. G., H. J. ENEA, and D. C. SMITH [1973], "The LISP70 Pattern Matching System," *Proc. Third Intern. Joint Conf. on Artificial Intelligence*, Stanford, Calif.

195. THOMPSON, K. [1968], "Regular Expression Search Algorithm," *CACM*, *11*, no. 6, 419–422.

196. TURSKI, W. M. [1971], "A Model for Data Structures and Its Applications I," *Acta Informatica*, *1*, 26–34.

197. VALIANT, L. G. [1975], "General Context-Free Recognition in Less Than Cubic Time," *Journal of Computing and Systems Science*, *10*, no. 2, 308–315.

198. VAN WIJNGAARDEN, A. (ed.), B. J. MALLOUX, J. E. L. PECK, and C. H. A. KOSTER [1969], "Report on the Algorithmic Language ALGOL 68," *Numerische Mathematik*, *14*, 79–218.

199. WEGBREIT, B. [1970], *Studies in Extensible Languages*, Ph.D. Thesis, Harvard University.

200. WEGBREIT, B. [1974a], "The ECL Programming System," *EJCC*, 253–262.

201. WEGBREIT, B. [1974b], "The Treatment of Data Types in EL1," *CACM*, *17*, no. 5, 251–264.

202. WEGBREIT, B., and J. SPITZEN [1977], "Proving Properties of Complex Data Structures," *JACM*.

203. WEGNER, P. [1972], "The Vienna Definition Language," *Computing Surveys*, *4*, no. 1, 5–63.

204. WILLIAM, R. [1971], "A Survey of Data Structures for Computer Graphics Systems," *Computing Surveys*, *3*, no. 1, 1–21.

205. WINOGRAD, T. [1976], "Parsing Natural Language via Recursive Transition Net," in *Applied Computation Theory* (ed. R. T. Yeh), Prentice-Hall, Englewood Cliffs, N.J.

206. WIRTH, N. [1971a], "Program Development by Stepwise Refinement, *CACM*, *14*, no. 4, 221.

207. WIRTH, N. [1971b], "The Programming Language PASCAL," *Acta Informatica*, *1*, 35–63.

208. WIRTH, N. [1975], "An Assessment of the Programming Language Pascal," *Proc. International Conference on Reliable Software*, 23–30.

209. WONG, C. K., and T. W. MADDOCKS [1975], "A Generalized Pascal's Triangle," *Fibonacci Quarterly*, *13*, 134–136.

210. WOODS, W. A. [1970], "Transition Network Grammars for Natural Language Analysis," *CACM*, *13*, no. 10, 591–606.

211. WULF, W. [1974], "ALPHARD: Toward a Language to Support Structured Programs," Technical Report, Carnegie-Mellon University.

212. WULF, W. [1975], *The Design of an Optimizing Compiler*, American Elsevier, New York.

213. YEH, R. T. [1968], "Generalized Pair Algebra with Applications to Automata Theory," *JACM*, *15*, no. 2, 304–316.

214. YEH, R. T. [1973], "Toward an Algebraic Theory of Fuzzy Relational Systems," Technical Report TR-25, Department of Computer Sciences, University of Texas at Austin.

215. ZILLES, S. N. [1973], "Procedural Encapsulation: A Linguistic Protection Technique," *SIGPLAN Notices*, *8*, no. 9, 140–146.

216. ZILLES, S. N. [1974], "Algebraic Specification of Data Types," Project MAC Progress Report 11, MIT, Cambridge, Mass., 28–52.

217. ZILLES, S. N. [1975], "An Introduction to Data Algebras," working draft paper, IBM Research Laboratory, San Jose, Calif.